REVISED THIRD EDITION

Cassandra: The Definitive Guide
Distributed Data at Web Scale

Jeff Carpenter and Eben Hewitt

Beijing · Boston · Farnham · Sebastopol · Tokyo

Cassandra: The Definitive Guide
by Jeff Carpenter and Eben Hewitt

Published by O'Reilly Media, Inc., 1005 Gravenstein Highway North, Sebastopol, CA 95472.

O'Reilly books may be purchased for educational, business, or sales promotional use. Online editions are also available for most titles (*http://oreilly.com*). For more information, contact our corporate/institutional sales department: 800-998-9938 or *corporate@oreilly.com*.

Acquisitions Editor: Jess Haberman	**Indexer:** Potomac Indexing, LLC
Development Editor: Sarah Grey	**Interior Designer:** David Futato
Production Editor: Deborah Baker	**Cover Designer:** Karen Montgomery
Copyeditor: Sonia Saruba	**Illustrator:** Rebecca Demarest
Proofreader: Kim Cofer	

December 2010:	First Edition
July 2016:	Second Edition
April 2020:	Third Edition
January 2022:	Revised Third Edition

Revision History for the Revised Third Edition

2022-01-21:   First Release

See *http://oreilly.com/catalog/errata.csp?isbn=9781492097143* for release details.

978-1-492-09714-3

[LSI]

This book is dedicated to my sweetheart, Alison Brown. I can hear the sound of violins, long before it begins.

—E.H.

For Stephanie, my inspiration, unfailing support, and the love of my life.

—J.C.

Table of Contents

Foreword

I first came across Apache Cassandra at the start of 2009. As a beta tester for push alerts on the iPhone, our mobile news application was having a difficult time handling millions of user lookups to send timely updates. After evaluating several different approaches, I stumbled onto Cassandra. Here was a database where I had to model my data for the query I was going to make, optimizing the "fetch" to return the whole result set in a single disk seek. What had been taking up to 30 minutes, impacting latencies across the site, sped up to a matter of seconds—so fast that our development contacts at Apple had to ask us to lower our throughput!

Almost every aspect of Cassandra has changed substantially since then. What was initially a niche group of power users and distributed systems enthusiasts has blossomed into a thriving, diverse community. Over the years, Cassandra has proved itself time and again, running some of the largest workloads on the internet for services you use every day. An equally valid maturity signal is that you now have in front of you a third edition of this book.

Through all its successes, Cassandra is still a difficult system to use. From installation to integration and operationalization, it remains nuanced, with plenty of gotchas. This book does a fantastic job of walking the reader through common pitfalls, with detailed explanations of important concepts.

No matter what your focus, read all the way through this book, so you understand the Cassandra system as a whole. As a developer, you may never need to care about anti-entropy repair (that's the ops team's job!), but you still need to understand its impact on maintaining data consistency. This may be the first time you have used a system where the operational mechanics affect how you configure your application for data consistency. You'll also need to communicate the failure boundaries and cluster topology to your application team so they can configure data distribution and consistency levels correctly.

Regardless of your role, these concepts are difficult. This book, more than any single resource I've come across to date, does an excellent job of explaining things. We all learn differently, though, and I encourage you to supplement what this volume offers by engaging with Apache Cassandra's thriving community, full of experienced power users, developers, and application architects who contribute code and documentation, participate in discussion lists and Slack channels, and speak at meetups and events. Use this book as your gateway into the world of Apache Cassandra.

— Nate McCall
Vice President, Apache Cassandra
Apache Software Foundation
Raumati South, New Zealand
March 25, 2020

Preface

Why Apache Cassandra?

Apache Cassandra is a free, open source, distributed data storage system that differs sharply from relational database management systems (RDBMSs).

Cassandra first started as an Incubator project at Apache in January of 2009. Shortly thereafter, the committers, led by Apache Cassandra Project Chair Jonathan Ellis, released version 0.3 of Cassandra, and steadily made releases up to the milestone 3.0 release. Since 2017, the project has been led by Apache Cassandra Project Chair Nate McCall, producing releases 3.1 through the latest 4.0 release. Cassandra is being used in production by some of the biggest companies on the web, including Facebook, Twitter, and Netflix.

Its popularity is due in large part to the outstanding technical features it provides. It is durable, seamlessly scalable, and tuneably consistent. It performs blazingly fast writes, can store hundreds of terabytes of data, and is decentralized and symmetrical so there's no single point of failure. It is highly available and offers a data model based on the Cassandra Query Language (CQL).

Is This Book for You?

This book is intended for a variety of audiences. It should be useful to you if you are:

- A developer working with large-scale, high-volume applications, such as Web 2.0 social applications, ecommerce sites, financial services, or sensor-based Internet of Things (IoT) systems

- An application architect or data architect who needs to understand the available options for high-performance, decentralized, elastic data stores

- A database administrator or database developer currently working with standard relational database systems who needs to understand how to implement a fault-tolerant, eventually consistent data store

- A manager who wants to understand the advantages (and disadvantages) of Cassandra to help make decisions about technology strategy

- A student, analyst, or researcher who is designing a project related to Cassandra or other nonrelational data store options

This book is a technical guide. In many ways, Cassandra and other NoSQL databases represent a new way of thinking about data. Many developers who gained their professional chops in the last 15–20 years have become well versed in thinking about data in purely relational or object-oriented terms. Cassandra's data model is different and can be difficult to wrap your mind around at first, especially for those of us with entrenched ideas about what a database is (and should be).

Using Cassandra does not mean that you have to be a Java developer. However, Cassandra is written in Java, so if you're going to dive into the source code, a solid understanding of Java is crucial. Many of the examples in this book are in Java, but Cassandra drivers are available in a wide variety of languages, including Java, Node.js, Python, C#, PHP, Ruby, and Go.

Finally, it is assumed that you have a good understanding of how the web works, can use an integrated development environment (IDE), and are somewhat familiar with the typical concerns of data-driven applications. You might be a well-seasoned developer or administrator but still, on occasion, encounter tools used in the Cassandra world that you're not familiar with. For example, Apache Ant is used to build Cassandra, and the Cassandra source code is available via Git. In cases where we speculate that you'll need to do a little setup of your own in order to work with the examples, we try to support that.

What's in This Book?

This book is designed with the chapters acting, to a reasonable extent, as standalone guides. This is important for a book on Cassandra, which has a variety of audiences in different job roles and industries. To borrow from the software world, the book is designed to be modular. If you're new to Cassandra, it makes sense to read the book in order; if you've passed the introductory stages, you will still find value in later chapters, which you can read as standalone guides.

Here is how the book is organized:

Chapter 1, "Beyond Relational Databases"
> This chapter reviews the history of the enormously successful relational database and the rise of nonrelational database technologies like Cassandra.

Chapter 2, "Introducing Cassandra"
This chapter introduces Cassandra and discusses what's exciting and different about it, where it came from, and what its advantages are.

Chapter 3, "Installing Cassandra"
This chapter walks you through installing Cassandra, getting it running, and trying out some of its basic features.

Chapter 4, "The Cassandra Query Language"
Here we look at Cassandra's data model, highlighting how it differs from the traditional relational model. We also explore how this data model is expressed in the Cassandra Query Language (CQL).

Chapter 5, "Data Modeling"
This chapter introduces principles and processes for data modeling in Cassandra. We analyze a well-understood domain to produce a working schema.

Chapter 6, "The Cassandra Architecture"
This chapter helps you understand what happens during read and write operations and how the database accomplishes some of its notable aspects, such as durability and high availability. We go under the hood to understand some of the more complex inner workings, such as the gossip protocol, hinted handoffs, read repairs, Merkle trees, and more.

Chapter 7, "Designing Applications with Cassandra"
In order to help make some of Cassandra's architecture concepts more concrete, we'll explore some of the common ways in which Cassandra figures into the architecture and design of modern cloud applications.

Chapter 8, "Application Development with Drivers"
There are a variety of drivers available for different languages, including Java, Node.js, Python, Ruby, C#, and PHP, in order to abstract Cassandra's lower-level API. We help you understand how to use common driver features to develop applications with Cassandra.

Chapter 9, "Writing and Reading Data"
We build on the previous chapters to learn how Cassandra works "under the covers" to read and write data. We'll also discuss concepts such as batches, lightweight transactions, and paging.

Chapter 10, "Configuring and Deploying Cassandra"
This chapter shows you how to specify partitioners, replica placement strategies, and snitches. We set up a cluster and see the implications of different configuration choices. We'll discuss how to plan your cluster deployments, including hybrid and multicloud deployments using providers such as Amazon, Microsoft,

and Google, as well as deploying and managing clusters using Docker and Kubernetes.

Chapter 11, "Monitoring"

Once your cluster is up and running, you'll want to monitor its usage, memory patterns, and thread patterns, and understand its general activity. Cassandra has a rich Java Management Extensions (JMX) interface baked in, which we put to use to monitor all of these and more.

Chapter 12, "Maintenance"

The ongoing maintenance of a Cassandra cluster is made somewhat easier by some tools that ship with the server. We see how to decommission a node, load balance the cluster, get statistics, and perform other routine operational tasks.

Chapter 13, "Performance Tuning"

One of Cassandra's most notable features is its speed—it's very fast. But there are a number of things, including memory settings, data storage, hardware choices, caching, and buffer sizes, that you can tune to squeeze out even more performance.

Chapter 14, "Security"

NoSQL technologies are often slighted as being weak on security. Thankfully, Cassandra provides authentication, authorization, and encryption features, which we'll learn how to configure in this chapter.

Chapter 15, "Migrating and Integrating"

We close the book with a summary of the steps involved in bringing Cassandra into your enterprise, from the perspective of migrating from a relational database to Cassandra. We'll look at the implications for data modeling, application development, and deployment as well as how Cassandra integrates with other popular technologies, including:

- Streaming systems such as Apache Kafka
- Search engines such as Apache Lucene, Apache Solr, and ElasticSearch
- Analytics platforms such as Apache Spark

Cassandra Versions Used in This Book

This book was developed using Apache Cassandra 4.0 and the DataStax Java Driver version 4.1. The formatting and content of tool output, log files, configuration files, and error messages are as they appear in the 4.0 release, and may change in future releases.

When discussing features added in releases 2.0 and later, we cite the release in which the feature was added for readers who may be using earlier versions and are considering whether to upgrade.

New for the Third Edition

For this third edition, there is not quite as much of a time gap to cover as there was between the first and second editions, but there have been several key changes we'd like to note:

A grown-up database
> The conventional wisdom in the software engineering community has been that it takes 5–10 years for a new database engine to fully mature. Thankfully, Cassandra has reached this maturity milestone, and while the 4.0 release certainly has some stability and availability improvements, the bulk of the new features are focused on features that make the database easier to understand and maintain. This edition covers new 4.0 features including: virtual tables (covered in Chapter 11), audit logging (covered in Chapter 14), and change data capture (CDC) (covered in Chapter 15).

Cassandra in cloud applications
> The types of applications in which Cassandra is used continue to increase. To help bridge the gap between concept and reality, we've added a new chapter on this, Chapter 7. We've also updated Chapter 15 to include discussion of several patterns for using Kafka and Cassandra together.

Changes in cloud deployment
> When the second edition was published, Docker had already become a popular choice for application deployment, but the verdict was still out on running databases on Docker. Since then, there have been sufficient advances that we now feel comfortable recommending deployment of Cassandra on Docker. Kubernetes has emerged as the key technology for orchestrating the deployment and maintenance of containers across clusters of machines. In this edition we've updated Chapter 10 with new guidance on deployment of Cassandra to Docker and added coverage of Kubernetes to reflect the changing landscape.

Note on the Revised Third Edition

This revised third edition contains several updates to help bring the Cassandra story up to date as of 2022:

- The Cassandra community has continued to innovate since the 4.0 release. This edition highlights efforts under the Apache project umbrella, as reflected in the Cassandra Enhancement Proposal (CEP) process. We also highlight companion ventures, including K8ssandra (*https://k8ssandra.io*), a project for deploying Cassandra in Kubernetes.

- The experience of developing applications with Cassandra continues to improve. We've extended our coverage of development with Cassandra in Chapter 8, including API access with Stargate (*https://stargate.io*) and driver examples in additional popular languages.

Conventions Used in This Book

The following typographical conventions are used in this book:

Italic
: Indicates new terms, URLs, email addresses, filenames, and file extensions.

`Constant width`
: Used for program listings, as well as within paragraphs to refer to program elements such as variable or function names, databases, data types, environment variables, statements, and keywords.

`Constant width bold`
: Shows commands or other text that should be typed literally by the user.

 This element signifies a tip or suggestion.

 This element signifies a general note.

 This element indicates a warning or caution.

Using Code Examples

The code examples found in this book are available for download at *https://github.com/jeffreyscarpenter/cassandra-guide* and *https://github.com/jeffreyscarpenter/reservation-service*.

This book is here to help you get your job done. In general, you may use the code in this book in your programs and documentation. You do not need to contact us for permission unless you're reproducing a significant portion of the code. For example, writing a program that uses several chunks of code from this book does not require permission. Selling or distributing examples from O'Reilly books does require permission. Answering a question by citing this book and quoting example code does not require permission. Incorporating a significant amount of example code from this book into your product's documentation does require permission.

We appreciate, but generally do not require, attribution. An attribution usually includes the title, author, publisher, and ISBN. For example: "*Cassandra: The Definitive Guide*, Revised Edition, by Jeff Carpenter and Eben Hewitt (O'Reilly). Copyright 2022 Jeff Carpenter, 978-1-492-09714-3."

If you feel your use of code examples falls outside fair use or the permission given here, feel free to contact us at *permissions@oreilly.com*.

O'Reilly Interactive Katacoda Scenarios

Interactive Katacoda scenarios mimic real-world production environments and let you write and run code as you learn, right in your browser. The author has developed a collection of Katacoda scenarios to give you hands-on practice with the tools and practices outlined in this book. Visit *http://oreilly.com* for more information about our interactive content, to view the ebook format for this title, and also to learn about all our learning platform has to offer.

O'Reilly Online Learning

 For more than 40 years, *O'Reilly Media* has provided technology and business training, knowledge, and insight to help companies succeed.

Our unique network of experts and innovators share their knowledge and expertise through books, articles, and our online learning platform. O'Reilly's online learning platform gives you on-demand access to live training courses, in-depth learning paths, interactive coding environments, and a vast collection of text and video from O'Reilly and 200+ other publishers. For more information, please visit *http://oreilly.com*.

How to Contact Us

Please address comments and questions concerning this book to the publisher:

O'Reilly Media, Inc.
1005 Gravenstein Highway North

Sebastopol, CA 95472

800-998-9938 (in the United States or Canada)

707-829-0515 (international or local)

707-829-0104 (fax)

We have a web page for this book, where we list errata, examples, and any additional information. You can access this page at *https://oreil.ly/cassandra_revisedEd*.

Send an email to *bookquestions@oreilly.com* to comment or ask technical questions about this book.

For more information about our books, courses, and news, see our website at *http://www.oreilly.com*.

Find us on Facebook: *http://facebook.com/oreilly*

Follow us on Twitter: *http://twitter.com/oreillymedia*

Watch us on YouTube: *http://www.youtube.com/oreillymedia*

Acknowledgments

There are many wonderful people to whom we are grateful for helping bring this book to life.

Thank you to our technical reviewers: Stu Hood, Robert Schneider, and Gary Dusbabek contributed thoughtful reviews to the first edition, while Andrew Baker, Ewan Elliot, Kirk Damron, Corey Cole, Jeff Jirsa, Chris Judson, and Patrick McFadin reviewed the second edition. The third edition was reviewed by Pankaj Gallar, Cedrick Lunven, Alex Ott, and Wei Deng.

Thank you to Jonathan Ellis and Patrick McFadin for writing forewords for the first and second editions, respectively, and to Nate McCall for the third edition foreword. Thanks also to Patrick for his contributions to the Spark integration section in Chapter 15.

Thanks to our editors, Mike Loukides, Marie Beaugureau, Nicole Taché, Jess Haberman, and Sarah Grey, for their constant support and making this a better book.

Jeff would like to thank Eben for entrusting him with the opportunity to update such a well-regarded, foundational text, and for Eben's encouragement from start to finish.

Finally, we've been inspired by the many terrific developers who have contributed to Cassandra. Hats off for making such an elegant and powerful database.

## CHAPTER 1

Beyond Relational Databases

If at first the idea is not absurd, then there is no hope for it.

—Albert Einstein

Welcome to *Cassandra: The Definitive Guide*. The aim of this book is to help developers and database administrators understand this important database technology. During the course of this book, we will explore how Cassandra compares to traditional relational database management systems, and help you put it to work in your own environment.

What's Wrong with Relational Databases?

If I had asked people what they wanted, they would have said faster horses.

—Henry Ford

We ask you to consider a certain model for data, invented by a small team at a company with thousands of employees. It was accessible over a TCP/IP interface and was available from a variety of languages, including Java and web services. This model was difficult at first for all but the most advanced computer scientists to understand, until broader adoption helped make the concepts clearer. Using the database built around this model required learning new terms and thinking about data storage in a different way. But as products sprang up around it, more businesses and government agencies put it to use, in no small part because it was fast—capable of processing thousands of operations a second. The revenue it generated was tremendous.

And then a new model came along.

The new model was threatening, chiefly for two reasons. First, the new model was very different from the old model, which it pointedly controverted. It was threatening because it can be hard to understand something different and new. Ensuing debates can help entrench people stubbornly further in their views—views that might have been largely inherited from the climate in which they learned their craft and the circumstances in which they work. Second, and perhaps more importantly, as a barrier, the new model was threatening because businesses had made considerable investments in the old model and were making lots of money with it. Changing course seemed ridiculous, even impossible.

Of course, we are talking about the Information Management System (IMS) hierarchical database, invented in 1966 at IBM.

IMS was built for use in the Saturn V moon rocket. Its architect was Vern Watts, who dedicated his career to it. Many of us are familiar with IBM's database DB2. IBM's wildly popular DB2 database gets its name as the successor to DB1—the product built around the hierarchical data model IMS. IMS was released in 1968, and subsequently enjoyed success in Customer Information Control System (CICS) and other applications. It is still used today.

But in the years following the invention of IMS, the new model, the disruptive model, the threatening model, was the relational database.

In his 1970 paper, "A Relational Model of Data for Large Shared Data Banks" (*https:// oreil.ly/IM50v*), Dr. Edgar F. Codd also advanced his theory of the relational model for data while working at IBM's San Jose research laboratory. This paper became the foundational work for relational database management systems.

Codd's work was antithetical to the hierarchical structure of IMS. Understanding and working with a relational database required learning new terms, including *relations, tuples,* and *normal form,* all of which must have sounded very strange indeed to users of IMS. It presented certain key advantages over its predecessor, such as the ability to express complex relationships between multiple entities, well beyond what could be represented by hierarchical databases.

While these ideas and their application have evolved in four decades, the relational database still is clearly one of the most successful software applications in history. It's used in the form of Microsoft Access in sole proprietorships, and in giant multinational corporations with clusters of hundreds of finely tuned instances representing multiterabyte data warehouses. Relational databases store invoices, customer records, product catalogs, accounting ledgers, user authentication schemes—the very world, it might appear. There is no question that the relational database is a key facet of the modern technology and business landscape, and one that will be with us in its various forms for many years to come, as will IMS in its various forms. The relational model presented an alternative to IMS, and each has its uses.

So the short answer to the question, "What's Wrong with Relational Databases?" is "Nothing."

There is, however, a rather longer answer, which says that every once in a while an idea is born that ostensibly changes things, and engenders a revolution of sorts. And yet, in another way, such revolutions, viewed structurally, are simply history's business as usual. IMS, RDBMS, NoSQL. The horse, the car, the plane. They each build on prior art, they each attempt to solve certain problems, and so they're each good at certain things—and less good at others. They coexist, even now.

So let's examine for a moment why you might consider an alternative to the relational database, just as Codd himself four decades ago looked at the Information Management System and thought that maybe it wasn't the only legitimate way of organizing information and solving data problems, and that maybe, for certain problems, it might prove fruitful to consider an alternative.

You encounter scalability problems when your relational applications become successful and usage goes up. The need to gather related data from multiple tables via *joins* is inherent in any relatively normalized relational database of even modest size, and joins can be slow. The way that databases gain consistency is typically through the use of transactions, which require locking some portion of the database so it's not available to other clients. This can become untenable under very heavy loads, as the locks mean that competing users start queuing up, waiting for their turn to read or write the data.

You typically address these problems in one or more of the following ways, sometimes in this order:

- Throw hardware at the problem by adding more memory, adding faster processors, and upgrading disks. This is known as *vertical scaling*. This can relieve you for a time.

- When the problems arise again, the answer appears to be similar: now that one box is maxed out, you add hardware in the form of additional boxes in a database cluster. Now you have the problem of data replication and consistency during regular usage and in failover scenarios. You didn't have that problem before.

- Now you need to update the configuration of the database management system. This might mean optimizing the channels the database uses to write to the underlying filesystem. You turn off logging or journaling, which frequently is not a desirable (or, depending on your situation, legal) option.

- Having put what attention you could into the database system, you turn to your application. You try to improve your indexes. You optimize the queries. But presumably at this scale you weren't wholly ignorant of index and query optimization, and already had them in pretty good shape. So this becomes a painful process of picking through the data access code to find any opportunities for fine-tuning. This might include reducing or reorganizing joins, throwing out resource-intensive features such as XML processing within a stored procedure, and so forth. Of course, presumably you were doing that XML processing for a reason, so if you have to do it somewhere, you move that problem to the application layer, hoping to solve it there and crossing your fingers that you don't break something else in the meantime.

- You employ a caching layer. For larger systems, this might include distributed caches such as Redis, memcached, Hazelcast, Aerospike, Ehcache, or Riak. Now you have a consistency problem between updates in the cache and updates in the database, which is exacerbated over a cluster.

- You turn your attention to the database again and decide that, now that the application is built and you understand the primary query paths, you can duplicate some of the data to make it look more like the queries that access it. This process, called denormalization, is antithetical to the five normal forms that characterize the relational model, and violates Codd's 12 Rules for relational data. You remind yourself that you live in this world, and not in some theoretical cloud, and then undertake to do what you must to make the application start responding at acceptable levels again, even if it's no longer "pure."

Codd's 12 Rules

Codd provided a list of 12 rules (there are actually 13, numbered 0 to 12) formalizing his definition of the relational model as a response to the divergence of commercial databases from his original concepts. Codd introduced his rules in a pair of articles in *CompuWorld* magazine in October 1985, and formalized them in the second edition of his book *The Relational Model for Database Management*, which is now out of print. Although Codd's rules represent an ideal system which commercial databases have typically implemented only partially, they have continued to exert a key influence over relational data modeling to the present day.

This likely sounds familiar to you. At web scale, engineers may legitimately ponder whether this situation isn't similar to Henry Ford's assertion that at a certain point, it's not simply a faster horse that you want. And they've done some impressive, interesting work.

We must therefore begin here in recognition that the relational model is simply a model. That is, it's intended to be a useful way of looking at the world, applicable to certain problems. It does not purport to be exhaustive, closing the case on all other ways of representing data, never again to be examined, leaving no room for alternatives. If you take the long view of history, Dr. Codd's model was a rather disruptive one in its time. It was new, with strange new vocabulary and terms such as *tuples*—familiar words used in a new and different manner. The relational model was held up to suspicion, and doubtless suffered its vehement detractors. It encountered opposition even in the form of Dr. Codd's own employer, IBM, which had a very lucrative product set around IMS and didn't need a young upstart cutting into its pie.

But the relational model now arguably enjoys the best seat in the house within the data world. SQL is widely supported and well understood. It is taught in introductory university courses. Cloud-based Platform-as-a-Service (PaaS) providers such as Amazon Web Services, Google Cloud Platform, Microsoft Azure, Alibaba, and Rackspace provide relational database access as a service, including automated monitoring and maintenance features. Often the database you end up using is dictated by architectural standards within your organization. Even absent such standards, it's prudent to learn whatever your organization already has for a database platform. Your colleagues in development and infrastructure have considerable hard-won knowledge.

If by nothing more than osmosis (or inertia), you have learned over the years that a relational database is a one-size-fits-all solution.

So perhaps a better question is not, "What's Wrong with Relational Databases?" but rather, "What problem do you have?"

That is, you want to ensure that your solution matches the problem that you have. There are certain problems that relational databases solve very well. But the explosion of the web, and in particular social networks, means a corresponding explosion in the sheer volume of data you must deal with. When Tim Berners-Lee first worked on the web in the early 1990s, it was for the purpose of exchanging scientific documents between PhDs at a physics laboratory. Now, of course, the web has become so ubiquitous that it's used by everyone, from those same scientists to legions of five-year-olds exchanging emoji about kittens. That means in part that it must support enormous volumes of data; the fact that it does stands as a monument to the ingenious architecture of the web.

But as the traditional relational databases started to bend under the weight, it became clear that new solutions were needed.

A Quick Review of Relational Databases

Though you are likely familiar with them, let's briefly turn our attention to some of the foundational concepts in relational databases. This will give us a basis on which to consider more recent advances in thought around the trade-offs inherent in distributed data systems, especially very large distributed data systems, such as those that are required at web scale.

There are many reasons that the relational database has become so overwhelmingly popular over the last four decades. An important one is the Structured Query Language (SQL), which is feature-rich and uses a simple, declarative syntax. SQL was first officially adopted as an American National Standards Institute (ANSI) standard in 1986; since that time, it's gone through several revisions and has also been extended with vendor-proprietary syntax such as Microsoft's T-SQL and Oracle's PL/SQL to provide additional implementation-specific features.

SQL is powerful for a variety of reasons. It allows the user to represent complex relationships with the data, using statements that form the Data Manipulation Language (DML) to insert, select, update, delete, truncate, and merge data. You can perform a rich variety of operations using functions based on relational algebra to find a maximum or minimum value in a set, for example, or to filter and order results. SQL statements support grouping aggregate values and executing summary functions. SQL provides a means of directly creating, altering, and dropping schema structures at runtime using Data Definition Language (DDL). SQL also allows you to grant and revoke rights for users and groups of users using the same syntax.

SQL is easy to use. The basic syntax can be learned quickly, and conceptually SQL and RDBMSs offer a low barrier to entry. Junior developers can become proficient readily, and as is often the case in an industry beset by rapid changes, tight deadlines, and exploding budgets, ease of use can be very important. And it's not just the syntax that's easy to use; there are many robust tools that include intuitive graphical interfaces for viewing and working with your database.

In part because it's a standard, SQL allows you to easily integrate your RDBMS with a wide variety of systems. All you need is a driver for your application language, and you're off to the races in a very portable way. If you decide to change your application implementation language (or your RDBMS vendor), you can often do that painlessly, assuming you haven't backed yourself into a corner using lots of proprietary extensions.

Transactions, ACID-ity, and Two-Phase Commit

In addition to the features mentioned already, RDBMSs and SQL also support *transactions*. A key feature of transactions is that they execute virtually at first, allowing the programmer to undo (using rollback) any changes that may have gone awry during execution; if all has gone well, the transaction can be reliably committed. As Jim Gray puts it, a transaction is "a transformation of state" that has the ACID properties (see "The Transaction Concept: Virtues and Limitations" (*https://oreil.ly/ AMarh*)).

ACID is an acronym for Atomic, Consistent, Isolated, Durable, which are the gauges you can use to assess that a transaction has executed properly and that it was successful:

Atomic

Atomic means "all or nothing"; that is, when a statement is executed, every update within the transaction must succeed in order to be called successful. There is no partial failure where one update was successful and another related update failed. The common example here is with monetary transfers at an ATM: the transfer requires a debit from one account and a credit to another account. This operation cannot be subdivided; they must both succeed.

Consistent

Consistent means that data moves from one correct state to another correct state, with no possibility that readers could view different values that don't make sense together. For example, if a transaction attempts to delete a customer and their order history, it cannot leave order rows that reference the deleted customer's primary key; this is an inconsistent state that would cause errors if someone tried to read those order records.

Isolated

Isolated means that transactions executing concurrently will not become entangled with each other; they each execute in their own space. That is, if two different transactions attempt to modify the same data at the same time, then one of them will have to wait for the other to complete.

Durable

Once a transaction has succeeded, the changes will not be lost. This doesn't imply another transaction won't later modify the same data; it just means that writers can be confident that the changes are available for the next transaction to work with as necessary.

The debate about support for transactions comes up very quickly as a sore spot in conversations around nonrelational data stores, so let's take a moment to revisit what this really means. On the surface, ACID properties seem so obviously desirable as to not even merit conversation. Presumably no one who runs a database would suggest that data updates don't have to endure for some length of time; that's the very point of making updates—that they're there for others to read. However, a more subtle examination might lead you to want to find a way to tune these properties a bit and control them slightly. There is, as they say, no free lunch on the internet, and once you see how you're paying for transactions, you may start to wonder whether there's an alternative.

Transactions become difficult under heavy load. When you first attempt to horizontally scale a relational database, making it distributed, you must now account for *distributed transactions*, where the transaction isn't simply operating inside a single table or a single database, but is spread across multiple systems. In order to continue to honor the ACID properties of transactions, you now need a transaction manager to orchestrate across the multiple nodes.

In order to account for successful completion across multiple hosts, the idea of a two-phase commit (sometimes referred to as "2PC") is introduced. The two-phase commit is a commonly used algorithm for achieving consensus in distributed systems, involving two sets of interactions between hosts known as the prepare phase and commit phase. Because the two-phase commit locks all associated resources, it is useful only for operations that can complete very quickly. Although it may often be the case that your distributed operations can complete in subsecond time, it is certainly not always the case. Some use cases require coordination between multiple hosts that you may not control yourself. Operations coordinating several different but related activities can take hours to update.

Two-phase commit *blocks*; that is, clients ("competing consumers") must wait for a prior transaction to finish before they can access the blocked resource. The protocol will wait for a node to respond, even if it has died. It's possible to avoid waiting forever in this event, because a timeout can be set that allows the transaction coordinator node to decide that the node isn't going to respond and that it should abort the transaction. However, an infinite loop is still possible with 2PC; that's because a node can send a message to the transaction coordinator node agreeing that it's OK for the coordinator to commit the entire transaction. The node will then wait for the coordinator to send a commit response (or a rollback response if, say, a different node can't commit); if the coordinator is down in this scenario, that node conceivably will wait forever.

So in order to account for these shortcomings in two-phase commit of distributed transactions, the database world turned to the idea of *compensation*. Compensation, often used in web services, means in simple terms that the operation is immediately committed, and then in the event that some error is reported, a new operation is invoked to restore proper state.

There are a few basic, well-known patterns for compensatory action that architects frequently have to consider as an alternative to two-phase commit. These include writing off the transaction if it fails, deciding to discard erroneous transactions and reconciling later. Another alternative is to retry failed operations later on notification. In a reservation system or a stock sales ticker, these are not likely to meet your requirements. For other kinds of applications, such as billing or ticketing applications, this can be acceptable.

The Problem with Two-Phase Commit

Gregor Hohpe, a Google architect, wrote a wonderful and often-cited blog entry titled "Starbucks Does Not Use Two-Phase Commit" (*https://oreil.ly/0rnad*). It shows in real-world terms how difficult it is to scale two-phase commit and highlights some of the alternatives that are mentioned here. It's an easy, fun, and enlightening read. If you're interested in digging deeper, Martin Kleppman's comprehensive book *Designing Data-Intensive Applications* (O'Reilly) contains an excellent in-depth discussion of two-phase commit and other consensus algorithms.

The problems that 2PC introduces for application developers include loss of availability and higher latency during partial failures. Neither of these is desirable. So once you've had the good fortune of being successful enough to necessitate scaling your database past a single machine, you now have to figure out how to handle transactions across multiple machines and still make the ACID properties apply. Whether you have 10 or 100 or 1,000 database machines, atomicity is still required in transactions as if you were working on a single node. But it's now a much, much bigger pill to swallow.

Schema

One often-lauded feature of relational database systems is the rich schemas they afford. You can represent your domain objects in a relational model. A whole industry has sprung up around (expensive) tools such as the CA ERwin Data Modeler to support this effort. In order to create a properly normalized schema, however, you are forced to create tables that don't exist as business objects in your domain. For example, a schema for a university database might require a "student" table and a "course" table. But because of the "many-to-many" relationship here (one student can take many courses at the same time, and one course has many students at the same time), you have to create a join table. This pollutes a pristine data model, where you'd prefer to just have students and courses. It also forces you to create more complex SQL statements to join these tables together. The join statements, in turn, can be slow.

Again, in a system of modest size, this isn't much of a problem. But complex queries and multiple joins can become burdensomely slow once you have a large number of rows in many tables to handle.

Finally, not all schemas map well to the relational model. One type of system that has risen in popularity in the last decade is the *complex event processing system* or *stream processing system*, which represents state changes in a very fast stream. It's often useful to contextualize events at runtime against other events that might be related in order to infer some conclusion to support business decision-making. Although event streams can be represented in terms of a relational database, as with Apache Kafka's KSQL, it is often an uncomfortable stretch.

If you're an application developer, you'll no doubt be familiar with the many object-relational mapping (ORM) frameworks that have sprung up in recent years to help ease the difficulty in mapping application objects to a relational model. Again, for small systems, ORM can be a relief. But it also introduces new problems of its own, such as extended memory requirements, and it often pollutes the application code with increasingly unwieldy mapping code. Here's an example of a Java method using Hibernate to "ease the burden" of having to write the SQL code:

```
@CollectionOfElements
@JoinTable(name="store_description",
  joinColumns = @JoinColumn(name="store_code"))
@MapKey(columns={@Column(name="for_store",length=3)})
@Column(name="description")
private Map<String, String> getMap() {
  return this.map;
}
//... etc.
```

Is it certain that we've done anything but move the problem here? Of course, with some systems, such as those that make extensive use of document exchange, as with services or XML-based applications, there are not always clear mappings to a relational database. This exacerbates the problem.

Sharding and Shared-Nothing Architecture

If you can't split it, you can't scale it.

—Randy Shoup, Distinguished Architect, eBay

Another way to attempt to scale a relational database is to introduce *sharding* to your architecture. This has been used to good effect at large websites such as eBay, which supports billions of SQL queries a day, and in other modern web applications. The idea here is that you split the data so that instead of hosting all of it on a single server or replicating all of the data on all of the servers in a cluster, you divide up portions of the data horizontally and host them each separately.

For example, consider a large customer table in a relational database. The least disruptive thing (for the programming staff, anyway) is to vertically scale by adding CPU, adding memory, and getting faster hard drives, but if you continue to be successful and add more customers, at some point (perhaps into the tens of millions of rows), you'll likely have to start thinking about how you can add more machines. When you do so, do you just copy the data so that all of the machines have it? Or do you instead divide up that single customer table so that each database has only some of the records, with their order preserved? Then, when clients execute queries, they put load only on the machine that has the record they're looking for, with no load on the other machines.

It seems clear that in order to shard, you need to find a good key by which to order your records. For example, you could divide your customer records across 26 machines, one for each letter of the alphabet, with each hosting only the records for customers whose last names start with that particular letter. It's likely this is not a good strategy, however—there probably aren't many last names that begin with "Q" or "Z," so those machines will sit idle while the "J," "M," and "S" machines spike. You could shard according to something numeric, like phone number, "member since" date, or the name of the customer's state. It all depends on how your specific data is likely to be distributed.

There are three basic strategies for determining shard structure:

Feature-based shard or functional segmentation
> This is the approach taken by Randy Shoup, Distinguished Architect at eBay, who in 2006 helped bring the site's architecture into maturity to support many billions of queries per day. Using this strategy, the data is split not by dividing records in a single table (as in the customer example discussed earlier), but rather by splitting into separate databases the features that don't overlap with each other very much. For example, at eBay, the users are in one shard, and the items for sale are in another. This approach depends on understanding your domain so that you can segment data cleanly.

Key-based sharding
> In this approach, you find a key in your data that will evenly distribute it across shards. So instead of simply storing one letter of the alphabet for each server as in the (naive and improper) earlier example, you use a one-way hash on a key data element and distribute data across machines according to the hash. It is common in this strategy to find time-based or numeric keys to hash on.

Lookup table
> In this approach, also known as *directory-based sharding*, one of the nodes in the cluster acts as a "Yellow Pages" directory and looks up which node has the data you're trying to access. This has two obvious disadvantages. The first is that you'll take a performance hit every time you have to go through the lookup table as an additional hop. The second is that the lookup table not only becomes a bottleneck, but a single point of failure.

Sharding can minimize contention depending on your strategy and allows you not just to scale horizontally, but then to scale more precisely, as you can add power to the particular shards that need it.

Sharding could be termed a kind of *shared-nothing* architecture that's specific to databases. A shared-nothing architecture is one in which there is no centralized (shared) state, but each node in a distributed system is independent, so there is no client contention for shared resources.

Shared-nothing architecture was more recently popularized by Google, which has written systems such as its Bigtable database and its MapReduce implementation that do not share state, and are therefore capable of near-infinite scaling. The Cassandra database is a shared-nothing architecture, as it has no central controller and no notion of primary/secondary replicas; all of its nodes are the same.

More on Shared-Nothing Architecture

The term was first coined by Michael Stonebraker at the University of California at Berkeley in his 1986 paper "The Case for Shared Nothing." (*https://oreil.ly/prH9l*). It's only a few pages. If you take a look, you'll see that many of the features of shared-nothing distributed data architecture, such as ease of high availability and the ability to scale to a very large number of machines, are the very things that Cassandra excels at.

Many nonrelational databases offer this automatically and out of the box is very handy; creating and maintaining custom data shards by hand is a wicked proposition. For example, MongoDB, which we'll discuss later, provides auto-sharding capabilities to manage failover and node balancing. It's good to understand sharding in terms of data architecture in general, but especially in terms of Cassandra more specifically. Cassandra uses an approach similar to key-based sharding to distribute data across nodes, but does so automatically.

Web Scale

In summary, relational databases are very good at solving certain data storage problems, but because of their focus, they also can create problems of their own when it's time to scale. Then, you often need to find a way to get rid of your joins, which means denormalizing the data, which means maintaining multiple copies of data and seriously disrupting your design, both in the database and in your application. Further, you almost certainly need to find a way around distributed transactions, which will quickly become a bottleneck. These compensatory actions are not directly supported in any but the most expensive RDBMSs. And even if you can write such a huge check, you still need to carefully choose partitioning keys to the point where you can never entirely ignore the limitation.

Perhaps more importantly, as you see some of the limitations of RDBMSs and consequently some of the strategies that architects have used to mitigate their scaling issues, a picture slowly starts to emerge. It's a picture that makes some NoSQL solutions seem perhaps less radical and less scary than you may have thought at first, and more like a natural expression and encapsulation of some of the work that was already being done to manage very large databases.

Because of some of the inherent design decisions in RDBMSs, it is not always as easy to scale as some other, more recent possibilities that take the structure of the web into consideration. However, it's not only the structure of the web you need to consider, but also its phenomenal growth, because as more and more data becomes available, you need architectures that allow your organization to take advantage of this data in near real time to support decision making, and to offer new and more powerful features and capabilities to your customers.

Data Scale, Then and Now

It has been said, though it is hard to verify, that the 17th-century English poet John Milton had actually read every published book on the face of the earth. Milton knew many languages (he was even learning Navajo at the time of his death), and given that the total number of published books at that time was in the thousands, this would have been possible. The size of the world's data stores have grown somewhat since then.

With the rapid growth in the web, there is great variety to the kinds of data that need to be stored, processed, and queried, and some variety to the businesses that use such data. Consider not only customer data at familiar retailers or suppliers, and not only digital video content, but also the required move to digital television and the explosive growth of email, messaging, mobile phones, RFID, Voice Over IP (VoIP) usage, and the Internet of Things (IoT). Companies that provide content—and the third-party value-add businesses built around them—require very scalable data solutions. Consider too that a typical business application developer or database administrator may be used to thinking of relational databases as the center of the universe. You might then be surprised to learn that within corporations, around 80% of data is unstructured.

The Rise of NoSQL

The recent interest in nonrelational databases reflects the growing sense of need in the software development community for web scale data solutions. The term "NoSQL" began gaining popularity around 2009 as a shorthand way of describing these databases. The term has historically been the subject of much debate, but a consensus has emerged that the term refers to nonrelational databases that support "not only SQL" semantics.

Various experts have attempted to organize these databases in a few broad categories; let's examine a few of the most common:

Key-value stores

In a key-value store, the data items are keys that have a set of attributes. All data relevant to a key is stored with the key; data is frequently duplicated. Popular key-value stores include Amazon's Dynamo DB, Riak, and Voldemort. Additionally, many popular caching technologies act as key-value stores, including Oracle Coherence, Redis, and Memcached.

Column stores

In a column store, also known as a *wide-column store* or *column-oriented store*, data is stored by column rather than by row. For example, in a column store, all customer addresses might be stored together, allowing them to be retrieved in a single query. Popular column stores include Apache Hadoop's HBase, Apache Kudu, and Apache Druid.

Document stores

The basic unit of storage in a document database is the complete document, often stored in a format such as JSON, XML, or YAML. Popular document stores include MongoDB, CouchDB, and several public cloud offerings.

Graph databases

Graph databases represent data as a graph—a network of nodes and edges that connect the nodes. Both nodes and edges can have properties. Because they give heightened importance to relationships, graph databases such as Neo4j, JanusGraph, and DataStax Graph have proven popular for building social networking and semantic web applications.

Object databases

Object databases store data not in terms of relations and columns and rows, but in terms of objects as understood from the discipline of object-oriented programming. This makes it straightforward to use these databases from object-oriented applications. Object databases such as db4o and InterSystems Caché allow you to avoid techniques like stored procedures and object-relational mapping (ORM) tools. The most widely used object database is Amazon Web Services' Simple Storage Service (S3).

XML databases

XML databases are a special form of document databases, optimized specifically for working with data described in the eXtensible Markup Language (XML). So-called "XML native" databases include BaseX and eXist.

Multimodel databases

Databases that support more than one of these styles have been growing in popularity. These "multimodel" databases are based on a primary underlying database (most often a relational, key-value, or column store) and expose additional models as APIs on top of that underlying database. Examples of these include

Microsoft Azure Cosmos DB, which exposes document, wide column, and graph APIs on top of a key-value store, and DataStax Enterprise, which offers a graph API on top of Cassandra's wide column model. Multimodel databases are often touted for their ability to support an approach known as *polyglot persistence*, in which different microservices or components of an application can interact with data using more than one of the models we've described here. We'll discuss an example of polyglot persistence in Chapter 7.

Learning More About NoSQL Databases

For a comprehensive list of NoSQL databases, see the NoSQL site (*https://oreil.ly/KLChH*). The DB-Engines site (*https://oreil.ly/qdJnx*) also provides popularity rankings of popular databases by type, updated monthly.

There is wide variety in the goals and features of these databases, but they tend to share a set of common characteristics. The most obvious of these is implied by the name NoSQL—these databases support data models, Data Definition Languages (DDLs), and interfaces beyond the standard SQL available in popular relational databases. In addition, these databases are typically distributed systems without centralized control. They emphasize horizontal scalability and high availability, in some cases at the cost of strong consistency and ACID semantics. They tend to support rapid development and deployment. They take flexible approaches to schema definition, in some cases not requiring any schema to be defined up front. They provide support for Big Data and analytics use cases.

Over the past decade, there have been a large number of open source and commercial offerings in the NoSQL space. The adoption and quality of these have varied widely, but leaders have emerged in the categories just discussed, and many have become mature technologies with large installation bases and commercial support. We're happy to report that Cassandra is one of those technologies, as we'll dig into more in the next chapter.

New Relational Architectures and NewSQL

Many of the challenges with previous approaches to scale relational databases that we've described in this chapter can be attributed to designs that attempted to graft distributed systems principles on top of existing database engines, with generally unsatisfactory results.

In response to the criticisms of traditional RDBMS that we've summarized in this chapter, database researchers began to explore new approaches for creating more scalable relational systems. In 2012, two key papers were published, proposing new approaches for providing transactional guarantees at scale. The first was the Calvin transaction protocol (*https://oreil.ly/Dsqm8*) developed at Yale University described an approach based on a global consensus protocol used by all transactions on a database. FaunaDB is an example of a database that implements the approach on the Calvin paper.

Google's Spanner paper (*https://oreil.ly/fuxLh*), published a couple of months later, proposed an approach in which the database is divided into shards and a separate consensus protocol is applied to shards to support transactional guarantees. Google Cloud Spanner, CockroachDB, and YugaByteDB are examples of databases that follow this approach.

Don't worry if the references to consistency don't make sense yet; we'll dive into this more in "Brewer's CAP Theorem" on page 23. The main takeaway for now is that these so called *NewSQL* databases were designed from the ground up to support ACID transaction semantics at scale. Note that the reference to SQL is possibly misleading, as not all of these databases provide full ANSI SQL support.

Summary

The relational model has served the software industry well over the past four decades, but the level of availability and scalability required for modern applications has stretched traditional relational database technology to the breaking point.

The intention of this book is not to convince you by clever argument to adopt a non-relational database such as Apache Cassandra. It is only our intention to present what Cassandra can do and how it does it so that you can make an informed decision and get started working with it in practical ways if you find it applies.

Perhaps the ultimate question, then, is not "What's Wrong with Relational Databases?" but rather, "What kinds of things would I do with data if it wasn't a problem?" In a world now working at web scale and looking to the future, Apache Cassandra might be one part of the answer.

## CHAPTER 2

Introducing Cassandra

An invention has to make sense in the world in which it is finished, not the world in which it is started.

—Ray Kurzweil

In the previous chapter, we discussed the emergence of nonrelational database technologies in order to meet the increasing demands of modern web scale applications. In this chapter, we'll focus on Cassandra's value proposition and key tenets to show how it rises to the challenge. You'll also learn about Cassandra's history and how you can get involved in the open source community that maintains Cassandra.

The Cassandra Elevator Pitch

Hollywood screenwriters and software entrepreneurs are often advised to have their "elevator pitch" ready. This is a summary of exactly what their product is all about—concise, clear, and brief enough to deliver in just a minute or two, in the lucky event that they find themselves sharing an elevator with an executive, agent, or investor who might consider funding their project. Cassandra has a compelling story, so let's boil it down to an elevator pitch that you can present to your manager or colleagues should the occasion arise.

Cassandra in 50 Words or Less

"Apache Cassandra is an open source, distributed, decentralized, elastically scalable, highly available, fault-tolerant, tuneably consistent, row-oriented database. Cassandra bases its distribution design on Amazon's Dynamo and its data model on Google's Bigtable, with a query language similar to SQL. Created at Facebook, it now powers cloud-scale applications across many industries." That's exactly 50 words.

Of course, if you were to recite that to your boss in the elevator, you'd probably get a blank look in return. So let's break down the key points in the following sections.

Distributed and Decentralized

Cassandra is *distributed*, which means that it is capable of running on multiple machines while appearing to users as a unified whole. In fact, there is little point in running a single Cassandra node. Although you can do it, and that's acceptable for getting up to speed on how it works, you quickly realize that you'll need multiple machines to really realize any benefit from running Cassandra. Much of its design and codebase is specifically engineered toward not only making it work across many different machines, but also for optimizing performance across multiple data center racks, and even for a single Cassandra cluster running across geographically dispersed data centers. You can confidently write data to anywhere in the cluster and Cassandra will get it.

Once you start to scale many other data stores (MySQL, Bigtable), some nodes need to be set up as primary replicas in order to organize other nodes, which are set up as secondary replicas. Cassandra, however, is decentralized, meaning that every node is identical; no Cassandra node performs certain organizing operations distinct from any other node. Instead, Cassandra features a peer-to-peer architecture and uses a gossip protocol to maintain and keep in sync a list of nodes that are alive or dead. We'll discuss this more in "Gossip and Failure Detection" on page 108.

The fact that Cassandra is *decentralized* means that there is no single point of failure. All of the nodes in a Cassandra cluster function exactly the same. This is sometimes referred to as "server symmetry." Because they are all doing the same thing, by definition there can't be a special host that is coordinating activities, as with the primary/secondary setup that you see in MySQL, Bigtable, and so many other databases.

In many distributed data solutions (such as RDBMS clusters), you set up multiple copies of data on different servers in a process called replication, which copies the data to multiple machines so that they can all serve simultaneous requests and improve performance. Typically this process is not decentralized, as in Cassandra, but is rather performed by defining a *primary/secondary relationship*. That is, all of the servers in this kind of cluster don't function in the same way. You configure your cluster by designating one server as the primary (or *primary replica*) and others as *secondary replicas*. The primary replica acts as the authoritative source of the data, and operates in a unidirectional relationship with the secondary replicas, which must synchronize their copies. If the primary node fails, the whole database is in jeopardy. To work around the situation of the primary as a single point of failure, you often need to add complexity to the environment in the form of multiple primary nodes. Note that while we frequently understand primary/secondary replication in the RDBMS world, there are NoSQL databases such as MongoDB that follow the primary/secondary scheme as well. Even Mongo's "replica set" mechanism is essentially a primary/secondary scheme in which the primary can be replaced by an automated leader election process.

Decentralization, therefore, has two key advantages: it's simpler to use than primary/secondary, and it helps you avoid outages. It is simpler to operate and maintain a decentralized store than a primary/secondary store because all nodes are the same. That means that you don't need any special knowledge to scale; setting up 50 nodes isn't much different from setting up one. There's next to no configuration required to support it. Because all of the replicas in Cassandra are identical, failures of a node won't disrupt service.

In short, because Cassandra is distributed and decentralized, there is no single point of failure, which supports high availability.

Elastic Scalability

Scalability is an architectural feature of a system that can continue serving a greater number of requests with little degradation in performance. *Vertical scaling*—simply adding more processing capacity and memory to your existing machine—is the easiest way to achieve this. *Horizontal scaling* means adding more machines that have all or some of the data on them so that no one machine has to bear the entire burden of serving requests. But then the software itself must have an internal mechanism for keeping its data in sync with the other nodes in the cluster.

Elastic scalability refers to a special property of horizontal scalability. It means that your cluster can seamlessly scale up and scale back down. To do this, the cluster must be able to accept new nodes that can begin participating by getting a copy of some or all of the data and start serving new user requests without major disruption or reconfiguration of the entire cluster. You don't have to restart your process. You don't have to change your application queries. You don't have to manually rebalance the data yourself. Just add another machine—Cassandra will find it and start sending it work.

Scaling down, of course, means removing some of the processing capacity from your cluster. You might do this for business reasons, such as adjusting to seasonal workloads in retail or travel applications. Or perhaps there will be technical reasons such as moving parts of your application to another platform. As much as we try to minimize these situations, they still happen. But when they do, you won't need to upset the entire apple cart to scale back.

High Availability and Fault Tolerance

In general architecture terms, the availability of a system is measured according to its ability to fulfill requests. But computers can experience all manner of failure, from hardware component failure to network disruption to corruption. Any computer is susceptible to these kinds of failure. There are of course very sophisticated (and often prohibitively expensive) computers that can themselves mitigate many of these circumstances, as they include internal hardware redundancies and facilities to send notification of failure events and hot swap components. But anyone can accidentally break an Ethernet cable, and catastrophic events can beset a single data center. So for a system to be highly available, it must typically include multiple networked computers, and the software they're running must then be capable of operating in a cluster and have some facility for recognizing node failures and failing over requests to another part of the system.

Cassandra is highly available. You can replace failed nodes in the cluster with no downtime, and you can replicate data to multiple data centers to offer improved local performance and prevent downtime if one data center experiences a catastrophe such as fire or flood.

Tuneable Consistency

Consistency is an overloaded term in the database world, but for our purposes we will use the definition that a read always returns the most recently written value. Consider the case of two customers attempting to put the same item into their shopping carts on an ecommerce site. If I place the last item in stock into my cart an instant after you do, you should get the item added to your cart, and I should be informed that the item is no longer available for purchase. This is guaranteed to happen when the state of a write is consistent among all nodes that have that data.

But as we'll see later, scaling data stores means making certain trade-offs among data consistency, node availability, and partition tolerance. Cassandra is frequently called "eventually consistent," which is a bit misleading. Out of the box, Cassandra trades some consistency in order to achieve total availability. But Cassandra is more accurately termed "tuneably consistent," which means it allows you to easily decide the level of consistency you require, in balance with the level of availability.

Let's take a moment to unpack this, as the term "eventual consistency" has caused some uproar in the industry. Some practitioners hesitate to use a system that is described as "eventually consistent."

For detractors of eventual consistency, the broad argument goes something like this: eventual consistency is maybe OK for social web applications where data doesn't *really* matter. After all, you're just posting to Mom what little Billy ate for breakfast, and if it gets lost, it doesn't really matter. But the data *I* have is actually really important, and it's ridiculous to think that I could allow eventual consistency in my model.

Set aside the number of large-scale web applications (Amazon, Facebook, Google, Twitter) that use this model, and perhaps there's something to this argument. Presumably such data is very important indeed to the companies running these applications, because that data is their primary product, and they are multibillion-dollar companies with billions of users to satisfy in a sharply competitive world. It may be possible to gain guaranteed, immediate, and perfect consistency throughout a highly trafficked system running in parallel on a variety of networks, but if you want clients to get their results sometime this year, it's a very tricky proposition.

The detractors claim that databases like Cassandra have merely eventual consistency, and that all other distributed systems have *strict* consistency. As with so many things in the world, however, the reality is not so black and white, and the binary opposition between consistent and not-consistent is not truly reflected in practice. There are instead *degrees* of consistency, and in the real world they are very susceptible to external circumstance.

Eventual consistency is one of several consistency models available to architects. Let's take a look at these models so we can understand the trade-offs:

Strict consistency
> This is sometimes called sequential consistency, and is the most stringent level of consistency. It requires that any read will always return the most recently written value. That sounds perfect, and it's exactly what I'm looking for. I'll take it! However, upon closer examination, what do we find? What precisely is meant by "most recently written"? Most recently to whom? In one single-processor machine, this is no problem to observe, as the sequence of operations is known to the one clock. But in a system executing across a variety of geographically dispersed data centers, it becomes much more slippery. Achieving this implies some sort of global clock that is capable of timestamping all operations, regardless of the location of the data or the user requesting it or how many (possibly disparate) services are required to determine the response.

Causal consistency
> This is a slightly weaker form of strict consistency. It does away with the fantasy of the single global clock that can magically synchronize all operations without creating an unbearable bottleneck. Instead of relying on timestamps, causal consistency takes a more semantic approach, attempting to determine the cause of events to create some consistency in their order. It means that writes that are potentially related must be read in sequence. If two different, unrelated operations suddenly write to the same field at the same time, then those writes are inferred not to be causally related. But if one write occurs after another, we might infer that they are causally related. Causal consistency dictates that causal writes must be read in sequence.

Weak (eventual) consistency
> Eventual consistency means on the surface that all updates will propagate throughout all of the replicas in a distributed system, but that this may take some time. Eventually, all replicas will be consistent.

Eventual consistency becomes suddenly very attractive when you consider what is required to achieve stronger forms of consistency.

When considering consistency, availability, and partition tolerance, we can achieve only two of these goals in a given distributed system, a trade-off known as the CAP theorem (we explore this theorem in more depth in "Brewer's CAP Theorem"). At the center of the problem is data update replication. To achieve a strict consistency, all update operations will be performed synchronously, meaning that they must block, locking all replicas until the operation is complete, and forcing competing clients to wait. A side effect of such a design is that during a failure, some of the data will be entirely unavailable. As Amazon CTO Werner Vogels (*https://oreil.ly/CtOZw*) puts it, "rather than dealing with the uncertainty of the correctness of an answer, the data is made unavailable until it is absolutely certain that it is correct."

We could alternatively take an optimistic approach to replication, propagating updates to all replicas in the background in order to avoid blowing up on the client. The difficulty this approach presents is that now we are forced into the situation of detecting and resolving conflicts. A design approach must decide whether to resolve these conflicts at one of two possible times: during reads or during writes. That is, a distributed database designer must choose to make the system either always readable or always writable.

Dynamo and Cassandra choose to be always writable, opting to defer the complexity of reconciliation to read operations, and realize tremendous performance gains. The alternative is to reject updates amidst network and server failures.

In Cassandra, consistency is not an all-or-nothing proposition. A more accurate term is "tuneable consistency" because the client can control the number of replicas to block on for all updates. This is done by setting the consistency level against the replication factor.

You set the *replication factor* to the number of nodes in the cluster you want the updates to propagate to (remember that an update means any add, update, or delete operation).

The *consistency level* is a setting that clients must specify on every operation and that allows you to decide how many replicas in the cluster must acknowledge a write operation or respond to a read operation in order to be considered successful. That's the part where Cassandra has pushed the decision for determining consistency out to the client.

So if you like, you could set the consistency level to a number equal to the replication factor, and gain stronger consistency at the cost of synchronous blocking operations that wait for all nodes to be updated and declare success before returning. This is not often done in practice with Cassandra, however, for reasons that should be clear (it defeats the availability goal, would impact performance, and generally goes against the grain of why you'd want to use Cassandra in the first place). So if the client sets the consistency level to a value less than the replication factor, the update is considered successful even if some nodes are down.

Brewer's CAP Theorem

In order to understand Cassandra's design and its label as an "eventually consistent" database, we need to understand the CAP theorem. The CAP theorem is sometimes called Brewer's theorem after its author, Eric Brewer.

While working at the University of California at Berkeley, Eric Brewer posited his CAP theorem in 2000 at the ACM Symposium on the Principles of Distributed Computing. The theorem states that within a large-scale distributed data system, there are three requirements that have a relationship of sliding dependency:

Consistency
> All database clients will read the same value for the same query, even given concurrent updates.

Availability
> All database clients will always be able to read and write data.

Partition tolerance
> The database can be split into multiple machines; it can continue functioning in the face of network segmentation breaks.

Brewer's theorem is that in any given system, you can strongly support only two of the three. This is analogous to the saying you may have heard in software development: "You can have it good, you can have it fast, you can have it cheap: pick two."

We have to choose between them because of this sliding mutual dependency. The more consistency you demand from your system, for example, the less partition-tolerant you're likely to be able to make it, unless you make some concessions around availability.

The CAP theorem was formally proved to be true by Seth Gilbert and Nancy Lynch of MIT in 2002. In distributed systems, however, it is very likely that you will have network partitioning, and that at some point, machines will fail and cause others to become unreachable. Networking issues such as packet loss or high latency are nearly inevitable and have the potential to cause temporary partitions. This leads us to the conclusion that a distributed system must do its best to continue operating in the face of network partitions (to be partition tolerant), leaving us with only two real options to compromise on: availability and consistency.

Figure 2-1 illustrates visually that there is no overlapping segment where all three are obtainable.

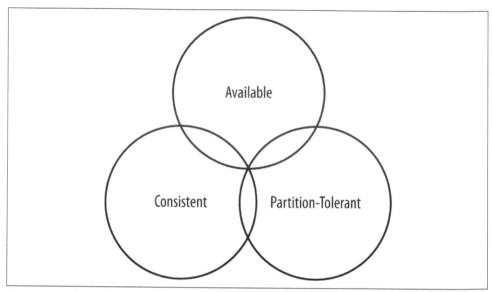

Figure 2-1. CAP theorem indicates that you can realize only two of these properties at once

It might prove useful at this point to see a graphical depiction of where each of the nonrelational data stores we'll look at falls within the CAP spectrum. The graphic in Figure 2-2 was inspired by a slide in a 2009 talk given by Dwight Merriman, CEO and founder of MongoDB (*https://oreil.ly/CXv5c*), to the MySQL User Group in New York City. However, we have modified the placement of some systems based on research.

Figure 2-2 shows the general focus of some of the different databases we discuss in this chapter. Note that placement of the databases in this chart could change based on configuration. As Stu Hood points out, a distributed MySQL database can count as a consistent system only if you're using Google's synchronous replication patches; otherwise, it can only be available and partition tolerant (AP).

It's interesting to note that the design of the system around CAP placement is independent of the orientation of the data storage mechanism; for example, the CP edge is populated by graph databases and document-oriented databases alike.

In this depiction, relational databases are on the line between consistency and availability, which means that they can fail in the event of a network failure (including a cable breaking). This is typically achieved by defining a single primary replica, which could itself go down, or an array of servers that simply don't have sufficient mechanisms built in to continue functioning in the case of network partitions.

Graph databases such as Neo4j and the set of databases derived at least in part from the design of Google's Bigtable database (such as MongoDB, HBase, Hypertable, and

Redis) all are focused slightly less on availability and more on ensuring consistency and partition tolerance.

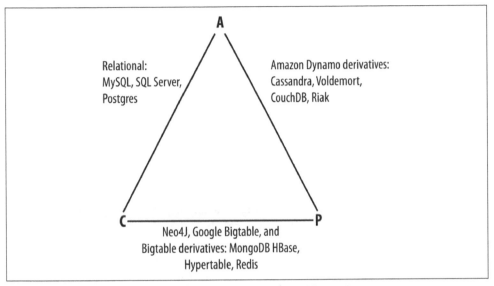

Figure 2-2. Where different databases appear on the CAP continuum

Finally, the databases derived from Amazon's Dynamo design include Cassandra, Project Voldemort, CouchDB, and Riak. These are more focused on availability and partition tolerance. However, this does not mean that they dismiss consistency as unimportant, any more than Bigtable dismisses availability. According to the Bigtable paper, the average percentage of server hours that "some data" was unavailable is 0.0047% (section 4), so this is relative, as we're talking about very robust systems already. If you think of each of these letters (C, A, P) as knobs you can tune to arrive at the system you want, Dynamo derivatives are intended for employment in the many use cases where "eventual consistency" is tolerable and where "eventual" is a matter of milliseconds, read repairs mean that reads will return consistent values, and you can achieve strong consistency if you want to.

So what does it mean in practical terms to support only two of the three facets of CAP?

CA

To primarily support consistency and availability means that you're likely using two-phase commit for distributed transactions. It means that the system will block when a network partition occurs, so it may be that your system is limited to a single data center cluster in an attempt to mitigate this. If your application needs only this level of scale, this is easy to manage and allows you to rely on familiar, simple structures.

CP

> To primarily support consistency and partition tolerance, you may try to advance your architecture by setting up data shards in order to scale. Your data will be consistent, but you still run the risk of some data becoming unavailable if nodes fail.

AP

> To primarily support availability and partition tolerance, your system may return inaccurate data, but the system will always be available, even in the face of network partitioning. DNS is perhaps the most popular example of a system that is massively scalable, highly available, and partition tolerant.

Note that this depiction is intended to offer an overview that helps draw distinctions between the broader contours in these systems; it is not strictly precise. For example, it's not entirely clear where Google's Bigtable should be placed on such a continuum. The Google paper describes Bigtable as "highly available," but later goes on to say that if Chubby (the Bigtable persistent lock service) "becomes unavailable for an extended period of time [caused by Chubby outages or network issues], Bigtable becomes unavailable" (section 4). On the matter of data reads, the paper says that "we do not consider the possibility of multiple copies of the same data, possibly in alternate forms due to views or indices." Finally, the paper indicates that "centralized control and Byzantine fault tolerance are not Bigtable goals" (section 10). Given such variable information, you can see that determining where a database falls on this sliding scale is not an exact science.

The CAP Theorem—An Ongoing Conversation

In February 2012, Eric Brewer provided an updated perspective on his CAP theorem in the article "CAP Twelve Years Later: How the *Rules* Have Changed" (*https://oreil.ly/6qToG*) in IEEE's *Computer*. Brewer now describes the "pick two" axiom as somewhat misleading. He notes that designers only need sacrifice consistency or availability in the presence of partitions, and that advances in partition recovery techniques have made it possible for designers to achieve high levels of both consistency and availability.

These advances in partition recovery certainly would include Cassandra's usage of mechanisms such as hinted handoff and read repair. We'll explore these in Chapter 6. However, it is important to recognize that these partition recovery mechanisms are not infallible. There is still immense value in Cassandra's tuneable consistency, allowing Cassandra to function effectively in a diverse set of deployments in which it is not possible to completely prevent partitions.

In recent years Eric Brewer has joined the Google Cloud Platform team. In his 2017 blog post "Inside Cloud Spanner and the CAP Theorem" (*https://oreil.ly/S5LAs*), he evaluates Google Spanner in terms of the CAP theorem. While Brewer cites the high

---

availability of Google's infrastructure as a justification for arguing that Spanner effectively behaves as a CA system, he acknowledges that since partitions still occasionally occur, it is technically a CP system.

Row-Oriented

Cassandra's data model can be described as a *partitioned row store*, in which data is stored in sparse multidimensional hash tables. "Sparse" means that for any given row you can have one or more columns, but each row doesn't need to have all the same columns as other rows like it (as in a relational model). "Partitioned" means that each row has a unique partition key used to distribute the rows across multiple data stores. Somewhat confusingly, this type of data model is also frequently referred to as a *wide column store*, for example by the DB-Engines (*https://oreil.ly/yCwcY*) website.

Row-Oriented Versus Column-Oriented

Cassandra has frequently been referred to as a *column-oriented* or *columnar* database, but this is not technically correct. The mistake is based on confusion between similar sounding terms. A column-oriented database is one in which the data is stored by columns, as opposed to relational databases, which store data in rows (hence the term *row-oriented*). Column-oriented databases such as Apache HBase or Apache Kudu are designed for analytic use cases.

In the relational storage model, all of the columns for a table are defined beforehand and space is allocated for each column whether it is populated or not. In contrast, Cassandra stores data in a multidimensional, sorted hash table. As data is stored in each column, it is stored as a separate entry in the hash table. Column values are stored according to a consistent sort order, omitting columns that are not populated, which enables more efficient storage and query processing. We'll examine Cassandra's data model in more detail in Chapter 4.

Is Cassandra "Schema-Free"?

In its early versions, Cassandra was faithful to the original Bigtable whitepaper in supporting a "schema-free" data model in which new columns can be defined dynamically. Schema-free databases such as Bigtable and MongoDB have the advantage of being very extensible and highly performant in accessing large amounts of data. The major drawback of schema-free databases is the difficulty in determining the meaning and format of data, which limits the ability to perform complex queries. These disadvantages proved a barrier to adoption for many, especially as startup projects that benefited from the initial flexibility matured into more complex enterprises involving multiple developers and administrators.

The solution for those users was the introduction of the Cassandra Query Language (CQL), which provides a way to define schema via a syntax similar to the Structured Query Language (SQL) familiar to those coming from a relational background. Initially, CQL was provided as another interface to Cassandra alongside the schema-free interface based on the Apache Thrift project. During this transitional phase, the term "schema-optional" was used to describe that data models could be defined by schema using CQL, but could also be dynamically extended to add new columns via the Thrift API. During this period, the underlying data storage continued to be based on the Bigtable model.

For the 3.0 release, Cassandra's underlying storage was re-implemented to more closely align with CQL. The Thrift-based API that supported dynamic column creation was marked as deprecated in 3.0, and removed entirely in the 4.0 release. Cassandra does not entirely limit the ability to dynamically extend the schema on the fly, but the way it works is significantly different. CQL collections such as lists, sets, and maps provide the ability to add a variable number of values of a given type. CQL also provides the ability to change the type of columns in certain instances, and facilities to support the storage of JSON-formatted text.

So perhaps the best way to describe Cassandra's current posture is that it supports "flexible schema."

High Performance

Cassandra was designed specifically from the ground up to take full advantage of multiprocessor/multicore machines, and to run across many dozens of these machines housed in multiple data centers. It scales consistently and seamlessly to hundreds of terabytes. Cassandra has been shown to perform exceptionally well under heavy load. It consistently can show very fast throughput for writes per second on basic commodity computers, whether physical hardware or virtual machines. As you add more servers, you can maintain all of Cassandra's desirable properties without sacrificing performance.

Where Did Cassandra Come From?

The Cassandra data store is an open source Apache project (*http://cassan dra.apache.org*). Cassandra originated at Facebook in 2007 to solve its inbox search problem—the company had to deal with large volumes of data in a way that was difficult to scale with traditional methods. Specifically, the team had requirements to handle huge volumes of data in the form of message copies, reverse indices of messages, and many random reads and many simultaneous random writes.

The team was led by Jeff Hammerbacher, with Avinash Lakshman, Karthik Ranganathan, and Facebook engineer on the Search Team Prashant Malik as key engineers.

The code was released as an open source Google Code project in July 2008. During its tenure as a Google Code project in 2008, the code was updatable only by Facebook engineers, and little community was built around it as a result. So in March 2009, it was moved to an Apache Incubator project, and on February 17, 2010, it was voted into a top-level project. The committers, many of whom have been with the project since 2010/2011, represent companies, including Twitter, LinkedIn, and Apple, as well as independent developers.

The Paper that Introduced Cassandra to the World

"Cassandra—A Decentralized Structured Storage System" (*https:// oreil.ly/GpNBG*) by Facebook's Lakshman and Malik was a central paper on Cassandra. An updated commentary (*https://oreil.ly/ I4p5Z*) on this paper was provided by Jonathan Ellis corresponding to the 2.0 release, noting changes to the technology since the transition to Apache.

How Did Cassandra Get Its Name?

In Greek mythology, Cassandra was the daughter of King Priam and Queen Hecuba of Troy. Cassandra was so beautiful that the god Apollo gave her the ability to see the future. But when she refused his amorous advances, he cursed her such that she would still be able to accurately predict everything that would happen—but no one would believe her. Cassandra foresaw the destruction of her city of Troy, but was powerless to stop it. The Cassandra distributed database is named for her. We speculate that it is also named as kind of a joke on the Oracle at Delphi, another seer for whom a database is named.

As commercial interest in Cassandra grew, the need for production support became apparent. Jonathan Ellis, the first Apache Project Chair for Cassandra, and his colleague Matt Pfeil formed a services company called DataStax (originally known as Riptano) in April of 2010. DataStax provided leadership and support for the Cassandra project, employing several Cassandra committers, as well as free products, including Cassandra drivers for various languages and tools for development and administration of Cassandra. Paid product offerings include enterprise versions of the Cassandra server and tools, integrations with other data technologies, and product support.

During the period from 2010 to 2016, the Apache Project matured Cassandra over a series of releases from 0.6 to 3.0. While the original API provided by Cassandra was based on Apache Thrift, the introduction of the Cassandra Query Language in the 0.8 release marked a major shift toward improved usability and developer productivity due to its similarity with SQL known by many from their previous RDBMS experience. With the completion of a new storage engine in the 3.0 release, the Cassandra codebase was fully aligned from top to bottom around the CQL data model.

After the 3.0 release in 2016, Nate McCall took on the role of Apache Project Chair for Cassandra. This period has been marked by continued growth in the community, with enterprises including Apple, Facebook/Instagram, Netflix, and Uber providing increased contributions to the project, as well as significant contributions from consultancies such as The Last Pickle and Pythian toward both the core database and supporting tooling, and stability improvements and other bug fixes from DataStax. These efforts have culminated in the Cassandra 4.0 release scheduled for 2020.

A well-known axiom in the software industry is that it takes 5 to 10 years for a new database engine to reach a true battle-hardened level of maturity, and it has become clear that Cassandra has reached this milestone. As Patrick McFadin, VP of Developer Relations at DataStax, is fond of saying, "Everyone seems to have a bit of Cassandra running somewhere in their infrastructure."

Is Cassandra a Good Fit for My Project?

We have now unpacked the elevator pitch and have an understanding of Cassandra's advantages. Despite Cassandra's sophisticated design and smart features, it is not the right tool for every job. So in this section, let's take a quick look at what kind of projects Cassandra is a good fit for.

Large Deployments

You probably don't drive a semitruck to pick up your dry cleaning; semis aren't well suited for that sort of task. Lots of careful engineering has gone into Cassandra's high availability, tuneable consistency, peer-to-peer protocol, and seamless scaling, which are its main selling points. None of these qualities is even meaningful in a single-node deployment, let alone allowed to realize its full potential.

There are, however, a wide variety of situations where a single-node relational database is all we may need. So do some measuring. Consider your expected traffic, throughput needs, and SLAs. There are no hard-and-fast rules here, but if you expect that you can reliably serve traffic with an acceptable level of performance with just a few relational databases, it might be a better choice to do so, simply because RDBMSs are easier to run on a single machine and are more familiar.

If you think you'll need at least several nodes to support your efforts, however, Cassandra might be a good fit. If your application is expected to require dozens of nodes, Cassandra might be a great fit.

Lots of Writes, Statistics, and Analysis

Consider your application from the perspective of the ratio of reads to writes. Cassandra is optimized for excellent throughput on writes.

Many of the early production deployments of Cassandra involved storing user activity updates, social network usage, recommendations/reviews, and application statistics. These are strong use cases for Cassandra because they involve lots of writing with less predictable read operations, and because updates can occur unevenly with sudden spikes. In fact, the ability to handle application workloads that require high performance at significant write volumes with many concurrent client threads is one of the primary features of Cassandra.

According to the project wiki, Cassandra has been used to create a variety of applications, including a windowed time-series store, an inverted index for document searching, and a distributed job priority queue.

Geographical Distribution

Cassandra has out-of-the-box support for geographical distribution of data. You can easily configure Cassandra to replicate data across multiple data centers. If you have a globally deployed application that could see a performance benefit from putting the data near the user, Cassandra could be a great fit.

Hybrid Cloud and Multicloud Deployment

Another benefit of Cassandra's flexible deployment means that not only can you deploy it across multiple data centers, these data centers can be from multiple different providers. This makes Cassandra a great choice for a variety of different topologies. In a hybrid cloud architecture, you might use Cassandra to replicate data from a traditional on-premises data center to data centers within your favorite public cloud provider as part of a digital transformation effort.

Further down the road, you might adopt a multicloud architecture and leverage Cassandra to replicate data between clouds in order to make that data accessible to best-of-breed managed services offered by the top providers, such as a machine learning service. Or perhaps you need your data accessible in multiple clouds in order to ensure the highest possible availability for a mission-critical application. After all, even the big public clouds have been known to have occasional region-wide outages. The good news is that the challenging part of a multicloud Cassandra deployment is more likely to be the network configuration, not the database.

Getting Involved

The strength and relevance of any technology depend on the investment of individuals in a vibrant community environment. Thankfully, the Cassandra community is active and healthy, offering a number of ways for you to participate. The awesome-cassandra (*https://oreil.ly/3STpn*) list maintained by Rahul Singh is a great resource that provides a comprehensive list of Cassandra resources; we'll highlight a few items here:

Forums

Cassandra is a popular topic on forums including Stack Overflow (*https://oreil.ly/QrE8X*) and Quora (*https://oreil.ly/iJlGw*). DataStax maintains a community site (*https://community.datastax.com*), which features areas for both the open source project as well as DataStax products.

Mailing lists

The Apache project hosts several mailing lists to which you can subscribe to learn about various topics of interest:

- *user@cassandra.apache.org* provides a general discussion list for users and is frequently used by new users or those needing assistance.

- *dev@cassandra.apache.org* is used by developers to discuss changes, prioritize work, and approve releases.

- *client-dev@cassandra.apache.org* is used for discussion specific to development of Cassandra clients for various programming languages.

- *commits@cassandra.apache.org* tracks Cassandra code commits. This is a fairly high-volume list and is primarily of interest to committers.

Releases are typically announced to both the developer and user mailing lists.

Chat

Many of the Cassandra developers and community members hang out in the `cassandra` and `cassandra-dev` channels on the Apache Software Foundation's Slack. This informal environment is a great place to get your questions answered or offer up some answers of your own. You can get an invitation to join the Slack workspace at *https://oreil.ly/FLD8r*.

Blogs

The Apache Cassandra blog (*https://oreil.ly/o70Ei*) provides deep-dive technical articles on Cassandra implementation details and features under development. Other blogs that reference Cassandra frequently include the DataStax blog (*https://oreil.ly/IAsy4*), the Instaclustr blog (*https://oreil.ly/Rb4xb*) and the Last Pickle blog (*https://oreil.ly/fg_QG*).

Issues and improvements

If you encounter issues using Cassandra and feel you have discovered a defect, feel free to submit an issue to the Cassandra JIRA (*https://oreil.ly/JwmUg*). In fact, users who identify defects on the *user@cassandra.apache.org* list are frequently encouraged to create JIRA issues.

In November 2019, the Cassandra community formally approved a Cassandra Enhancement Proposal (CEP) process to promote effective collaboration between project contributors toward development of new features and significant changes. You can read more about the CEP on the Apache website (*https://oreil.ly/0vaZ0*).

Meetups

A *meetup* group is a local community of people who meet face to face to discuss topics of common interest. These groups provide an excellent opportunity to network, learn, or share your knowledge by offering a presentation of your own. There are Cassandra meetups on every continent (*https://meetup.com*), so you stand a good chance of being able to find one in your area.

Conferences

Cassandra is a popular topic at the ApacheCon conferences hosted by the Apache Software Foundation, as well as the Strata Data Conferences hosted by O'Reilly. The Cassandra Project Management Committee (PMC) periodically hosts Next Generation Cassandra Conferences (NGCC) where Cassandra committers and other contributors share research and proposals for enhancements and new features. After hosting a Cassandra Summit from 2012 to 2016, DataStax resumed hosting conferences in 2019 with Accelerate, a conference focused on Cassandra and DataStax technologies.

Training

DataStax offers training and certification on Apache Cassandra and DataStax Enterprise at DataStax Academy (*https://academy.datastax.com*).

A Marketable Skill

There continues to be increased demand for Cassandra developers and administrators. A 2015 Dice.com salary survey (*https://oreil.ly/Gjgzl*) placed Cassandra as the second most highly compensated software skill set. (More recent surveys are available but require login.)

Summary

In this chapter, we've taken an introductory look at Cassandra's defining characteristics, history, and major features. We have learned about the Cassandra user community and how companies are using Cassandra. Now we're ready to start getting some hands-on experience.

## CHAPTER 3

Installing Cassandra

For those among us who like instant gratification, let's start by installing Cassandra. Because Cassandra introduces a lot of new vocabulary, there might be some unfamiliar terms as you walk through this. That's OK; the idea here is to get set up quickly in a simple configuration to make sure everything is running properly. This will serve as an orientation. Then, we'll take a step back and explain Cassandra in its larger context.

Installing the Apache Distribution

While there are a number of options available for installing Cassandra on various operating systems, let's start your journey by downloading the Apache distribution from *http://cassandra.apache.org* so you can get a good look at what's inside. We'll explore other installation options in "Other Cassandra Distributions" on page 44.

Click the link on the Cassandra home page to download a version as a gzipped archive. Typically, multiple versions of Cassandra are provided. The *latest version* is the current recommended version for use in production. There are *other supported releases* that are still viable for production usage and receive bug fixes. The project goal is to limit the number of supported releases, but reasonable accommodations are made. For example, the 2.2 and 2.1 releases were considered to be officially maintained through the release of 4.0. For all releases, the prebuilt binary is named *apache-cassandra-x.x.x-bin.tar.gz*, where *x.x.x* represents the version number. The download for Cassandra 4.0 is around 40 MB.

Extracting the Download

You can unpack the compressed file using any regular ZIP utility. On Unix-based systems such as Linux or macOS, gzip extraction utilities should be preinstalled; on Windows, you'll need to get a program such as WinZip, which is commercial, or something like 7-Zip (*http://www.7-zip.org*), which is freeware.

Open your extracting program. You might have to extract the ZIP file and the TAR file in separate steps. Once you have a folder on your filesystem called *apache-cassandra-x.x.x*, you're ready to run Cassandra.

What's in There?

Once you decompress the tarball, you'll see that the Cassandra binary distribution includes several files and directories.

The files include the *NEWS.txt* file, which includes the release notes describing features included in the current and prior releases, and the *CHANGES.txt* file, which is similar but focuses on bug fixes. You'll want to make sure to review these files whenever you are upgrading to a new version so you know what changes to expect. The *LICENSE.txt* and *NOTICE.txt* files contain the Apache 2.0 license used by Cassandra, and copyright notices for Cassandra and included software, respectively.

Let's take a moment now to look around in the different directories and see what's there:

bin

> This directory contains the executables to run Cassandra as well as clients, including the query language shell (`cqlsh`). It also has scripts to run the `node tool`, which is a utility for inspecting a cluster to determine whether it is properly configured, and to perform a variety of maintenance operations. We look at `node tool` in depth later. The directory also contains several utilities for performing operations on SSTables, the files in which Cassandra stores its data on disk. We'll discuss these utilities in Chapter 12.

conf

> This directory contains the files for configuring your Cassandra instance. The configuration files you may use most frequently include the *cassandra.yaml* file, which is the primary configuration for running Cassandra, and the *logback.xml* file, which lets you change the logging settings to suit your needs. Additional files can be used to configure Java Virtual Machine (JVM) settings, the network topology, metrics reporting, archival and restore commands, and triggers. You'll learn how to use these configuration files in Chapter 10.

doc

Traditionally, documentation has been one of the weaker areas of the project, but a concerted effort for the 4.0 release, including sponsorship from the Google Season of Docs (*https://oreil.ly/p2jP2*) project, yielded significant progress to the documentation included in the Cassandra distribution as well as the documentation on the Cassandra website (*https://oreil.ly/THfB6*). The documentation includes a getting started guide, an architectural overview, and instructions for configuring and operating Cassandra.

javadoc

This directory contains a documentation website generated using Java's JavaDoc tool. Note that JavaDoc reflects only the comments that are stored directly in the Java code, and as such does not represent comprehensive documentation. It's helpful if you want to see how the code is laid out. Moreover, Cassandra is a wonderful project, but the code contains relatively few comments, so you might find the JavaDoc's usefulness limited. It may be more fruitful to simply read the class files directly if you're familiar with Java. Nonetheless, to read the JavaDoc, open the *javadoc/index.html* file in a browser.

lib

This directory contains all of the external libraries that Cassandra needs to run. For example, it uses two different JSON serialization libraries, the Google collections project, and several Apache Commons libraries.

pylib

This directory contains Python libraries that are used by `cqlsh`.

tools

This directory contains tools that are used to maintain your Cassandra nodes. You'll learn about these tools in Chapter 12.

Additional Directories

If you've already run Cassandra using the default configuration, you will notice two additional directories under the main Cassandra directory: *data* and *log*. We'll discuss the contents of these directories momentarily.

Building from Source

Cassandra uses Apache Ant for its build scripting language and Maven for dependency management.

Downloading Ant

You can download Ant from *http://ant.apache.org*. You don't need to download Maven separately just to build Cassandra.

Building from source requires a complete Java 8 JDK (or later version), not just the Java Runtime Environment (JRE). If you see a message about how Ant is missing *tools.jar*, either you don't have the full JDK or you're pointing to the wrong path in your environment variables. Maven downloads files from the internet, so if your connection is invalid or Maven cannot determine the proxy, the build will fail.

Downloading Development Builds

If you want to download the latest Cassandra builds or view test results, you can find these in Jenkins, which the Cassandra project uses as its continuous integration tool. See this Jenkins page (*https://oreil.ly/FBgt7*) for the latest builds and test coverage information.

If you are interested in having a look at the Cassandra source, you can get the trunk version of the Cassandra source using this command:

```
$ git clone https://github.com/apache/cassandra.git
```

Because Maven takes care of all the dependencies, it's easy to build Cassandra once you have the source. Just make sure you're in the root directory of your source download and execute the `ant` program, which will look for a file called *build.xml* in the current directory and execute the default build target. Ant and Maven take care of the rest. To execute the Ant program and start compiling the source, just type:

```
$ ant
```

That's it. Maven will retrieve all of the necessary dependencies, and Ant will build the hundreds of source files and execute the tests. If all went well, you should see a BUILD SUCCESSFUL message. If all did not go well, make sure that your path settings are all correct, that you have the most recent versions of the required programs, and that you downloaded a stable Cassandra build. You can check the Jenkins report to make sure that the source you downloaded actually can compile.

More Build Output

If you want to see detailed information on what is happening during the build, you can pass Ant the -v option to cause it to output verbose details regarding each operation it performs.

Additional Build Targets

To compile the server, you can simply execute ant, as shown previously. This command executes the default target, *jar*. This target will perform a complete build, including unit tests, and output a file into the *build* directory called *apache-cassandra-x.x.x.jar*.

If you want to see a list of all of the targets supported by the build file, simply pass Ant the -p option to get a description of each target. Here are a few others you might be interested in:

test

> Users will probably find this the most helpful, as it executes the battery of unit tests. You can also check out the unit test sources themselves for some useful examples of how to interact with Cassandra.

stress-build

> This target builds the Cassandra stress tool, which you will learn to use in Chapter 13.

clean

> This target removes locally created artifacts such as generated source files and classes and unit test results. The related target *realclean* performs a *clean* and additionally removes the Cassandra distribution JAR files and JAR files downloaded by Maven.

Running Cassandra

The Cassandra developers have done a terrific job of making it very easy for new users to start using Cassandra immediately, as you can start a single node without making any changes to the default configuration. We'll note some of the available configuration options in Chapter 10.

Required Java Version

Cassandra versions from 3.0 onward require a Java 8 JVM or later, preferably the latest stable version. It has been tested on both the OpenJDK and Oracle's JDK. Cassandra 4.0 has been compiled and tested against both Java 8 and Java 11. You can check your installed Java version by opening a command prompt and executing `java -version`. If you need a JDK, you can get one at this Java SE Downloads page (*https://oreil.ly/tuA7P*) or the jdk.java.net page (*https://jdk.java.net*).

Setting the Environment

Once you have the binary (or the source downloaded and compiled), you're ready to start the database server.

Setting the `JAVA_HOME` environment variable is recommended. To do this on a Windows system, click the Start button and then right-click Computer. Click Advanced System Settings, and then click the Environment Variables… button. Click New… to create a new system variable. In the Variable Name field, type `JAVA_HOME`. In the Variable Value field, type the path to your Java installation. This is probably something like *C:\Program Files\Java\jre1.8.0_25* or */usr/java/jre1.8.0_*.

Once you've started the server for the first time, Cassandra will add directories to your system to store its datafiles. The default configuration creates directories under the *CASSANDRA_HOME* directory:

data

>This directory is where Cassandra stores its data. By default, there are subdirectories under the *data* directory, corresponding to the various datafiles Cassandra uses: *commitlog*, *data*, *hints*, and *saved_caches*. We'll explore the significance of each of these datafiles in Chapter 6. If you've been trying different versions of the database and aren't worried about losing data, you can delete these directories and restart the server as a last resort.

logs

>This directory is where Cassandra stores its logs in a file called *system.log*. If you encounter any difficulties, consult the log to see what might have happened.

Datafile Locations

The datafile locations are configurable in the *cassandra.yaml* file, located in the *conf* directory. The properties are called `data_file_directories`, `commit_log_directory`, `hints_directory`, and `saved_caches_directory`. We'll discuss the recommended configuration of these directories in Chapter 10.

Many users on Unix-based systems prefer to use the */var/lib* directory for data storage. If you are changing this configuration, you will need to edit the *conf/cassandra.yaml* file and create the referenced directories for Cassandra to store its data, making sure to configure write permissions for the user that will be running Cassandra:

```
$ sudo mkdir -p /var/lib/cassandra
$ sudo chown -R username /var/lib/cassandra
```

Instead of *username*, substitute your own username, of course.

Starting the Server

To start the Cassandra server on any OS, open a command prompt or terminal window, navigate to the *<cassandra-directory>/bin* where you unpacked Cassandra, and run the command cassandra -f to start your server.

Starting Cassandra in the Foreground

Using the -f switch tells Cassandra to stay in the foreground instead of running as a background process, so that all of the server logs will print to standard out (stdout in Unix systems) and you can see them in your terminal window, which is useful for testing. In either case, the logs will append to the *system.log* file.

In a clean installation, you should see quite a few log statements as the server gets running. The exact syntax of logging statements will vary depending on the release you're using, but there are a few highlights you can look for. If you search for cassandra.yaml, you'll quickly run into the following:

```
INFO  [main] 2019-08-25 17:42:11,712 YamlConfigurationLoader.java:89 -
  Configuration location:
  file:/Users/jeffreycarpenter/cassandra/conf/cassandra.yaml
INFO  [main] 2019-08-25 17:42:11,855 Config.java:598 - Node configuration:[
  allocate_tokens_for_keyspace=null;
  ...
```

These log statements indicate the location of the *cassandra.yaml* file containing the configured settings. The Node configuration statement lists out the settings read from the config file.

Now search for JVM and you'll find something like this:

```
INFO  [main] 2019-08-25 17:42:12,308 CassandraDaemon.java:487 -
  JVM vendor/version: OpenJDK 64-Bit Server VM/12.0.1
INFO  [main] 2019-08-25 17:42:12,309 CassandraDaemon.java:488 -
  Heap size: 3.900GiB/3.900GiB
```

These log statements provide information describing the JVM being used, including memory settings.

Next, search for the versions in use—Cassandra version, CQL version, Native protocol supported versions:

```
INFO  [main] 2019-08-25 17:42:17,847 StorageService.java:610 -
  Cassandra version: 4.0.0
INFO  [main] 2019-08-25 17:42:17,848 StorageService.java:611 -
  CQL version: 3.4.5
INFO  [main] 2019-08-25 17:42:17,848 StorageService.java:612 -
  Native protocol supported versions: 3/v3, 4/v4, 5/v5-beta (default: 4/v4)
```

You can also find statements where Cassandra is initializing internal data structures, such as caches:

```
INFO [main] 2015-12-08 06:02:43,633 CacheService.java:115 -
  Initializing key cache with capacity of 24 MBs.
INFO [main] 2015-12-08 06:02:43,679 CacheService.java:137 -
  Initializing row cache with capacity of 0 MBs
INFO [main] 2015-12-08 06:02:43,686 CacheService.java:166 -
  Initializing counter cache with capacity of 12 MBs
```

If you search for terms like JMX, gossip, and listening, you'll find statements like the following:

```
WARN  [main] 2019-08-25 17:42:12,363 StartupChecks.java:168 -
  JMX is not enabled to receive remote connections.
  Please see cassandra-env.sh for more info.
INFO  [main] 2019-08-25 17:42:18,354 StorageService.java:814 -
  Starting up server gossip
INFO  [main] 2019-08-25 17:42:18,070 InboundConnectionInitiator.java:130 -
  Listening on address: (127.0.0.1:7000), nic: lo0, encryption: enabled (openssl)
```

These log statements indicate the server is beginning to initiate communications with other servers in the cluster and expose publicly available interfaces. By default, the management interface via the Java Management Extensions (JMX) is disabled for remote access. We'll explore the management interface in Chapter 11.

Finally, search for state jump and you'll see the following:

```
INFO  [main] 2019-08-25 17:42:18,581 StorageService.java:1507 -
  JOINING: Finish joining ring
INFO  [main] 2019-08-25 17:42:18,591 StorageService.java:2508 -
  Node 127.0.0.1:7000 state jump to NORMAL
```

Congratulations! Now your Cassandra server should be up and running with a new single-node cluster called "Test Cluster," ready to interact with other nodes and clients. If you continue to monitor the output, you'll begin to see periodic output such as memtable flushing and compaction, which you'll learn about soon.

Starting Over

The committers work hard to ensure that data is readable from one minor dot release to the next and from one major version to the next. The commit log, however, needs to be completely cleared out from version to version (even minor versions).

If you have any previous versions of Cassandra installed, you may want to clear out the data directories for now, just to get up and running. If you've messed up your Cassandra installation and want to get started cleanly again, you can delete the data folders.

Stopping Cassandra

Now that you've successfully started a Cassandra server, you may be wondering how to stop it. You may have noticed the `stop-server` command in the *bin* directory. Let's try running that command. Here's what you'll see on Unix systems:

```
$ ./stop-server
please read the stop-server script before use
```

So you see that the server has not been stopped, but instead you are directed to read the script. Taking a look inside with your favorite code editor, you'll learn that the way to stop Cassandra is to kill the JVM process that is running Cassandra. The file suggests a couple of different techniques by which you can identify the JVM process and kill it.

The first technique is to start Cassandra using the `-p` option, which provides Cassandra with the name of a file to which it should write the process identifier (PID) upon starting up. This is arguably the most straightforward approach to making sure you kill the right process.

However, because you did not start Cassandra with the `-p` option, you'll need to find the process yourself and kill it. The script suggests using `pgrep` to locate processes for the current user containing the term "cassandra":

```
user=`whoami`
pgrep -u $user -f cassandra | xargs kill -9
```

Stopping Cassandra on Windows

On Windows installations, you can find the JVM process and kill it using the Task Manager.

Other Cassandra Distributions

The preceding instructions showed you how to install the Apache distribution of Cassandra. In addition to the Apache distribution, there are a couple of other ways to get Cassandra:

DataStax Enterprise Edition

DataStax provides a fully supported version certified for production use. The product line provides an integrated database platform with support for complementary data technologies such as Apache Solr for search, Apache Spark for analytics, Apache TinkerPop for graph, as well as advanced security and other enterprise features. We'll explore some of these integrations in Chapter 15.

Virtual machine images

A frequent model for deployment of Cassandra is to package one of the preceding distributions in a virtual machine image. For example, multiple such images are available in the Amazon Web Services (AWS) Marketplace.

Containers

It has become increasingly popular to run Cassandra in Docker containers, especially in development environments. We'll provide some simple instructions for running the Apache distribution in Docker in "Running Cassandra in Docker" on page 53.

Managed services

There are a few providers of Cassandra as a managed service, where the provider provides hosting and management of Cassandra clusters. These include Instaclustr (*https://www.instaclustr.com/platform/managed-apache-cassandra/*) and Aiven (*https://aiven.io/cassandra*). DataStax provides an Apache Cassandra as a service called Astra (*https://astra.datastax.com*).

> **Verifying CQL Compatibility on Managed Services**
>
> Multiple public cloud providers claim to offer Cassandra support by enabling CQL on top of their existing database service offerings. Before migrating Cassandra workloads to these services, make sure to check the fine print to confirm that all the features that your workloads need are fully supported.

We'll take a deeper look at several options for deploying Cassandra in production environments, including Kubernetes and cloud computing environments, in Chapter 10.

Selecting the right distribution will depend on your deployment environment; your needs for scale, stability, and support; and your development and maintenance budgets. Having both open source and commercial deployment options provides the flexibility to make the right choice for your organization.

Running the CQL Shell

Now that you have a Cassandra installation up and running, let's give it a quick try to make sure everything is set up properly. You'll use the CQL shell (cqlsh) to connect to your server and have a look around.

Deprecation of the CLI

If you've used Cassandra in releases prior to 3.0, you may also be familiar with the command-line client interface known as cassandra-cli. The CLI was removed in the 3.0 release because it depends on the legacy Thrift API, which was deprecated in 3.0 and removed entirely in 4.0.

To run the shell, create a new terminal window, change to the Cassandra home directory, and type the following command (you should see output similar to that shown here):

```
$ bin/cqlsh
Connected to Test Cluster at 127.0.0.1:9042.
[cqlsh 6.0.0 | Cassandra 4.0.0 | CQL spec 3.4.5 | Native protocol v5]
Use HELP for help.
```

Because you did not specify a node to which you wanted to connect, the shell helpfully checks for a node running on the local host, and finds the node you started earlier. The shell also indicates that you're connected to a Cassandra server cluster called "Test Cluster." That's because this cluster of one node at localhost is set up for you by default.

Renaming the Default Cluster

In a production environment, be sure to change the cluster name to something more suitable to your application.

To connect to a specific node, specify the hostname and port on the command line. For example, the following will connect to your local node:

```
$ bin/cqlsh localhost 9042
```

The port number can be omitted if the node uses the default value (9042). Another alternative for configuring the cqlsh connection is to set the environment variables $CQLSH_HOST and $CQLSH_PORT. This approach is useful if you will be frequently connecting to a specific node on another host. The environment variables will be overriden if you specify the host and port on the command line.

Connection Errors

Have you run into an error like this while trying to connect to a server?

```
Exception connecting to localhost/9042. Reason:
    Connection refused.
```

If so, make sure that a Cassandra instance is started at that host and port, and that you can ping the host you're trying to reach. There may be firewall rules preventing you from connecting.

To see a complete list of the command-line options supported by cqlsh, type the command cqlsh -help.

Basic cqlsh Commands

Let's take a quick tour of cqlsh to learn what kinds of commands you can send to the server. You'll see how to use the basic environment commands and how to do a round trip of inserting and retrieving some data.

Case in cqlsh

The cqlsh commands are all case insensitive. For the examples in this book, we adopt the convention of uppercase to be consistent with the way the shell describes its own commands in help topics and output.

cqlsh Help

To get help for cqlsh, type HELP or ? to see the list of available commands:

```
cqlsh> HELP

Documented shell commands:
===========================
CAPTURE   CLS          COPY  DESCRIBE  EXPAND  LOGIN    SERIAL  SOURCE   UNICODE
CLEAR     CONSISTENCY  DESC  EXIT      HELP    PAGING   SHOW    TRACING

CQL help topics:
================
AGGREGATES                    CREATE_KEYSPACE           DROP_TRIGGER    TEXT
ALTER_KEYSPACE                CREATE_MATERIALIZED_VIEW  DROP_TYPE       TIME
ALTER_MATERIALIZED_VIEW       CREATE_ROLE               DROP_USER       TIMESTAMP
ALTER_TABLE                   CREATE_TABLE              FUNCTIONS       TRUNCATE
ALTER_TYPE                    CREATE_TRIGGER            GRANT           TYPES
```

ALTER_USER	CREATE_TYPE	INSERT	UPDATE
APPLY	CREATE_USER	INSERT_JSON	USE
ASCII	DATE	INT	UUID
BATCH	DELETE	JSON	
BEGIN	DROP_AGGREGATE	KEYWORDS	
BLOB	DROP_COLUMNFAMILY	LIST_PERMISSIONS	
BOOLEAN	DROP_FUNCTION	LIST_ROLES	
COUNTER	DROP_INDEX	LIST_USERS	
CREATE_AGGREGATE	DROP_KEYSPACE	PERMISSIONS	
CREATE_COLUMNFAMILY	DROP_MATERIALIZED_VIEW	REVOKE	
CREATE_FUNCTION	DROP_ROLE	SELECT	
CREATE_INDEX	DROP_TABLE	SELECT_JSON	

cqlsh Help Topics

You'll notice that the help topics listed differ slightly from the actual command syntax. The CREATE_TABLE help topic describes how to use the syntax > CREATE TABLE ..., for example.

To get additional documentation about a particular command, type HELP <command>. Many cqlsh commands may be used with no parameters, in which case they print out the current setting. Examples include CONSISTENCY, EXPAND, and PAGING.

Describing the Environment in cqlsh

Now that you have connected to your Cassandra instance Test Cluster, to learn more about the cluster you're working in, type:

```
cqlsh> DESCRIBE CLUSTER;
Cluster: Test Cluster
Partitioner: Murmur3Partitioner
```

To see which keyspaces are available in the cluster, issue this command:

```
cqlsh> DESCRIBE KEYSPACES;
system_traces  system_auth  system_distributed    system_views
system_schema  system       system_virtual_schema
```

Initially this list will consist of several system keyspaces. Once you have created your own keyspaces, they will be shown as well. The system keyspaces are managed internally by Cassandra, and aren't for you to put data into. In this way, these keyspaces are similar to the master and temp databases in Microsoft SQL Server. Cassandra uses these keyspaces to store the schema, tracing, and security information. We'll learn more about these keyspaces in Chapter 6.

You can use the following command to learn the client, server, and protocol versions in use:

```
cqlsh> SHOW VERSION;
[cqlsh 6.0.0 | Cassandra 4.0.0 | CQL spec 3.4.5 | Native protocol v5]
```

You may have noticed that this version info is printed out when cqlsh starts. There are a variety of other commands with which you can experiment. For now, let's add some data to the database and get it back out again.

Creating a Keyspace and Table in cqlsh

A Cassandra keyspace is sort of like a relational database. It defines one or more tables. When you start cqlsh without specifying a keyspace, the prompt will look like this: cqlsh>, with no keyspace specified.

Now you'll create your own keyspace so you have something to write data to. In creating your keyspace, there are some required options. To walk through these options, you could use the command HELP CREATE_KEYSPACE, but instead you can use the helpful command-completion features of cqlsh. Type the following and then press the Tab key:

```
cqlsh> CREATE KEYSPACE my_keyspace WITH
```

When you press the Tab key, cqlsh begins completing the syntax of your command:

```
cqlsh> CREATE KEYSPACE my_keyspace WITH replication = {'class': '
```

This is informing you that in order to specify a keyspace, you also need to specify a replication strategy. Tab again to see what options you have:

```
cqlsh> CREATE KEYSPACE my_keyspace WITH replication = {'class': '
NetworkTopologyStrategy    OldNetworkTopologyStrategy SimpleStrategy
```

Now cqlsh is giving you three strategies to choose from. You'll learn more about these strategies in Chapter 6. For now, choose the SimpleStrategy by typing the name, and indicate you're done with a closing quote and Tab again:

```
cqlsh> CREATE KEYSPACE my_keyspace WITH replication = {'class':
    'SimpleStrategy', 'replication_factor':
```

The next option you're presented with is a replication factor. For the simple strategy, this indicates how many nodes the data in this keyspace will be written to. For a production deployment, you'll want copies of your data stored on multiple nodes, but because you're just running a single node at the moment, you'll ask for a single copy. Specify a value of "1" and a space and Tab again:

```
cqlsh> CREATE KEYSPACE my_keyspace WITH replication = {'class':
    'SimpleStrategy', 'replication_factor': 1};
```

You see that cqlsh has now added a closing bracket, indicating you've completed all of the required options. Complete the command with a semicolon and return, and your keyspace will be created.

Keyspace Creation Options

For a production keyspace, you would probably never want to use a value of 1 for the replication factor. There are additional options on creating a keyspace depending on the replication strategy that is chosen. The command completion feature will walk through the different options.

Have a look at your keyspace using the DESCRIBE KEYSPACE command:

```
cqlsh> DESCRIBE KEYSPACE my_keyspace
CREATE KEYSPACE my_keyspace WITH replication = {'class':
  'SimpleStrategy', 'replication_factor': '1'} AND
  durable_writes = true;
```

We see that the table has been created with the SimpleStrategy, a replication_fac
tor of one, and durable writes. Notice that your keyspace is described in much the same syntax that we used to create it, with one additional option that we did not specify: durable_writes = true. Don't worry about this option now; we'll return to it in Chapter 6.

After you have created your own keyspace, you can switch to it in the shell by typing:

```
cqlsh> USE my_keyspace;
cqlsh:my_keyspace>
```

Notice that the prompt has changed to indicate that we're using the keyspace.

Using Snake Case

You may have wondered why we directed you to name your keyspace in "snake case" (my_keyspace) as opposed to "camel case" (MyKeyspace), which is familiar to developers using Java and other languages.

As it turns out, Cassandra naturally handles keyspace, table, and column names as lowercase. When you enter names in mixed case, Cassandra stores them as all lowercase.

This behavior can be overridden by enclosing your names in double quotes (e.g., CRE
ATE KEYSPACE "MyKeyspace"). However, it tends to be a lot simpler to use snake case than to go against the grain.

Now that you have a keyspace, you can create a table in your keyspace. To do this in cqlsh, use the following command:

```
cqlsh:my_keyspace> CREATE TABLE user ( first_name text ,
  last_name text, title text, PRIMARY KEY (last_name, first_name)) ;
```

This creates a new table called "user" in your current keyspace with three columns to store first and last names and a title, all of type text. The text and varchar types are synonymous and are used to store strings. You've specified a primary key for this table consisting of the first_name and last_name and taken the defaults for other table options. You'll learn more about primary keys and the significance of your choice of primary key in Chapter 4, but for now let's think of that combination of names as identifying unique rows in your table. The title column is the only one in your table that is not part of the primary key.

Using Keyspace Names in cqlsh

You could have also created this table without switching to your keyspace by using the syntax CREATE TABLE my_keyspace.user.

You can use cqlsh to get a description of a the table you just created using the DESCRIBE TABLE command:

```
cqlsh:my_keyspace> DESCRIBE TABLE user;
CREATE TABLE my_keyspace.user (
    first_name text,
    last_name text,
    title text,
    PRIMARY KEY (last_name, first_name)
) WITH bloom_filter_fp_chance = 0.01
    AND caching = {'keys': 'ALL', 'rows_per_partition': 'NONE'}
    AND comment = ''
    AND compaction = {'class': 'org.apache.cassandra.db.compaction.
      SizeTieredCompactionStrategy', 'max_threshold': '32',
      'min_threshold': '4'}
    AND compression = {'chunk_length_in_kb': '16', 'class':
      'org.apache.cassandra.io.compress.LZ4Compressor'}
    AND crc_check_chance = 1.0
    AND dclocal_read_repair_chance = 0.0
    AND default_time_to_live = 0
    AND gc_grace_seconds = 864000
    AND max_index_interval = 2048
    AND memtable_flush_period_in_ms = 0
    AND min_index_interval = 128
    AND read_repair_chance = 0.0
    AND speculative_retry = '99p';
```

You'll notice that cqlsh prints a nicely formatted version of the CREATE TABLE command that you just typed in but also includes default values for all of the available table options that you did not specify. We'll describe these settings later. For now, you have enough to get started.

Writing and Reading Data in cqlsh

Now that you have a keyspace and a table, you can write some data to the database and read it back out again. It's OK at this point not to know quite what's going on. You'll come to understand Cassandra's data model in depth later. For now, you have a keyspace (database), which has a table, which holds columns, the atomic unit of data storage.

To write rows, you use the INSERT command:

```
cqlsh:my_keyspace> INSERT INTO user (first_name, last_name, title)
    VALUES ('Bill', 'Nguyen', 'Mr.');
```

Here you have created a new row with two columns for the key Bill, to store a set of related values. The column names are first_name and last_name.

Now that you have written some data, you can read it back using the SELECT command:

```
cqlsh:my_keyspace> SELECT * FROM user WHERE first_name='Bill' AND
    last_name='Nguyen';

 last_name | first_name | title
-----------+------------+-------
    Nguyen |       Bill |   Mr.

(1 rows)
```

In this command, you requested to return rows matching the primary key including all columns. For this query, you specified both of the columns referenced by the primary key. What happens when you only specify one of the values? Let's find out:

```
cqlsh:my_keyspace> SELECT * FROM user where last_name = 'Nguyen';

 last_name | first_name | title
-----------+------------+-------
    Nguyen |       Bill |   Mr.

(1 rows)
cqlsh:my_keyspace> SELECT * FROM user where first_name = 'Bill';
InvalidRequest: Error from server: code=2200 [Invalid query]
message="Cannot execute this query as it might involve data
filtering and thus may have unpredictable performance.
If you want to execute this query despite the
performance unpredictability, use ALLOW FILTERING"
```

This behavior might not seem intuitive at first, but it has to do with the composition of the primary key you used for this table. This is your first clue that there might be something a bit different about accessing data in Cassandra as compared to what you might be used to in SQL. We'll explain the significance of your primary key selection and the ALLOW FILTERING option in Chapter 4 and other chapters.

Counting Data and Full Table Scans

Many new Cassandra users, especially those who are coming from a relational background, will be inclined to use the SELECT COUNT command as a way to ensure data has been written. For example, you could use the following command to verify your write to the user table:

```
cqlsh:my_keyspace> SELECT COUNT (*) FROM user;
 count
-------
     1

(1 rows)

Warnings :
Aggregation query used without partition key
```

Note that when you execute this command, cqlsh gives you the correct count of rows, but also gives you a warning. This is because you've asked Cassandra to perform a full table scan. In a multi-node cluster with potentially large amounts of data, this COUNT could be a very expensive operation. Throughout the rest of the book, you'll encounter various ways in which Cassandra tries to warn you or constrain your ability to perform operations that will perform poorly at scale in a distributed architecture.

You can delete a column using the DELETE command. Here you will delete the title column from the row inserted previously:

```
cqlsh:my_keyspace> DELETE title FROM USER WHERE
    first_name='Bill' AND last_name='Nguyen';
```

You can perform this delete because the title column is not part of the primary key. To make sure that the value has been removed, you can query again:

```
cqlsh:my_keyspace> SELECT * FROM user WHERE first_name='Bill'
    AND last_name='Nguyen';

 last_name | first_name | title
-----------+------------+-------
    Nguyen |       Bill |  null

(1 rows)
```

Now you'll clean up after yourself by deleting the entire row. It's the same command, but you don't specify a column name:

```
cqlsh:my_keyspace> DELETE FROM USER WHERE first_name='Bill'
    AND last_name='Nguyen';
```

To make sure that it's removed, you can query again:

```
cqlsh:my_keyspace> SELECT * FROM user WHERE first_name='Bill'
  AND last_name='Nguyen';

 last_name | first_name | title
-----------+------------+-------
```

(0 rows)

If you really want to clean things up, you can remove all data from the table using the TRUNCATE command, or even delete the table schema using the DROP TABLE command:

```
cqlsh:my_keyspace> TRUNCATE user;
cqlsh:my_keyspace> DROP TABLE user;
```

cqlsh Command History

Now that you've been using cqlsh for a while, you may have noticed that you can navigate through commands you've executed previously with the up and down arrow keys. This history is stored in a file called *cqlsh_history*, which is located in a hidden directory called *.cassandra* within your home directory. This acts like your bash shell history, listing the commands in a plain-text file in the order Cassandra executed them. Nice!

Running Cassandra in Docker

Over the past few years, containers have become a very popular alternative to full machine virtualization for deployment of applications and supporting infrastructure such as databases.

Given the high popularity of Docker and its image format, the Apache project has begun supporting official Docker images of Cassandra.

If you have a Docker environment installed on your machine, it's extremely simple to start a Cassandra node. After making sure you've stopped any Cassandra node started previously, start a new node in Docker using the following two commands:

```
$ docker pull cassandra
$ docker run --name my-cassandra cassandra
```

The first command pulls the Docker image marked with the tag *latest* from the Docker Hub *https://hub.docker.com/_/cassandra/*:

```
Using default tag: latest
latest: Pulling from library/cassandra
9fc222b64b0a: Pull complete
33b9abeacd73: Pull complete
d28230b01bc3: Pull complete
6e755ec31928: Pull complete
```

```
b881e4d8c78e: Pull complete
d8b058ab9240: Pull complete
3ddfff7126ed: Pull complete
94de8e3674c4: Pull complete
61d4f90c97c4: Pull complete
a3d009e31ea4: Pull complete
Digest: sha256:0f188d784235e1bedf191361096e6eeab330f9579eac7d2e68e14a5c29f75ad6
Status: Downloaded newer image for cassandra:latest
docker.io/library/cassandra:latest
```

The second command starts an instance of Cassandra with default options. Note that you could have used the -d option to start the container in the background without printing out the logs.

You used the --name option to specify a name for the container, which allows you to reference the container by name when using other Docker commands. For example, you can stop the container by using the command:

```
$ docker stop my-cassandra
```

If you don't provide a name for the container, the Docker runtime will assign a randomly selected name such as breezy_ensign. Docker also creates a unique identifier for each container, which is returned from the initial run command. Either the name or ID may be used to reference a specific container in Docker commands.

If you'd like to start an instance of cqlsh, the simplest way is to use the copy inside the instance by executing a command on the instance:

```
$ docker exec -it my-cassandra cqlsh
```

This will give you a cqlsh prompt, with which you could execute the same commands you've practiced in this chapter, or any other commands you'd like.

Up to this point, you've only created a single Cassandra node in Docker, which is not accessible from outside Docker's internal network. In order to access this node from outside Docker for CQL queries, you'll want to make sure the standard CQL port is exposed when the node is created:

```
$ docker start cassandra -p 9042:9042
```

There are several other configuration options available for running Cassandra in Docker, documented on the Docker Hub page referenced earlier. One exercise you may find interesting is to launch multiple nodes in Docker to create a small cluster.

Summary

Now you should have a Cassandra installation up and running. You've worked with the cqlsh client to insert and retrieve some data, and you're ready to take a step back and get the big picture on Cassandra before really diving into the details.

## CHAPTER 4

The Cassandra Query Language

In this chapter, you'll gain an understanding of Cassandra's data model and how that data model is implemented by the Cassandra Query Language (CQL). We'll show how CQL supports Cassandra's design goals and look at some general behavior characteristics.

For developers and administrators coming from the relational world, the Cassandra data model can be difficult to understand initially. Some terms, such as *keyspace*, are completely new, and some, such as *column*, exist in both worlds but have slightly different meanings. The syntax of CQL is similar in many ways to SQL, but with some important differences. For those familiar with NoSQL technologies such as Dynamo or Bigtable, it can also be confusing, because although Cassandra may be based on those technologies, its own data model is significantly different.

So in this chapter, we start from relational database terminology and introduce Cassandra's view of the world. Along the way you'll get more familiar with CQL and learn how it implements this data model.

The Relational Data Model

In a relational database, the database itself is the outermost container that might correspond to a single application. The database contains tables. Tables have names and contain one or more columns, which also have names. When you add data to a table, you specify a value for every column defined; if you don't have a value for a particular column, you use null. This new entry adds a row to the table, which you can later read if you know the row's unique identifier (primary key), or by using a SQL statement that expresses some criteria that row might meet. If you want to update values in the table, you can update all of the rows or just some of them, depending on the filter you use in a "where" clause of your SQL statement.

After this review, you're in good shape to look at Cassandra's data model in terms of its similarities and differences.

Cassandra's Data Model

In this section, we'll take a bottom-up approach to understanding Cassandra's data model.

The simplest data store you would conceivably want to work with might be an array or list. It would look like Figure 4-1.

Figure 4-1. A list of values

If you persisted this list, you could query it later, but you would have to either examine each value in order to know what it represented, or always store each value in the same place in the list and then externally maintain documentation about which cell in the array holds which values. That would mean you might have to supply empty placeholder values (nulls) in order to keep the predetermined size of the array in case you didn't have a value for an optional attribute (such as a fax number or apartment number). An array is a clearly useful data structure, but not semantically rich.

Now let's add a second dimension to this list: names to match the values. Give names to each cell, and now you have a map structure, as shown in Figure 4-2.

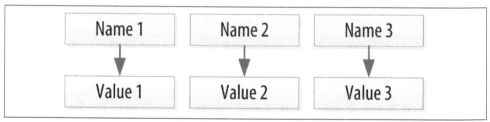

Figure 4-2. A map of name/value pairs

This is an improvement because you can know the names of your values. So if you decided that your map would hold user information, you could have column names like first_name, last_name, phone, email, and so on. This is a somewhat richer structure to work with.

But the structure you've built so far works only if you have one instance of a given entity, such as a single person, user, hotel, or tweet. It doesn't give you much if you want to store multiple entities with the same structure, which is certainly what you want to do. There's nothing to unify some collection of name/value pairs, and no way to repeat the same column names. So you need something that will group some of the column values together in a distinctly addressable group. You need a key to reference a group of columns that should be treated together as a set. You need rows. Then, if you get a single row, you can get all of the name/value pairs for a single entity at once, or just get the values for the names you're interested in. You could call these name/value pairs *columns*. You could call each separate entity that holds some set of columns *rows*. And the unique identifier for each row could be called a *row key* or *primary key*. Figure 4-3 shows the contents of a simple row: a primary key, which is itself one or more columns, and additional columns. Let's come back to the primary key shortly.

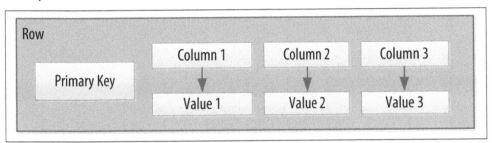

Figure 4-3. A Cassandra row

Cassandra defines a *table* to be a logical division that associates similar data. For example, you might have a user table, a hotel table, an address book table, and so on. In this way, a Cassandra table is analogous to a table in the relational world.

You don't need to store a value for every column every time you store a new entity. Maybe you don't know the values for every column for a given entity. For example, some people have a second phone number and some don't, and in an online form backed by Cassandra, there may be some fields that are optional and some that are required. That's OK. Instead of storing null for those values you don't know, which would waste space, you just don't store that column at all for that row. So now you have a sparse, multidimensional array structure that looks like Figure 4-4. This flexible data structure is characteristic of Cassandra and other databases classified as *wide column* stores.

Now let's return to the discussion of primary keys in Cassandra, as this is a fundamental topic that will affect your understanding of Cassandra's architecture and data model, how Cassandra reads and writes data, and how it is able to scale.

Cassandra uses a special type of primary key called a *composite key* (or *compound key*) to represent groups of related rows, also called *partitions*. The composite key consists of a *partition key*, plus an optional set of *clustering columns*. The partition key is used to determine the nodes on which rows are stored and can itself consist of multiple columns. The clustering columns are used to control how data is sorted for storage within a partition. Cassandra also supports an additional construct called a *static column*, which is for storing data that is not part of the primary key but is shared by every row in a partition.

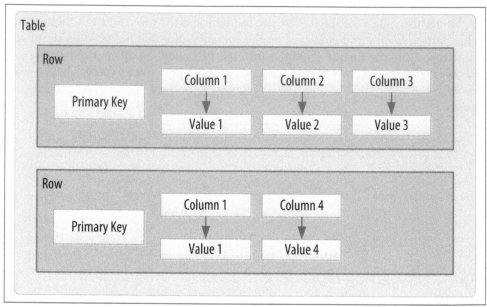

Figure 4-4. A Cassandra table

Figure 4-5 shows how each partition is uniquely identified by a partition key, and how the clustering keys are used to uniquely identify the rows within a partition. Note that in the case where no clustering columns are provided, each partition consists of a single row.

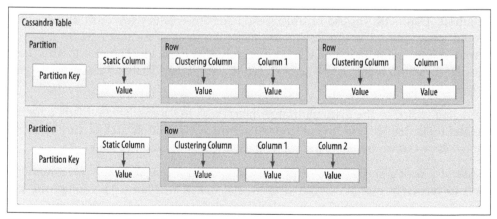

Figure 4-5. A Cassandra table with partitions

Putting these concepts all together, we have the basic Cassandra data structures:

- The *column*, which is a name/value pair
- The *row*, which is a container for columns referenced by a primary key
- The *partition*, which is a group of related rows that are stored together on the same nodes
- The *table*, which is a container for rows organized by partitions
- The *keyspace*, which is a container for tables
- The *cluster*, which is a container for keyspaces that spans one or more nodes

So that's the bottom-up approach to looking at Cassandra's data model. Now that you know the basic terminology, let's examine each structure in more detail.

Clusters

As previously mentioned, the Cassandra database is specifically designed to be distributed over several machines operating together that appear as a single instance to the end user. So the outermost structure in Cassandra is the *cluster*, sometimes called the *ring*, because Cassandra assigns data to nodes in the cluster by arranging them in a ring.

Keyspaces

A cluster is a container for keyspaces. A *keyspace* is the outermost container for data in Cassandra, corresponding closely to a *database* in the relational model. In the same way that a database is a container for tables in the relational model, a keyspace is a container for tables in the Cassandra data model. Like a relational database, a keyspace has a name and a set of attributes that define keyspace-wide behavior such as replication.

Because we're currently focusing on the data model, we'll leave questions about setting up and configuring clusters and keyspaces until later. We'll examine these topics in Chapter 10.

Tables

A *table* is a container for an ordered collection of rows, each of which is itself an ordered collection of columns. Rows are organized in partitions and assigned to nodes in a Cassandra cluster according to the column(s) designated as the partition key. The ordering of data within a partition is determined by the clustering columns.

When you write data to a table in Cassandra, you specify values for one or more columns. That collection of values is called a *row*. You must specify a value for each of the columns contained in the *primary key* as those columns taken together will uniquely identify the row.

Let's go back to the user table from the previous chapter. Remember how you wrote a row of data and then read it using the SELECT command in cqlsh:

```
cqlsh:my_keyspace> SELECT * FROM user where last_name = 'Nguyen';

last_name | first_name | title
-----------+------------+-------
   Nguyen |       Bill |   Mr.

(1 rows)
```

You'll notice in the last line of output that one row was returned. It turns out to be the row identified by the last_name "Nguyen" and first_name "Bill." This is the primary key that uniquely identifies this row.

One interesting point about the preceding query is that it is only specifying the partition key, which makes it a query that could potentially return multiple rows. To illustrate this point, let's add another user with the same last_name and then repeat the SELECT command from above:

```
cqlsh:my_keyspace> INSERT INTO user (first_name, last_name, title)
  VALUES ('Wanda', 'Nguyen', 'Mrs.');
cqlsh:my_keyspace> SELECT * FROM user WHERE last_name='Nguyen';

last_name | first_name | title
-----------+------------+-------
   Nguyen |       Bill |   Mr.
   Nguyen |      Wanda |  Mrs.

(2 rows)
```

As you can see, by partitioning users by last_name, you've made it possible to load the entire partition in a single query by providing that last_name. To access just one single row, you'd need to specify the entire primary key:

```
cqlsh:my_keyspace> SELECT * FROM user WHERE last_name='Nguyen' AND
  first_name='Bill';

last_name | first_name | title
-----------+------------+-------
   Nguyen |       Bill |   Mr.

(1 rows)
```

Data Access Requires a Primary Key

To summmmarize this important detail: the SELECT, INSERT, UPDATE, and DELETE commands in CQL all operate in terms of rows. For INSERT and UPDATE commands, all of the primary key columns must be specified using the WHERE clause in order to identify the specific row that is affected. The SELECT and DELETE commands can operate in terms of one or more rows within a partition, an entire partition, or even multiple partitions by using the WHERE and IN clauses. We'll explore these commands in more detail in Chapter 9.

While you do need to provide a value for each primary key column when you add a new row to the table, you are not required to provide values for nonprimary key columns. To illustrate this, let's insert another row with no title:

```
cqlsh:my_keyspace> INSERT INTO user (first_name, last_name)
               ... VALUES ('Mary', 'Rodriguez');
cqlsh:my_keyspace> SELECT * FROM user WHERE last_name='Rodriguez';

 last_name | first_name | title
-----------+------------+-------
 Rodriguez |       Mary |  null

(1 rows)
```

Since you have not set a value for title, the value returned is null.

Now if you decide later that you would also like to keep track of users' middle initials, you can modify the user table using the ALTER TABLE command and then view the results using the DESCRIBE TABLE command:

```
cqlsh:my_keyspace> ALTER TABLE user ADD middle_initial text;
cqlsh:my_keyspace> DESCRIBE TABLE user;

CREATE TABLE my_keyspace.user (
    last_name text,
    first_name text,
    middle_initial text,
    title text,
    PRIMARY KEY (last_name, first_name)
) ...
```

You see that the middle_initial column has been added. Note that we've shortened the output to omit the various table settings. You'll learn more about these settings and how to configure them throughout the rest of the book.

Now, let's write some additional rows, populate different columns for each, and read the results:

```
cqlsh:my_keyspace> INSERT INTO user (first_name, middle_initial, last_name,
  title)
  VALUES ('Bill', 'S', 'Nguyen', 'Mr.');
cqlsh:my_keyspace> INSERT INTO user (first_name, middle_initial, last_name,
  title)
  VALUES ('Bill', 'R', 'Nguyen', 'Mr.');
cqlsh:my_keyspace> SELECT * FROM user WHERE first_name='Bill' AND
  last_name='Nguyen';

 last_name | first_name | middle_initial | title
-----------+------------+----------------+-------
    Nguyen |       Bill |              R |   Mr.

(1 rows)
```

Was this the result that you expected? If you're following closely, you may have noticed that both of the INSERT statements here specify a previous row uniquely identified by the primary key columns first_name and last_name. As a result, Cassandra has faithfully updated the row you indicated, and your SELECT will only return the single row that matches that primary key. The two INSERT statements have only served to first set and then overwrite the middle_initial.

Insert, Update, and Upsert

Because Cassandra uses an append model, there is no fundamental difference between the insert and update operations. If you insert a row that has the same primary key as an existing row, the row is replaced. If you update a row and the primary key does not exist, Cassandra creates it.

For this reason, it is often said that Cassandra supports *upsert*, meaning that inserts and updates are treated the same, with one minor exception that we'll discuss in "Lightweight Transactions" on page 193.

Let's visualize the data you've inserted up to this point in Figure 4-6. Notice that there are two partitions, identified by the last_name values of "Nguyen" and "Rodriguez." The "Nguyen" partition contains the two rows, "Bill" and "Wanda," and the row for "Bill" contains values in the title and middle_initial columns, while "Wanda" has only a title and no middle_initial specified.

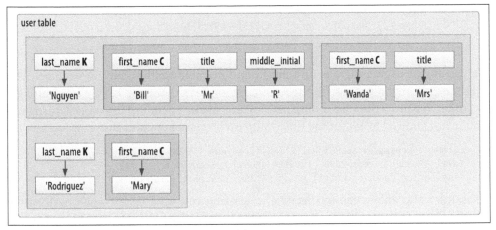

Figure 4-6. Data inserted into the user *table*

Now that you've learned more about the structure of a table and done some data modeling, let's dive deeper into columns.

Columns

A *column* is the most basic unit of data structure in the Cassandra data model. So far you've seen that a column contains a name and a value. You constrain each of the values to be of a particular type when you define the column. You'll want to dig into the various types that are available for each column, but first let's take a look into some other attributes of a column that we haven't discussed yet: timestamps and time to live. These attributes are key to understanding how Cassandra uses time to keep data current.

Timestamps

Each time you write data into Cassandra, a timestamp, in microseconds, is generated for each column value that is inserted or updated. Internally, Cassandra uses these timestamps for resolving any conflicting changes that are made to the same value, in what is frequently referred to as a *last write wins* approach.

Let's view the timestamps that were generated for previous writes by adding the write time() function to the SELECT command for the title column, plus a couple of other values for context:

```
cqlsh:my_keyspace> SELECT first_name, last_name, title, writetime(title)
  FROM user;

 first_name | last_name | title | writetime(title)
------------+-----------+-------+------------------
       Mary | Rodriguez |  null |             null
```

```
       Bill |    Nguyen |   Mr. | 1567876680189474
      Wanda |    Nguyen |  Mrs. | 1567874109804754
```

(3 rows)

As you might expect, there is no timestamp for a column that has not been set. You might expect that if you ask for the timestamp on first_name or last_name, you'd get a similar result to the values obtained for the title column. However, it turns out you're not allowed to ask for the timestamp on primary key columns:

```
cqlsh:my_keyspace> SELECT WRITETIME(first_name) FROM user;
InvalidRequest: code=2200 [Invalid query] message="Cannot use
    selection function writeTime on PRIMARY KEY part first_name"
```

Cassandra also allows you to specify a timestamp you want to use when performing writes. To do this, you'll use the CQL UPDATE command for the first time. Use the optional USING TIMESTAMP option to manually set a timestamp (note that the timestamp must be later than the one from your SELECT command, or the UPDATE will be ignored):

```
cqlsh:my_keyspace> UPDATE user USING TIMESTAMP 1567886623298243
    SET middle_initial = 'Q' WHERE first_name = 'Mary' AND last_name = 'Rodriguez';
cqlsh:my_keyspace> SELECT first_name, middle_initial, last_name,
    WRITETIME(middle_initial) FROM user WHERE first_name = 'Mary' AND
    last_name = 'Rodriguez';

 first_name | middle_initial | last_name | writetime(middle_initial)
------------+----------------+-----------+---------------------------
       Mary |              Q | Rodriguez |          1567886623298243
```

(1 rows)

This statement has the effect of adding the middle_initial column and setting the timestamp to the value you provided.

Working with Timestamps

Setting the timestamp is not required for writes. This functionality is typically used for writes in which there is a concern that some of the writes may cause fresh data to be overwritten with stale data. This is advanced behavior and should be used with caution.

There is currently not a way to convert timestamps produced by writetime() into a more friendly format in cqlsh.

Time to live (TTL)

One very powerful feature that Cassandra provides is the ability to expire data that is no longer needed. This expiration is very flexible and works at the level of individual column values. The time to live (or TTL) is a value that Cassandra stores for each column value to indicate how long to keep the value.

The TTL value defaults to null, meaning that data that is written will not expire. Let's show this by adding the TTL() function to a SELECT command in cqlsh to see the TTL value for Mary's title:

```
cqlsh:my_keyspace> SELECT first_name, last_name, TTL(title)
  FROM user WHERE first_name = 'Mary' AND last_name = 'Rodriguez';

 first_name | last_name | ttl(title)
------------+-----------+------------
       Mary | Rodriguez |       null

(1 rows)
```

Now let's set the TTL on the middle_initial column to an hour (3,600 seconds) by adding the USING TTL option to your UPDATE command:

```
cqlsh:my_keyspace> UPDATE user USING TTL 3600 SET middle_initial =
  'Z' WHERE first_name = 'Mary' AND last_name = 'Rodriguez';
cqlsh:my_keyspace> SELECT first_name, middle_initial,
  last_name, TTL(middle_initial)
  FROM user WHERE first_name = 'Mary' AND last_name = 'Rodriguez';

 first_name | middle_initial | last_name | ttl(middle_initial)
------------+----------------+-----------+---------------------
       Mary |              Z | Rodriguez |                3574

(1 rows)
```

As you can see, the clock is already counting down your TTL, reflecting the several seconds it took to type the second command. If you run this command again in an hour, Mary's middle_initial will be shown as null. You can also set TTL on INSERTS using the same USING TTL option, in which case the entire row will expire.

You can try inserting a row using TTL of 60 seconds and check that the row is initially there:

```
cqlsh:my_keyspace> INSERT INTO user (first_name, last_name)
  VALUES ('Jeff', 'Carpenter') USING TTL 60;
cqlsh:my_keyspace> SELECT * FROM user WHERE first_name='Jeff' AND
  last_name='Carpenter';

 last_name | first_name | middle_initial | title
-----------+------------+----------------+-------
```

```
    Carpenter |       Jeff |         null |  null
```

(1 rows)

After you wait a minute, the row is no longer there:

```
cqlsh:my_keyspace> SELECT * FROM user WHERE first_name='Jeff' AND
  last_name='Carpenter';

last_name | first_name | middle_initial | title
----------+------------+----------------+-------
```

(0 rows)

Using TTL

Remember that TTL is stored on a per-column level for nonprimary key columns. There is currently no mechanism for setting TTL at a row level directly after the initial insert; you would instead need to reinsert the row, taking advantage of Cassandra's upsert behavior. As with the timestamp, there is no way to obtain or set the TTL value of a *primary key* column, and the TTL can only be set for a column when you provide a value for the column.

The behavior of Cassandra's TTL feature can be somewhat nonintuitive, especially in cases where you are updating an existing row. Rahul Kumar's blog "Cassandra TTL intricacies and usage by examples" (*https://oreil.ly/BVZLM*) does a great job of summarizing the effects of TTL in a number of different cases.

CQL Types

Now that we've taken a deeper dive into how Cassandra represents columns, including time-based metadata, let's look at the various types that are available to you for representing values.

As you've seen previously, each column in a table is of a specified type. Up until this point, you've only used the varchar type, but there are plenty of other options available in CQL, so let's explore them.

CQL supports a flexible set of data types, including simple character and numeric types, collections, and user-defined types. We'll describe these data types and provide some examples of how they might be used to help you learn to make the right choice for your data model.

Numeric Data Types

CQL supports the numeric types you'd expect, including integer and floating-point numbers. These types are similar to standard types in Java and other languages:

int
  A 32-bit signed integer (as in Java)

bigint
  A 64-bit signed long integer (equivalent to a Java long)

smallint
  A 16-bit signed integer (equivalent to a Java short)

tinyint
  An 8-bit signed integer (as in Java)

varint
  A variable precision signed integer (equivalent to java.math.BigInteger)

float
  A 32-bit IEEE-754 floating point (as in Java)

double
  A 64-bit IEEE-754 floating point (as in Java)

decimal
  A variable precision decimal (equivalent to java.math.BigDecimal)

Additional Integer Types

The smallint and tinyint types were added in the Cassandra 2.2 release.

While enumerated types are common in many languages, there is no direct equivalent in CQL. A common practice is to store enumerated values as strings. For example, in Java you might use the Enum.name() method to convert an enumerated value to a String for writing to Cassandra as text, and the Enum.valueOf() method to convert from text back to the enumerated value.

Textual Data Types

CQL provides two data types for representing text, one of which you've made quite a bit of use of already (text):

```
text, varchar
```
Synonyms for a UTF-8 character string

```
ascii
```
An ASCII character string

UTF-8 is the more recent and widely used text standard and supports internationalization, so we recommend using `text` over `ascii` when building tables for new data. The `ascii` type is most useful if you are dealing with legacy data that is in ASCII format.

Setting the Locale in cqlsh

By default, `cqlsh` prints out control and other unprintable characters using a backslash escape. You can control how `cqlsh` displays non-ASCII characters by setting the locale with the `$LANG` environment variable before running the tool. See the `cqlsh` command `HELP TEXT_OUTPUT` for more information.

Time and Identity Data Types

The identity of data elements such as rows and partitions is important in any data model in order to be able to access the data. Cassandra provides several types that prove quite useful in defining unique partition keys. Let's take some time (pun intended) to dig into these:

```
timestamp
```
While we noted earlier that each column has a timestamp indicating when it was last modified, you can also use a timestamp as the value of a column itself. The time can be encoded as a 64-bit signed integer, but it is typically much more useful to input a timestamp using one of several supported ISO 8601 date formats. For example:

```
2015-06-15 20:05-0700
   2015-06-15 20:05:07-0700
   2015-06-15 20:05:07.013-0700
   2015-06-15T20:05-0700
   2015-06-15T20:05:07-0700
   2015-06-15T20:05:07.013+-0700
```

The best practice is to always provide time zones rather than relying on the operating system time zone configuration.

```
date, time
```
Releases through Cassandra 2.1 only had the `timestamp` type to represent times, which included both a date and a time of day. The 2.2 release introduced `date`

and `time` types that allowed these to be represented independently; that is, a date without a time, and a time of day without reference to a specific date. As with `timestamp`, these types support ISO 8601 formats.

Although there are new `java.time` types available in Java 8, the `date` type maps to a custom type in Cassandra in order to preserve compatibility with older JDKs. The `time` type maps to a Java `long` representing the number of nanoseconds since midnight.

`uuid`

A *universally unique identifier* (UUID) is a 128-bit value in which the bits conform to one of several types, of which the most commonly used are known as Type 1 and Type 4. The CQL `uuid` type is a Type 4 UUID, which is based entirely on random numbers. UUIDs are typically represented as dash-separated sequences of hex digits. For example:

```
1a6300ca-0572-4736-a393-c0b7229e193e
```

The `uuid` type is often used as a surrogate key, either by itself or in combination with other values.

Because UUIDs are of a finite length, they are not absolutely guaranteed to be unique. However, most operating systems and programming languages provide utilities to generate IDs that provide adequate uniqueness. You can also obtain a Type 4 UUID value via the CQL `uuid()` function and use this value in an `INSERT` or `UPDATE`.

`timeuuid`

This is a Type 1 UUID, which is based on the MAC address of the computer, the system time, and a sequence number used to prevent duplicates. This type is frequently used as a conflict-free timestamp. CQL provides several convenience functions for interacting with the `timeuuid` type: `now()`, `dateOf()`, and `unixTimestampOf()`.

The availability of these convenience functions is one reason why `timeuuid` tends to be used more frequently than `uuid`.

Building on the previous examples, you might determine that you'd like to assign a unique ID to each user, as `first_name` is perhaps not a sufficiently unique key for the user table. After all, it's very likely that you'll run into users with the same first name at some point. If you were starting from scratch, you might have chosen to make this identifier your primary key, but for now you'll add it as another column.

Primary Keys Are Forever

After you create a table, there is no way to modify the primary key, because this controls how data is distributed within the cluster, and even more importantly, how it is stored on disk.

Let's add the identifier using a `uuid`:

```
cqlsh:my_keyspace> ALTER TABLE user ADD id uuid;
```

Next, insert an ID for Mary using the `uuid()` function and then view the results:

```
cqlsh:my_keyspace> UPDATE user SET id = uuid() WHERE first_name =
  'Mary' AND last_name = 'Rodriguez';
cqlsh:my_keyspace> SELECT first_name, id FROM user WHERE
  first_name = 'Mary' AND last_name = 'Rodriguez';

 first_name | id
------------+--------------------------------------
       Mary | ebf87fee-b372-4104-8a22-00c1252e3e05

(1 rows)
```

Notice that the `id` is in UUID format.

Now you have a more robust table design, which you can extend with even more columns as you learn about more types.

Other Simple Data Types

CQL provides several other simple data types that don't fall nicely into one of the preceding categories:

boolean

This is a simple true/false value. The `cqlsh` is case insensitive in accepting these values but outputs `True` or `False`.

blob

A *binary large object* (blob) is a colloquial computing term for an arbitrary array of bytes. The CQL blob type is useful for storing media or other binary file types. Cassandra does not validate or examine the bytes in a blob. CQL represents the data as hexadecimal digits—for example, `0x00000ab83cf0`. If you want to encode arbitrary textual data into the blob, you can use the `textAsBlob()` function in order to specify values for entry. See the `cqlsh` help function `HELP BLOB_INPUT` for more information.

inet

This type represents IPv4 or IPv6 internet addresses. `cqlsh` accepts any legal format for defining IPv4 addresses, including dotted or nondotted representations containing decimal, octal, or hexadecimal values. However, the values are represented using the dotted decimal format in `cqlsh` output—for example, `192.0.2.235`.

IPv6 addresses are represented as eight groups of four hexadecimal digits, separated by colons—for example, `2001:0db8:85a3:0000:0000:8a2e:0370:7334`. The IPv6 specification allows the collapsing of consecutive zero hex values, so the preceding value is rendered as follows when read using SELECT: `2001:db8:85a3:a::8a2e:370:7334`.

counter

The `counter` data type provides a 64-bit signed integer, whose value cannot be set directly, but only incremented or decremented. Cassandra is one of the few databases that provides race-free increments across data centers. Counters are frequently used for tracking statistics such as numbers of page views, tweets, log messages, and so on. The `counter` type has some special restrictions. It cannot be used as part of a primary key. If a counter is used, all of the columns other than primary key columns must be counters.

For example, you could create an additional table to count the number of times a user has visited a website:

```
cqlsh:my_keyspace> CREATE TABLE user_visits (
   user_id uuid PRIMARY KEY, visits counter);
```

You'd then increment the value for user "Mary" according to the unique ID assigned previously each time she visits the site:

```
cqlsh:my_keyspace> UPDATE user_visits SET visits = visits + 1
   WHERE user_id=ebf87fee-b372-4104-8a22-00c1252e3e05;
```

And you could read out the value of the counter just as you read any other column:

```
cqlsh:my_keyspace> SELECT visits from user_visits WHERE
   user_id=ebf87fee-b372-4104-8a22-00c1252e3e05;

 visits
--------
      1

(1 rows)
```

There is no operation to reset a counter directly, but you can approximate a reset by reading the counter value and decrementing by that value. Unfortunately, this is not guaranteed to work perfectly, as the counter may have been changed elsewhere in between reading and writing.

A Warning About Idempotence

The counter increment and decrement operators are not *idempotent*. An idempotent operation is one that will produce the same result when executed multiple times. Incrementing and decrementing are not idempotent because executing them multiple times could result in different results as the stored value is increased or decreased.

To see how this is possible, consider that Cassandra is a distributed system in which interactions over a network may fail when a node fails to respond to a request indicating success or failure. A typical client response to this request is to retry the operation. The result of retrying a nonidempotent operation such as incrementing a counter is not predictable. Since it is not known whether the first attempt succeeded, the value may have been incremented twice. This is not a fatal flaw, but something you'll want to be aware of when using counters.

The only other CQL operation that is not idempotent besides incrementing or decrementing a counter is adding an item to a `list`, which we'll discuss next.

Collections

Let's say you wanted to extend the `user` table to support multiple email addresses. One way to do this would be to create additional columns such as `email2`, `email3`, and so on. While this approach will work, it does not scale very well and might cause a lot of rework. It is much simpler to deal with the email addresses as a group or "collection." CQL provides three collection types to help you with these situations: sets, lists, and maps. Let's now take a look at each of them:

set

> The `set` data type stores a collection of elements. The elements are unordered when stored, but are returned in sorted order. For example, text values are returned in alphabetical order. Sets can contain the simple types you've learned previously, as well as user-defined types (which we'll discuss momentarily) and even other collections. One advantage of using `set` is the ability to insert additional items without having to read the contents first.

You can modify the `user` table to add a set of email addresses:

```
cqlsh:my_keyspace> ALTER TABLE user ADD emails set<text>;
```

Then add an email address for Mary and check that it was added successfully:

```
cqlsh:my_keyspace> UPDATE user SET emails = { 'mary@example.com' }
   WHERE first_name = 'Mary' AND last_name = 'Rodriguez';
cqlsh:my_keyspace> SELECT emails FROM user WHERE first_name =
```

```
  'Mary' AND last_name = 'Rodriguez';

 emails
---------------------
 {'mary@example.com'}
```

(1 rows)

Note that in adding that first email address, you replaced the previous contents of the set, which in this case was null. You can add another email address later without replacing the whole set by using concatenation:

```
cqlsh:my_keyspace> UPDATE user
  SET emails = emails + {'mary.rodriguez.AZ@gmail.com' }
  WHERE first_name = 'Mary' AND last_name = 'Rodriguez';
cqlsh:my_keyspace> SELECT emails FROM user
  WHERE first_name = 'Mary' AND last_name = 'Rodriguez';

 emails
---------------------------------------------------------
 {'mary.mcdonald.AZ@gmail.com', 'mary@example.com'}
```

(1 rows)

Other Set Operations

You can also clear items from the set by using the subtraction operator: SET emails = emails - {'*mary@example.com*'}.

Alternatively, you could clear out the entire set by using the empty set notation: SET emails = {}.

list

The list data type contains an ordered list of elements. By default, the values are stored in order of insertion. You can modify the user table to add a list of phone numbers:

```
cqlsh:my_keyspace> ALTER TABLE user ADD phone_numbers list<text>;
```

Then add a phone number for Mary and check that it was added successfully:

```
cqlsh:my_keyspace> UPDATE user SET phone_numbers = ['1-800-999-9999' ]
  WHERE first_name = 'Mary' AND last_name = 'Rodriguez';
cqlsh:my_keyspace> SELECT phone_numbers FROM user WHERE
  first_name = 'Mary' AND last_name = 'Rodriguez';

 phone_numbers
---------------------
 ['1-800-999-9999']
```

```
(1 rows)
```

Let's add a second number by appending it:

```
cqlsh:my_keyspace> UPDATE user SET phone_numbers =
  phone_numbers + [ '480-111-1111' ]
  WHERE first_name = 'Mary' AND last_name = 'Rodriguez';
cqlsh:my_keyspace> SELECT phone_numbers FROM user WHERE
  first_name = 'Mary' AND last_name = 'Rodriguez';

 phone_numbers
------------------------------------
 ['1-800-999-9999', '480-111-1111']

(1 rows)
```

The second number you added now appears at the end of the list.

 You could also have prepended the number to the front of the
list by reversing the order of the values: SET phone_numbers =
['4801234567'] + phone_numbers.

You can replace an individual item in the list when you reference it by its index:

```
cqlsh:my_keyspace> UPDATE user SET phone_numbers[1] = '480-111-1111'
  WHERE first_name = 'Mary' AND last_name = 'Rodriguez';
```

As with sets, you can also use the subtraction operator to remove items that
match a specified value:

```
cqlsh:my_keyspace> UPDATE user SET phone_numbers =
  phone_numbers - [ '480-111-1111' ]
  WHERE first_name = 'Mary' AND last_name = 'Rodriguez';
```

Finally, you can delete a specific item directly using its index:

```
cqlsh:my_keyspace> DELETE phone_numbers[0] from user WHERE
  first_name = 'Mary' AND last_name = 'Rodriguez';
```

Expensive List Operations

Because a list stores values according to position, there is the potential that updating or deleting a specific item in a list could require Cassandra to read the entire list, perform the requested operation, and write out the entire list again. This could be an expensive operation if you have a large number of values in the list. For this reason, many users prefer to use the set or map types, especially in cases where there is the potential to update the contents of the collection.

map

The map data type contains a collection of key-value pairs. The keys and the values can be of any type except counter. Let's try this out by using a map to store information about user logins. Create a column to track login session time, in seconds, with a timeuuid as the key:

```
cqlsh:my_keyspace> ALTER TABLE user ADD
  login_sessions map<timeuuid, int>;
```

Then you can add a couple of login sessions for Mary and see the results:

```
cqlsh:my_keyspace> UPDATE user SET login_sessions =
  { now(): 13, now(): 18}
  WHERE first_name = 'Mary' AND last_name = 'Rodriguez';
cqlsh:my_keyspace> SELECT login_sessions FROM user
  WHERE first_name = 'Mary' AND last_name = 'Rodriguez';

 login_sessions
------------------------------------------------
 {839b2660-d1c0-11e9-8309-6d2c86545d91: 13,
  839b2661-d1c0-11e9-8309-6d2c86545d91: 18}

(1 rows)
```

We can also reference an individual item in the map by using its key.

Collection types are very useful in cases where we need to store a variable number of elements within a single column.

Tuples

Now you might decide that you need to keep track of physical addresses for your users. You could just use a single text column to store these values, but that would put the burden of parsing the various components of the address on the application. It would be better if you could define a structure in which to store the addresses to maintain the integrity of the different components.

Fortunately, Cassandra provides two different ways to manage more complex data structures: tuples and user-defined types.

First, let's have a look at tuples, which provide a way to have a fixed-length set of values of various types. For example, you could add a tuple column to the user table that stores an address. You could have added a tuple to define addresses, assuming a three-line address format and an integer postal code such as a US zip code:

```
cqlsh:my_keyspace> ALTER TABLE user ADD
   address tuple<text, text, text, int>;
```

Then you could populate an address using the following statement:

```
cqlsh:my_keyspace> UPDATE user SET address =
   ('7712 E. Broadway', 'Tucson', 'AZ', 85715 )
   WHERE first_name = 'Mary' AND last_name = 'Rodriguez';
```

This does provide you the ability to store an address, but it can be a bit awkward to try to remember the positional values of the various fields of a tuple without having a name associated with each value. There is also no way to update individual fields of a tuple; the entire tuple must be updated. For these reasons, tuples are infrequently used in practice, because Cassandra offers an alternative that provides a way to name and access each value, which we'll examine next.

But first, let's use the CQL DROP command to get rid of the address column so that you can replace it with something better:

```
cqlsh:my_keyspace> ALTER TABLE user DROP address;
```

User-Defined Types

Cassandra gives you a way to define your own types to extend its data model. These user-defined types (UDTs) are easier to use than tuples since you can specify the values by name rather than position. Create your own address type:

```
cqlsh:my_keyspace> CREATE TYPE address (
   street text,
   city text,
   state text,
   zip_code int);
```

A UDT is scoped by the keyspace in which it is defined. You could have written CRE ATE TYPE my_keyspace.address. If you run the command DESCRIBE KEYSPACE my_keyspace, you'll see that the address type is part of the keyspace definition.

Now that you have defined the address type, you can use it in the user table. Rather than simply adding a single address, you can use a map to store multiple addresses to which you can give names such as "home," "work," and so on. However, you immediately run into a problem:

```
cqlsh:my_keyspace> ALTER TABLE user ADD
  addresses map<text, address>;
InvalidRequest: code=2200 [Invalid query] message="Non-frozen
  collections are not allowed inside collections: map<text,
  address>"
```

What is going on here? It turns out that a user-defined data type is considered a collection, as its implementation is similar to a `set`, `list`, or `map`. You've asked Cassandra to nest one collection inside another.

Freezing Collections

Cassandra releases prior to 2.2 do not fully support the nesting of collections. Specifically, the ability to access individual attributes of a nested collection is not yet supported, because the nested collection is serialized as a single object by the implementation. Therefore, the entire nested collection must be read and written in its entirety.

Freezing is a concept that was introduced as a forward compatibility mechanism. For now, you can nest a collection within another collection by marking it as `frozen`, which means that Cassandra will store that value as a blob of binary data. In the future, when nested collections are fully supported, there will be a mechanism to "unfreeze" the nested collections, allowing the individual attributes to be accessed.

You can also use a collection as a primary key if it is frozen.

Now that we've taken a short detour to discuss freezing and nested collections, let's get back to modifying your table, this time marking the address as frozen:

```
cqlsh:my_keyspace> ALTER TABLE user ADD addresses map<text,
  frozen<address>>;
```

Now let's add a home address for Mary:

```
cqlsh:my_keyspace> UPDATE user SET addresses = addresses +
  {'home': { street: '7712 E. Broadway', city: 'Tucson',
  state: 'AZ', zip_code: 85715 } }
  WHERE first_name = 'Mary' AND last_name = 'Rodriguez';
cqlsh:my_keyspace> SELECT addresses FROM user
  WHERE first_name = 'Mary' AND last_name = 'Rodriguez';

 addresses
--------------------------------------------------------
 {'home': {street: '7712 E. Broadway',
           city: 'Tucson', state: 'AZ', zip_code: 85715}}

(1 rows)
```

Now that you've learned about the various types, let's take a step back and look at the tables you've created so far by describing my_keyspace:

```
cqlsh:my_keyspace> DESCRIBE KEYSPACE my_keyspace ;

CREATE KEYSPACE my_keyspace WITH replication = {'class':
  'SimpleStrategy', 'replication_factor': '1') AND
  durable_writes = true;

CREATE TYPE my_keyspace.address (
    street text,
    city text,
    state text,
    zip_code int
);

CREATE TABLE my_keyspace.user (
    last_name text,
    first_name text,
    addresses map<text, frozen<address>>,
    emails set<text>,
    id uuid,
    login_sessions map<timeuuid, int>,
    middle_initial text,
    phone_numbers list<text>,
    title text,
    PRIMARY KEY (last_name, first_name)
) WITH CLUSTERING ORDER BY (first_name ASC)
    AND bloom_filter_fp_chance = 0.01
    AND caching = {'keys': 'ALL', 'rows_per_partition': 'NONE'}
    AND comment = ''
    AND compaction = {'class': 'org.apache.cassandra.db.compaction
      .SizeTieredCompactionStrategy', 'max_threshold': '32',
      'min_threshold': '4'}
    AND compression = {'chunk_length_in_kb': '16', 'class':
      'org.apache.cassandra.io.compress.LZ4Compressor'}
    AND crc_check_chance = 1.0
    AND dclocal_read_repair_chance = 0.1
    AND default_time_to_live = 0
    AND gc_grace_seconds = 864000
    AND max_index_interval = 2048
    AND memtable_flush_period_in_ms = 0
    AND min_index_interval = 128
    AND read_repair_chance = 0.0
    AND speculative_retry = '99PERCENTILE';

CREATE TABLE my_keyspace.user_visits (
    user_id uuid PRIMARY KEY,
    visits counter
) WITH bloom_filter_fp_chance = 0.01
    AND caching = {'keys': 'ALL', 'rows_per_partition': 'NONE'}
    AND comment = ''
```

```
AND compaction = {'class': 'org.apache.cassandra.db.compaction
  .SizeTieredCompactionStrategy', 'max_threshold': '32',
  'min_threshold': '4'}
AND compression = {'chunk_length_in_kb': '16', 'class':
  'org.apache.cassandra.io.compress.LZ4Compressor'}
AND crc_check_chance = 1.0
AND dclocal_read_repair_chance = 0.1
AND default_time_to_live = 0
AND gc_grace_seconds = 864000
AND max_index_interval = 2048
AND memtable_flush_period_in_ms = 0
AND min_index_interval = 128
AND read_repair_chance = 0.0
AND speculative_retry = '99PERCENTILE';
```

Practicing CQL Commands

The commands listed in this chapter to operate on the user table are available as a gist on GitHub (*https://git.io/fjihw*) to make it easier for you to execute them. The file is named *cqlsh_intro.cql*.

Summary

In this chapter, you took a quick tour of Cassandra's data model of clusters, keyspaces, tables, keys, rows, and columns. In the process, you learned a lot of CQL syntax and gained more experience working with tables and columns in cqlsh. If you're interested in diving deeper into CQL, you can read the full language specification (*https://oreil.ly/fWE0X*).

## CHAPTER 5

Data Modeling

The data model you use is the most important factor in your success with Cassandra.

—Patrick McFadin

More than any configuration or tuning you can perform, your data model is the main factor that will affect your application performance and cluster maintenance. In this chapter, you'll learn how to design data models for Cassandra, including a data modeling process and notation. To apply this knowledge, you'll design the data model for a sample application, which you'll build over the next several chapters. This will help show how all the parts fit together. Along the way, you'll see some tools to help you manage your CQL scripts.

Conceptual Data Modeling

First, let's create a simple domain model that is easy to understand in the relational world, and then see how you might map it from a relational to a distributed hash table model in Cassandra.

To create the example, we want to use something that is complex enough to show the various data structures and design patterns, but not something that will bog you down with details. Also, a domain that's familiar to everyone will allow you to concentrate on how to work with Cassandra, not on what the application domain is all about.

Let's use a domain that is easily understood and that everyone can relate to: making hotel reservations.

Our conceptual domain includes hotels, guests that stay in the hotels, a collection of rooms for each hotel, the rates and availability of those rooms, and a record of reservations booked for guests. Hotels typically also maintain a collection of "points of interest," which are parks, museums, shopping galleries, monuments, or other places near the hotel that guests might want to visit during their stay. Both hotels and points of interest need to maintain geolocation data so that they can be found on maps for mashups, and to calculate distances.

The conceptual domain is shown in Figure 5-1 using the entity–relationship model popularized by Peter Chen. This simple diagram represents the entities in the domain with rectangles, and attributes of those entities with ovals. Attributes that represent unique identifiers for items are underlined. Relationships between entities are represented as diamonds, and the connectors between the relationship and each entity show the multiplicity of the connection.

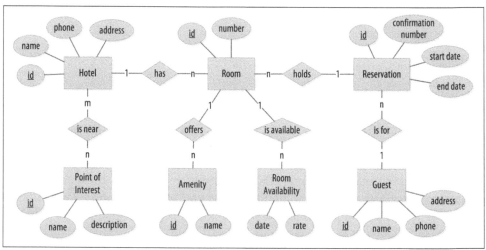

Figure 5-1. Hotel domain entity-relationship diagram

Obviously, in the real world, there would be many more considerations and much more complexity. For example, hotel rates are notoriously dynamic, and calculating them involves a wide array of factors. Here you'll define something complex enough to be interesting and touch on the important points, but simple enough to maintain the focus on learning Cassandra.

RDBMS Design

When you set out to build a new data-driven application that will use a relational database, you might start by modeling the domain as a set of properly normalized tables and use foreign keys to reference related data in other tables.

Figure 5-2 shows how you might represent the data storage for an application using a relational database model. The relational model includes a couple of "join" tables in order to realize the many-to-many relationships from the conceptual model of hotels-to-points of interest, rooms-to-amenities, rooms-to-availability, and guests-to-rooms (via a reservation).

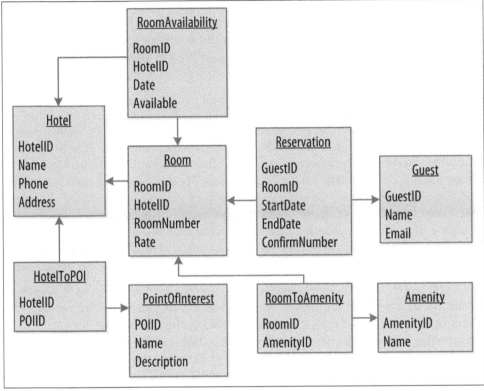

Figure 5-2. A simple hotel search system using RDBMS

Design Differences Between RDBMS and Cassandra

Of course, because this is a Cassandra book, what you really want is to model your data so you can store it in Cassandra. Before you start creating a Cassandra data model, let's take a minute to highlight some of the key differences in doing data modeling for Cassandra versus a relational database.

No joins

You cannot perform joins in Cassandra. If you have designed a data model and find that you need something like a join, you'll have to either do the work on the client side, or create a denormalized second table that represents the join results for you. This latter option is preferred in Cassandra data modeling. Performing joins on the client should be a very rare case; you really want to duplicate (denormalize) the data instead.

No referential integrity

Although Cassandra supports features such as lightweight transactions and batches, Cassandra itself has no concept of referential integrity across tables. In a relational database, you could specify foreign keys in a table to reference the primary key of a record in another table. But Cassandra does not enforce this. It is still a common design requirement to store IDs related to other entities in your tables, but operations such as cascading deletes are not available.

Denormalization

In relational database design, you are often taught the importance of normalization. This is not an advantage when working with Cassandra because it performs best when the data model is denormalized. It is often the case that companies end up denormalizing data in relational databases as well. There are two common reasons for this. One is performance. Companies simply can't get the performance they need when they have to do so many joins on years' worth of data, so they denormalize along the lines of known queries. This ends up working, but goes against the grain of how relational databases are intended to be designed, and ultimately makes one question whether using a relational database is the best approach in these circumstances.

A second reason that relational databases get denormalized on purpose is a business document structure that requires retention. That is, you have an enclosing table that refers to a lot of external tables whose data could change over time, but you need to preserve the enclosing document as a snapshot in history. The common example here is with invoices. You already have customer and product tables, and you'd think that you could just make an invoice that refers to those tables. But this should never be done in practice. Customer or price information could change, and then you would lose the integrity of the invoice document as it was on the invoice date, which could violate audits, reports, or laws, and cause other problems.

In the relational world, denormalization violates Codd's normal forms, and you try to avoid it. But in Cassandra, denormalization is, well, perfectly normal. It's not required if your data model is simple. But don't be afraid of it.

Server-Side Denormalization with Materialized Views

Historically, denormalization in Cassandra has required designing and managing multiple tables using techniques we will introduce momentarily. Beginning with the 3.0 release, Cassandra provides an experimental feature known as *materialized views*, which allows you to create multiple denormalized views of data based on a base table design. Cassandra manages materialized views on the server, including the work of keeping the views in sync with the table. We'll share examples of classic denormalization in this chapter, and discuss materialized views in Chapter 7.

Query-first design

Relational modeling, in simple terms, means that you start from the conceptual domain and then represent the nouns in the domain in tables. You then assign primary keys and foreign keys to model relationships. When you have a many-to-many relationship, you create the join tables that represent just those keys. The join tables don't exist in the real world, and are a necessary side effect of the way relational models work. After you have all your tables laid out, you can start writing queries that pull together disparate data using the relationships defined by the keys. The queries in the relational world are very much secondary. It is assumed that you can always get the data you want as long as you have your tables modeled properly. Even if you have to use several complex subqueries or join statements, this is usually true.

By contrast, in Cassandra you don't start with the data model; you start with the query model. Instead of modeling the data first and then writing queries, with Cassandra you model the queries and let the data be organized around them. Think of the most common query paths your application will use, and then create the tables that you need to support them.

Detractors have suggested that designing the queries first is overly constraining on application design, not to mention database modeling. But it is perfectly reasonable to expect that you should think hard about the queries in your application, just as you would, presumably, think hard about your relational domain. You may get it wrong, and then you'll have problems in either world. Or your query needs might change over time, and then you'll have to work to update your data set. But this is no different from defining the wrong tables, or needing additional tables, in an RDBMS.

Designing for optimal storage

In a relational database, it is frequently transparent to the user how tables are stored on disk, and it is rare to hear of recommendations about data modeling based on how the RDBMS might store tables on disk. However, that is an important consideration in Cassandra. Because Cassandra tables are each stored in separate files on disk, it's important to keep related columns defined together in the same table.

A key goal as you begin creating data models in Cassandra is to minimize the number of partitions that must be searched in order to satisfy a given query. Because the partition is a unit of storage that does not get divided across nodes, a query that searches a single partition will typically yield the best performance.

Sorting is a design decision

In an RDBMS, you can easily change the order in which records are returned to you by using ORDER BY in your query. The default sort order is not configurable; by default, records are returned in the order in which they are written. If you want to change the order, you just modify your query, and you can sort by any list of columns.

In Cassandra, however, sorting is treated differently; it is a design decision. The sort order available on queries is fixed, and is determined entirely by the selection of clustering columns you supply in the CREATE TABLE command. The CQL SELECT statement does support ORDER BY semantics, but only in the order specified by the clustering columns (ascending or descending).

Defining Application Queries

Let's try the query-first approach to start designing the data model for your hotel application. The user interface design for the application is often a great artifact to use to begin identifying queries. Let's assume that you've talked with the project stakeholders, and your UX designers have produced user interface designs or wireframes for the key use cases. You'll likely have a list of shopping queries like the following:

- Q1. Find hotels near a given point of interest.
- Q2. Find information about a given hotel, such as its name and location.
- Q3. Find points of interest near a given hotel.
- Q4. Find an available room in a given date range.
- Q5. Find the rate and amenities for a room.

Number Your Queries

It is often helpful to be able to refer to queries by a shorthand number rather that explaining them in full. The queries listed here are numbered Q1, Q2, and so on, which is how we will reference them in diagrams throughout this example.

Now if your application is to be a success, you'll certainly want your customers to be able to book reservations at your hotels. This includes steps such as selecting an available room and entering their guest information. So clearly you will also need some queries that address the reservation and guest entities from the conceptual data model. Even here, however, you'll want to think not only from the customer perspective in terms of how the data is written, but also in terms of how the data will be queried by downstream use cases.

Our natural tendency as data modelers would be to focus first on designing the tables to store reservation and guest records, and only then start thinking about the queries that would access them. You may have felt a similar tension already when we began discussing the shopping queries before, thinking "but where did the hotel and point of interest data come from?" Don't worry, we will get to this soon enough. Here are some queries that describe how your users will access reservations:

- Q6. Look up a reservation by confirmation number.
- Q7. Look up a reservation by hotel, date, and guest name.
- Q8. Look up all reservations by guest name.
- Q9. View guest details.

Examine the queries in the context of the workflow of the application in Figure 5-3. Each box on the diagram represents a step in the application workflow, with arrows indicating the flows between steps and the associated query. If you've modeled your application well, each step of the workflow accomplishes a task that "unlocks" subsequent steps. For example, the "View hotels near POI" task helps the application learn about several hotels, including their unique keys. The key for a selected hotel may be used as part of Q2, in order to obtain a detailed description of the hotel. The act of booking a room creates a reservation record that may be accessed by the guest and hotel staff at a later time through various additional queries.

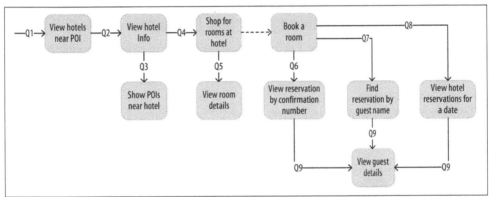

Figure 5-3. Hotel application queries

Logical Data Modeling

Now that you have defined your queries, you're ready to begin designing Cassandra tables. First, you'll create a logical model containing a table for each query, capturing entities and relationships from the conceptual model.

To name each table, identify the primary entity type for which you are querying, and use that to start the entity name. If you are querying by attributes of other related entities, you append those to the table name, separated with _by_; for example, `hotels_by_poi`.

Next, identify the primary key for the table, adding partition key columns based on the required query attributes, and clustering columns in order to guarantee uniqueness and support desired sort ordering.

The Importance of Primary Keys in Cassandra

The design of the primary key is extremely important, as it will determine how much data will be stored in each partition and how that data is organized on disk, which in turn will affect how quickly Cassandra processes read queries.

You complete the design of each table by adding any additional attributes identified by the query. If any of these additional attributes are the same for every instance of the partition key, mark the column as static.

Now that was a pretty quick description of a fairly involved process, so it will be worth your time to work through a detailed example. First, let's introduce a notation that you can use to represent your logical models.

Introducing Chebotko Diagrams

Several individuals within the Cassandra community have proposed notations for capturing data models in diagrammatic form. We've elected to use a notation popularized by Artem Chebotko that provides a simple, informative way to visualize the relationships between queries and tables in your designs. Figure 5-4 shows the Chebotko notation for a logical data model.

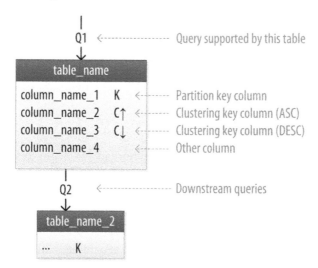

Figure 5-4. A Chebotko logical diagram

Each table is shown with its title and a list of columns. Primary key columns are identified via symbols such as K for partition key columns and C↑ or C↓ to represent clustering columns. Lines are shown entering tables or between tables to indicate the
queries that each table is designed to support.

Hotel Logical Data Model

Figure 5-5 shows a Chebotko logical data model for the queries involving hotels,
points of interest, rooms, and amenities. One thing you'll notice immediately is that
the Cassandra design doesn't include dedicated tables for rooms or amenities, as you
had in the relational design. This is because your workflow didn't identify any queries
requiring this direct access.

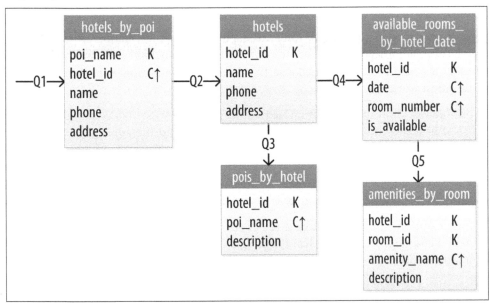

Figure 5-5. Hotel domain logical model

Let's explore the details of each of these tables.

The first query (Q1) is to find hotels near a point of interest, so you'll call the table
hotels_by_poi. You're searching by a named point of interest, so that is a clue that
the point of interest should be a part of the primary key. Let's reference the point of
interest by name, because according to your workflow that is how your users will start
their search.

You'll note that you certainly could have more than one hotel near a given point of
interest, so you'll need another component in your primary key in order to make sure

you have a unique partition for each hotel. So you add the hotel key as a clustering column.

Let's also assume that according to your application workflow, your user will provide a name of a point of interest, but would benefit from seeing the description of the point of interest alongside hotel results. Therefore you include the poi_description as a column in the hotels_by_poi table, and designate this value as a static column since the point of interest description is the same for all rows in a partition.

Make Your Primary Keys Unique

An important consideration in designing your table's primary key is making sure that it defines a unique data element. Otherwise you run the risk of accidentally overwriting data.

Now for the second query (Q2), you'll need a table to get information about a specific hotel. One approach would be to put all of the attributes of a hotel in the hotels_by_poi table, but you choose to add only those attributes required by your application workflow.

From the workflow diagram, you note that the hotels_by_poi table is used to display a list of hotels with basic information on each hotel, and the application knows the unique identifiers of the hotels returned. When the user selects a hotel to view details, you can then use Q2, which is used to obtain details about the hotel. Because you already have the hotel_id from Q1, you use that as a reference to the hotel you're looking for. Therefore the second table is just called hotels.

Another option would be to store a set of poi_names in the hotels table. This is an equally valid approach. You'll learn through experience which approach is best for your application.

Q3 is just a reverse of Q1—looking for points of interest near a hotel, rather than hotels near a point of interest. This time, however, you need to access the details of each point of interest, as represented by the pois_by_hotel table. As you did previously, you add the point of interest name as a clustering key to guarantee uniqueness.

At this point, let's now consider how to support query Q4 to help your users find available rooms at a selected hotel for the nights they are interested in staying. Note that this query involves both a start date and an end date. Because you're querying over a range instead of a single date, you know that you'll need to use the date as a clustering key. You use the hotel_id as a primary key to group room data for each hotel on a single partition, which should help your search be super fast. Let's call this the available_rooms_by_hotel_date table.

Searching Over a Range

Use clustering columns to store attributes that you need to access in a range query. Remember that the order of the clustering columns is important. You'll learn more about range queries in Chapter 9.

The Wide Partition Pattern

The design of the `available_rooms_by_hotel_date` table is an instance of the *wide partition* pattern. This pattern is sometimes called the *wide row* pattern when discussing databases that support similar models, but wide partition is a more accurate description from a Cassandra perspective. The essence of the pattern is to group multiple related rows in a partition in order to support fast access to multiple rows within the partition in a single query.

In order to round out the shopping portion of your data model, you add the `ameni ties_by_room` table to support Q5. This will allow your user to view the amenities of one of the rooms that is available for the desired stay dates.

Reservation Logical Data Model

Now let's switch gears to look at the reservation queries. Figure 5-6 shows a logical data model for reservations. You'll notice that these tables represent a denormalized design; the same data appears in multiple tables, with differing keys.

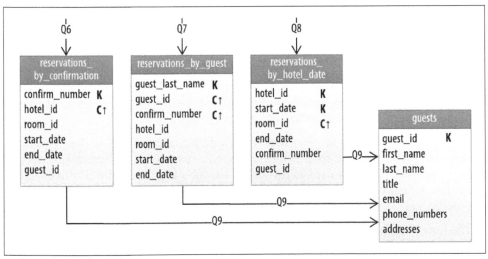

Figure 5-6. A denormalized logical model for reservations

In order to satisfy Q6, the `reservations_by_confirmation` table supports the lookup of reservations by a unique confirmation number provided to the customer at the time of booking.

If the guest doesn't have the confirmation number, the `reservations_by_guest` table can be used to look up the reservation by guest name. You could envision query Q7 being used on behalf of a guest on a self-serve website or a call center agent trying to assist the guest. Because the guest name might not be unique, you include the guest ID here as a clustering column as well.

The hotel staff might wish to see a record of upcoming reservations by date in order to get insight into how the hotel is performing, such as the dates the hotel is sold out or undersold. Q8 supports the retrieval of reservations for a given hotel by date.

Finally, you create a `guests` table. You'll notice that it has similar attributes to the `user` table from Chapter 4. This provides a single location that you can use to store data about guests. In this case, you specify a separate unique identifier for your guest records, as it is not uncommon for guests to have the same name. In many organizations, a customer database such as the `guests` table would be part of a separate customer management application, which is why we've omitted other guest access patterns from this example.

Design Queries for All Stakeholders

Q8 and Q9 in particular help to remind you that you need to create queries that support various stakeholders of your application, not just customers but staff as well, and perhaps even the analytics team, suppliers, and so on.

More Patterns and Anti-Patterns

As with other types of software design, there are some well-known patterns and anti-patterns for data modeling in Cassandra. You've already used one of the most common patterns in your hotel model—the *wide partition* pattern.

The *time series* pattern is an extension of the wide partition pattern. In this pattern, a series of measurements at specific time intervals are stored in a wide partition, where the measurement time is used as part of the partition key. This pattern is frequently used in domains including business analysis, sensor data management, and scientific experiments.

The time series pattern is also useful for data other than measurements. Consider the example of a banking application. You could store each customer's balance in a row, but that might lead to a lot of read and write contention as various customers check their balance or make transactions. You'll probably be tempted to wrap a transaction

---

around your writes just to protect the balance from being updated in error. In contrast, a time series–style design would store each transaction as a timestamped row and leave the work of calculating the current balance to the application.

One design trap that many new users fall into is attempting to use Cassandra as a queue. Each item in the queue is stored with a timestamp in a wide partition. Items are appended to the end of the queue and read from the front, being deleted after they are read. This is a design that seems attractive, especially given its apparent similarity to the time series pattern. The problem with this approach is that the deleted items are now tombstones that Cassandra must scan past in order to read from the front of the queue. Over time, a growing number of tombstones begins to degrade read performance. We'll discuss tombstones in Chapter 6.

The queue anti-pattern serves as a reminder that any design that relies on the deletion of data is potentially a poorly performing design.

Physical Data Modeling

Once you have a logical data model defined, creating the physical model is a relatively simple process.

You walk through each of your logical model tables, assigning types to each item. You can use any of the types you learned in Chapter 4, including the basic types, collections, and user-defined types. You may identify additional user-defined types that can be created to simplify your design.

After you've assigned data types, you analyze your model by performing size calculations and testing out how the model works. You may make some adjustments based on your findings. Once again, let's cover the data modeling process in more detail by working through an example.

First, let's look at a few additions to the Chebotko notation for physical data models.

Chebotko Physical Diagrams

To draw physical models, you need to be able to add the typing information for each column. Figure 5-7 shows the addition of a type for each column in a sample table.

The figure includes a designation of the keyspace containing each table, and visual cues for columns represented using collections and user-defined types. Note also the designation of static columns and secondary index columns (we'll discuss secondary indexes in Chapter 7). There is no restriction on assigning these as part of a logical model, but they are typically more of a physical data modeling concern.

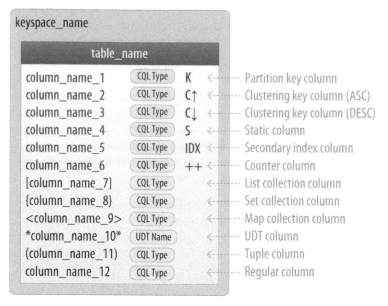

Figure 5-7. Extending the Chebotko notation for physical data models

Hotel Physical Data Model

Now let's get to work on your physical model. First, you need keyspaces to contain your tables. To keep the design relatively simple, you create a `hotel` keyspace to contain tables for hotel and availability data, and a `reservation` keyspace to contain tables for reservation and guest data. In a real system, you might divide the tables across even more keyspaces in order to separate concerns.

For the `hotels` table, you use Cassandra's `text` type to represent the hotel's `id`. For the address, you use the `address` type similar to the one you created in Chapter 4. You use the `text` type to represent the phone number, as there is considerable variance in the formatting of numbers between countries.

Using Unique Identifiers as References

While it would make sense to use the uuid type for attributes such as the hotel_id, for the purposes of this book we mostly use text attributes as identifiers, to keep the samples simple and readable. For example, a common convention in the hospitality industry is to reference properties by short codes like "AZ123" or "NY229." We'll use these values for hotel_ids, while acknowledging they are not necessarily globally unique.

You'll find that it's often helpful to use unique IDs to uniquely reference elements, and to use these uuids as references in tables representing other entities. This helps to minimize coupling between different entity types. This may prove especially effective if you are using a microservice architectural style for your application, in which there are separate services responsible for each entity type.

As you work to create physical representations of various tables in your logical hotel data model, you use the same approach. The resulting design is shown in Figure 5-8.

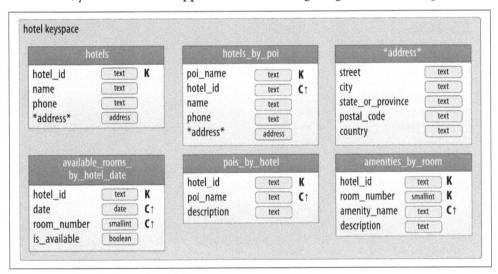

Figure 5-8. Hotel physical model

The address type is also included in the design, designated with an asterisk to denote that it is a user-defined type, and has no primary key columns identified. You make use of this type in the hotels and hotels_by_poi tables.

Taking Advantage of User-Defined Types

User-defined types are frequently used to create logical groupings of nonprimary key columns, as you have done with the `address` user-defined type. UDTs can also be stored in collections to further reduce complexity in the design.

Remember that the scope of a UDT is the keyspace in which it is defined. To use `address` in the `reservation` keyspace you're about to design, you'll have to declare it again.

Reservation Physical Data Model

Now, let's examine the reservation tables in your design. Remember that your logical model contained three denormalized tables to support queries for reservations by confirmation number, guest, and hotel and date. For the first iteration of your physical data model design, let's assume you're going to manage this denormalization manually (see Figure 5-9). (We'll revisit this design choice in Chapter 7 to consider using Cassandra's materialized view feature.)

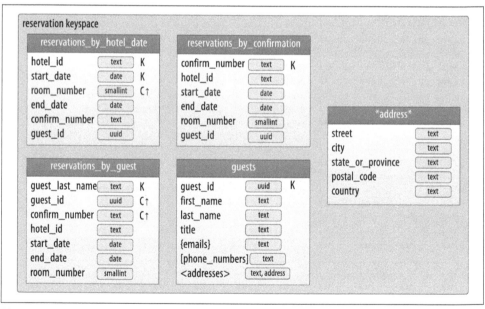

Figure 5-9. Reservation physical model

Note that you have reproduced the `address` type in this keyspace and modeled the `guest_id` as a `uuid` type in all of your tables.

Evaluating and Refining

Once you've created your physical model, there are some steps you'll want to take to evaluate and refine your table designs to help ensure optimal performance.

Calculating Partition Size

The first thing that you want to look for is whether your tables will have partitions that will be overly large, or to put it another way, too wide. Partition size is measured by the number of cells (values) that are stored in the partition. Cassandra's hard limit is two billion cells per partition, but you'll likely run into performance issues before reaching that limit. The recommended size of a partition is not more than 100,000 cells.

In order to calculate the size of your partitions, you use the following formula:

$$N_v = N_r\left(N_c - N_{pk} - N_s\right) + N_s$$

The number of values (or cells) in the partition (N_v) is equal to the number of static columns (N_s) plus the product of the number of rows (N_r) and the number of of values per row. The number of values per row is defined as the number of columns (N_c) minus the number of primary key columns (N_{pk}) and static columns (N_s).

The number of columns tends to be relatively static, although as you have seen, it is quite possible to alter tables at runtime. For this reason, a primary driver of partition size is the number of rows in the partition. This is a key factor that you must consider in determining whether a partition has the potential to get too large. Two billion values sounds like a lot, but in a sensor system where tens or hundreds of values are measured every millisecond, the number of values starts to add up pretty fast.

Let's take a look at one of your tables to analyze the partition size. Because it has a wide partition design with one partition per hotel, you choose the avail able_rooms_by_hotel_date table. The table has four columns total ($N_c = 4$), including three primary key columns ($N_{pk} = 3$) and no static columns ($N_s = 0$). Plugging these values into the formula, you get:

$$N_v = N_r(4 - 3 - 0) + 0 = 1N_r$$

Therefore the number of values for this table is equal to the number of rows. You still need to determine a number of rows. To do this, you make some estimates based on the application you're designing. The table is storing a record for each room, in each of your hotels, for every night. Let's assume that your system will be used to store 2 years of inventory at a time, and there are 5,000 hotels in the system, with an average of 100 rooms in each hotel.

Since there is a partition for each hotel, the estimated number of rows per partition is as follows:

$$N_r = 100 \text{ rooms/hotel} \times 730 \text{ days} = 73,000 \text{ rows}$$

This relatively small number of rows per partition is not an issue, but the number of cells may be. If you start storing more dates of inventory, or don't manage the size of your inventory well using TTL, you could start having issues. You still might want to look at breaking up this large partition, which you'll learn how to do shortly.

Estimate for the Worst Case

When performing sizing calculations, it is tempting to assume the nominal or average case for variables, such as the number of rows. Consider calculating the worst case as well, as these sorts of predictions have a way of coming true in successful systems.

Calculating Size on Disk

In addition to calculating the size of your partitions, it is also an excellent idea to estimate the amount of disk space that will be required for each table you plan to store in the cluster. In order to determine the size, you use the following formula to determine the size S_t of a partition:

$$S_t = \sum_i sizeOf\left(c_{k_i}\right) + \sum_j sizeOf\left(c_{s_j}\right) + N_r \times \left(\sum_k sizeOf\left(c_{r_k}\right) + \sum_l sizeOf\left(c_{c_l}\right)\right) + N_v \times sizeOf\left(t_{avg}\right)$$

This is a bit more complex than the previous formula, but let's break it down a bit at a time, starting with the notation:

- In this formula, c_k refers to partition key columns, c_s to static columns, c_r to regular columns, and c_c to clustering columns.

- The term$_{avg}$ refers to the average number of bytes of metadata stored per cell, such as timestamps. It is typical to use an estimate of 8 bytes for this value.

- You recognize the number of rows N_r and number of values N_v from previous calculations.

- The *sizeOf()* function refers to the size, in bytes, of the CQL data type of each referenced column.

The first term asks you to sum the size of the partition key columns. For this design, the `available_rooms_by_hotel_date` table has a single partition key column, the `hotel_id`, which you chose to make of type `text`. Assuming your hotel identifiers are simple 5-character codes, you have a 5-byte value, so the sum of the partition key column sizes is 5 bytes.

The second term asks you to sum the size of your static columns. This table has no static columns, so in your case this is 0 bytes.

The third term is the most involved, and for good reason—it is calculating the size of the cells in the partition. You sum the size of the clustering columns and regular columns. The clustering columns are the `date`, which is 4 bytes, and the `room_number`, which is a 2-byte short integer, giving a sum of 6 bytes. There is only a single regular column, the boolean `is_available`, which is 1 byte in size. Summing the regular column size (1 byte) plus the clustering column size (6 bytes) gives a total of 7 bytes. To finish up the term, you multiply this value by the number of rows (73,000), giving a result of 511,000 bytes (0.51 MB).

The fourth term is simply counting the metadata that Cassandra stores for each cell. In the storage format used by Cassandra 3.0 and later, the amount of metadata for a given cell varies based on the type of data being stored, and whether or not custom timestamp or TTL values are specified for individual cells. For your table, you reuse the number of values from the previous calculation (73,000) and multiply by 8, which gives a result of 0.58 MB.

Adding these terms together, you get the final estimate:

```
Partition size = 16 bytes + 0 bytes + 0.51 MB + 0.58 MB = 1.1 MB
```

This formula is an approximation of the uncompressed size of a partition on disk, but is accurate enough to be quite useful. (Note that if you make use of SSTable compression, as discussed in Chapter 13, the storage space required will be reduced.) Remembering that the partition must be able to fit on a single node, it looks like your table design will not put a lot of strain on your disk storage.

A More Compact Storage Format

As mentioned in Chapter 2, Cassandra's storage engine was re-implemented for the 3.0 release, including a new format for SSTable files. The previous format stored a separate copy of the clustering columns as part of the record for each cell. The newer format eliminates this duplication, which reduces the size of stored data and simplifies the formula for computing that size.

Keep in mind also that this estimate only counts a single replica of your data. You will need to multiply the value obtained here by the number of partitions and the number of replicas specified by the keyspace's replication strategy in order to determine the total required capacity for each table. This will come in handy when you learn how to plan cluster deployments in Chapter 10.

Breaking Up Large Partitions

As discussed previously, your goal is to design tables that can provide the data you need with queries that touch a single partition, or failing that, the minimum possible number of partitions. However, as you have seen in previous examples, it is quite possible to design wide partition–style tables that approach Cassandra's built-in limits. Performing sizing analysis on tables may reveal partitions that are potentially too large, either in number of values, size on disk, or both.

The technique for splitting a large partition is straightforward: add an additional column to the partition key. In most cases, moving one of the existing columns into the partition key will be sufficient. Another option is to introduce an additional column to the table to act as a sharding key, but this requires additional application logic.

Continuing to examine the available rooms example, if you add the `date` column to the partition key for the `available_rooms_by_hotel_date` table, each partition would then represent the availability of rooms at a specific hotel on a specific date. This will certainly yield partitions that are significantly smaller, perhaps too small, as the data for consecutive days will likely be on separate nodes. This also increases your effort to do queries that span multiple days, as you will have to query multiple partitions.

Another technique, known as *bucketing*, is often used to break the data into moderate-size partitions. For example, you could bucketize the `avail able_rooms_by_hotel_date` table by adding a `month` column to the partition key, perhaps represented as an integer. The comparision with the original design is shown in Figure 5-10. While the `month` column is partially duplicative of the `date`, it provides a nice way of grouping related data in a partition that will not get too large.

If you really felt strongly about preserving a wide partition design, you could instead add the `room_id` to the partition key, so that each partition would represent the availability of the room across all dates. Because you haven't identified a query that involves searching availability of a specific room, the first or second design approach is most suitable to your application needs.

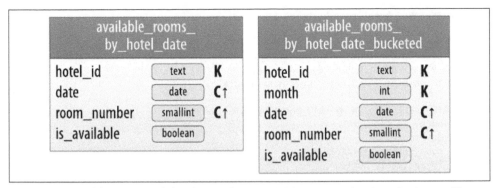

Figure 5-10. Adding a month bucket to the `available_rooms_by_hotel_date` *table*

Defining Database Schema

Once you have finished evaluating and refining your physical model, you're ready to implement the schema in CQL. Here is the schema for the `hotel` keyspace, using CQL's comment feature to document the query pattern supported by each table:

```
CREATE KEYSPACE hotel
    WITH replication = {'class': 'SimpleStrategy', 'replication_factor' : 3};

CREATE TYPE hotel.address (
    street text,
    city text,
    state_or_province text,
    postal_code text,
    country text
);

CREATE TABLE hotel.hotels_by_poi (
    poi_name text,
    poi_description text STATIC,
    hotel_id text,
    name text,
    phone text,
    address frozen<address>,
    PRIMARY KEY ((poi_name), hotel_id)
) WITH comment = 'Q1. Find hotels near given poi'
AND CLUSTERING ORDER BY (hotel_id ASC) ;

CREATE TABLE hotel.hotels (
    id text PRIMARY KEY,
    name text,
    phone text,
    address frozen<address>,
    pois set<text>
) WITH comment = 'Q2. Find information about a hotel';
```

```
CREATE TABLE hotel.pois_by_hotel (
    poi_name text,
    hotel_id text,
    description text,
    PRIMARY KEY ((hotel_id), poi_name)
) WITH comment = 'Q3. Find pois near a hotel';

CREATE TABLE hotel.available_rooms_by_hotel_date (
    hotel_id text,
    date date,
    room_number smallint,
    is_available boolean,
    PRIMARY KEY ((hotel_id), date, room_number)
) WITH comment = 'Q4. Find available rooms by hotel / date';

CREATE TABLE hotel.amenities_by_room (
    hotel_id text,
    room_number smallint,
    amenity_name text,
    description text,
    PRIMARY KEY ((hotel_id, room_number), amenity_name)
) WITH comment = 'Q5. Find amenities for a room';
```

 Identify Partition Keys Explicitly

We recommend representing tables by surrounding the elements of your partition key with parentheses, even though the partition key consists of the single column poi_name. This is a best practice that makes your selection of partition key more explicit to others reading your CQL.

Similarly, here is the schema for the reservation keyspace:

```
CREATE KEYSPACE reservation
    WITH replication = {'class': 'SimpleStrategy', 'replication_factor' : 3};

CREATE TYPE reservation.address (
    street text, city text,
    state_or_province text,
    postal_code text,
    country text
);

CREATE TABLE reservation.reservations_by_confirmation (
    confirm_number text,
    hotel_id text,
    start_date date,
    end_date date,
    room_number smallint,
    guest_id uuid,
    PRIMARY KEY (confirm_number)
```

```
) WITH comment = 'Q6. Find reservations by confirmation number';

CREATE TABLE reservation.reservations_by_hotel_date (
    hotel_id text,
    start_date date,
    room_number smallint,
    end_date date,
    confirm_number text,
    guest_id uuid,
    PRIMARY KEY ((hotel_id, start_date), room_number)
) WITH comment = 'Q7. Find reservations by hotel and date';

CREATE TABLE reservation.reservations_by_guest (
    guest_last_name text,
    guest_id uuid,
    confirm_number text,
    hotel_id text,
    start_date date,
    end_date date,
    room_number smallint,
    PRIMARY KEY ((guest_last_name), guest_id, confirm_number)
) WITH comment = 'Q8. Find reservations by guest name';

CREATE TABLE reservation.guests (
    guest_id uuid PRIMARY KEY,
    first_name text,
    last_name text,
    title text,
    emails set<text>,
    phone_numbers list<text>,
    addresses map<text, frozen<address>>
) WITH comment = 'Q9. Find guest by ID';
```

You now have a complete Cassandra schema for storing data for your hotel application.

Cassandra Data Modeling Tools

You've already had quite a bit of practice creating schema and manipluating data using cqlsh, but now that you're starting to create an application data model with more tables, it starts to be more of a challenge to keep track of all of that CQL.

Thankfully, there are several tools available to help you design and manage your Cassandra schema and build queries:

Hackolade

Hackolade (*https://oreil.ly/kvjI8*) is a data modeling tool that supports schema design for Cassandra and many other NoSQL databases. Hackolade supports the unique concepts of CQL, such as partition keys and clustering columns, as well as data types, including collections and UDTs. It also provides the ability to create

Chebotko diagrams, as described in this chapter. Figure 5-11 shows an entity-relationship diagram representing the conceptual data model from this chapter.

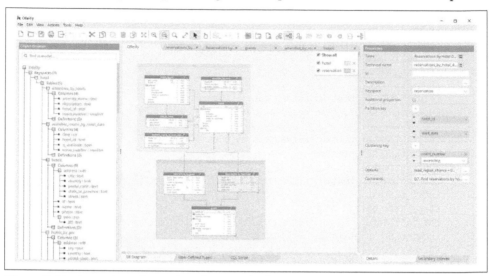

Figure 5-11. An entity-relationship diagram for hotel and reservation data in Hackolade

Kashlev Data Modeler

The Kashlev Data Modeler (*https://oreil.ly/d1mIN*) is a Cassandra data modeling tool that automates the data modeling methodology described in this chapter, including identifying access patterns; conceptual, logical, and physical data modeling; and schema generation. It also includes model patterns that you can optionally leverage as a starting point for your designs.

DataStax DevCenter

DataStax DevCenter is a tool for managing schema, executing queries, and viewing results. While the tool is no longer actively supported, it is still popular with many developers and is available as a free download from DataStax (*https://oreil.ly/ftiob*). Figure 5-12 shows the hotel schema being edited in DevCenter.

The middle pane shows the currently selected CQL file, featuring syntax highlighting for CQL commands, CQL types, and name literals. DevCenter provides command completion as you type out CQL commands, and interprets the commands you type, highlighting any errors you make. The tool provides panes for managing multiple CQL scripts and connections to multiple clusters. The connections are used to run CQL commands against live clusters and view the results. The tool also has a query trace feature that is useful for gaining insight into the performance of your queries.

Figure 5-12. Editing the hotel schema in DataStax DevCenter

IDE plug-ins

CQL plug-ins are available for several integrated development environments (IDEs), such as IntelliJ IDEA and Apache NetBeans. These plug-ins typically provide features such as schema management and query execution.

Make Sure Your Tools Have Full CQL Support

Some IDEs and tools that claim to support Cassandra do not actually support CQL natively, but instead access Cassandra using a JDBC/ODBC driver and interact with Cassandra as if it were a relational database with SQL support. When selecting tools for working with Cassandra, you'll want to make sure they support CQL and reinforce Cassandra best practices for data modeling, as discussed in this chapter.

Summary

In this chapter, you learned how to create a complete, working Cassandra data model and compared it with an equivalent relational model. You represented the data model in both logical and physical forms, and learned about tools for realizing your data models in CQL. Now that you have a working data model, you're ready to continue building a hotel application in the coming chapters.

## CHAPTER 6

The Cassandra Architecture

3.2 Architecture—fundamental concepts or properties of a system in its environment embodied in its elements, relationships, and in the principles of its design and evolution.

—ISO/IEC/IEEE 42010

In this chapter, we examine several aspects of Cassandra's architecture in order to understand how it does its job. We'll explain the topology of a cluster, and how nodes interact in a peer-to-peer design to maintain the health of the cluster and exchange data, using techniques like gossip, repair, hinted handoff, and lightweight transactions. Looking inside the design of a node, we examine architecture techniques Cassandra uses to support reading, writing, and deleting data, and examine how these choices affect architectural considerations such as scalability, durability, availability, manageability, and more. We'll also learn about the data structures inside a node, including commit logs, memtables, caches, and SSTables.

As we introduce these topics, we also provide references to where you can find their implementations in the Cassandra source code.

Data Centers and Racks

Cassandra is frequently used in systems spanning physically separate locations. Cassandra provides two levels of grouping that are used to describe the topology of a cluster: data center and rack. A *rack* is a logical set of nodes in close proximity to each other, perhaps on physical machines in a single rack of equipment. A *data center* is a logical set of racks, perhaps located in the same building and connected by reliable network. A sample topology with multiple data centers and racks is shown in Figure 6-1.

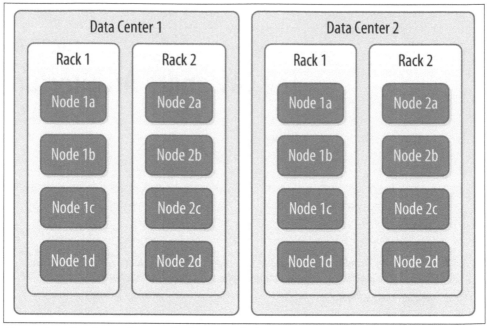

Figure 6-1. Topology of a sample cluster with data centers, racks, and nodes

Out of the box, Cassandra comes with a simple default configuration of a single data center ("datacenter1") containing a single rack ("rack1"). We'll learn in Chapter 10 how to build a larger cluster and define its topology.

Cassandra leverages the information you provide about your cluster's topology to determine where to store data, and how to route queries efficiently. Cassandra stores copies of your data in the data centers you request to maximize availability and partition tolerance, while preferring to route queries to nodes in the local data center to maximize performance.

Gossip and Failure Detection

To support decentralization and partition tolerance, Cassandra uses a gossip protocol that allows each node to keep track of state information about the other nodes in the cluster. The gossiper runs every second on a timer.

Gossip protocols (sometimes called *epidemic protocols*) generally assume a faulty network, are commonly employed in very large, decentralized network systems, and are often used as an automatic mechanism for replication in distributed databases. They take their name from the concept of human gossip, a form of communication in which peers can choose with whom they want to exchange information.

The gossip protocol in Cassandra is primarily implemented by the `org.apache.cassandra.gms.Gossiper` class, which is responsible for managing gossip for the local node. When a server node is started, it registers itself with the gossiper to receive endpoint state information.

Because Cassandra gossip is used for failure detection, the `Gossiper` class maintains a list of nodes that are alive and dead.

Here is how the gossiper works:

1. Once per second, the gossiper will choose a random node in the cluster and initialize a gossip session with it. Each round of gossip requires three messages.

2. The gossip initiator sends its chosen friend a `GossipDigestSyn` message.

3. When the friend receives this message, it returns a `GossipDigestAck` message.

4. When the initiator receives the `ack` message from the friend, it sends the friend a `GossipDigestAck2` message to complete the round of gossip.

When the gossiper determines that another endpoint is dead, it "convicts" that endpoint by marking it as dead in its local list and logging that fact.

Cassandra has robust support for failure detection, as specified by a popular algorithm for distributed computing called Phi Accrual Failure Detector. This manner of failure detection originated at the Advanced Institute of Science and Technology in Japan in 2004.

Accrual failure detection is based on two primary ideas. The first general idea is that failure detection should be flexible, which is achieved by decoupling it from the application being monitored. The second and more novel idea challenges the notion of traditional failure detectors, which are implemented by simple "heartbeats" and decide whether a node is dead or not dead based on whether a heartbeat is received or not. But accrual failure detection decides that this approach is naive, and finds a place in between the extremes of dead and alive—a *suspicion level*.

Therefore, the failure monitoring system outputs a continuous level of "suspicion" regarding how confident it is that a node has failed. This is desirable because it can take into account fluctuations in the network environment. For example, just because one connection gets caught up doesn't necessarily mean that the whole node is dead. So suspicion offers a more fluid and proactive indication of the weaker or stronger possibility of failure based on interpretation (the sampling of heartbeats), as opposed to a simple binary assessment.

Phi Threshold and Accrual Failure Detectors

Accrual failure detectors output a value associated with each process (or node) called Phi. The Phi value represents the level of *suspicion* that a server might be down. The computation of this value is designed to be adaptive in the face of volatile network conditions, so it's not a binary condition that simply checks whether a server is up or down.

The Phi convict threshold in the configuration adjusts the sensitivity of the failure detector. Lower values increase the sensitivity and higher values decrease it, but not in a linear fashion. With default settings, Cassandra can generally detect a failed node in about 10 seconds using this mechanism.

The original paper, "The Phi Accrual Failure Detector" (*https://oreil.ly/jMubA*), is by Naohiro Hayashibara et al.

Failure detection is implemented in Cassandra by the `org.apache.cassandra.gms.FailureDetector` class, which implements the `org.apache.cassandra.gms.IFailureDetector` interface. Together, they allow operations including:

`isAlive(InetAddressAndPort)`
What the detector will report about a given node's alive-ness.

`interpret(InetAddressAndPort)`
Used by the gossiper to help it decide whether a node is alive or not based on the suspicion level reached by calculating Phi (as described in the Hayashibara et al. paper).

`report(InetAddressAndPort)`
When a node receives a heartbeat, it invokes this method.

Snitches

The job of a snitch is to provide information about your network topology so that Cassandra can efficiently route requests. The snitch will figure out where nodes are in relation to other nodes. The snitch will determine relative host proximity for each node in a cluster, which is used to determine which nodes to read and write from.

As an example, let's examine how the snitch participates in a read operation. When Cassandra performs a read, it must contact a number of replicas determined by the consistency level. In order to support the maximum speed for reads, Cassandra selects a single replica to query for the full object, and asks additional replicas for hash values in order to ensure the latest version of the requested data is returned. The snitch helps to help identify the replica that will return the fastest, and this is the replica that is queried for the full data.

The default snitch (the `SimpleSnitch`) is topology unaware; that is, it does not know about the racks and data centers in a cluster, which makes it unsuitable for multiple data center deployments. For this reason, Cassandra comes with several snitches for different network topologies and cloud environments, including Amazon EC2, Google Cloud, and Apache Cloudstack.

The snitches can be found in the package `org.apache.cassandra.locator`. Each snitch implements the `IEndpointSnitch` interface. We'll learn how to select and configure an appropriate snitch for your environment in Chapter 10.

While Cassandra provides a pluggable way to statically describe your cluster's topology, it also provides a feature called *dynamic snitching* that helps optimize the routing of reads and writes over time. Here's how it works. Your selected snitch is wrapped with another snitch called the `DynamicEndpointSnitch`. The dynamic snitch gets its basic understanding of the topology from the selected snitch. It then monitors the performance of requests to the other nodes, even keeping track of things like which nodes are performing compaction. The performance data is used to select the best replica for each query. This enables Cassandra to avoid routing requests to replicas that are busy or performing poorly.

The dynamic snitching implementation uses a modified version of the Phi failure detection mechanism used by gossip. The *badness threshold* is a configurable parameter that determines how much worse a preferred node must perform than the best-performing node in order to lose its preferential status. The scores of each node are reset periodically in order to allow a poorly performing node to demonstrate that it has recovered and reclaim its preferred status.

Rings and Tokens

So far we've been focusing on how Cassandra keeps track of the physical layout of nodes in a cluster. Let's shift gears and look at how Cassandra distributes data across these nodes.

Cassandra represents the data managed by a cluster as a *ring*. Each node in the ring is assigned one or more ranges of data described by a *token*, which determines its position in the ring. For example, in the default configuration, a token is a 64-bit integer ID used to identify each partition. This gives a possible range for tokens from -2^{63} to $2^{63}-1$. We'll discuss other possible configurations under "Partitioners" on page 113.

A node claims ownership of the range of values less than or equal to each token and greater than the last token of the previous node, known as a *token range*. The node with the lowest token owns the range less than or equal to its token and the range greater than the highest token, which is also known as the *wrapping range*. In this way, the tokens specify a complete ring. Figure 6-2 shows a notional ring layout including the nodes in a single data center. This particular arrangement is structured such that consecutive token ranges are spread across nodes in different racks.

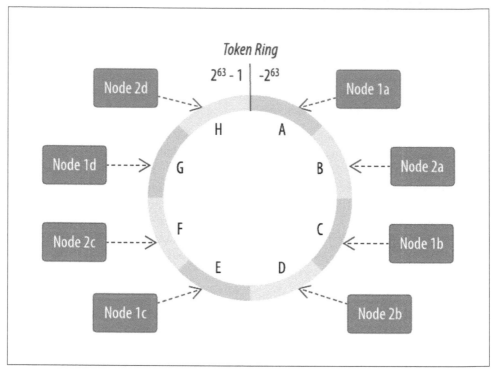

Figure 6-2. Example ring arrangement of nodes in a data center

Data is assigned to nodes by using a hash function to calculate a token for the partition key. This partition key token is compared to the token values for the various nodes to identify the range, and therefore the node, that owns the data. Token ranges are represented by the `org.apache.cassandra.dht.Range` class.

To see an example of tokens in action, let's revisit our `user` table from Chapter 4. The CQL language provides a `token()` function that we can use to request the value of the token corresponding to a partition key, in this case the `last_name`:

```
cqlsh:my_keyspace> SELECT last_name, first_name, token(last_name) FROM user;

 last_name | first_name | system.token(last_name)
-----------+------------+-------------------------
 Rodriguez |       Mary |    -7199267019458681669
     Scott |     Isaiah |     1807799317863611380
    Nguyen |       Bill |     6000710198366804598
```

```
    Nguyen  |      Wanda  |     6000710198366804598
```

(5 rows)

As you might expect, we see a different token for each partition, and the same token appears for the two rows represented by the partition key value "Nguyen."

Virtual Nodes

Early versions of Cassandra assigned a single token (and therefore by implication, a single token range) to each node, in a fairly static manner, requiring you to calculate tokens for each node. Although there are tools available to calculate tokens based on a given number of nodes, it was still a manual process to configure the `ini tial_token` property for each node in the *cassandra.yaml* file. This also made adding or replacing a node an expensive operation, as rebalancing the cluster required moving a lot of data.

Cassandra's 1.2 release introduced the concept of *virtual nodes*, also called *vnodes* for short. Instead of assigning a single token to a node, the token range is broken up into multiple smaller ranges. Each physical node is then assigned multiple tokens. Historically, each node has been assigned 256 of these tokens, meaning that it represents 256 virtual nodes (although we'll discuss possible changes to this value in Chapter 10). Virtual nodes have been enabled by default since 2.0.

Vnodes make it easier to maintain a cluster containing heterogeneous machines. For nodes in your cluster that have more computing resources available to them, you can increase the number of vnodes by setting the `num_tokens` property in the *cassandra.yaml* file. Conversely, you might set `num_tokens` lower to decrease the number of vnodes for less capable machines.

Cassandra automatically handles the calculation of token ranges for each node in the cluster in proportion to their `num_tokens` value. Token assignments for vnodes are calculated by the `org.apache.cassandra.dht.tokenallocator.ReplicationAware TokenAllocator` class.

A further advantage of virtual nodes is that they speed up some of the more heavyweight Cassandra operations such as bootstrapping a new node, decommissioning a node, and repairing a node. This is because the load associated with operations on multiple smaller ranges is spread more evenly across the nodes in the cluster.

Partitioners

A *partitioner* determines how data is distributed across the nodes in the cluster. As we learned in Chapter 4, Cassandra organizes rows in partitions. Each row has a partition key that is used to identify the partition to which it belongs. A partitioner, then, is a hash function for computing the token of a partition key. Each row of data is distributed within the ring according to the value of the partition key token. As shown in Figure 6-3, the role of the partitioner is to compute the token based on the partition key columns. Any clustering columns that may be present in the primary key are used to determine the ordering of rows within a given node that owns the token representing that partition.

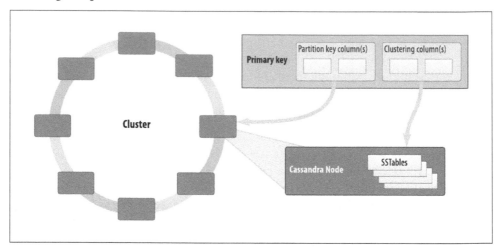

Figure 6-3. The role of the partitioner

Cassandra provides several different partitioners in the `org.apache.cassandra.dht` package (DHT stands for *distributed hash table*). The `Murmur3Partitioner` was added in 1.2 and has been the default partitioner since then; it is an efficient Java implementation on the murmur algorithm developed by Austin Appleby. It generates 64-bit hashes. The previous default was the `RandomPartitioner`.

Because of Cassandra's generally pluggable design, you can also create your own partitioner by implementing the `org.apache.cassandra.dht.IPartitioner` class and placing it on Cassandra's classpath. Note, however, that the default partitioner is not frequently changed in practice, and that you can't change the partitioner after initializing a cluster.

Replication Strategies

A node serves as a *replica* for different ranges of data. If one node goes down, other replicas can respond to queries for that range of data. Cassandra replicates data across nodes in a manner transparent to the user, and the *replication factor* is the number of nodes in your cluster that will receive copies (replicas) of the same data. If your replication factor is 3, then three nodes in the ring will have copies of each row.

The first replica will always be the node that claims the range in which the token falls, but the remainder of the replicas are placed according to the *replication strategy* (sometimes also referred to as the *replica placement strategy*).

For determining replica placement, Cassandra implements the Gang of Four strategy pattern, which is outlined in the common abstract class `org.apache.cassandra.loca tor.AbstractReplicationStrategy`, allowing different implementations of an algorithm (different strategies for accomplishing the same work). Each algorithm implementation is encapsulated inside a single class that extends the `AbstractRepli cationStrategy`.

Out of the box, Cassandra provides two primary implementations of this interface (extensions of the abstract class): `SimpleStrategy` and `NetworkTopologyStrategy`. The `SimpleStrategy` places replicas at consecutive nodes around the ring, starting with the node indicated by the partitioner. The `NetworkTopologyStrategy` allows you to specify a different replication factor for each data center. Within a data center, it allocates replicas to different racks in order to maximize availability. The `NetworkTo pologyStrategy` is recommended for keyspaces in production deployments, even those that are initially created with a single data center, since it is more straightforward to add an additional data center should the need arise.

Legacy Replication Strategies

A third strategy, `OldNetworkTopologyStrategy`, is provided for backward compatibility. It was previously known as the `RackAwar eStrategy`, while the `SimpleStrategy` was previously known as the `RackUnawareStrategy`. `NetworkTopologyStrategy` was previously known as `DataCenterShardStrategy`. These changes were effective in the 0.7 release.

The strategy is set independently for each keyspace and is a required option to create a keyspace, as we saw in Chapter 4.

Consistency Levels

In Chapter 2, we discussed Brewer's CAP theorem, in which consistency, availability, and partition tolerance are traded off against one another. Cassandra provides tuneable consistency levels that allow you to make these trade-offs at a fine-grained level. You specify a consistency level on each read or write query that indicates how much consistency you require. A higher consistency level means that more nodes need to respond to a read or write query, giving you more assurance that the values present on each replica are the same.

For read queries, the consistency level specifies how many replica nodes must respond to a read request before returning the data. For write operations, the consistency level specifies how many replica nodes must respond for the write to be reported as successful to the client. Because Cassandra is eventually consistent, updates to other replica nodes may continue in the background.

The available consistency levels include ONE, TWO, and THREE, each of which specify an absolute number of replica nodes that must respond to a request. The QUORUM consistency level requires a response from a majority of the replica nodes. This is sometimes expressed as:

$$Q = floor(RF/2 + 1)$$

In this equation, Q represents the number of nodes needed to achieve quorum for a replication factor RF. It may be simpler to illustrate this with a couple of examples: if RF is 3, Q is 2; if RF is 4, Q is 3; if RF is 5, Q is 3, and so on.

The ALL consistency level requires a response from all of the replicas. We'll examine these consistency levels and others in more detail in Chapter 9.

Consistency is tuneable in Cassandra because clients can specify the desired consistency level on both reads and writes. There is an equation that is popularly used to represent the way to achieve *strong consistency* in Cassandra: *R + W > RF = strong consistency*. In this equation, *R*, *W*, and *RF* are the read replica count, the write replica count, and the replication factor, respectively; all client reads will see the most recent write in this scenario, and you will have strong consistency. As we discuss in more detail in Chapter 9, the recommended way to achieve strong consistency in Cassandra is to write and read using the QUORUM or LOCAL_QUORUM consistency levels.

Distinguishing Consistency Levels and Replication Factors

If you're new to Cassandra, it can be easy to confuse the concepts of replication factor and consistency level. The replication factor is set per keyspace. The consistency level is specified per query, by the client. The replication factor indicates how many nodes you want to use to store a value during each write operation. The consistency level specifies how many nodes the client has decided must respond in order to feel confident of a successful read or write operation. The confusion arises because the consistency level is based on the replication factor, not on the number of nodes in the system.

Queries and Coordinator Nodes

Let's bring these concepts together to discuss how Cassandra nodes interact to support reads and writes from client applications. Figure 6-4 shows the typical path of interactions with Cassandra.

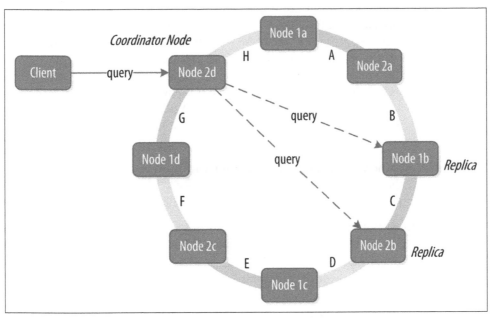

Figure 6-4. Clients, coordinator nodes, and replicas

A client may connect to any node in the cluster to initiate a read or write query. This node is known as the *coordinator node*. The coordinator identifies which nodes are replicas for the data that is being written or read and forwards the queries to them.

For a write, the coordinator node contacts all replicas, as determined by the consistency level and replication factor, and considers the write successful when a number of replicas commensurate with the consistency level acknowledge the write.

For a read, the coordinator contacts enough replicas to ensure the required consistency level is met, and returns the data to the client.

These, of course, are the "happy path" descriptions of how Cassandra works. In order to get a full picture of Cassandra's architecture, we'll now discuss some of Cassandra's high availability mechanisms that it uses to mitigate failures, including hinted handoff and repair.

Hinted Handoff

Consider the following scenario: a write request is sent to Cassandra, but a replica node where the write properly belongs is not available due to network partition, hardware failure, or some other reason. In order to ensure general availability of the ring in such a situation, Cassandra implements a feature called *hinted handoff*. You might think of a *hint* as a little Post-it Note that contains the information from the write request. If the replica node where the write belongs has failed, the coordinator will create a hint, which is a small reminder that says, "I have the write information that is intended for node B. I'm going to hang on to this write, and I'll notice when node B comes back online; when it does, I'll send it the write request." That is, once it detects via gossip that node B is back online, node A will "hand off" to node B the "hint" regarding the write. Cassandra holds a separate hint for each partition that is to be written.

This allows Cassandra to be always available for writes, and generally enables a cluster to sustain the same write load even when some of the nodes are down. It also reduces the time that a failed node will be inconsistent after it does come back online.

In general, hints do not count as writes for the purposes of consistency level. The exception is the consistency level ANY, which was added in 0.6. This consistency level means that a hinted handoff alone will count as sufficient toward the success of a write operation. That is, even if only a hint was able to be recorded, the write still counts as successful. Note that the write is considered durable, but the data may not be readable until the hint is delivered to the target replica.

Hinted Handoff and Guaranteed Delivery

Hinted handoff is used in Amazon's Dynamo, which inspired the design of databases, including Cassandra and Amazon's DynamoDB. It is also familiar to those who are aware of the concept of guaranteed delivery in messaging systems such as the Java Message Service (JMS). In a durable guaranteed-delivery JMS queue, if a message cannot be delivered to a receiver, JMS will wait for a given interval and then resend the request until the message is received.

There is a practical problem with hinted handoffs (and guaranteed delivery approaches, for that matter): if a node is offline for some time, the hints can build up considerably on other nodes. Then, when the other nodes notice that the failed node has come back online, they tend to flood that node with requests, just at the moment it is most vulnerable (when it is struggling to come back into play after a failure). To address this problem, Cassandra limits the storage of hints to a configurable time window. It is also possible to disable hinted handoff entirely.

As its name suggests, `org.apache.cassandra.hints.HintsService` is the class that implements hinted handoffs internally.

Although hinted handoff helps increase Cassandra's availability, due to the limitations mentioned it is not sufficient on its own to ensure consistency of data across replicas.

Anti-Entropy, Repair, and Merkle Trees

Cassandra uses an *anti-entropy* protocol as an additional safeguard to ensure consistency. Anti-entropy protocols are a type of gossip protocol for repairing replicated data. They work by comparing replicas of data and reconciling differences observed between the replicas. Anti-entropy is used in Amazon's Dynamo, and Cassandra's implementation is modeled on that (see Section 4.7 of the Dynamo paper (*https://oreil.ly/gSRpy*)).

Anti-Entropy in Cassandra

In Cassandra, the term *anti-entropy* is often used in two slightly different contexts, with meanings that have some overlap:

- The term is often used as a shorthand for the replica synchronization mechanism for ensuring that data on different nodes is updated to the newest version.
- At other times, Cassandra is described as having an anti-entropy *capability* that includes replica synchronization as well as hinted handoff.

Replica synchronization is supported via two different modes known as *read repair* and *anti-entropy repair*. Read repair refers to the synchronization of replicas as data is read. Cassandra reads data from multiple replicas in order to achieve the requested consistency level, and detects if any replicas have out-of-date values. If an insufficient number of nodes have the latest value, a read repair is performed immediately to update the out-of-date replicas. Otherwise, the repairs can be performed in the background after the read returns. This design is observed by Cassandra as well as by straight key-value stores such as Project Voldemort and Riak.

Anti-entropy repair (sometimes called *manual repair*) is a manually initiated operation performed on nodes as part of a regular maintenance process. This type of repair is executed by using a tool called `nodetool`, as we'll learn about in Chapter 12. Running `nodetool repair` causes Cassandra to execute a *validation compaction* (see "Compaction" on page 125). During a validation compaction, the server initiates a TreeRequest/TreeReponse conversation to exchange Merkle trees with neighboring replicas. The Merkle tree is a hash representing the data in that table. If the trees from the different nodes don't match, they have to be reconciled (or "repaired") to determine the latest data values they should all be set to. This tree comparison validation is the responsibility of the `org.apache.cassandra.service.reads.AbstractReadExe cutor` class.

What's a Merkle Tree?

A Merkle tree, named for its inventor, Ralph Merkle, is also known as a *hash tree*. It's a data structure represented as a binary tree, and it's useful because it summarizes in short form the data in a larger data set. In a hash tree, the leaves are the data blocks (typically files on a filesystem) to be summarized. Every parent node in the tree is a hash of its direct child nodes, which tightly compacts the summary.

In Cassandra, the Merkle tree is implemented in the `org.apache.cassan dra.utils.MerkleTree` class.

Merkle trees are used in Cassandra to ensure that the peer-to-peer network of nodes receives data blocks unaltered and unharmed. They are also used in cryptography to verify the contents of files and transmissions.

Both Cassandra and Dynamo use Merkle trees for anti-entropy, but their implementations are a little different. In Cassandra, each table has its own Merkle tree; the tree is created as a snapshot during a validation compaction, and is kept only as long as is required to send it to the neighboring nodes on the ring. The advantage of this implementation is that it reduces network I/O.

Lightweight Transactions and Paxos

As we discussed in "Consistency Levels" on page 115, Cassandra provides the ability to achieve strong consistency by specifying sufficiently high consistency levels on writes and reads. However, strong consistency is not enough to prevent race conditions in cases where clients need to read, then write data.

To help explain this with an example, let's revisit our `my_keyspace.user` table from Chapter 4. Imagine we are building a client that wants to manage user records as part of an account management application. In creating a new user account, we'd like to make sure that the user record doesn't already exist, lest we unintentionally overwrite existing user data. So first we do a read to see if the record exists, and then only perform the create if the record doesn't exist.

The behavior we're looking for is called *linearizable consistency*, meaning that we'd like to guarantee that no other client can come in between our read and write queries with their own modification. Since the 2.0 release, Cassandra supports a *lightweight transaction* (LWT) mechanism that provides linearizable consistency.

Cassandra's LWT implementation is based on Paxos. Paxos is a consensus algorithm that allows distributed peer nodes to agree on a proposal, without requiring a leader to coordinate a transaction. Paxos and other consensus algorithms emerged as alternatives to traditional two-phase commit-based approaches to distributed transactions (see the note, "The Problem with Two-Phase Commit" on page 9).

The basic Paxos algorithm consists of two stages: prepare/promise and propose/accept. To modify data, a coordinator node can propose a new value to the replica nodes, taking on the role of leader. Other nodes may act as leaders simultaneously for other modifications. Each replica node checks the proposal, and if the proposal is the latest it has seen, it promises to not accept proposals associated with any prior proposals. Each replica node also returns the last proposal it received that is still in progress. If the proposal is approved by a majority of replicas, the leader commits the proposal, but with the caveat that it must first commit any in-progress proposals that preceded its own proposal.

The Cassandra implementation extends the basic Paxos algorithm to support the desired read-before-write semantics (also known as *check-and-set*), and to allow the state to be reset between transactions. It does this by inserting two additional phases into the algorithm, so that it works as follows:

1. Prepare/Promise
2. Read/Results
3. Propose/Accept
4. Commit/Ack

Thus, a successful transaction requires four round-trips between the coordinator node and replicas. This is more expensive than a regular write, which is why you should think carefully about your use case before using LWTs.

More on Paxos

Several papers have been written about the Paxos protocol. One of the best explanations available is Leslie Lamport's "Paxos Made Simple" (*https://oreil.ly/pczBj*).

Cassandra's lightweight transactions are limited to a single partition. Internally, Cassandra stores a Paxos state for each partition. This ensures that transactions on different partitions cannot interfere with each other.

You can find Cassandra's implementation of the Paxos algorithm in the package `org.apache.cassandra.service.paxos`. These classes are leveraged by the `Storage Service`, which we will learn about soon. We discuss LWTs in more detail in Chapter 9.

Memtables, SSTables, and Commit Logs

Now let's take a look inside a Cassandra node at some of the internal data structures and files, summarized in Figure 6-5. Cassandra stores data both in memory and on disk to provide both high performance and durability. In this section, we'll focus on Cassandra's *storage engine* and its use of constructs called *memtables*, *SSTables*, and *commit logs* to support the writing and reading of data from tables.

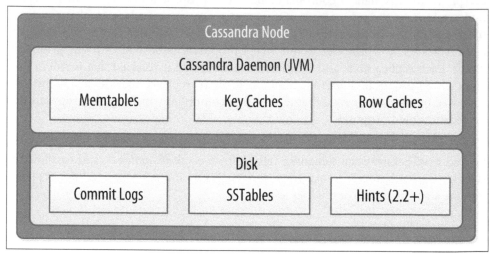

Figure 6-5. Internal data structures and files of a Cassandra node

When a node receives a write operation, it immediately writes the data to a *commit log*. The commit log is a crash-recovery mechanism that supports Cassandra's durability goals. A write will not count as successful on the node until it's written to the commit log, to ensure that if a write operation does not make it to the in-memory store (the memtable, discussed in a moment), it will still be possible to recover the data. If you shut down the node or it crashes unexpectedly, the commit log can ensure that data is not lost. That's because the next time you start the node, the commit log gets replayed. In fact, that's the only time the commit log is read; clients never read from it.

```
cqlsh> DESCRIBE KEYSPACE my_keyspace ;

CREATE KEYSPACE my_keyspace WITH replication =
  {'class': 'SimpleStrategy',
   'replication_factor': '1'}  AND durable_writes = true;
```

What Are Durable Writes?

Now that we've introduced the concept of the commit log, it's a good time for us to demystify a property of a keyspace that we first noticed in Chapter 3:

```
cqlsh> DESCRIBE KEYSPACE my_keyspace ;

CREATE KEYSPACE my_keyspace WITH replication =
    {'class': 'SimpleStrategy',
     'replication_factor': '1'}  AND durable_writes = true;
```

The `durable_writes` property controls whether Cassandra will use the commit log for writes to the tables in the keyspace. This value defaults to `true`, meaning that the commit log will be updated on modifications. Setting the value to `false` increases the speed of writes, but also risks losing data if the node goes down before the data is flushed from memtables into SSTables.

After it's written to the commit log, the value is written to a memory-resident data structure called the *memtable*. Each memtable contains data for a specific table. In early implementations of Cassandra, memtables were stored on the JVM heap, but improvements starting with the 2.1 release have moved some memtable data to native memory, with configuration options to specify the amount of on-heap and native memory available. This makes Cassandra less susceptible to fluctuations in performance due to Java garbage collection. Optionally, Cassandra may also write data to in memory caches, which we'll discuss in "Caching" on page 125.

When the number of objects stored in the memtable reaches a threshold, the contents of the memtable are flushed to disk in a file called an *SSTable*. A new memtable is then created. This flushing is a nonblocking operation; multiple memtables may exist for a single table, one current and the rest waiting to be flushed. They typically should not have to wait very long, as the node should flush them very quickly unless it is overloaded.

Why Are They Called "SSTables"?

The term "SSTable" originated in Google Bigtable as a compaction of "Sorted String Table." Cassandra borrows this term even though it does not store data as strings on disk.

Each commit log maintains an internal bit flag to indicate whether it needs flushing. When a write operation is first received, it is written to the commit log and its bit flag is set to 1. There is only one bit flag per table, because only one commit log is ever being written to across the entire server. All writes to all tables will go into the same commit log, so the bit flag indicates whether a particular commit log contains anything that hasn't been flushed for a particular table. Once the memtable has been properly flushed to disk, the corresponding commit log's bit flag is set to 0, indicating that the commit log no longer has to maintain that data for durability purposes. Like regular log files, commit logs have a configurable rollover threshold, and once this file size threshold is reached, the log will roll over, carrying with it any extant dirty bit flags.

Once a memtable is flushed to disk as an SSTable, it is immutable and cannot be changed by the application. Despite the fact that SSTables are compacted, this compaction changes only their on-disk representation; it essentially performs the "merge" step of a mergesort into new files and removes the old files on success.

Since the 1.0 release, Cassandra has supported the compression of SSTables in order to maximize use of the available storage. This compression is configurable per table.

All writes are sequential, which is the primary reason that writes perform so well in Cassandra. No reads or seeks of any kind are required for writing a value to Cassandra because all writes are append operations. This makes the speed of your disk one key limitation on performance. Compaction is intended to amortize the reorganization of data, but it uses sequential I/O to do so. So the performance benefit is gained by splitting; the write operation is just an immediate append, and then compaction helps to organize for better future read performance. If Cassandra naively inserted values where they ultimately belonged, writing clients would pay for seeks up front.

On reads, Cassandra will read both SSTables and memtables to find data values, as the memtable may contain values that have not yet been flushed to disk. Memtables are implemented by the `org.apache.cassandra.db.Memtable` class.

Bloom Filters

Bloom filters are used to boost the performance of reads. They are named for their inventor, Burton Bloom. Bloom filters are very fast, nondeterministic algorithms for testing whether an element is a member of a set. They are nondeterministic because it is possible to get a false-positive read from a Bloom filter, but not a false-negative. Bloom filters work by mapping the values in a data set into a bit array and condensing a larger data set into a digest string using a hash function. The digest, by definition, uses a much smaller amount of memory than the original data would. The filters are stored in memory and are used to improve performance by reducing the need for disk access on key lookups. Disk access is typically much slower than memory access. So, in a way, a Bloom filter is a special kind of key cache.

Cassandra maintains a Bloom filter for each SSTable. When a query is performed, the Bloom filter is checked first before accessing disk. Because false-negatives are not possible, if the filter indicates that the element does not exist in the set, it certainly doesn't; but if the filter thinks that the element is in the set, the disk is accessed to make sure.

Bloom filters are implemented by the `org.apache.cassandra.utils.BloomFilter` class. Cassandra provides the ability to increase Bloom filter accuracy (reducing the number of false-positives) by increasing the filter size, at the cost of more memory. This false-positive chance is tuneable per table.

Other Uses of Bloom Filters

Bloom filters are used in other distributed database and caching technologies, including Apache Hadoop, Google Bigtable, and the Squid proxy cache.

Caching

As an additional mechanism to boost read performance, Cassandra provides three optional forms of caching:

- The *key cache* stores a map of partition keys to row index entries, facilitating faster read access into SSTables stored on disk. The key cache is stored on the JVM heap.

- The *row cache* caches entire rows and can greatly speed up read access for frequently accessed rows, at the cost of more memory usage. The row cache is stored in off-heap memory.

- The *chunk cache* was added in the 3.6 release to store uncompressed chunks of data read from SSTable files that are accessed frequently. The chunk cache is stored in off-heap memory.

- The *counter cache* was added in the 2.1 release to improve counter performance by reducing lock contention for the most frequently accessed counters.

By default, key and counter caching are enabled, while row caching is disabled, as it requires more memory. Cassandra saves its caches to disk periodically in order to warm them up more quickly on a node restart. We'll investigate how to tune these caches in Chapter 13.

Compaction

As we already discussed, SSTables are immutable, which helps Cassandra achieve such high write speeds. However, periodic compaction of these SSTables is important in order to support fast read performance and clean out stale data values. A compaction operation in Cassandra is performed in order to merge SSTables. During compaction, the data in SSTables is merged: the keys are merged, columns are combined, obsolete values are discarded, and a new index is created.

Compaction is the process of freeing up space by merging large accumulated data-files. This is roughly analogous to rebuilding a table in the relational world. But the primary difference in Cassandra is that it is intended as a transparent operation that is amortized across the life of the server.

On compaction, the merged data is sorted, a new index is created over the sorted data, and the freshly merged, sorted, and indexed data is written to a single new SSTable (each SSTable consists of multiple files, including *Data*, *Index*, and *Filter*). This process is managed by the class `org.apache.cassandra.db.compaction.Compac tionManager`.

Another important function of compaction is to improve performance by reducing the number of required seeks. There is a bounded number of SSTables to inspect to find the column data for a given key. If a key is frequently mutated, it's very likely that the mutations will all end up in flushed SSTables. Compacting them prevents the database from having to perform a seek to pull the data from each SSTable in order to locate the current value of each column requested in a read request.

When compaction is performed, there is a temporary spike in disk I/O and the size of data on disk while old SSTables are read and new SSTables are being written.

Cassandra supports multiple algorithms for compaction via the strategy pattern. The compaction strategy is an option that is set for each table. The compaction strategy extends the `AbstractCompactionStrategy` class. The available strategies include:

- `SizeTieredCompactionStrategy` (STCS) is the default compaction strategy and is recommended for write-intensive tables.

- `LeveledCompactionStrategy` (LCS) is recommended for read-intensive tables.

- `TimeWindowCompactionStrategy` (TWCS) is intended for time series or otherwise date-based data.

We'll revisit these strategies in Chapter 13 to discuss selecting the best strategy for each table.

One interesting feature of compaction relates to its intersection with incremental repair. A feature called *anticompaction* was added in 2.1. As the name implies, anti-compaction is somewhat of an opposite operation to regular compaction in that the result is the division of an SSTable into two SSTables, one containing repaired data, and the other containing unrepaired data.

The trade-off is that more complexity is introduced into the compaction strategies, which must handle repaired and unrepaired SSTables separately so that they are not merged together.

What About Major Compaction?

Users with prior experience may recall that Cassandra exposes an administrative operation called *major compaction* (also known as *full compaction*) that consolidates multiple SSTables into a single SSTable. While this feature is still available, the utility of performing a major compaction has been greatly reduced over time. In fact, usage is actually discouraged in production environments, as it tends to limit Cassandra's ability to remove stale data. We'll learn more about this and other administrative operations on SSTables available via nodetool in Chapter 12.

Log Structured Merge Trees

The basic design of Cassandra's storage engine that we've described in this chapter is shared with several other databases modeled after the Google Bigtable paper, which itself draws inspiration from the 1996 paper by Patrick O'Neil et al., "The Log-Structured Merge-Tree (LSM-Tree)" (*https://oreil.ly/xYRvw*).

The LSM-Tree paper describes a data structure proposed as an improvement over the B-Trees previously dominant in storage design in which data is updated in place. The basic idea of the design is that data is stored first in memory and then over time is cascaded, or *merged* into one or more stages of files on disk using a merge-sort algorithm. The design was originally intended to take advantage of the fact that sequential writes to spinning disk are faster than random access, although it works equally well on modern SSD-based storage.

The Bigtable paper introduced the terms *memtable* and *SSTable* for the in-memory and on-disk components of the pattern, and established common design elements, including the initial storage of data in memtables, the use of a write-ahead log for durability, periodic storage of sorted data on disk in immutable SSTables, the use of memtables and Bloom filters to index into SSTables for fast reads, and compaction as a background process to consolidate SSTables.

Databases that conform to this pattern are commonly referred to as LSM-Tree databases and include both simple storage engines such as RocksDB and LevelDB, as well as distributed databases such as Cassandra and HBase. LSM-Tree databases are known for their high write throughput due to the append-only storage model. Reads are not quite as fast but are aided by the use of Bloom filters and SSTable indexes.

Deletion and Tombstones

We've already discussed several common distributed system approaches that Cassandra uses to handle failure gracefully. Another interesting case has to do with deleting data. Because a node could be down or unreachable when data is deleted, that node could miss a delete. When that node comes back online later and a repair occurs, the node could "resurrect" the data that had been previously deleted by re-sharing it with other nodes.

To prevent deleted data from being reintroduced, Cassandra uses a concept called a *tombstone*. A tombstone is a marker that is kept to indicate data that has been deleted. When you execute a delete operation, the data is not immediately deleted. Instead, it's treated as an update operation that places a tombstone on the value.

A tombstone is similar to the idea of a "soft delete" from the relational world. Instead of actually executing a delete SQL statement, the application will issue an update statement that changes a value in a column called something like "deleted." Programmers sometimes do this to support audit trails, for example.

Tombstones are not kept forever; instead, they are removed as part of compaction. There is a setting per table called gc_grace_seconds (Garbage Collection Grace Seconds), which represents the amount of time that nodes will wait to garbage collect (or compact) tombstones. By default, it's set to 864,000 seconds, the equivalent of 10 days. Cassandra keeps track of tombstone age, and once a tombstone is older than gc_grace_seconds, it will be garbage collected. The purpose of this delay is to give a node that is unavailable time to recover; if a node is down longer than this value, then it should be treated as failed and replaced.

Managers and Services

While we've referenced several locations in the Cassandra source code in this chapter, it's a good idea to get an overall sense of how the codebase is structured. There is a set of classes that form Cassandra's basic internal control mechanisms. We've encountered a few of them already, including the HintedHandOffManager, the Compaction Manager, and the StageManager. We'll present a brief overview of a few other classes here so that you can become familiar with some of the more important ones. Many of these expose MBeans via the Java Management Extension (JMX) in order to report status and metrics, and in some cases to allow configuration and control of their activities. We'll learn more about interacting with these MBeans in Chapter 11.

Cassandra Daemon

The org.apache.cassandra.service.CassandraDaemon interface represents the life cycle of the Cassandra service running on a single node. It includes the typical life cycle operations that you might expect: start, stop, activate, deactivate, and destroy.

You can also create an in-memory Cassandra instance programmatically by using the class `org.apache.cassandra.service.EmbeddedCassandraService`. Creating an embedded instance can be useful for unit testing programs using Cassandra.

Storage Engine

Cassandra's core data storage functionality is commonly referred to as the storage engine, which consists primarily of classes in the `org.apache.cassandra.db` package. The main entry point is the `ColumnFamilyStore` class, which manages all aspects of table storage, including commit logs, memtables, SSTables, and indexes.

What's a Column Family?

Tables were known as *column families* in early versions of Cassandra.

A History of Changes to the Storage Engine

The storage engine was largely rewritten for the 3.0 release to bring Cassandra's in-memory and on-disk representations of data in alignment with the CQL. An excellent summary of the changes is provided in the CASSANDRA-8099 Jira issue (*https://oreil.ly/iieXt*).

The storage engine rewrite was a precursor for many other changes, most importantly, support for materialized views, which was implemented under CASSANDRA-6477 (*https://oreil.ly/pkYsW*). These two Jira issues make for interesting reading if you want to better understand the changes required "under the hood" to enable these powerful new features.

Engineers at Instagram have created a Cassandra fork known as Rocksandra in which the native storage engine is replaced by RocksDB, with the goal of improving Cassandra's tail write latency. Their proposal to define an API to make the storage engine pluggable is documented as CASSANDRA-13474 (*https://oreil.ly/XiULB*).

Storage Service

Cassandra wraps the storage engine with a service that is represented by the `org.apache.cassandra.service.StorageService` class. The storage service contains the node's token, which is a marker indicating the range of data that the node is responsible for.

The server starts up with a call to the `initServer` method of this class, upon which the server registers the thread pools used to manage various tasks, makes some determinations about its state (such as whether it was bootstrapped or not, and what its partitioner is), and registers an `MBean` with the JMX server.

Storage Proxy

The `org.apache.cassandra.service.StorageProxy` sits in front of the `StorageService` to handle the work of responding to client requests. It coordinates with other nodes to store and retrieve data, including storage of hints when needed. The `StorageProxy` also helps manage lightweight transaction processing.

Direct Invocation of the Storage Proxy

Although it is possible to invoke the `StorageProxy` programmatically, as an in-memory instance, note that this is not considered an officially supported API for Cassandra and therefore has undergone changes between releases.

Messaging Service

The purpose of `org.apache.cassandra.net.MessagingService` is to manage all inbound and outbound messages from this node to and from other nodes, except for SSTable streaming, which we'll examine next. Incoming messages are routed to the other services referenced in this section for handling. Outgoing messages may optionally have callbacks, which are invoked when a response is received from the other node.

4.0 Feature: Asynchronous Internode Messaging

The `MessagingService` was rewritten for the 4.0 release to make all of its communications asynchronous using Netty, a nonblocking I/O client-server framework used to simplify networking for Java applications.

Stream Manager

Streaming is Cassandra's optimized way of sending SSTable files from one node to another via a persistent TCP connection; all other communication between nodes occurs via serialized messages. Streaming may occur when tokens need to be reallocated across the cluster, such as when a node is added or removed. Streaming may also occur during repair processing or when a node is being replaced or rebuilt. We'll learn more about these operations in Chapter 12.

The `org.apache.cassandra.streaming.StreamManager` handles these streaming messages, including connection management, message compression, progress tracking, and statistics.

Zero-Copy Streaming

Traditionally, SSTables have been streamed one partition at a time. The Cassandra 4.0 release introduced a zero-copy streaming feature to stream SSTables in their entirety using zero-copying APIs of the host operating system. These APIs allow files to be transferred over the network without first copying them into the CPU. This feature is enabled by default and has been estimated to improve streaming speed by a factor of 5 (*https://oreil.ly/ACmGM*).

CQL Native Transport Server

The CQL Native Protocol is the binary protocol used by clients to communicate with Cassandra. The `org.apache.cassandra.transport` package contains the classes that implement this protocol, including the `Server`. This native transport server manages client connections and routes incoming requests, delegating the work of performing queries to the `StorageProxy`.

There are several other classes that manage key features of Cassandra. Table 6-1 shows a few to investigate if you're interested.

Table 6-1. Classes implementing key Cassandra features

Key feature	Class
Repair	`org.apache.cassandra.service.ActiveRepairService`
Caching	`org.apache.cassandra.service.CacheService`
Migration	`org.apache.cassandra.schema.MigrationManager`
Materialized views	`org.apache.cassandra.db.view.ViewManager`
Secondary indexes	`org.apache.cassandra.index.SecondaryIndexManager`
Authentication and authorization	`org.apache.cassandra.auth.PasswordAuthenticator, CassandraAuthorizer, CassandraRoleManager`

System Keyspaces

In true "dogfooding" style, Cassandra makes use of its own storage to keep track of metadata about the cluster and local node. This is similar to the way in which Microsoft SQL Server maintains the meta-databases `master` and `tempdb`. The `master` is used to keep information about disk space, usage, system settings, and general server installation notes; the `tempdb` is used as a workspace to store intermediate results and perform general tasks. The Oracle database always has a tablespace called SYSTEM, used for similar purposes. The Cassandra `system` keyspaces are used much like these.

Let's go back to `cqlsh` and use DESCRIBE TABLES to get a quick overview of the tables in Cassandra's `system` keyspaces:

```
cqlsh> DESCRIBE TABLES;

Keyspace system_traces
----------------------
events  sessions

Keyspace system_schema
----------------------
tables     triggers    views    keyspaces  dropped_columns
functions  aggregates  indexes  types      columns

Keyspace system_auth
--------------------
resource_role_permissons_index  network_permissions  role_permissions
role_members                    roles

Keyspace system
---------------
repairs                view_builds_in_progress  paxos
available_ranges       prepared_statements      size_estimates
batches                peers                    built_views
peer_events_v2         compaction_history       local
available_ranges_v2    sstable_activity         transferred_ranges
peers_v2               peer_events
"IndexInfo"            transferred_ranges_v2

Keyspace system_distributed
---------------------------
repair_history  view_build_status  parent_repair_history
```

Seeing Different System Keyspaces?

If you're using a version of Cassandra prior to 4.0, you may not see some of these keyspaces listed. The basic `system` keyspace has been around since the beginning, but other keyspaces have been added:

- The `system_traces` keyspace was added in 1.2 to support request tracing.

- The `system_auth` and `system_distributed` keyspaces were added in 2.2 to support role-based access control (RBAC) and persistence of repair data, respectively.

- Tables related to schema definition were migrated from `system` to the `system_schema` keyspace in 3.0.

Let's dig a bit deeper into the contents of Cassandra's `system` keyspace:

```
cqlsh> USE system;

cqlsh:system> DESCRIBE KEYSPACE;
```

```
CREATE KEYSPACE system WITH replication =
  {'class': 'LocalStrategy'} AND durable_writes = true;

...
```

We've truncated the output here because it lists the complete structure of each table. We'll summarize some of the key tables next. Looking at the first statement in the output, we see that the system keyspace is using the replication strategy LocalStrat egy, meaning that this information is intended for internal use and not replicated to other nodes.

Immutability of the System Keyspaces

Describing the system keyspaces produces similar output to describing any other keyspace, in that the tables are described using the CREATE TABLE command syntax. This may be somewhat mis- leading in this case, as you cannot modify the schema of these sys tem keyspaces.

Looking over the contents of the tables in the system keyspace, we see that many of them are related to the concepts discussed in this chapter:

- Information about the structure of the cluster communicated via gossip is stored in system.local and system.peers. These tables hold information about the local node and other nodes in the cluster, including IP addresses, locations by data center and rack, token ranges, CQL, and protocol versions.

- The system.transferred_ranges and system.available_ranges track token ranges previously managed by each node and any ranges needing allocation.

- The construction of materialized views is tracked in the sys tem.view_builds_in_progress and system.built_views tables, resulting in the views available in system_schema.views.

- User-provided extensions include system_schema.types for user-defined types, system_schema.triggers for triggers configured per table, system_schema.func tions for user-defined functions, and system_schema.aggregates for user- defined aggregates.

- The system.paxos table stores the status of transactions in progress, while the system.batches table stores the status of batches.

- The system.size_estimates stores the estimated number of partitions per table and mean partition size.

Removal of the system.hints Table

Hinted handoffs have traditionally been stored in the `sys tem.hints` table. As thoughtful developers have noted, the fact that hints are really messages to be kept for a short time and deleted means this usage is actually an instance of the well-known anti-pattern of using Cassandra as a queue, which is discussed in Chapter 5. Hint storage was moved to flat files in the 3.0 release.

Feel free to explore the contents of some of the other `system_*` keyspaces using the `DESCRIBE KEYSPACE` or `DESCRIBE TABLE` commands:

- The cluster's definitions of the keyspaces, tables, and indexes are stored by the `system_schema.keyspaces`, `system_schema.tables`, and `system_schema.col umns`.

- The `system_traces` keyspace contains tables that store information about query traces, which we'll learn how to view and interpret in Chapter 13.

- The `system_auth` keyspace contains tables that store information about the users, roles, and permissions Cassandra uses to provide authentication and authorization features we'll learn about in Chapter 14.

Summary

In this chapter, we examined the main pillars of Cassandra's architecture, including gossip, snitches, partitioners, replication, consistency, anti-entropy, hinted handoff, and lightweight transactions. We also looked at some of Cassandra's internal data structures, including memtables, SSTables, and commit logs, and how Cassandra executes various operations, such as deletion and compaction. Finally, we surveyed some of the major classes and interfaces, pointing out key points of interest in case you want to dive deeper into the codebase.

## CHAPTER 7

Designing Applications with Cassandra

In the previous chapters you learned how Cassandra represents data, how to create Cassandra data models, and how Cassandra's architecture works to distribute data across a cluster so that you can access it quickly and reliably. Now it's time to take this knowledge and start to apply it in the context of real-world application design.

Hotel Application Design

Let's return to the hotel domain you began working with in Chapter 5. Imagine that you've been asked to develop an application that leverages the Cassandra data models you created to represent hotels, their room availability, and reservations.

How will you get from a data model to the application? After all, data models don't exist in a vacuum. There must be software applications responsible for writing and reading data from the tables that you design. While you could take many architectural approaches to developing such an application, we'll focus in this chapter on the microservice architectural style.

Cassandra and Microservice Architecture

Over the past several years, the microservice architectural style has been foundational to the discipline of cloud-native applications. As a database designed for the cloud from the ground up, Cassandra is a natural fit for cloud-native applications.

We don't intend to provide a full discussion of the benefits of a microservice architecture here, but will reference a subset of the principles introduced in Sam Newman's book *Building Microservices* (O'Reilly), an excellent source on this topic:

Encapsulation

> *Encapsulation* could also be phrased as "services that are focused on doing one thing well" or the "single responsibility principle."

By contrast, in many enterprises the database serves as a central integration point. An application might expose interfaces to other applications such as remote procedure call (RPC) or messaging interfaces, but it's also common for one application to access another application's database directly, which violates encapsulation and produces dependencies between applications that can be difficult to isolate and debug (see Figure 7-1).

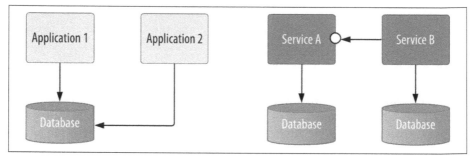

Figure 7-1. Integration by database contrasted with microservices

Autonomy

> In a microservice architecture, *autonomy* refers to the ability to independently deploy each microservice without dependence on any other microservices. This flexibility has significant advantages in allowing you to independently evolve portions of a deployed application without downtime, gradually introducing new versions of a service and minimizing the risk of these deployments.
>
> Another implication of autonomy is that each microservice can have its own data store using the most appropriate technology for that service. We'll examine this flexibility in more detail in "Polyglot persistence" on page 140.

Scalability

> Microservice architecture provides a lot of flexibility by giving you the ability to run more or fewer instances of a service dynamically according to demand. This allows you to scale different aspects of an application independently.
>
> For example, in a hotel domain there is a large disparity between *shopping* (the amount of traffic devoted to looking for hotel rooms) and *booking* (the much lower level of traffic associated with customers actually committing to a reservation). For this reason, you might expect to scale the services associated with hotel and inventory data to a higher degree than the services associated with storing reservations.

Microservice Architecture for a Hotel Application

To create a microservice architecture for the hotel application, you'll need to identify services, their interfaces, and how they interact. Although it was written well before microservices became popular, Eric Evans' book *Domain-Driven Design* (Addison-Wesley Professional) has proven to be a useful reference. One of the key principles Evans articulates is beginning with a domain model and identifying bounded contexts. This process has become a widely recommended approach for identifying microservices.

In Figure 7-2, you can see some of the key architecture and design artifacts that are often produced when building new applications. Rather than a strict workflow, these are presented in an approximate order. The influences between these artifacts are sometimes sequential or *waterfall* style, but are more often iterative in nature as designs are refined.

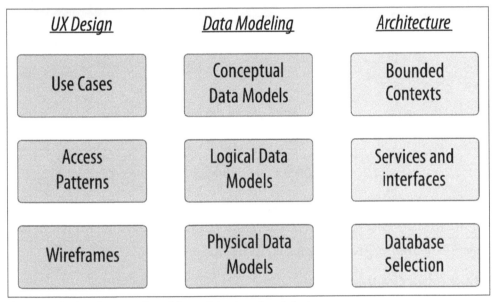

Figure 7-2. Artifacts produced by architectural and design processes

Use cases and access patterns are user experience (UX) design artifacts that also influence the data modeling and software architecture processes. We discussed the special role of access patterns in Cassandra data modeling in Chapter 5, so let's focus here on the interactions between data modeling and software architecture.

To define a microservice architecture, let's use a process that complements the data modeling processes you've already learned. As you begin to identify entities as part of a conceptual data modeling phase, you can begin to identify bounded contexts that represent groupings of related entities. As you progress into logical data modeling, you'll refine the bounded contexts in order to identify specific services that will be responsible for each table (or group of related, denormalized tables). During the final stage of the design process, you confirm the design of each service, the selection of database, the physical data models, and actual database schema.

Identifying Bounded Contexts

Let's see how this high-level process works in practice for your hotel application. Reusing the conceptual data model from Chapter 5, you might choose to identify a Hotel Domain encompassing the information about hotels, their rooms and availability, and a Reservation Domain to include information about reservations and guests, as shown in Figure 7-3. These happen to correspond to the keyspaces identified in your initial data model.

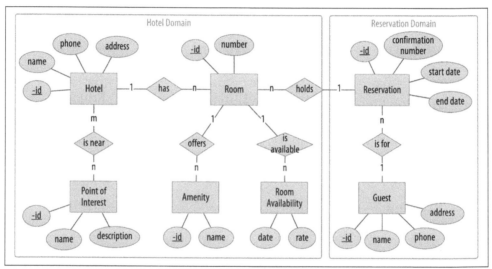

Figure 7-3. Identifying bounded contexts for a hotel application

Identifying Services

The next step is to formalize the bounded contexts you've identified into specific services that will own specific tables within your logical data model. For example, the Hotel Domain identified previously might decompose into separate services focused on hotels, points of interest, and inventory availability, as shown in Figure 7-4.

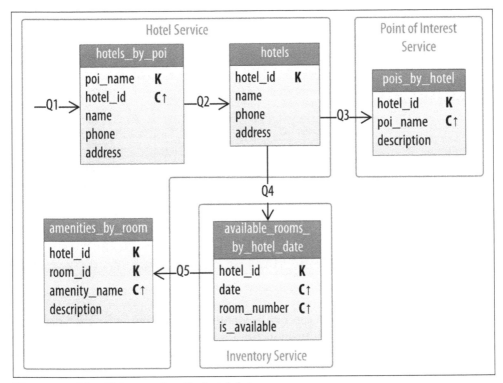

Figure 7-4. Identifying services for hotel data

There are multiple possible designs, but a good general design principle is to assign tables that have a high degree of correspondence to the same service. In particular, when working with Cassandra, a natural approach is to assign denormalized tables representing the same basic data type to the same service.

Services should embody classic object-oriented principles of coupling and cohesion: there should be a high degree of cohesion or relatedness between tables owned by a service, and a low amount of coupling or dependence between contexts. The query arrows on your Chebotko diagrams are helpful here in identifying relationships between services, whether they are direct invocation dependencies, or data flows orchestrated through user interfaces or events.

Using the same principles as described here, examine the tables in your logical data model within the Reservation Domain. You might identify a Reservation Service and a Guest Service, as shown in Figure 7-5. In many cases there will be a one-to-one relationship between bounded contexts and services, although with more complex domains there could be further decomposition into services.

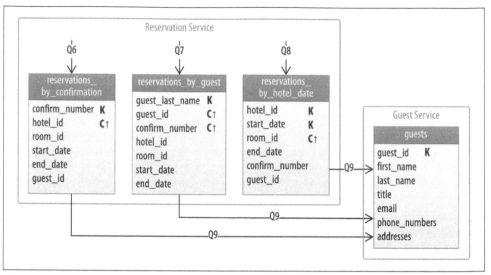

Figure 7-5. Identifying services for reservation data

While the initial design did not specifically identify access patterns for guest data outside of navigating to guest information from a reservation, it's not a big stretch to imagine that your business stakeholders will at some point want to allow guests to create and manage accounts on your application.

Designing Microservice Persistence

The final stage in the data modeling process consists of creating physical data models. This corresponds to the architectural tasks of designing services, including database-related design choices such as selecting a database and creating database schema.

Polyglot persistence

One of the benefits of microservice architecture is that each service is independently deployable. This gives you the ability to select a different database for each microservice, an approach known as *polyglot persistence.*

While you might be surprised to read this in a book on Cassandra, it is nonetheless true that Cassandra may not be the ideal backing store for every microservice, especially those that do not require the scalability that Cassandra offers.

Let's examine the services you've identified in the design of your hotel application to identify some options for polyglot persistence. We'll summarize these in Table 7-1.

Table 7-1. Polyglot persistence example

Service	Data characteristics	Database options
Hotel Service	Descriptive text about hotels and their amenities, changes infrequently	Document database (i.e., MongoDB), Cassandra, or Elasticsearch/Solr for full text search
Point of Interest Service	Geographic locations and descriptions of points of interest	Cassandra or other tabular databases supporting geospatial indexes such as DataStax Enterprise
Inventory Service	Counts of available rooms by date, large volume of reads and writes	Cassandra or other tabular databases
Reservation Service	Rooms reserved on behalf of guests, lower volume of reads and writes than inventory	Cassandra or other tabular databases
Guest Service	Guest identity and contact information, possible extension point for customer and fraud analytics systems	Cassandra, graph databases

You might make some of your selections with an eye to future extensibility and scalability of the system.

Representing other database models in CQL

When choosing to use Cassandra as the primary underlying database across multiple services, it is still possible to achieve some of the characteristics of other data models such as key-value models, document models, and graph models:

Key-value models

> Key-value models can be represented in Cassandra by treating the key as the partition key. The remaining data can be stored in a value column as a *text* or *blob* type. It's recommended not to exceed 5 MB for a single value, so consider breaking up large documents into multiple rows.

Document models

> There are two primary approaches in which Cassandra can behave like a document database, one based on having a well-defined schema, and the other approximating a flexible schema approach. Both involve identifying primary key columns according to standard Cassandra data modeling practices discussed in Chapter 5.

The flexible schema approach involves storing nonprimary key columns in a blob, as in the following table definition:

```
CREATE TABLE hotel.hotels_document (
    id text PRIMARY KEY,
    document text);
```

With this design, the document column could contain arbitrary descriptive data in JavaScript Object Notation (JSON) or some other format, which would be left to the application to interpret. This could be somewhat error prone and is not a very elegant solution.

A better approach is to use CQL support for reading and writing data in JSON format, introduced in Cassandra 2.2. For example, you could insert data into the hotels table with this query:

```
cqlsh:hotel> INSERT INTO hotels JSON '{ "id": "AZ123",
  "name": "Super Hotel Suites at WestWorld",
  "phone": "1-888-999-9999",
  "address": {
    "street": "10332 E. Bucking Bronco",
    "city": "Scottsdale",
    "state_or_province": "AZ",
    "postal_code": "85255"
  }
}';
```

Similarly, you can request data in JSON format from a CQL query. The response will contain a single text field labeled json that includes the requested columns—in this case, all of them (note that no formatting is provided for the output):

```
cqlsh:hotel> SELECT JSON * FROM hotels WHERE id = 'AZ123';

 [json]
---------------------------------------------------
 { "id": "AZ123", "name": "Super Hotel Suites at WestWorld",
 "phone": "1-888-999-9999", "address": {
 "street": "10332 E. Bucking Bronco", "city": "Scottsdale",
 "state_or_province": "AZ", "postal_code": 85255 }
```

The INSERT JSON and SELECT JSON commands are particularly useful for web applications or other JavaScript applications that use JSON representations. While the ability to read and write data in JSON format does make Cassandra appear to behave more like a document database, remember that all of the referenced attributes must be defined in the table schema.

Graph models

Graph data models are a powerful way of representing domains where the relationships between entities are as important or more important than the properties of the entities themselves. Common graph representations include *property graphs*. A property graph consists of vertexes that represent the entities in a domain, while edges represent the relationships between vertices and can be navigated in either direction. Both vertices and edges can have properties, hence the name property graph.

Property graphs between related entities can be represented on top of Cassandra using an approach in which each vertex type and edge type is stored in a dedicated table. To interact with the graph, applications use a graph query language such as Gremlin or Cypher. Graph databases provide a processing engine that interprets these queries and executes them, including data access to an underlying storage layer. DataStax Enterprise is an example of a database that provides a graph API with Cassandra as the underlying storage layer.

Extending Designs

Anyone who has built and maintained an application of significant size knows that change is inevitable. Business stakeholders come up with new requirements that cause you to extend systems.

For example, let's say your business stakeholder approaches you after your initial hotel data model to identify additional ways that customers should be able to search for hotels in your application. You might represent these as additional access patterns, such as searching for hotels by name, location, or amenities, as shown in Figure 7-6.

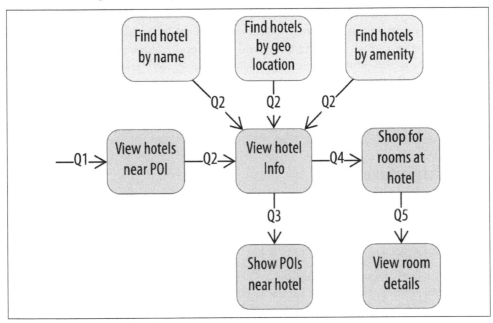

Figure 7-6. Additional hotel access patterns

According to the principles you learned in Chapter 5, your first thought might be to continue the practice of denormalization, creating new tables that will be able to support each of these access patterns, as shown in Figure 7-7.

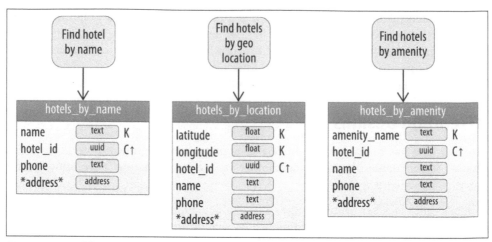

Figure 7-7. Additional hotel tables

At this point, you now have five different access patterns for hotel data, and it's reasonable to begin to ask how many denormalized tables is too many. The correct answer for your domain is going to depend on several factors, including the volume of reads and writes, and the amount of data. However, let's assume in this case that you'd like to explore some other options besides just automatically adding new tables to your design.

Cassandra provides two mechanisms that you can use as alternatives to managing multiple denormalized tables: secondary indexes and materialized views.

Secondary Indexes

If you try to query on a column in a Cassandra table that is not part of the primary key, you'll soon realize that this is not allowed. For example, consider the `hotels` table, which uses the `id` as the primary key. Attempting to query by the hotel's `name` results in the following output:

```
cqlsh:hotel> SELECT * FROM hotels
  WHERE name = 'Super Hotel Suites at WestWorld';
InvalidRequest: Error from server: code=2200 [Invalid query] message=
  "Cannot execute this query as it might involve data filtering and
  thus may have unpredictable performance. If you want to execute this
  query despite the performance unpredictability, use ALLOW FILTERING"
```

As the error message instructs, you could override Cassandra's default behavior in order to force it to query based on this column using the `ALLOW FILTERING` keyword. However, the implication of such a query is that Cassandra would need to ask all of the nodes in the cluster to scan all stored SSTable files for hotels matching the provided name, because Cassandra has no indexing built on that particular column. This could yield some undesirable side effects on larger or more heavily loaded clusters, including query timeouts and additional processing load on your Cassandra nodes.

One way to address this situation without adding an additional table using the hotel's name as a primary key is to create a *secondary index* for the name column. A secondary index is an index on a column that is not part of the primary key:

```
cqlsh:hotel> CREATE INDEX ON hotels ( name );
```

You can also give an optional name to the index with the syntax CREATE INDEX <name> ON.... If you don't specify a name, cqlsh creates a name automatically according to the form *<table name>_<column name>_idx*. For example, you can learn the name of the index you just created using DESCRIBE KEYSPACE:

```
cqlsh:hotel> DESCRIBE KEYSPACE;
...
CREATE INDEX hotels_name_idx ON hotel.hotels (name);
```

Now that you've created the index, your query will work as expected:

```
cqlsh:hotel> SELECT id, name FROM hotels
   WHERE name = 'Super Hotel Suites at WestWorld';

 id    | name
-------+-----------------------------------
 AZ123 | Super Hotel Suites at WestWorld

(1 rows)
```

You're not limited just to indexes based only on simple type columns. It's also possible to create indexes that are based on user-defined types or values stored in collections. For example, you might wish to be able to search based on the address column (based on the address UDT) or the pois column (a set of unique identifiers for points of interest):

```
cqlsh:hotel> CREATE INDEX ON hotels ( address );
cqlsh:hotel> CREATE INDEX ON hotels ( pois );
```

Note that for maps in particular, you have the option of indexing either the keys (via the syntax KEYS(addresses)), the values (which is the default), or both (in Cassandra 2.2 or later).

Now let's look at the resulting updates to the design of hotel tables, taking into account the creation of indexes on the hotels table as well as the service and updated keyspace assignments for each table, as shown in Figure 7-8. Note here the assignment of a keyspace per service, which we'll discuss more in depth in "Services, Keyspaces, and Clusters" on page 153.

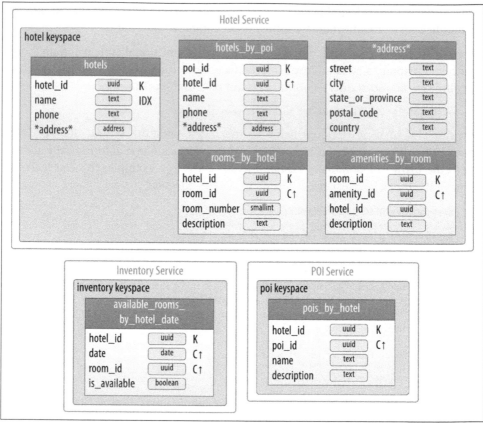

Figure 7-8. Revised hotel physical model

If you change your mind at a later time about these indexes, you can remove them using the DROP INDEX command:

```
cqlsh:hotels> DROP INDEX hotels_name_idx;
cqlsh:hotels> DROP INDEX hotels_address_idx;
cqlsh:hotels> DROP INDEX hotels_pois_idx;
```

Secondary Index Pitfalls

Because Cassandra partitions data across multiple nodes, each node must maintain its own copy of a secondary index based on the data stored in partitions it owns. For this reason, queries involving a secondary index typically involve more nodes, making them significantly more expensive.

Secondary indexes are not recommended for several specific cases:

- Columns with high cardinality. For example, indexing on the `hotel.address` column could be very expensive, as the vast majority of addresses are unique.

- Columns with very low data cardinality. For example, it would make little sense to index on the `user.title` column (from the user table in Chapter 4) in order to support a query for every "Mrs." in the `user` table, as this would result in a massive row in the index.

- Columns that are frequently updated or deleted. Indexes built on these columns can generate errors if the amount of deleted data (tombstones) builds up more quickly than the compaction process can handle.

For optimal read performance, denormalized table designs or materialized views (which we'll discuss in the next section) are generally preferred to using secondary indexes. However, secondary indexes can be a useful way of supporting queries that were not considered in the initial data model design.

SASI: A New Secondary Index Implementation

The Cassandra 3.4 release introduced an experimental, alternative implementation of secondary indexes known as the SSTable Attached Secondary Index (SASI). SASI was developed by Apple and released as an open source implementation of Cassandra's secondary index API. As the name implies, SASI indexes are calculated and stored as part of each SSTable file, differing from the original Cassandra implementation, which stores indexes in separate, "hidden" tables.

The SASI implementation exists alongside traditional secondary indexes, and you can create a SASI index with the CQL `CREATE CUSTOM INDEX` command:

```
cqlsh:my_keyspace> CREATE CUSTOM INDEX hotel_name_sasi_idx
  ON hotels (name)
  USING 'org.apache.cassandra.index.sasi.SASIIndex'
  WITH OPTIONS= {'mode': 'CONTAINS'};
```

SASI indexes do offer functionality beyond the traditional secondary index implementation, such as the ability to do inequality (greater than or less than) searches on indexed columns. You can also use the CQL `LIKE` keyword to do text searches against indexed columns. For example, you could use the following query to find hotels whose name contains the substring "world" (case insensitive):

```
cqlsh:hotel> SELECT id, name FROM hotels
  WHERE name LIKE '%world%';

 id    | name
-------+----------------------------------
 AZ123 | Super Hotel Suites at WestWorld

(1 rows)
```

While SASI indexes do perform better than traditional indexes by eliminating the need to read from additional tables, they still require reads from a greater number of nodes than a denormalized design.

Materialized Views

Materialized views were introduced to help address some of the shortcomings of secondary indexes that we've discussed. Creating indexes on columns with high cardinality tends to result in poor performance, because most or all of the nodes in the ring are queried.

Materialized views address this problem by storing preconfigured views that support queries. Each materialized view supports queries based on a single column that is not part of the original primary key. Materialized views simplify application development: instead of the application having to keep multiple denormalized tables in sync, Cassandra takes on the responsibility of updating views in order to keep them consistent with the base table.

Materialized views incur a performance impact on writes to the base table because some reads are required to maintain this consistency. However, materialized views demonstrate more efficient performance compared to managing denormalized tables in application clients. Internally, materialized view updates are implemented using batching, which we will discuss in Chapter 9.

As you work with physical data model designs, you will want to consider whether to manage the denormalization manually or use Cassandra's materialized view capability.

The design shown for the `reservation` keyspace in Figure 5-9 uses both approaches. The `reservations_by_hotel_date` and `reservations_by_guest` are represented as regular tables, and `reservations_by_confirmation` as a materialized view on the `reservations_by_hotel_date` table. We'll discuss the reasoning behind this design choice momentarily.

Similar to secondary indexes, materialized views are created on existing tables. To understand the syntax and constraints associated with materialized views, let's take a look at a CQL command that creates the `reservations_by_confirmation` table from the reservation physical model as a materialized view:

```
cqlsh> CREATE MATERIALIZED VIEW reservation.reservations_by_confirmation
  AS SELECT *
  FROM reservation.reservations_by_hotel_date
  WHERE confirm_number IS NOT NULL and hotel_id IS NOT NULL and
    start_date IS NOT NULL and room_number IS NOT NULL
  PRIMARY KEY (confirm_number, hotel_id, start_date, room_number);
```

The order of the clauses in the `CREATE MATERIALIZED VIEW` command can appear somewhat inverted, so let's walk through these clauses in an order that is a bit easier to process.

The first parameter after the command is the name of the materialized view—in this case, `reservations_by_confirmation`. The `FROM` clause identifies the base table for the materialized view, `reservations_by_hotel_date`.

The `PRIMARY KEY` clause identifies the primary key for the materialized view, which must include all of the columns in the primary key of the base table. This restriction keeps Cassandra from collapsing multiple rows in the base table into a single row in the materialized view, which would greatly increase the complexity of managing updates.

The grouping of the primary key columns uses the same syntax as an ordinary table. The most common usage is to place the additional column first as the partition key, followed by the base table primary key columns, used as clustering columns for purposes of the materialized view.

The `WHERE` clause provides support for filtering. Note that a filter must be specified for every primary key column of the materialized view, even if it is as simple as designating that the value `IS NOT NULL`.

The `AS SELECT` clause identifies the columns from the base table that you want your materialized view to contain. You can reference individual columns, but in this case the wildcard `*` indicates that all columns will be part of the view.

Enhanced Materialized View Capabilities

The initial implementation of materialized views in the 3.0 release has some limitations on the selection of primary key columns and filters. There are several Jira issues currently in progress to add capabilities, such as multiple nonprimary key columns in materialized view primary keys, CASSANDRA-9928 (*https://oreil.ly/yVlBi*), or using aggregates in materialized views, CASSANDRA-9778 (*https://oreil.ly/6J7ix*). If you're interested in these features, track the Jira issues to see when they will be included in a release.

Now that you have a better understanding of the design and use of materialized views, let's revisit the reservation physical design. Specifically, `reservations_by_con` `firmation` is a good candidate for implementation as a materialized view due to the high cardinality of the confirmation numbers—after all, you can't get any higher cardinality than a unique value per reservation.

Here is the schema for this materialized view:

```
CREATE MATERIALIZED VIEW reservation.reservations_by_confirmation AS
SELECT * FROM reservation.reservations_by_hotel_date
WHERE confirm_number IS NOT NULL and hotel_id IS NOT NULL and
start_date IS NOT NULL and room_number IS NOT NULL
PRIMARY KEY (confirm_number, hotel_id, start_date, room_number);
```

An alternate design would be to use `reservations_by_confirmation` as the base table and `reservations_by_hotel_date` as a materialized view. However, because you cannot create a materialized view with multiple nonprimary key columns from the base table, this would have required you to designate either `hotel_id` or `date` as a clustering column in `reservations_by_confirmation`. Both designs might be acceptable based on the anticipated amount of data, but this should give some insight into the trade-offs you'll want to consider in selecting which of several denormalized table designs to use as the base table.

An updated physical data model reflecting the design of tables used by the Reservation Service and Guest Service is shown in Figure 7-9. In this view, the contents of the `reservations_by_confirmation` table are shown in italics to indicate it is a materialized view based on `reservations_by_hotel_date`.

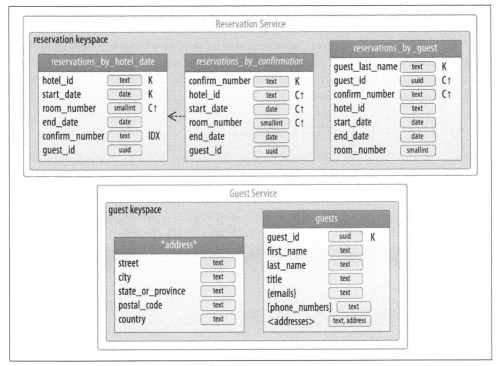

Figure 7-9. Revised Reservation physical model

Experimental Features

Materialized views were a major selling point of the Cassandra 3.0 release and drove a number of significant design changes under the hood, such as the new storage engine we'll discuss in Chapter 9. However, there were several rough edges and some corner cases that were not well handled in the initial implementation.

While there have been significant improvements on these issues in releases in the 3.X series, the Cassandra community has clarified the process for introducing new features entailing significant architectural change. These new features will now be designated as *experimental features* and disabled by default. Enabling an experimental feature will require a change in the *cassandra.yaml* file.

Other experimental features include the SASI indexes discussed earlier as well as transient replicas, a feature introduced in Cassandra 4.0 as a cost-saving measure for extremely large clusters. You'll learn more about transient replicas in Chapter 9.

Reservation Service: A Sample Microservice

So far, you've learned how a microservice architecture is a natural fit for using Cassandra, identified candidate services for a hotel application, and considered how service design might influence your Cassandra data models. The final subject to examine is the design of individual microservices.

Design Choices for a Java Microservice

Let's narrow the focus to the design of a single service: the Reservation Service. As we've discussed, the Reservation Service will be responsible for reading and writing data using the tables in the `reservation` keyspace.

A candidate design for a Java implementation of the Reservation Service using popular libraries and frameworks is shown in Figure 7-10. This implementation uses Apache Cassandra for its data storage via the DataStax Java Driver and the Spring Boot project for managing the service life cycle. It exposes a RESTful API documented via Swagger.

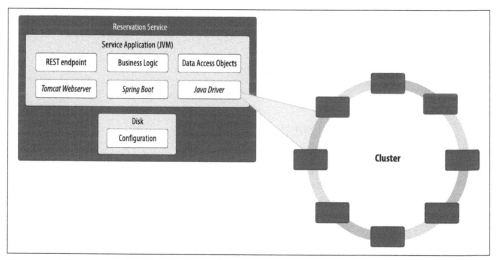

Figure 7-10. Reservation Service Java design

The Reservation Service Java implementation can be found on this GitHub site (*https://github.com/jeffreyscarpenter/reservation-service*). The goal of this project is to provide a minimally functional implementation of a Java microservice using the DataStax Java Driver that can be used as a reference or starting point for other applications. We'll be referencing this source code in Chapter 8 as we examine the functionality provided by the various DataStax drivers.

Deployment and Integration Considerations

As you proceed into implementation, there are a couple of factors you'll want to consider related to how the service will be deployed and integrated with other services and supporting infrastructure.

Services, Keyspaces, and Clusters

First, you'll want to consider the relationship of services to keyspaces. A good rule of thumb is to use a keyspace per service to promote encapsulation. You'll learn about Cassandra's access control features in Chapter 14 that allow you to create a database user per keyspace, such that each service can be easily configured to have exclusive read and write access to all of the tables in its associated keyspace.

Next, you'll want to consider whether a given service will have its own dedicated Cassandra cluster or share a cluster with other services. Figure 7-11 depicts a shared deployment in which Reservation and Inventory Services are using a shared cluster for data storage.

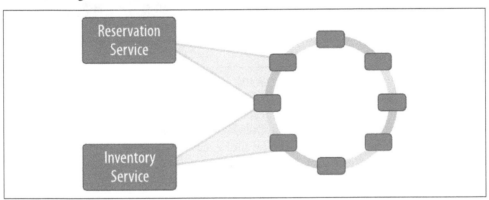

Figure 7-11. Service mapping to clusters

Companies that use both microservice architectures and Cassandra at large scale, such as Netflix, are known to use dedicated clusters per service. The decision of how many clusters to use will depend on the workload of each service. A flexible approach is to use a mix of shared and dedicated clusters, in which services that have lower demand share a cluster, while services with higher demand are deployed with their own dedicated cluster. Sharing a cluster across multiple services makes sense when the usage patterns of the services do not conflict.

Data Centers and Load Balancing

A second consideration is the selection of data centers where each service will be deployed. The corresponding cluster for a service should also have nodes in each data center where the service will be deployed, to enable the fastest possible access. Figure 7-12 shows a sample deployment across two data centers. The service instances should be made aware of the name of the local data center. The keyspace used by a service will need to be configured with a number of replicas to be stored per data center, assuming the `NetworkTopologyStrategy` is the replication strategy in use.

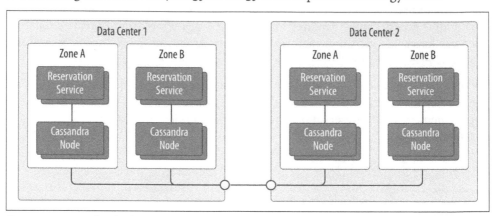

Figure 7-12. Multiple data center deployment

As you will learn in Chapter 8, most of these options, such as keyspace names, database access credentials, and cluster topology, can be externalized from application code into configuration files that can be more readily changed. Even so, it's wise to begin thinking about these choices in the design phase.

Interactions Between Microservices

One question that arises when developing microservices that manage related types is how to maintain data consistency between the different types. If you want to maintain strict ownership of data by different microservices, how can you maintain a consistency relationship for data types owned by different services? Cassandra does not provide a mechanism to enforce transactions across table or keyspace boundaries. But this problem is not unique to Cassandra, since you'd have a similar design challenge whenever you need consistency between data types managed by different services, regardless of the backing store.

Let's look at the hotel application for an example. Given the separate services to manage inventory and reservation data, how do you ensure that the inventory records are correctly updated when a customer makes a reservation? Two common approaches to this challenge are shown in Figure 7-13.

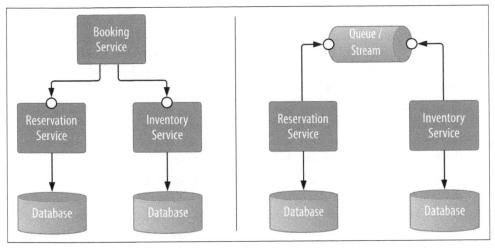

Figure 7-13. Service integration patterns

The approach on the left side is to create a Booking Service to help coordinate the changes to reservation and inventory data. This is an instance of a technique known as *orchestration*, often seen in architectures that distinguish between so-called *CRUD services* (responsible for creating, reading, updating, and deleting a specific data type) and services that implement business processes. In this example, the Reservation and Inventory Services are more CRUD services, while the Booking Service implements the business process of booking a reservation, reserving inventory, and possibly other activities such as notifying the customer and hotel.

An alternative approach is depicted on the right side of the figure, in which a message queue or streaming platform such as Apache Kafka is used to create a stream of data change events that can be consumed asynchronously by other services and applications. For example, the Inventory Service might choose to subscribe to events related to reservations published by the Reservation Service in order to make corresponding adjustments to inventory. Because there is no central entity orchestrating these changes, this approach is instead known as *choreography*. We'll examine integrating Cassandra with Kafka and other complementary technologies in more detail in Chapter 15.

It's important to note that both orchestration and choreography can exhibit the trade-offs between consistency, availability, and partition tolerance discussed in Chapter 2, and will require careful planning to address error cases such as service and infrastructure failures. While a detailed treatment of these approaches, including error-handling scenarios, is beyond scope here, techniques and technologies are available to address error cases such as service failure and data inconsistency. These include:

- Using a distributed transaction framework to coordinate changes across multiple services and databases. This can be a good approach when strong consistency is required. Scalar DB (*https://oreil.ly/4WSZt*) is an interesting library for implementing distributed ACID transactions that is built using Cassandra's lightweight transactions as a locking primitive.

- Using a distributed analytics tool such as Apache Spark to check data for consistency as a background processing task. This approach is useful as a backstop for catching data inconsistencies caused by software errors, in situations in which there is tolerance for temporary data inconsistencies.

- A variant of the event-based choreography approach is to leverage the change data capture (CDC) feature of a database as the source of events, rather than relying on a service to reliably persist data to a database and then post an event. This approach is typically used to guarantee highly consistent interactions at the interface between applications, although it could be used between individual services.

KillrVideo: A Reference Application for Video Sharing

The DataStax Developer Relations team and other contributors have created a video-sharing application called KillrVideo (*http://www.killrvideo.com*). KillrVideo is an open source reference application built using features of Apache Cassandra and DataStax Enterprise, including Search and Graph. It uses a microservice architecture, providing another example of the design principles discussed here. You can download the source on GitHub (*https://github.com/killrvideo*) and run your own copy of the application.

Summary

In this chapter, we've looked at why Cassandra is a natural fit within a microservice-style architecture, and discussed how to ensure your architecture and data modeling processes can work together. We examined techniques for putting Cassandra-based services in context of other data models. Now that we have examined the design of a particular microservice architecture, we're ready to dive into the details of implementing applications using Cassandra.

Application Development with Drivers

Now that we've looked at how to design a microservice architecture for a hotel application, let's look at how you might implement one of the services within that application—the Reservation Service. To write an application using Cassandra, you're going to need a driver, and thankfully you are in good hands.

You're likely used to connecting to relational databases using drivers. For example, in Java, JDBC is an API that abstracts the vendor implementation of the relational database to present a consistent way of storing and retrieving data using `Statements`, `PreparedStatements`, `ResultSets`, and so forth. To interact with the database, you get a driver that works with the particular database you're using, such as Oracle, SQL Server, or MySQL; the implementation details of this interaction are hidden from the developer.

There are a number of client drivers available for Cassandra as well, including support for most popular languages. There are benefits to these clients, in that you can easily embed them in your own applications, and that they frequently offer more features than the CQL native interface does, including connection pooling and JMX integration and monitoring. In the following sections, you'll learn about the various clients available and the features they offer.

Hector, Astyanax, and Other Legacy Clients

In the early days of Cassandra, the community produced a number of client drivers for different languages. These contributions were a key enabler of Cassandra adoption. We'll mention a few of these clients here to pay tribute:

- Hector (*https://oreil.ly/rmoJP*) was one of the first Cassandra clients. Hector provided a simple Java interface that helped many early developers avoid the challenges of writing to the Thrift API, and served as the inspiration for several other drivers.

- Astyanax (*https://oreil.ly/EakEz*) was a Java client originally built by Netflix on top of the Thrift API as a logical successor to the Hector driver. This driver helped many users transition from Thrift to CQL. The project was retired in 2016.

- Other clients included Pycassa for Python, Perlcassa for Perl, Helenus for Node.js, and Cassandra-Sharp for the Microsoft .NET framework and C#. Most of these clients are no longer actively maintained, as they were based on the now-removed Thrift interface.

This Apache Cassandra page (*https://oreil.ly/XaTY-*) has a comprehensive list of both current and legacy drivers.

DataStax Java Driver

The introduction of CQL was the impetus for a major shift in the landscape of Cassandra client drivers. The simplicity and familiar syntax of CQL made the development of client programs similar to traditional relational database drivers. DataStax made a strategic investment of open source drivers for Java and several additional languages in order to fuel Cassandra adoption. These drivers quickly became the de facto standard for new development projects.

Focusing on the Java Driver

The DataStax Java Driver is the oldest and most popular driver, and typically the driver in which new features appear first. For this reason, in this book we'll focus on using the Java driver and use this as an opportunity to learn about the features that are provided by the DataStax drivers across multiple languages.

You can access the drivers as well as additional connectors and tools at *https://github.com/datastax*. Visit the driver matrix page (*https://oreil.ly/6pPmY*) to access documentation and identify driver versions that are compatible with your server version.

Development Environment Configuration

First, you'll need to access the driver in your development environment. You could download the driver directly from the URL listed and manage the dependencies manually, but it is more typical in modern Java development to use a tool like Maven or Gradle to manage dependencies. If you're using Maven, you'll need to add something like the following to your project *pom.xml* file, while specifying a value for the driver version:

```
<dependency>
  <groupId>com.datastax.oss</groupId>
  <artifactId>java-driver-core</artifactId>
  <version>${driver.version}</version>
</dependency>
```

You can find information in the online documentation manuals for the Java drivers (*https://oreil.ly/evJRW*), as well as for the documentation for Javadoc for the Java driver (*https://oreil.ly/znyF2*). Alternatively, the Javadocs are also part of the source distribution.

All of the DataStax drivers are managed as open source projects on GitHub. If you're interested in seeing the Java driver source, you can get a read-only trunk version using this command:

```
$ git clone https://github.com/datastax/java-driver.git
```

If you're interested in learning more about the internals of the driver, or even potentially contributing to the project, the DataStax documentation site also has a developer guide (*https://oreil.ly/VeR6N*).

Driver API Changes

The 4.0 release of the Java driver included significant breaking changes to the API and configuration of the driver in order to simplify application development and discourage configurations contrary to best practices. This book conforms to the newer APIs. The "Clients" chapter in the second edition of this book remains a good resource for those using the Java Driver 3.x and earlier.

In September 2019, DataStax announced a significant change to its strategy for drivers for all languages. Prior to that point, DataStax had maintained separate open source and enterprise drivers for use with Apache Cassandra and DataStax Enterprise, respectively. In early 2020, the codebases for the drivers in each of the supported languages were merged, bringing the benefits of several performance and availability improvements that were previously only available to DSE customers. DSE-specific driver features are out of the scope of this book, but are well documented on the sites we've referenced.

DataStax Drivers also support the ability to connect to clusters running in Astra (*https://oreil.ly/KA9RY*), the Cassandra-as-a-Service provided by DataStax.

Connecting to a Cluster

Once you've configured your environment, it's time to start coding. We'll base the code samples for this chapter around the Reservation Service, a microservice implementation based on the hotel data model introduced in Chapter 5, and the corresponding application design discussed in Chapter 7. The source code for the Reservation Service is available at *https://github.com/jeffreyscarpenter/reservation-service*.

To start building your application, you'll use the driver's API to connect to a cluster. In the Java driver, connectivity to a cluster is represented by the `com.data stax.oss.driver.api.core.CqlSession` class.

The `CqlSession` class is the main entry point of the driver. It supports a fluent-style API using the builder pattern. For example, the following line creates a `CqlSession` that will attempt to connect to a Cassandra node on the local host at the default Cassandra native protocol port number:

```
CqlSession cqlSession = CqlSession.builder()
    .addContactPoint(new InetSocketAddress("127.0.0.1", 9042))
    .build()
```

Elimination of the Cluster Object

Many versions of DataStax drivers support the concept of a `Clus ter` object used to create `Session` objects. The 4.0 Java driver and later combine `Cluster` and `Session` into `CqlSession`.

In the terminology of the driver, the nodes you explicitly identify when creating a `CqlSession` are known as *contact points*. Contact points are similar to the concept of seed nodes that a Cassandra node uses to connect to other nodes in the same cluster.

The minimum required information to create a `CqlSession` is a single contact point. The driver defaults to a single contact point consisting of the local host and default port, so this statement is equivalent to the previous one (unless you are using file-based configuration, as we describe in "File-based configuration" on page 172):

```
CqlSession cqlSession = CqlSession.builder().build()
```

While this configuration is useful for development, when you might be running a Cassandra node on your local machine, for production environments you'll want to specify multiple contact points. This is a good practice in case one of the nodes you pick happens to be down when the client application is attempting to create a `CqlSes sion`. You'll also need to specify the name of the local data center. We'll discuss naming data centers in Chapter 10.

```
CqlSession cqlSession = CqlSession.builder()
    .addContactPoint(new InetSocketAddress("<some IP address>", 9042))
    .addContactPoint(new InetSocketAddress("<another IP address>", 9042))
    .withLocalDatacenter("<data center name>")
    .build()
```

When you create a CqlSession, the driver connects to one of the configured contact points to obtain metadata about the cluster. This action will throw a NoHostAvaila bleException if none of the contact points is available, or an AuthenticationExcep tion if authentication fails. We'll discuss authentication in more detail in Chapter 14.

You can optionally provide the name of a keyspace to connect to, as in this example that connects to the reservation keyspace:

```
CqlSession cqlSession = CqlSession.builder()
    .addContactPoint(new InetSocketAddress("<some IP address>", 9042))
    .addContactPoint(new InetSocketAddress("<another IP address>", 9042))
    .withKeyspace("reservation")
    .build()
```

If you do not specify a keyspace name when creating the CqlSession, you'll have to qualify every table reference in your queries with the appropriate keyspace name.

Each CqlSession manages connections to a Cassandra cluster, which are used to execute queries and control operations using the Cassandra native protocol. The CqlSes sion contains a pool of TCP connections for each host.

Sessions Are Expensive

Because a CqlSession maintains TCP connections to multiple nodes, it is a relatively heavyweight object. In most cases, you'll want to create a single CqlSession and reuse it throughout your application, rather than continually building up and tearing down CqlSessions. Another acceptable option is to create a CqlSession per keyspace, if your application is accessing multiple keyspaces.

Statements

Once you have created a CqlSession to connect to a cluster, you're ready to perform reads or writes. To begin doing some real application work, you'll create and execute CQL statements (*https://oreil.ly/RvcVY*) using implementations of Statement (*https://oreil.ly/BKmdd*). Statement is an interface with several implementations, including SimpleStatement, BoundStatement, and BatchStatement.

The simplest way to create and execute a statement is to call the CqlSession.exe cute() operation with a string representing the statement. Here's an example of a statement that will return the entire contents of the reservations table:

```
cqlSession.execute("SELECT * from reservation.reservations_by_confirmation");
```

This statement creates and executes a query in a single method call. In practice, this could turn out to be a very expensive query to execute in a large database, but it does serve as a useful example of a very simple query. Most queries will be more complex, as you'll have search criteria to specify, or specific values to insert. You can certainly use Java's various string utilities to build up the syntax of your query by hand, but this, of course, is error prone. It may even expose your application to injection attacks if you're not careful to sanitize strings that come from end users.

Simple Statements

Thankfully, the DataStax drivers make it easy to create parameterized statements. Let's see how to do this with the Java driver's SimpleStatement (*https://oreil.ly/ edwN_*) class. As it turns out, the execute() operation is a convenience method for creating a SimpleStatement. The previous code is equivalent to the following, using the SimpleStatement.newInstance() method:

```
cqlSession.execute(SimpleStatement.newInstance(
  "SELECT * from reservation.reservations_by_confirmation"));
```

The newInstance() is most useful in cases where you already have a set query string. Let's try building a query with variable parameters using a SimpleStatementBuilder. Here's an example of a statement that will insert a row in the reservations table, which you can then execute:

```
SimpleStatement reservationInsert = SimpleStatement.builder(
  "INSERT INTO reservations_by_confirmation (confirm_number, hotel_id,
    start_date, end_date, room_number, guest_id) VALUES (?, ?, ?, ?, ?, ?)")
  .addPositionalValue("RS2G0Z")
  .addPositionalValue("NY456")
  .addPositionalValue("2020-06-08")
  .addPositionalValue("2020-06-10")
  .addPositionalValue(111)
  .addPositionalValue("1b4d86f4-ccff-4256-a63d-45c905df2677")
  .build();
cqlSession.execute(reservationInsert);
```

The first parameter to the call is the basic syntax of your query, indicating the table and columns you are interested in. The question marks are used to indicate values that you'll be providing in additional parameters. You use simple strings to hold the values of columns such as the reservation ID, hotel ID, start and end dates, room number and guest ID, and an integer value for the room number.

If you've created your statement correctly, the insert will execute successfully (and silently). Now let's create another statement to read back the row you just inserted:

```
SimpleStatement reservationSelect = SimpleStatement.builder(
  "SELECT * FROM reservations_by_confirmation WHERE confirm_number=?")
  .addPositionalValue("RS2G0Z")
  .build();
ResultSet reservationSelectResult = cqlSession.execute(reservationSelect);
```

Again, you make use of parameterization to provide the ID for the search. This time, when you execute the query, make sure to receive the `ResultSet` that is returned from the `execute()` method. You can iterate through the rows returned by the `ResultSet` as follows:

```
for (Row row : reservationSelectResult) {
    System.out.format("confirm_number: %s, hotel_id: %, start_date: %s,
        end_date %s, room_number: %i, guest_id: %s\n",
        row.getString("confirm_number"), row.getString("hotel_id"),
        row.getLocalDate("start_date"), row.getLocalDate("end_date"),
        row.getInt("room_number"), row.getUuid("guest_id"));
}
```

This code uses the `ResultSet.iterator()` option to get an `Iterator` over the rows in the result set and loop over each row, printing out the desired column values. Note that you use special accessors to obtain the value of each column, depending on the desired type—in this case, `Row.getString()`, `getInt()`, and `getUuid()`. As you might expect, this will print out a result such as:

```
confirm_number: RS2G0Z, hotel_id: NY456, start_date: 2020-06-08,
    end_date: 2020-06-10, room_number: 111, guest_id:
    1b4d86f4-ccff-4256-a63d-45c905df2677
```

Of course, you typically will set columns to values you receive as variables, rather than the hardcoded value used here. You can find code samples for working with `Sim pleStatements` on the `simple-statement-solution` branch of the Reservation Service repository.

Prepared Statements

While `SimpleStatements` are quite useful for creating ad hoc queries, most applications tend to perform the same set of queries repeatedly. The `PreparedStatement` (*https://oreil.ly/ACGHk*) is designed to handle these queries more efficiently. The structure of the statement is sent to nodes a single time for preparation, and a handle for the statement is returned. To use the prepared statement, only the handle and the parameters need to be sent. Prepared statements are a core CQL feature supported by all DataStax drivers.

As you're building your application, you'll typically create `PreparedStatements` for reading data, corresponding to each access pattern you derive in your data model, plus others for writing data to your tables to support those access patterns.

Let's create some `PreparedStatements` to represent the same reservation queries as before, using the `CqlSession.prepare()` operation:

```
PreparedStatement reservationInsertPrepared = cqlSession.prepare(
    "INSERT INTO reservations_by_confirmation (confirm_number, hotel_id,
        start_date, end_date, room_number, guest_id) VALUES (?, ?, ?, ?, ?, ?)");
```

```
PreparedStatement reservationSelectPrepared = cqlSession.prepare(
  "SELECT * FROM reservations_by_confirmation WHERE confirm_number=?");
```

Note that the `PreparedStatement` uses the same parameterized syntax used earlier for the `SimpleStatement`. A key difference, however, is that a `PreparedStatement` is not a subtype of `Statement`. This prevents the error of trying to pass an unbound `PreparedStatement` to the `CqlSession` to execute. Note that there is also a variant of `CqlSession.prepare()` that accepts a parameterized `SimpleStatement` as input.

Let's take a step back and discuss what is happening behind the scenes of the `CqlSession.prepare()` operation:

- The driver passes the contents of your `PreparedStatement` to a Cassandra node and gets back a unique identifier for the statement. This unique identifier is referenced when you create a `BoundStatement`. If you're curious, you can actually see this reference by calling `PreparedStatement.getId()`.

- Once the driver prepares the statement on one node, it proceeds to prepare the statement on the other nodes in the cluster. Nodes keep track of prepared statements internally. In earlier releases, prepared statements were stored in a cache, but beginning with the 3.10 release, each Cassandra node stores prepared statements in a local table so that they are present if the node goes down and comes back up.

- The driver also provides the `advanced.prepared-statements.reprepare-on-up` configuration options; this is primarily useful if your cluster is using a release prior to Cassandra 3.10. If re-preparation is enabled (the default), the driver will re-prepare statements on nodes that have come back up.

- If the driver tries to execute a `PreparedStatement` on a node where it has not been prepared, the driver automatically prepares the statement, at the cost of an additional round trip between the driver and the node.

You can think of a `PreparedStatement` as a template for creating queries. In addition to specifying the form of your query, there are other attributes that you can set on a `PreparedStatement` that will be used as defaults for statements it is used to create, including a default consistency level, retry policy, and tracing.

In addition to improving efficiency, `PreparedStatements` also improve security by separating the query logic of CQL from the data. This provides protection against injection attacks, which attempt to embed commands into data fields in order to gain unauthorized access.

Bound statement

Now your PreparedStatement is available to use to create queries. In order to make use of a PreparedStatement, you bind it with actual values by calling the bind() operation. For example, you can bind the SELECT statement created earlier as follows:

```
BoundStatement reservationSelectBound = reservationSelectPrepared.bind("RS2G0Z");
```

The bind() operation used here allows you to provide values that match each variable in the PreparedStatement. It is possible to provide the first *n* bound values, in which case the remaining values must be bound separately before executing the statement. There is also a version of bind() that takes no parameters, in which case all of the parameters must be bound separately. There are several set() operations provided by BoundStatement that can be used to bind values of different types. For example, you can take the INSERT prepared statement from earlier and bind the values using the setString() operation:

```
BoundStatement reservationInsertBound = reservationInsertPrepared.bind()
  .setString("confirm_number", "RS2G0Z")
  .setString("hotel_id", "NY456")
  .setLocalDate("start_date", "2020-06-08")
  .setLocalDate("end_date", "2020-06-10")
  .setShort(111)
  .setUuid("1b4d86f4-ccff-4256-a63d-45c905df2677")
```

Once you have bound all of the values, execute a BoundStatement using CqlSession.execute(). If you have failed to bind any of the values, they will be ignored on the server side, if protocol v4 (Cassandra 3.0 or later) is in use. The driver behavior for older protocol versions is to throw an IllegalStateException if there are any unbound values.

You can find code samples for working with PreparedStatement and BoundStatement on the prepared-statement-solution branch of the Reservation Service repository.

Query Builder

The DataStax Java driver provides a unique feature not supported in other drivers called the QueryBuilder, which uses a fluent-style API for creating queries programmatically. This is especially useful for cases where there is variation in the query structure (such as optional parameters) that would make using PreparedStatements difficult. Similar to PreparedStatement, it also provides some protection against injection attacks.

To use the QueryBuilder, you'll need to include an additional dependency, for example, in a Maven POM file:

```
<dependency>
  <groupId>com.datastax.oss</groupId>
  <artifactId>java-driver-query-builder</artifactId>
  <version>${driver.version}</version>
</dependency>
```

The QueryBuilder provides a set of static methods to facilitate building different types of statements represented by different classes. The common usage is to import the static methods of the QueryBuilder class:

```
import static com.datastax.oss.driver.api.querybuilder.QueryBuilder.*;
```

Importing methods statically improves code readability, as you'll see as you look at some examples.

The QueryBuilder produces objects that implement the com.data stax.oss.driver.api.querybuilder.BuildableQuery interface and its sub-interfaces, such as Select, Insert, Update, Delete, and others. The methods on these interfaces return objects that represent the content of a query as it is being built up. You'll likely find your IDE quite useful in helping to identify the allowed operations as you're building queries.

Let's reproduce the queries from before using the QueryBuilder to see how it works. First, build a CQL INSERT query:

```
Insert reservationInsert =
  insertInto("reservation", "reservations_by_confirmation")
  .value("confirm_number", "RS2G0Z")
  .value("hotel_id", "NY456")
  .value("start_date", "2020-06-08")
  .value("end_date", "2020-06-10")
  .value("room_number", 111)
  .value("guest_id", "1b4d86f4-ccff-4256-a63d-45c905df2677");

SimpleStatement reservationInsertStatement = reservationInsert.build();
```

The first operation calls the QueryBuilder.insertInto() operation to create an Insert statement for the reservations_by_confirmation table. Then use the Insert.value() operation repeatedly to specify values for each column you are inserting. The Insert.build() operation returns a SimpleStatement you can then pass to CqlSession.execute().

The construction of the CQL SELECT command is similar:

```
Select reservationSelect =
  selectFrom("reservation", "reservations_by_confirmation")
  .all()
  .whereColumn("confirm_number").isEqualTo("RS2G0Z");

SimpleStatement reseravationSelectStatement = reservationSelect.build();
```

For this query, call `QueryBuilder.selectFrom()` to create a `Select` statement. You use the `Select.all()` operation to select all columns, although you could also have used the `column()` operation to select specific columns. Add a CQL `WHERE` clause via the `Select.whereColumn()` operation, to which you pass the name of the column and then add an equality check for the confirmation number, using the `isEqualTo()` operation.

This sample demonstrates how you can use the `QueryBuilder` to create a `Prepared Statement` instead of a `SimpleStatement`, using the concept of a *bind marker* as a placeholder for a value to be specified when the `PreparedStatement` is bound:

```
Select reservationSelect =
  selectFrom("reservation", "reservations_by_confirmation")
  .all()
  .whereColumn("confirm_number").isEqualTo(bindMarker());

PreparedStatement reservationSelectPrepared =
  cqlSession.prepare(reservationSelect.build());

// later
SimpleStatement reservationSelectStatement =
  reservationSelectPrepared.bind("RS2G0Z");
```

For a complete code sample using the `QueryBuilder`, see the `query-builder-solution` branch of the Reservation Service repository.

Object Mapper

You've learned several techniques for creating and executing query statements with the driver. There is one final technique to look at that provides a bit more abstraction. The DataStax drivers for Java, Python, and Node.js provide object mappers that allow you to focus on developing and interacting with domain models (or data types used on APIs).

The Java driver's object mapper works off of annotations in source code that are used to map Java classes to tables or user-defined types (UDTs). The object mapper is a useful tool for abstracting the details of interacting with Cassandra, especially if you have an existing domain model.

The mapper is provided in two separate libraries for use at compile time and runtime, so you will need to include additional Maven dependencies in order to use the mapper in your project. You'll add the following dependency to the compile path of your application:

```
<dependency>
  <groupId>com.datastax.oss</groupId>
  <artifactId>java-driver-mapper-processor</artifactId>
```

```
    <version>${driver.version}</version>
  </dependency>
```

You'll also add the runtime library as a runtime dependency:

```
<dependency>
  <groupId>com.datastax.oss</groupId>
  <artifactId>java-driver-mapper-runtime</artifactId>
  <version>${driver.version}</version>
</dependency>
```

The mapper API is based on standard design patterns for data access, including entity classes and Data Access Objects (DAOs). You create an entity class to represent each table in your design, a DAO interface to specify queries on entities, and a mapper interface that helps generate DAO instances. The mapper generates code based on the classes and interfaces you provide.

For a complete example of using the mapper, you'll want to look at the `mapper-solution` branch of the Reservation Service repository. We'll share some of the highlights here. Let's begin by creating a `ReservationsByConfirmation` entity class that will represent rows in the `reservations_by_confirmation` table:

```
import com.datastax.oss.driver.api.mapper.annotations.Entity;
import com.datastax.oss.driver.api.mapper.annotations.PartitionKey;
import com.datastax.oss.driver.api.mapper.annotations.NamingStrategy;
import static com.datastax.oss.driver.api.mapper.entity.naming.NamingConvention.
  SNAKE_CASE_INSENSITIVE;

@Entity
@NamingStrategy(convention = SNAKE_CASE_INSENSITIVE)
public class ReservationsByConfirmation {

    @PartitionKey
    private String confirmNumber;

    private String hotelId;
    private LocalDate startDate;
    private LocalDate endDate;
    private short roomNumber;
    private UUID guestId;

    // constructors, get/set methods, hashcode, equals
}
```

There are several annotations used in this example. The class is denoted as an `@Entity`, and also as having a `@NamingStrategy`, which is a way of specifying how the mapper should correlate Java identifiers to CQL. For example, you can specify a `SNAKE_CASE_INSENSITIVE` convention as in the preceding code, which means that the mapper will convert Java-style class and member names to lowercase, with underscores separating words, which is the recommended CQL naming style. Thus the class name `ReservationsByConfirmation` will be mapped to the `reserva` `tions_by_confirmation` table, the `confirmNumber` member will be mapped to the `confirm_number` column, and so on.

The Reservation Service uses an additional entity class `ReservationsByHotelDate` that is used with the `reservations_by_hotel_date` table. Its implementation is quite similar, so we won't reproduce it here.

You can also create entity classes corresponding to UDTs. If your domain model contains classes that reference other classes, you can annotate the referenced classes as user-defined types with the `@Entity` annotation. The object mapper processes objects recursively using your annotated types.

Next, you'll create a DAO interface to represent queries on these entity classes:

```
import com.datastax.oss.driver.api.core.PagingIterable;
import com.datastax.oss.driver.api.mapper.annotations.*;

@Dao
public interface ReservationDao {

    @SelectReservationsByConfirmation
  findByConfirmationNumber(
      String confirmNumber);

    @Query("SELECT * FROM ${tableId}")
    PagingIterable<ReservationsByConfirmation> findAll();

    @Insert
    void save(ReservationsByConfirmation reservationsByConfirmation);

    @Delete
    void delete(ReservationsByConfirmation reservationsByConfirmation);

    @Select (customWhereClause = "hotel_id = :hotelId AND start_date = :date")
    PagingIterable<ReservationsByHotelDate> findByHotelDate(
            @CqlName("hotel_id") String hotelId,
            @CqlName("start_date") LocalDate date);

    @Insert
    void save(ReservationsByHotelDate reservationsByHotelDate);

    @Delete
    void delete(ReservationsByHotelDate reservationsByHotelDate);
}
```

The `ReservationDao` interface is annotated as `@Dao`, and the various queries are marked with annotations such as `@Select`, `@Insert`, `@Delete`, and `@Query`.

The next step is to create a `Mapper` interface that can be used to obtain DAO instances:

```
import com.datastax.oss.driver.api.mapper.annotations.DaoFactory;
import com.datastax.oss.driver.api.mapper.annotations.Mapper;

@Mapper
public interface ReservationMapper {

    @DaoFactory
    ReservationDao reservationDao();

}
```

Annotate the interface with @Mapper, and each operation that returns a DAO with @DaoFactory. When you compile the application, the object mapper interprets your annotations to create a ReservationMapperBuilder class that you can invoke to obtain an implementation of ReservationMapper interface that wraps the CqlSes sion, and from there obtain an object implementing the ReservationDao interface:

```
ReservationMapper reservationMapper =
    new ReservationMapperBuilder(cqlSession).build();

ReservationDao reservationDao = reservationMapper.reservationDao();
```

Since the mapper and DAO objects are using your CqlSession, you should reuse them just as you do the CqlSession.

Now you can use the ReservationDao to perform queries using your entity classes. Create a ReservationsByConfirmation object using a simple constructor that you can save using the DAO:

```
ReservationsByConfirmation reservation = new ReservationsByConfirmation(
    "RS2G0Z", "NY456", "2020-06-08", "2020-06-10", 111,
    UUID.fromString("1b4d86f4-ccff-4256-a63d-45c905df2677"));

reservationDao.save(reservation);
```

You can use the java.util.UUID.fromString() operation here for convenience; in most applications, the value would have been passed in via a remote invocation.

The Mapper.save() operation is all you need to execute to perform a CQL INSERT or UPDATE, as these are really the same operation to Cassandra. The ReservationDao builds and executes the statement on your behalf.

To retrieve a specific reservation, use the ReservationDao.findByConfirmationNum ber() operation, passing in an argument list that matches the partition key:

```
ReservationsByConfirmation reservation =
    reservationDao.findByConfirmationNumber("RS2G0Z");
```

Deleting a reservation is also straightforward:

```
reservationDao.delete(reservation);
```

The object mapper documentation (*https://oreil.ly/7dRQb*) describes more advanced features, including DAO methods that execute asynchronously, the ability to configure CQL statement options such as TTL or consistency level, and customizing how the mapper handles annotations.

Asynchronous Execution

The `CqlSession.execute()` operation is synchronous, which means that it blocks until a result is obtained or an error occurs, such as a network timeout. The driver also provides the asynchronous `executeAsync()` operation to support non-blocking interactions with Cassandra. These non-blocking requests can make it simpler to send multiple queries in parallel to speed performance of your client application.

You could take any of the `Statements` from the preceding examples and execute them asynchronously:

```
CompletionStage<AsyncResultSet> resultStage = cqlSession.executeAsync(statement);
```

As of the 4.0 release of the DataStax Java driver, the result of `executeAsync()` and other asynchronous methods is of the type `CompletionStage` type introduced in Java 8. (Previous versions in the 3.x series relied on the `ListenableFuture` interface from Google's Guava framework.) The `CompletionStage` represents a stage of a computation. These stages can be chained together so that when a stage completes, other dependent stages are triggered.

With the Java driver, the asynchronous APIs can be used to assemble processing chains consisting of CQL queries and code that processes their results. Consider a chain in which the results of a SELECT query are used as inputs to perform a second query. In this example, you might load a reservation you wish to delete from the `res ervations_by_confirmation` table in a preliminary `selectStage`, in order to obtain the primary key columns you can then use to delete the reservation from the `reserva tions_by_hotel_date` table in a subsequent `deleteStage`:

```
// Load the reservation by confirmation number
CompletionStage<AsyncResultSet> selectStage = session.executeAsync(
  "SELECT * FROM reservations_by_confirmation WHERE
    confirm_number=RS2G0Z");

// Use fields of the reservation to delete from other table
CompletionStage<AsyncResultSet> deleteStage =
  selectStage.thenCompose(
    resultSet -> {
      Row reservationRow = resultSet.one();
      return session.executeAsync(SimpleStatement.newInstance(
        "DELETE FROM reservations_by_hotel_date WHERE hotel_id = ? AND
          start_date = ? AND room_number = ?",
        reservationRow.getString("confirm_number"),
        reservationRow.getLocalDate("start_date"),
```

```
            reservationRow.getInt("room_number"));
    });

    // Check results for success
    deleteStage.whenComplete(
        (resultSet, error) -> {
          if (error != null) {
            System.out.printf("Failed to delete: %s\n", error.getMessage());
          } else {
            System.out.println("Delete successful");
          }
```

We simplified this for readability, as you might wish to use prepared statements, or take advantage of a batch to delete from the `reservations_by_confirmation` and `reservations_by_hotel_date` tables at the same time.

In addition to the `CqlSession.executeAsync()` operation, the driver supports several other asynchronous operations, including `CqlSession.closeAsync()`, `CqlSession.prepareAsync()`, and several operations on the object mapper. You can also build the `CqlSession` asynchronously using `CqlSessionBuilder.buildAsync()`. For more information, see the Java driver's asynchronous programming documentation (*https://oreil.ly/jGaIy*).

 Reactive Style Programming

If you're interested in even more advanced asynchronous programming in Java, you may be familiar with reactive streams (*http://www.reactive-streams.org/*), an initiative to provide asynchronous stream processing with non-blocking back pressure. Reactive streams APIs became an official part of the Java platform in JDK 9 under the `java.util.concurrent.Flow.*` interfaces.

Beginning with the 4.4 release, the Java driver provides built-in support for reactive queries. The `CqlSession` interface extends a new `ReactiveSession` interface, which adds methods such as `exe cuteReactive()` to process queries expressed as reactive streams. To learn more about these APIs, see the Java driver reactive streams documentation (*https://oreil.ly/LGabZ*).

Driver Configuration

You've already looked at a few of the available options for configuring the Java driver, but now let's take a step back and look at its overall configuration approach.

File-based configuration

While all of the DataStax drivers support the configuration options listed in this section via their API, the Java driver also supports a file-based configuration approach.

File-based configuration is based on the Typesafe Config (*https://oreil.ly/F9Lae*) project, an open source library that provides configuration for JVM languages. In most cases it is preferable to use configuration values based on a configuration file rather than programmatic statements. For example, the configuration values provided previously could be specified in a configuration file such as the one provided for the Reservation Service:

```
datastax-java-driver {
  basic {
    contact-points = [ "127.0.0.1:9042", "127.0.0.2:9042" ]
    session-keyspace = reservation
  }
}
```

The configuration file here is written in the Human-Optimized Config Object Notation (HOCON) format. The Java driver uses the conventions of the Typesafe Config library for configuration file locations (*https://oreil.ly/QtmsK*); it searches the Java classpath for files named *application.conf*, *application.json*, or *application.properties*. The configuration loader is a pluggable interface that you can override to create your own implementation.

Basic configuration options

The Java driver divides configuration values into two categories: `basic` configuration values that are customized most frequently, and `advanced` configuration values that are used less frequently. The basic options include the following:

- Contact points and keyspace name, as discussed previously
- A `session-name` that will be used in log messages and metrics (if none is provided, they will be generated in the form `s1`, `s2`, and so on for each distinct `CqlSession` created)
- The `config-reload-interval` that specifies how often configuration values will be reloaded from the file (defaults to `5 minutes`)
- Default parameters applied to each `request`, including the `request.timeout`, the `request.consistency` (consistency level), and the `request.page-size`, which determines how many rows will be retrieved at a time for larger queries
- The `load-balancing-policy`, which we'll discuss in in the next section

You can configure advanced options on a `CqlSession`, including query execution, connection management, security, logging, and metrics. We'll examine several of these options in later sections. The DataStax documentation provides a reference configuration file (*https://oreil.ly/dPEIA*), which is an excellent resource for learning about all of the available configuration options.

Load balancing

As discussed in Chapter 6, a query can be made to any node in a cluster, which is then known as the coordinator node for that query. Depending on the contents of the query, the coordinator may communicate with other nodes in order to satisfy the query. If a client directs all of its queries at the same node, this will produce an unbalanced load on the cluster, especially if other clients are doing the same.

To get around this issue, the driver provides a pluggable mechanism that will balance the query load across multiple nodes. Load balancing (*https://oreil.ly/dPEIA*) is implemented by selecting an implementation of this interface:

```
com.datastax.oss.driver.api.core.loadbalancing.LoadBalancingPolicy
```

Each `LoadBalancingPolicy` must provide a `distance()` operation to classify each node in the cluster as local, remote, or ignored, according to the `HostDistance` enumeration. The driver prefers interactions with local nodes and maintains more connections to local nodes than remote nodes. The other key operation is `newQueryPlan()`, which returns a list of nodes in the order they should be queried. The `LoadBalancingPolicy` interface also contains operations that are used to inform the policy when nodes are added or removed, or go up or down. These operations help the policy avoid including down or removed nodes in query plans.

Versions of the Java driver through the 3.x series provided multiple `LoadBalancingPolicy` implementations with a composable API that allowed a custom selection of behaviors. Beginning with the 4.0 release, the DataStax Java Driver ships with a single default `LoadBalancingPolicy` to simplify the developer experience. This default implementation reflects an opinionated point of view based on best practices observed from many deployments, including the following behaviors:

Round-robin queries
> The policy allocates requests across the nodes in the cluster in a repeating pattern to spread the processing load (equivalent to the `RoundRobinPolicy` from the legacy driver).

Token awareness
> Whenever you use a `PreparedStatement`, the policy uses the token value of the partition key in order to select a node that is a replica for the desired data, thus minimizing the number of nodes that must be queried (equivalent to the `TokenAwarePolicy` from the legacy driver).

Data center awareness
> The policy requires setting a local data center. The default load balancing policy will only include nodes in the local data center as part of its query plans. The local data center must be identified explicitly when building the `CqlSession` via

the withLocalDataCenter() operation, or via the configuration property basic.load-balancing-policy.local-datacenter.

This is a difference from the legacy driver, which provided a DCAwareRoundRobin Policy that would include remote nodes in query plans after local nodes. This was intended as a reliability mechanism in case all replicas in the local data center were unavailable. In practice, however, if all the replicas in a local data center are down, it is typically a broader outage at the data center level, and shifting traffic to other nodes has proven to have undesirable side effects and be difficult to debug.

Should you wish to set a different default LoadBalancingPolicy, you may specify it when building a CqlSession via the withLoadBalancingPolicy() operation, or by configuring the properties in the basic.load-balancing-policy group.

Retrying failed queries

When Cassandra nodes fail or become unreachable, the driver automatically and transparently tries other nodes, and schedules reconnection to the dead nodes in the background according to the configured *reconnection policy* (*https://oreil.ly/5SekC*). The reconnection policy is determined according to the advanced.reconnection-policy configuration options. Two reconnection policies are provided: the Exponen tialReconnectionPolicy and the ConstantReconnectionPolicy.

Because temporary changes in network conditions can also make nodes appear off-line, the driver also provides a mechanism to retry queries (*https://oreil.ly/A_W-3*) that fail due to protocol or network-related errors. This removes the need to write retry logic in client code.

The driver retries failed queries according to the provided implementation of the com.datastax.oss.driver.api.core.retry.RetryPolicy interface. The onReadTi meout(), onWriteTimeout(), and onUnavailable() operations define the behavior that should be taken when a query fails with protocol- or network-related exceptions ReadTimeoutException, WriteTimeoutException, or UnavailableException, respectively. The onErrorResponse() operation describes the behavior for handling other recoverable server errors, and onRequestAborted() operation handles cases in which the driver aborts a request before the server responds.

The RetryPolicy operations return a RetryDecision, which indicates whether the query should be retried, and if so, at what consistency level. If the exception is not retried, it can be rethrown or ignored, in which case the query operation will return an empty ResultSet.

The 4.0 release of the driver provides a single opinionated implementation of the RetryPolicy based on best practices. Releases through 3.x had a FallthroughRetry

Policy that never recommended retries, and a DowngradingConsistencyRetryPo
licy that downgrades the consistency level required on retries, as an attempt to get
the query to succeed. The issue with the DowngradingConsistencyRetryPolicy was:
if you are willing to accept a downgraded consistency level under some circumstances, do you really require a higher consistency level for the general case?

The RetryPolicy implementation can be overridden using the advanced.retry-
policy configuration.

Speculative execution

While it's great to have a retry mechanism that automates the response to network
timeouts, you don't often have the luxury of being able to wait for timeouts or even
long garbage collection pauses. To speed things up, the driver provides a *speculative
execution* (*https://oreil.ly/al3ic*) feature. If the original coordinator node for a query
fails to respond in a predetermined interval, the driver can preemptively start an
additional execution of the query against a different coordinator node. When one of
the queries returns, the driver provides that response and cancels any other outstanding queries.

Speculative execution is disabled by default via the NoSpeculativeExecutionPolicy,
but can be enabled on a CqlSession by setting the ConstantSpeculativeExecution
Policy. Here's an example of how you configure this policy in the configuration file
by specifying a maximum number of executions and a constant delay between executions (in milliseconds):

```
advanced.speculative-execution-policy {
   class = ConstantSpeculativeExecutionPolicy
   max-executions = 3
   delay = 100 milliseconds
}
```

You may create your own policy by implementing the com.data
stax.oss.driver.api.core.specex.SpeculativeExecutionPolicy interface.

Connection pooling

Because the CQL native protocol is asynchronous, it allows multiple simultaneous
requests per connection; the maximum is 128 simultaneous requests in protocol v2,
while v3 and later allow up to 32,768 simultaneous requests. Because of this larger
number of simultaneous requests, fewer connections per node are required. In fact,
the default is a single connection per node.

Connection pool (*https://oreil.ly/zUY-B*) settings are configurable via the
advanced.connection configuration options, including the number of connections
to use for local and remote hosts, and the maximum number of simultaneous
requests per connection (defaults to 1,024). While the v4 driver does not provide the

ability to scale the number of connections up and down as with previous versions, you can adjust these settings by updating the configuration file, and the changes will be applied at the next time the configuration file is reloaded.

The driver uses a connection heartbeat to make sure that connections are not closed prematurely by intervening network devices. This defaults to 30 seconds but can be overridden using the `advanced.heartbeat` configuration options.

Protocol version

The driver supports multiple versions of the CQL native protocol (*https://oreil.ly/ 6xq3d*). Cassandra 4.0 uses CQL protocol version 5, while Cassandra 3.X releases support version 4.

By default, the driver negotiates the protocol version when establishing connections, even correctly handling connections to mixed clusters in which multiple versions of Cassandra are in use. You can force a protocol version using the `advanced.proto col.version` configuration option.

Compression

The driver provides the option of compressing messages between your client and Cassandra nodes according to the compression options supported by the CQL native protocol. Enabling compression reduces network bandwidth consumed by the driver, at the cost of additional CPU usage for the client and server.

Currently there are two compression algorithms available: `LZ4` and `SNAPPY`. The compression defaults to `NONE` but can be overridden by setting the `advanced.proto col.compression` configuration property.

Driver security

The driver provides a pluggable authentication mechanism that can be used to support a simple username/password login, or integration with other authentication systems. By default, no authentication is performed. An authentication provider can be selected by passing an implementation of the `com.data stax.oss.driver.api.core.auth.AuthProvider` interface, such as the `PlainTex tAuthProvider` to the `CqlSessionBuilder.withAuthProvider()` operation, or by setting the `advanced.auth-provider` section in your configuration file. You can configure the `PlainTextAuthProvider` and provide your username and password by using the `CqlSessionBuilder.withAuthCredentials()` operation.

The driver can also encrypt its communications with the server to ensure privacy. Client-server encryption options are specified by each node in its *cassandra.yaml* file. The driver complies with the encryption settings specified by each node.

We'll examine authentication, authorization, and encryption from both the client and server perspective in more detail in Chapter 14.

Execution profiles

While some of the configuration values that you've learned can be overridden on individual `Statements`, many of them cannot. So what can you do when the configuration values chosen are appropriate for some of your queries, but not others? The driver allows you to create *execution profiles*, which are settings of configuration values that can be applied to individual `Statements` as an overlay over the default configuration. To learn which configuration options can be set in a profile, see the reference configuration file (*https://oreil.ly/E6vbD*).

For example, let's say your default settings include a request timeout of one second and a consistency level of `LOCAL_QUORUM`. You could create an execution profile to use with requests that you want to give a stronger consistency by adding this to the `pro files` section of the configuration file:

```
datastax-java-driver {
  profiles {
    long_request {
      basic.request.timeout = 3 seconds
      basic.request.consistency = QUORUM
    }
  }
}
```

Then, you can apply the values to a `Statement`:

```
statement.setExecutionProfileName("long_request");
```

There is also a `setExecutionProfileName()` operation available when using the `Sim pleStatementBuilder`. Or, if you create a `PreparedStatement` from a `SimpleState ment` (using `CqlSession.prepare()`), any execution profile you have set will be inherited by any `BoundStatements` created from the `PreparedStatement`.

Metadata

To access the cluster metadata (*https://oreil.ly/WCYDb*), invoke the `CqlSession.get Metadata()` method, which returns an object implementing the `com.data stax.oss.driver.api.core.metadata.Metadata` interface. This object provides information about the cluster at a snapshot in time, including the nodes in the cluster, the tokens assigned to each node, and the schema, including keyspaces and tables.

Node discovery

A `CqlSession` maintains a *control connection* to the first node it connects with, which it uses to maintain information on the state and topology of the cluster. Using this connection, the driver will discover all the nodes currently in the cluster, and you can obtain this information through the `Metadata.getNodes()` operation, which returns a list of `com.datastax.oss.driver.api.core.metadata.Node` objects to represent each node. You can view the state of each node through the `Node.getState()` operation, or you can register an implementation of the `com.data stax.oss.driver.api.core.metadata.NodeStateListener` interface to receive callbacks when nodes are added or removed from the cluster, or when they are up or down. This state information is also viewable in the driver logs, which we'll discuss shortly.

Schema access

The `Metadata` class also allows the client to learn about the schema in a cluster, including operations that provide descriptions of individual keyspaces and tables. The schema version in use in a cluster can change over time as keyspaces and tables are created, altered, and deleted.

We discussed Cassandra's support for eventual consistency at great length in Chapter 2. Because schema information is itself stored using Cassandra, it is also eventually consistent, and as a result it is possible for different nodes to have temporarily different versions of the schema. The driver has internal safeguards to check for schema agreement before initiating any statement that would change the schema. The driver provides a notification mechanism for clients to learn about schema changes by registering a `com.datastax.oss.driver.api.core.metadata.schema.Schema ChangeListener` with the `CqlSession` as it is built using the `withSchemaChangeLis tener()` operation on the builder, or via the `advanced.schema-change-listener` configuration option.

In addition to the schema access you've just examined in the `Metadata` class, the Java driver also provides a facility for managing schema in the `com.data stax.oss.driver.api.querybuilder` package. The `SchemaBuilder` provides a fluent-style API for creating `Statements` representing operations such as `CREATE`, `ALTER`, and `DROP` on keyspaces, tables, indexes, and user-defined types (UDTs).

For example, you could create the `reservations_by_confirmation` table using the `createTable()` schema builder:

```
import static com.datastax.oss.driver.api.querybuilder.SchemaBuilder.createTable;
import com.datastax.oss.driver.api.core.type.DataTypes;

cqlSession.execute(createTable("reservation", "reservations_by_confirmation")
  .ifNotExists()
  .withPartitionKey("confirm_number, DataTypes.TEXT)
  .withColumn("hotel_id", DataTypes.TEXT)
  .withColumn("start_date", DataTypes.DATE)
  .withColumn("end_date", DataTypes.DATE)
```

```
.withColumn("room_number", DataTypes.SMALLINT)
.withColumn("guest_id", DataTypes.UUID)
.build());
```

Managing Case-Sensitive Identifiers with the Java Driver

As you learned in Chapter 4, CQL is case-sensitive by default.
While the practice is generally discouraged, it is possible to create
case-sensitive (*https://oreil.ly/vqv9A*) names for keyspaces, tables,
and columns by using quotes around identifiers in CQL. In order
to simplify the handling of case sensitivity, the Java driver uses the
CqlIdentifier class as a wrapper for all identifiers in its schema
API. If you are writing code that manipulates schema, it's a good
practice to make use of these identifiers as well. Java Driver APIs
that accept identifiers as arguments support both Java String (as
shown previously) and CqlIdentifier formats (as shown in the
Reservation Service implementation).

Debugging and Monitoring

The Java driver provides features for monitoring and debugging your client's use of
Cassandra, including facilities for logging and metrics. There are also capabilities for
query tracing and tracking slow queries, which you'll learn about in Chapter 13.

Driver logging

As you will learn in Chapter 11, Cassandra uses a logging API called Simple Logging
Facade for Java (SLF4J). The Java driver uses the SLF4J API for logging (*https://
oreil.ly/1Nr9a*) as well. In order to enable logging on your Java client application, you
need to provide a compliant SLF4J implementation on the classpath, such as Logback
(*http://logback.qos.ch/*) (used by the Reservation Service) or Log4j. The Java driver
provides information at multiple levels; the ERROR, WARN, and INFO levels are the most
useful to application developers.

You configure logging by taking advantage of Logback's configuration mechanism,
which supports separate configuration for test and production environments. Logback inspects the classpath first for the file *logback-test.xml* representing the test configuration, and then if no test configuration is found, it searches for the file
logback.xml. Here's an example extract from a *logback.xml* configuration file that enables the INFO log level for the Java driver:

```
<configuration>
  <!-- other appenders and loggers -->
  <logger name="com.datastax.oss.driver" level="INFO"/>
</configuration>
```

For more detail on Logback configuration, including sample configuration files for test and production environments, see the configuration page (*https://oreil.ly/wyKXy*) or the Reservation Service implementation.

Driver metrics

Sometimes it can be helpful to monitor the behavior of client applications over time in order to detect abnormal conditions and debug errors. The Java driver collects metrics (*https://oreil.ly/RL4tQ*) on its activities and makes these available using the Dropwizard Metrics library (*https://github.com/dropwizard/metrics*). The driver reports metrics on connections, task queues, queries, and errors such as connection errors, read and write timeouts, retries, and speculative executions. A full list of metrics is available in the reference configuration (*https://oreil.ly/ktuSE*).

You can access the Java driver metrics locally via the `CqlSession.getMetrics()` operation. The Metrics library can also integrate with the Java Management Extensions (JMX) to allow remote monitoring of metrics. We'll discuss the remote monitoring of metrics from Cassandra nodes in Chapter 11, and the same techniques apply to gathering metrics from client applications. JMX reporting is disabled by default in the v4 drivers (it was enabled by default in v3), but can be configured.

DataStax Python Driver

The DataStax Python Driver (*https://oreil.ly/Fn2_I*) was introduced in 2014, replacing the Pycassa client built on Cassandra's legacy Thrift interface as the primary Python driver for Cassandra. The driver supports Python 2.7 as well as current Python 3 versions back to 3.4. You can install the driver by running the Python installer *pip*:

```
$ pip install cassandra-driver
```

Installing Python and PIP

To use the example code, you'll need a compatible version of Python for your platform (as listed earlier), and `pip`. You can install `pip` by downloading the script (*https://bootstrap.pypa.io/get-pip.py*) and running the command `python get-pip.py`. You may need to run this command via `sudo` on Unix systems.

Here's a simple example of connecting to a cluster and inserting a row in the `hotels` table:

```
from cassandra.cluster import Cluster
cluster = Cluster(['127.0.0.1'])
session = cluster.connect('hotel')
session.execute("""
  insert into hotels (id, name, phone)
```

```
values (%s, %s, %s)
""",
('AZ123', 'Super Hotel at WestWorld', '1-888-999-9999')
)
```

The Python driver includes an object mapper called *cqlengine* and makes use of third-party libraries for performance, compression, and metrics. The driver source is available on GitHub (*https://oreil.ly/ujp48*). C extensions using Cython (*https://docs.datastax.com/en/developer/python-driver/latest/performance/#cython-extensions*) are used to speed up performance. The driver may also be run on PyPy (*https://docs.datastax.com/en/developer/python-driver/latest/performance/#pypy*), an alternative Python runtime that uses a JIT compiler. The reduced CPU consumption leads to improved throughput, up to two times better than regular Python.

DataStax Node.js Driver

The DataStax Node.js Driver (*https://oreil.ly/QFWc7*) was introduced in October 2014, based on the *node-cassandra-cql* project developed by Jorge Bay.

The Node.js driver is installed via the node package manager (NPM):

```
$ npm install cassandra-driver
```

Installing the Node.js Runtime and Package Manager

If you don't have experience using Node, you can get an installation for your platform at link:https://nodejs.org that includes both Node.js and NPM. These are typically installed at */usr/local/bin/node* and */usr/local/bin/npm* on Unix systems.

The syntax is a bit different, in that you access a `Client` object instead of a `Cluster` as in other language drivers, and the datacenter name is required. The other constructs are very similar:

```
const cassandra = require('cassandra-driver');
const client = new cassandra.Client({ contactPoints: ['127.0.0.1'],
  localDataCenter: 'datacenter1',
  keyspace: 'hotel'});
```

Building and executing a parameterized query looks like this:

```
const query = 'SELECT * FROM hotels WHERE id=?';
client.execute(query, ['AZ123'], function(err, result) {
  assert.ifError(err);
  console.log('got hotel with name ' + result.rows[0].name);
});
```

The Node.js driver also contains an object mapper (*https://docs.datastax.com/en/developer/nodejs-driver/latest/features/mapper/*) and provides built-in TypeScript support.

It provies both promise and callback-based APIs. As with other DataStax drivers, the source code is available on GitHub (*https://oreil.ly/0jmld*).

DataStax C# Driver

First released in July 2013, the DataStax C# Driver provides support for Windows clients using the .NET Framework and cross-platform development with .NET Core. For this reason, it is also frequently referred to as the ".NET Driver."

The C# Driver is available on NuGet, the package manager for the Microsoft development platform. Within PowerShell, run the following command at the Package Manager Console:

```
PM> Install-Package CassandraCSharpDriver
```

To use the driver, create a new project in Visual Studio and add a `using` directive that references the Cassandra namespace. The following example connects to our `hotel` keyspace and inserts a new record into the `hotels` table:

```
var cluster = Cluster.Builder()
.AddContactPoints("127.0.0.1")
.Build();

var session = cluster.Connect("hotel");
session.Execute(
  "INSERT INTO hotels (id, name, phone) " +
  "VALUES (" +
    "'AZ123'," +
    "'Super Hotel at WestWorld'," +
    "'1-888-999-9999'," +
    ";");
```

The C# Driver integrates with Language Integrated Query (LINQ), a Microsoft .NET Framework component that adds query capabilities to .NET languages; there is a separate object mapper available as well.

Other Cassandra Drivers

There are several drivers available for other programming languages:

GoCQL Driver
   The Go language created at Google has seen a rapid increase in popularity for server applications since its public introduction in 2009. The language is like C syntax but contains similar improvements in terms of memory management and concurrency.

   GoCQL (*https://gocql.github.io/*) is an open source (*https://github.com/gocql/gocql*) driver for the Go language. It is under active development and provides many of the same features as the DataStax drivers, including connection management, statement execution, paging, batches, and more.

DataStax C/C++ Driver

The DataStax C/C++ Driver (*https://oreil.ly/08zcO*) was released in February 2014. The C/C++ Driver is a bit different than the other drivers in that its API focuses on asynchronous operations to the exclusion of synchronous operations.

The C/C++ driver uses the *libuv* library for asynchronous I/O operations, and optionally uses the OpenSSL library if needed for encrypted client-node connections. Instructions for compilation and linking vary by platform, so see the driver documentation for details.

DataStax Ruby and PHP Drivers

DataStax also has drivers available for Ruby (*https://oreil.ly/SL3ds*) and PHP (*https://oreil.ly/bI0nK*), although these are considered to be in maintenance mode and are updated only for critical bug fixes.

JDBC and ODBC Drivers

Open Database Connectivity (ODBC) is a standard developed by Microsoft that allows applications to access data using SQL. Java Database Connectivity (JDBC) is a Java API that provides a SQL abstraction—see the `java.sql` package. JDBC and ODBC drivers (*https://oreil.ly/cgyv0*) are available from vendors, including Simba and Progress Software.

Stargate, An Open Source Data Gateway

While the development of CQL-based drivers has been a major boost to application development with Cassandra, many developers experience a significant learning curve in getting to know both CQL and the nuances of configuring and tuning performance with various drivers. Due to the continually evolving landscape of programming languages, there may not be an actively supported driver available for the language you are using.

Many organizations have dealt with these issues by building their own API frameworks on top of Cassandra, as recounted by Jeff Carpenter in the article "Data Services for the Masses" (*https://hackernoon.com/data-services-for-the-masses-jc4k35qa*). These frameworks tend to abstract the details of connecting with Cassandra clusters and executing queries behind more developer friendly APIs, and in some cases incorporate additional data stores.

In 2020, after observing many of these frameworks and noting their similar functionality, a team of engineers at DataStax created Stargate (*https://stargate.io*), an open source API framework (*https://oreil.ly/aiFss*) for data. Stargate launched with CQL and REST APIs, and subsequently added GraphQL (*https://oreil.ly/jmcbW*), gRPC (*https://oreil.ly/j4ACL*), and a document-style REST API (*https://oreil.ly/ofAlB*).

Stargate can be installed in front of Cassandra 3.11, Cassandra 4.0, and DataStax Enterprise 6.8 clusters, and Docker images are available. Stargate APIs are also available by default on Cassandra clusters in DataStax Astra.

While the REST and gRPC APIs are based on CQL and expose details of the underlying Cassandra tables, the Document and GraphQL APIs point to a future state in which Stargate APIs could be implemented by a pluggable selection of data stores.

Summary

You should now understand the various drivers available for Cassandra, the features they provide, and how to install and use them. We gave particular attention to the DataStax Java Driver in order to get some hands-on experience, which should serve you well even if you choose to use one of the other DataStax or community drivers. You'll continue to learn other driver features in the coming chapters as we discuss more details of reading and writing.

Writing and Reading Data

Now that you understand the data model and how to use a simple client, let's dig deeper into the different kinds of queries you can perform in Cassandra to write and read data. We'll also take a look behind the scenes to see how Cassandra handles your queries. Understanding these details will help you design queries that will perform well and provide the behavior you need.

As with the previous chapter, we've included code samples using the DataStax Java Driver to help illustrate how these concepts work in practice.

Writing

Let's start by noting some basic properties of writing data to Cassandra. First, writing data is very fast in Cassandra, because its design does not require performing disk reads or seeks. The memtables and SSTables save Cassandra from having to perform these operations on writes, which slows down many databases. All writes to disk in Cassandra are append only.

Because of the database commit log and hinted handoff design, the database is always writable, and within a row, writes are always atomic.

Write Consistency Levels

Cassandra's tuneable consistency levels mean that you can specify in your queries how much consistency you require on writes. A higher consistency level means that more replica nodes need to respond, indicating that the write has completed. Higher consistency levels also come with a reduction in availability, as more nodes must be operational for the write to succeed. The implications of using the different consistency levels on writes are shown in Table 9-1.

Table 9-1. Write consistency levels

Consistency level	Implication
ANY	Ensure that the value is written to a minimum of one replica node before returning to the client, allowing hints to count as a write.
ONE, TWO, THREE	Ensure that the value is written to the commit log and memtable of at least one, two, or three nodes before returning to the client.
LOCAL_ONE	Similar to ONE, with the additional requirement that the responding node is in the local data center.
QUORUM	Ensure that the write was received by at least a majority of replicas ((replication factor / 2) + 1).
LOCAL_QUORUM	Similar to QUORUM, where the responding nodes are in the local data center.
EACH_QUORUM	Ensure that a QUORUM of nodes respond in each data center.
ALL	Ensure that the number of nodes specified by replication factor received the write before returning to the client. If even one replica is unresponsive to the write operation, fail the operation.

The most notable consistency level for writes is the ANY level. This level means that the write is guaranteed to reach at least one node, but *it allows a hint to count as a successful write*. That is, if you perform a write operation and the node that the operation targets for that value is down, the server will make a note to itself, called a *hint*, which it will store until that node comes back up, or until the stored hint passes the expiration window specified by the max_hint_window_in_ms property defined for the node. Once the node is up, the server will detect this, look to see whether it has any writes that it saved for later in the form of a hint, and then write the value to the revived node.

Using the consistency level of ONE on writes means that the write operation will be written to both the commit log and the memtable. That means that writes at ONE are durable, so this level is the minimum level to use to achieve fast performance and durability. If this node goes down immediately after the write operation and before the memtable has been flushed to disk, the value will have been written to the commit log, which can be replayed when the server is brought back up to ensure that it still has the value.

Default Consistency Levels

Cassandra clients typically support setting a default consistency level for all queries, as well as a specific level for individual queries. For example, in cqlsh you can check and set the default consistency level using the CONSISTENCY command:

```
cqlsh> CONSISTENCY;
Current consistency level is ONE.
cqlsh> CONSISTENCY LOCAL_ONE;
Consistency level set to LOCAL_ONE.
```

In the DataStax Java Driver, the default consistency level can be set through the configuration option:

```
basic.request.consistency = QUORUM
```

If you do not configure this, it will be set to `LOCAL_ONE`. The default consistency level can be overridden on an individual statement:

```
Statement statement = ...
statement.setConsistencyLevel(ConsistencyLevel.LOCAL_QUORUM);
```

The Cassandra Write Path

The *write path* describes how data modification queries initiated by clients are processed, eventually resulting in the data being stored on disk. We'll examine the write path in terms of both interactions between nodes and the internal process of storing data on an individual node. An overview of the write path interactions between nodes in a multiple data center cluster is shown in Figure 9-1.

The write path begins when a client initiates a write query to a Cassandra node that serves as the coordinator for this request. The coordinator node uses the partitioner to identify which nodes in the cluster are replicas, according to the replication factor for the keyspace. The coordinator node may itself be a replica, especially if the client is using a token-aware load balancing policy. If the coordinator knows that there are not enough replicas up to satisfy the requested consistency level, it returns an error immediately.

Next, the coordinator node sends simultaneous write requests to all local replicas for the data being written. If the cluster spans multiple data centers, the *local coordinator* node selects a *remote coordinator* in each of the other data centers to forward the write to the replicas in that data center. Each of the remote replicas acknowledges the write directly to the original coordinator node.

This ensures that all nodes will get the write as long as they are up. Nodes that are down will not have consistent data, but they will be repaired via one of the anti-entropy mechanisms: hinted handoff, read repair, or anti-entropy repair.

The coordinator waits for the replicas to respond. Once a sufficient number of replicas have responded to satisfy the consistency level, the coordinator acknowledges the write to the client. If a replica doesn't respond within the timeout, it is presumed to be down, and a hint is stored for the write. A hint does not count as a successful replica write unless the consistency level `ANY` is used.

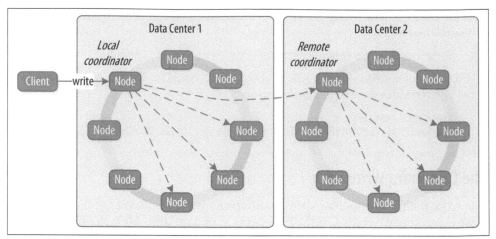

Figure 9-1. Interactions between nodes on the write path

Figure 9-2 depicts the interactions that take place within each replica node to process a write request. These steps are common in databases that share the log-structured merge tree design we explored in Chapter 6.

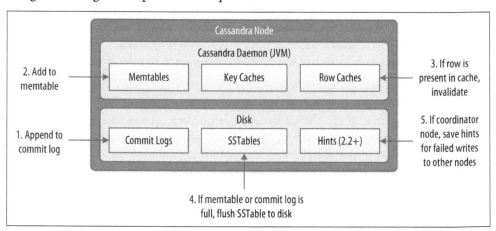

Figure 9-2. Interactions within a node on the write path

First, the replica node receives the write request and immediately writes the data to the commit log. Next, the replica node writes the data to a memtable. If row caching is used and the row is in the cache, the row is invalidated. We'll discuss caching in more detail under the read path.

If the write causes either the commit log or memtable to pass its maximum thresholds, a flush is scheduled to run. We'll learn how to tune these thresholds in Chapter 13.

At this point, the write is considered to have succeeded and the node can reply to the coordinator node or client.

After returning, the node executes a flush if one was scheduled. The contents of each memtable are stored as SSTables on disk, and the commit log is cleared. After the flush completes, additional tasks are scheduled to check if compaction is needed, and then a compaction is performed if necessary.

More Detail on the Write Path

Of course, this is a simple overview of the write path that doesn't take into account variants such as counter modifications and materialized views. For example, writes to tables with materialized views are more complex because partitions must be locked while consensus is negotiated between replicas. Cassandra leverages logged batches internally in order to maintain materialized views.

Writing Files to Disk

Let's examine a few more details on the files Cassandra writes to disk, including commit logs and SSTables.

Commit log files

Cassandra writes commit logs to the filesystem as binary files. By default, the commit log files are found under the *$CASSANDRA_HOME/data/commitlog* directory.

Commit log files are named according to the pattern *CommitLog-<version><timestamp>.log*. For example: *CommitLog-7-1566780133999.log*. The *version* is an integer representing the commit log format. For example, the version for the 4.0 release is 7. You can find the versions in use by release in the `org.apache.cassandra.db.commitlog.CommitLogDescriptor` class.

SSTable files

When SSTables are written to the filesystem during a flush, there are actually several files that are written per SSTable. Let's take a look at the default location under the *$CASSANDRA_HOME/data/data* directory to see how the files are organized on disk.

Forcing SSTables to Disk

If you're following along with the exercises in this book on a real Cassandra node, you may want to execute the `nodetool flush` command at this point, as you may not have entered enough data yet for Cassandra to have flushed data to disk automatically. You'll learn more about this command in Chapter 12.

Looking in the *data* directory, you'll see a directory for each keyspace. These directories, in turn, contain a directory for each table, consisting of the table name plus a UUID. The purpose of the UUID is to distinguish between multiple schema versions.

Each of these directories contains SSTable files that contain the stored data. Here is an example directory path: *hotel/hotels-3677bbb0155811e5899aa9fac1d00bce*.

Each SSTable is represented by multiple files that share a common naming scheme. The files are named according to the pattern *<version>-<generation>-<implementation>-<component>.db*. The significance of the pattern is as follows:

version

A two-character sequence representing the major/minor version of the SSTable format. For example, the version for the 4.0 release is *na*. You can learn more the about various versions in the `org.apache.cassandra.io.sstable.Descriptor` class

generation

An index number that is incremented every time a new SSTable is created for a table

implementation

A reference to the implementation of the `org.apache.cassandra.io.sstable.format.SSTableWriter` interface in use. As of the 4.0 release the value is "big," which references the "Bigtable format" found in the `org.apache.cassandra.io.sstable.format.big.BigFormat` class

Each SSTable is broken up into multiple files or *components*. These are the components as of the 3.0 release:

Data.db

These are the files that store the actual data and are the only files that are preserved by Cassandra's backup mechanisms, which you'll learn about in Chapter 12.

CompressionInfo.db

Provides metadata about the compression of the *Data.db* file.

Digest.crc32
>Contains a CRC32 checksum for the **-Data.db* file.

Filter.db
>Contains the Bloom filter for this SSTable.

Index.db
>Provides row and column offsets within the corresponding **-Data.db* file. The contents of this file are read into memory so that Cassandra knows exactly where to look when reading datafiles.

Summary.db
>A sample of the index for even faster reads.

Statistics.db
>Stores statistics about the SSTable that are used by the `nodetool tablehisto grams` command.

TOC.txt
>Lists the file components for this SSTable.

Older releases support different versions and filenames. Releases prior to 2.2 prepend the keyspace and table name to each file, while 2.2 and later releases leave these out because they can be inferred from the directory name.

We'll investigate some tools for working with SSTable files in Chapter 12.

Lightweight Transactions

As we've discussed previously in Chapter 1, Cassandra and many other NoSQL databases do not support transactions with full ACID semantics supported by relational databases. However, Cassandra does provide two mechanisms that offer some transactional behavior: *lightweight transactions* and *batches*.

Cassandra's lightweight transaction (LWT) mechanism uses the Paxos algorithm described in Chapter 6. LWTs were introduced in the 2.0 release. LWTs support the following semantics:

- On an `INSERT`, adding the `IF NOT EXISTS` clause will ensure that you do not overwrite an existing row with the same primary key. This is frequently used in cases where uniqueness is important, such as managing user identity or accounts, or maintaining unique reservation records, as you'll later see. Alternatively, the `IF EXISTS` clause will only update the row with the provided primary key if it is already present in the database. This is effectively limiting Cassandra's *upsert* behavior.

- On an UPDATE, adding an IF <conditions> clause will perform a check of one or more provided conditions, where multiple conditions are separated by an AND. Each condition is a check against a column in a WHERE clause using operators, including equality operators (=, !=), comparison operators (>, >=, <, ⇐), and the IN operator. This is frequently used to make sure that a row has an expected value that cannot change before a write occurs. If a transaction fails because the existing values did not match the ones you expected, Cassandra will include the current values so you can decide whether to retry or abort without needing to make an extra request. This form of lightweight transaction is frequently used for managing inventory counts.

Let's say you wanted to create a record for a new hotel, using the data model introduced in Chapter 5. You want to make sure that you're not overwriting a reservation with the same confirmation number, so you add the IF NOT EXISTS syntax to your INSERT command:

```
cqlsh> INSERT INTO reservation.reservations_by_confirmation (confirm_number,
    hotel_id, start_date, end_date, room_number, guest_id) VALUES (
    'RS2G0Z', 'NY456', '2020-06-08', '2020-06-10', 111,
    1b4d86f4-ccff-4256-a63d-45c905df2677) IF NOT EXISTS;

 [applied]
 -----------
       True
```

This command checks to see if there is a record with the partition key, which for this table consists of the confirm_number. So let's find out what happens when you execute this command a second time:

```
cqlsh> INSERT INTO reservation.reservations_by_confirmation (confirm_number,
    hotel_id, start_date, end_date, room_number, guest_id)
    VALUES ('RS2G0Z', 'NY456', '2020-06-08', '2020-06-10', 111,
    1b4d86f4-ccff-4256-a63d-45c905df2677) IF NOT EXISTS;

 [applied] | confirm_number | end_date   | guest_id     | hotel_id | ...
-----------+----------------+------------+--------------+----------+-----
     False |         RS2G0Z | 2020-06-10 | 1b4d86f4... |   NY456 | ...
```

In this case, the transaction fails, because there is already a reservation with the number "RS2G0Z," and cqlsh helpfully echoes back a row containing a failure indication and the original contents of the row.

It works in a similar way for updates. For example, you might use the following statement to make sure you're changing the end date for a reservation, but only if the previous value is the end date you expect:

```
cqlsh> UPDATE reservation.reservations_by_confirmation SET end_date='2020-06-12'
    WHERE confirm_number='RS2G0Z' IF end_date='2020-06-10';
```

```
[applied]
-----------
      True
```

Similar to what you saw with multiple INSERT statements, entering the same UPDATE statement again fails because the value has already been set. Because of Cassandra's upsert model, the IF NOT EXISTS syntax available on INSERT, and the IF x=y syntax on UPDATE represent the main semantic difference between these two operations.

Using Lightweight Transactions on Schema Creation

CQL also supports the use of the IF NOT EXISTS option on the creation of keyspaces and tables. This is especially useful if you are scripting multiple schema updates.

Let's implement the reservation INSERT using the DataStax Java Driver. When executing a conditional statement, the ResultSet will contain a single Row with a column named applied of type boolean. This tells you whether the conditional statement was successful or not. You can also use the wasApplied() operation on the statement:

```
cqlsh>SimpleStatement reservationInsert = SimpleStatement.builder(
  "INSERT INTO reservations_by_confirmation (confirm_number,
  hotel_id, start_date, end_date, room_number, guest_id)
  VALUES (?, ?, ?, ?, ?, ?)")
  .addPositionalValue("RS2G0Z")
  .addPositionalValue("NY456")
  .addPositionalValue("2020-06-08")
  .addPositionalValue("2020-06-10")
  .addPositionalValue(111)
  .addPositionalValue("1b4d86f4-ccff-4256-a63d-45c905df2677")
  .ifNotExists()
  .build();

ResultSet reservationInsertResult = session.execute(reservationInsert);

boolean wasApplied = reservationInsertResult.wasApplied();

if (wasApplied) {
  Row row = reservationInsertResult.one();
  row.getBool("applied");
}
```

This is a simple example using hardcoded values for readability rather than variables. You can find a working code sample for inserting reservation data using lightweight transactions on the lightweight-transaction-solution branch of the Reservation Service repository.

Conditional write statements use a *serial consistency level* in addition to the regular consistency level. The serial consistency level determines the number of nodes that must reply in the Paxos phase of the write, when the participating nodes are negotiating about the proposed write. The two available options are shown in Table 9-2.

Table 9-2. Serial consistency levels

Consistency level	Implication
SERIAL	This is the default serial consistency level, indicating that a quorum of nodes must respond.
LOCAL_SERIAL	Similar to SERIAL, but indicates that the transaction will only involve nodes in the local data center.

The serial consistency level can apply on reads as well. If Cassandra detects that a query is reading data that is part of an uncommitted transaction, it commits the transaction as part of the read, according to the specified serial consistency level.

You can set a default serial consistency level for all statements in cqlsh using the SERIAL CONSISTENCY statement, or in the DataStax Java Driver using the serial-consistency configuration option. To override the configured level on an individual statement, use the Statement.setSerialConsistencyLevel() operation.

Batches

While lightweight transactions are limited to a single partition, Cassandra provides a *batch* mechanism that allows you to group multiple modifications into a single statement, whether they address the same partition or different partitions.

The semantics of the batch operation are as follows:

- Only modification statements (INSERT, UPDATE, or DELETE) may be included in a batch.
- Batches may be *logged* or *unlogged*, where logged batches have more safeguards. We'll explain this in more detail below.
- Batches are not a transaction mechanism, but you can include lightweight transaction statements in a batch. Multiple lightweight transactions in a batch must apply to the same partition.
- Counter modifications are only allowed within a special form of batch known as a *counter batch*. A counter batch can only contain counter modifications.

Using a batch saves back-and-forth traffic between the client and the coordinator node, as the client is able to group multiple statements in a single query. However, the logged batch places additional work on the coordinator to orchestrate the execution of the various statements.

Cassandra's batches are a good fit for use cases such as making multiple updates to a single partition, or keeping multiple tables in sync. A good example is making modifications to denormalized tables that store the same data for different access patterns.

Batches Aren't for Bulk Loading

First-time users often confuse batches for a way to get faster performance for bulk updates. This is definitely not the case—batches
actually decrease performance and can cause garbage collection
pressure. We'll look at tools for bulk loading in Chapter 15.

In previous examples, you've inserted rows into the `reservations_by_confirmation`
table, but remember that there is also a denormalized table design for reservations:
`reservations_by_hotel_date`. Let's use a batch to group those writes together.

For a logged batch, use the CQL BEGIN BATCH and APPLY BATCH keywords to sur-
round the statements you wish to include:

```
cqlsh> BEGIN BATCH
  INSERT INTO reservation.reservations_by_confirmation (confirm_number,
  hotel_id, start_date, end_date, room_number, guest_id)
  VALUES ('RS2G0Z', 'NY456', '2020-06-08', '2020-06-10', 111,
  1b4d86f4-ccff-4256-a63d-45c905df2677);
  INSERT INTO reservation.reservations_by_hotel_date (confirm_number,
  hotel_id, start_date, end_date, room_number, guest_id)
  VALUES ('RS2G0Z', 'NY456', '2020-06-08', '2020-06-10', 111,
  1b4d86f4-ccff-4256-a63d-45c905df2677);
APPLY BATCH;
```

The DataStax Java Driver supports batches (*https://oreil.ly/UkFVT*) through the
`com.datastax.oss.driver.api.core.cql.BatchStatement` class. Here's an example
of what the same batch would look like in a Java client:

```
SimpleStatement reservationByConfirmationInsert = SimpleStatement.builder(
  "INSERT INTO reservations_by_confirmation (confirm_number, hotel_id,
  start_date, end_date, room_number, guest_id) VALUES (?, ?, ?, ?, ?, ?)")
  .addPositionalValue("RS2G0Z")
  .addPositionalValue("NY456")
  .addPositionalValue("2020-06-08")
  .addPositionalValue("2020-06-10")
  .addPositionalValue(111)
  .addPositionalValue("1b4d86f4-ccff-4256-a63d-45c905df2677")
  .build();

SimpleStatement reservationByHotelDateInsert = SimpleStatement.builder(
  "INSERT INTO reservations_by_hotel_date (confirm_number, hotel_id,
  start_date, end_date, room_number, guest_id) VALUES (?, ?, ?, ?, ?, ?)")
  .addPositionalValue("RS2G0Z")
  .addPositionalValue("NY456")
  .addPositionalValue("2020-06-08")
  .addPositionalValue("2020-06-10")
  .addPositionalValue(111)
  .addPositionalValue("1b4d86f4-ccff-4256-a63d-45c905df2677")
  .build();
```

```
BatchStatement reservationBatch = new BatchStatement();
reservationBatch.add(reservationByConfirmationInsert);
reservationBatch.add(reservationByHotelDateInsert);

cqlSession.execute(reservationBatch);
```

You can also create batches using a `BatchStatementBuilder`. You can find an example of working with `BatchStatement` on the `batch-statement-solution` branch of the Reservation Service repository.

Creating Counter Batches in DataStax Drivers

The DataStax drivers do not provide separate mechanisms for counter batches. Instead, you must simply remember to create batches that include only counter modifications or only non-counter modifications.

Logged batches are atomic—that is, if the batch is accepted, all of the statements in a batch will succeed eventually. This is why logged batches are sometimes referred to as *atomic batches*. Note that this is not the same definition of *atomicity* you might be used to if you have a relational database background. While all updates in a batch belonging to a given partition key are performed atomically, there is no guarantee across partitions. This means that modifications to different partitions may be read before the batch completes.

Here's how a logged batch works under the covers: the coordinator sends a copy of the batch called a *batchlog* to two other nodes, where it is stored in the `system.bat chlog` table. The coordinator then executes all of the statements in the batch, and deletes the batchlog from the other nodes after the statements are completed.

If the coordinator should fail to complete the batch, the other nodes have a copy in their batchlog and are therefore able to replay the batch. Each node checks its batchlog once a minute to see if there are any batches that should have completed. To give ample time for the coordinator to complete any in-progress batches, Cassandra uses a grace period from the timestamp on the batch statement equal to twice the value of the `write_request_timeout_in_ms` property. Any batches that are older than this grace period will be replayed and then deleted from the remaining node. The second batchlog node provides an additional layer of redundancy, ensuring high reliability of the batch mechanism.

In an unlogged batch, the steps involving the batchlog are skipped, allowing the write to complete more quickly. Users who are trying to rapidly insert a lot of data are often tempted to use unlogged batches. The trade-off you'll want to consider is that there is no guarantee that all of the writes to different partitions will complete successfully, which could leave the database in an inconsistent state. This risk does not exist when a batch contains mutations to a single partition. For this reason, if you request a logged batch with mutations to a single partition, Cassandra actually executes it as an unlogged batch to give you an extra boost of speed.

Another factor you should consider is the size of batches, measured in terms of the total data size, in bytes, rather than a specific number of statements. Cassandra enforces limits on the data size of batch statements to prevent them from becoming arbitrarily large and impacting the performance and stability of the cluster. The *cassandra.yaml* file contains two properties that control how this works: the `batch_size_warn_threshold_in_kb` property defines the level at which a node will log at the WARN log level that it has received a large batch, while any batch exceeding the value set `batch_size_fail_threshold_in_kb` will be rejected and result in error notification to the client. The batch size is measured in terms of the total amount of bytes to be sent. For simple statements, the size is the length of each CQL query, but the size will be lower for prepared statements since only the statement ID and parameter values are sent. The warning threshold defaults to 5 KB, while the fail threshold defaults to 50 KB.

Reading

There are a few basic properties of Cassandra's read capability that are worth noting. First, it's easy to read data because clients can connect to any node in the cluster to perform reads, without having to know whether a particular node acts as a replica for that data. If a client connects to a node that doesn't have the data it's trying to read, the node it's connected to will act as a coordinator node to read the data from a node that does have it, identified by token ranges.

In Cassandra, reads are generally slower than writes due to file I/O from reading SSTables. To fulfill read operations, Cassandra typically has to perform seeks, but you may be able to keep more data in memory by adding nodes, using compute instances with more memory, and using Cassandra's caches. Cassandra also has to wait for responses synchronously on reads (based on consistency level and replication factor), and then perform read repairs as necessary.

Read Consistency Levels

The consistency levels for read operations are similar to the write consistency levels, but the way they are handled behind the scenes is slightly different. A higher consistency level means that more nodes need to respond to the query, giving you more assurance that the values present on each replica are the same. If two nodes respond with different timestamps, the newest value wins, and that's what will be returned to the client. Cassandra will then perform what's called a *read repair*: it takes notice of the fact that one or more replicas responded to a query with an outdated value, and updates those replicas with the most current value so that they are all consistent.

The possible consistency levels, and the implications of specifying each one for read queries, are shown in Table 9-3.

Table 9-3. Read consistency levels

Consistency level	Implication
ONE, TWO, THREE	Immediately return the record held by the first node(s) that respond to the query. The record is checked against the same record on other replicas. If any are out of date, a *read repair* is then performed to sync them all to the most recent value.
LOCAL_ONE	Similar to ONE, with the additional requirement that the responding node is in the local data center.
QUORUM	Query all nodes. Once a majority of replicas ((replication factor / 2) + 1) respond, return to the client the value with the most recent timestamp. Then, if necessary, perform a read repair on all remaining replicas.
LOCAL_QUORUM	Similar to QUORUM, where the responding nodes are in the local data center.
EACH_QUORUM	Ensure that a QUORUM of nodes respond in each data center.
ALL	Query all nodes. Wait for all nodes to respond, and return to the client the record with the most recent timestamp. Then, if necessary, perform a read repair. If any nodes fail to respond, fail the read operation.

As you can see from the table, the ANY consistency level is not supported for read operations. Notice that the implication of consistency level ONE is that the first node to respond to the read operation is the value that the client will get—even if it is out of date. The read repair operation is performed after the record is returned, so any subsequent reads will all have a consistent value, regardless of the responding node.

Another item worth noting is in the case of consistency level ALL. If you specify ALL, then you're saying that you require all replicas to respond, so if any node with that record is down or otherwise fails to respond before the timeout, the read operation fails. A node is considered unresponsive if it does not respond to a query before the value specified by read_request_timeout_in_ms in the configuration file. The default is 5 seconds.

Aligning Read and Write Consistency Levels

The read and write consistency levels you choose to use in your applications are an example of the flexibility Cassandra provides us to make trade-offs among consistency, availability, and performance.

As you learned in Chapter 6, Cassandra can guarantee strong consistency on reads by using read and write consistency levels whose sum exceeds the replication factor. One simple way to achieve this is to require QUORUM for reads and writes. For example, on a keyspace with a replication factor of 3, QUORUM represents a response from two out of three nodes. Because 2 + 2 is greater than 3, strong consistency is guaranteed.

If you are willing to sacrifice strong consistency in order to support increased throughput and more tolerance for downed nodes, you can use lesser consistency levels. For example, using QUORUM for writes and ONE for reads doesn't guarantee strong consistency, as 2 + 1 is merely equal to 3.

Thinking this through practically, if you are only guaranteed writes to two out of three replicas, there is certainly a chance that one of the replicas did not receive the write and has not yet been repaired, and a read at consistency level ONE could go to that very node.

The Cassandra Read Path

Now let's take a look at what happens when a client requests data. This is known as the *read path*. We'll describe the read path from the perspective of a query for a single partition key, starting with the interactions between nodes shown in Figure 9-3.

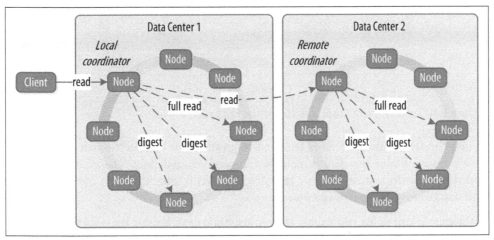

Figure 9-3. Interactions between nodes on the read path

The read path begins when a client initiates a read query to the coordinator node. As on the write path, the coordinator uses the partitioner to determine the replicas, and checks that there are enough replicas up to satisfy the requested consistency level. Another similarity to the write path is that a remote coordinator is selected per data center for any read queries that involve multiple data centers.

If the coordinator is not itself a replica, the coordinator then sends a read request to the fastest replica, as determined by the dynamic snitch. The coordinator node also sends a *digest request* to the other replicas. A digest request is similar to a standard read request, except the replicas return a digest, or hash, of the requested data.

The coordinator calculates the digest hash for data returned from the fastest replica and compares it to the digests returned from the other replicas. If the digests are consistent, and the desired consistency level has been met, then the data from the fastest replica can be returned. If the digests are not consistent, then the coordinator must perform a read repair, as discussed in the following section.

Figure 9-4 shows the interactions that take place within each replica node to process read requests.

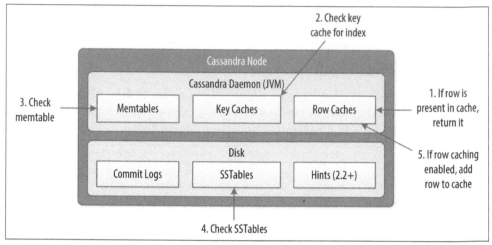

Figure 9-4. Interactions within a node on the read path

When the replica node receives the read request, it first checks the row cache. If the row cache contains the data, it can be returned immediately. The row cache helps speed read performance for rows that are accessed frequently. We'll discuss the pros and cons of row caching in Chapter 13.

If the data is not in the row cache, the replica node searches for the data in memtables and SSTables. There is only a single memtable for a given table, so that part of the search is straightforward. However, there are potentially many physical SSTables for a single Cassandra table, each of which may contain a portion of the requested data.

Cassandra implements several features to optimize the SSTable search: key caching, Bloom filters, SSTable indexes, and summary indexes.

The first step in searching SSTables on disk is to use a Bloom filter to determine whether the requested partition does not exist in a given SSTable, which would make it unnecessary to search that SSTable.

If the SSTable passes the Bloom filter, Cassandra checks the key cache to see if it contains the offset of the partition key in the SSTable. The key cache is implemented as a map structure in which the keys are a combination of the SSTable file descriptor and partition key, and the values are offset locations into SSTable files. The key cache helps to eliminate seeks within SSTable files for frequently accessed data, because the data can be read directly.

If the offset is not obtained from the key cache, Cassandra uses a two-level index stored on disk in order to locate the offset. The first-level index is the *partition summary*, which is used to obtain an offset for searching for the partition key within the second-level index, the *partition index*. The partition index is where the offset into the SSTable for the partition key is stored.

If the offset for the partition key is found, Cassandra accesses the SSTable at the specified offset and starts reading data. In the 3.6 release, a chunk cache was added to store chunks of data from SSTables that are accessed frequently; you'll learn more about this in Chapter 13.

Once data has been obtained from all of the SSTables, Cassandra merges the SSTable data and memtable data by selecting the value with the latest timestamp for each requested column.

Finally, the merged data can be added to the row cache (if enabled) and returned to the client or coordinator node. A digest request is handled in much the same way as a regular read request, with the additional step that a digest is calculated on the result data and returned instead of the data itself.

Read Repair

Here's how read repair works: the coordinator makes a full read request from all of the replica nodes. The coordinator node merges the data by selecting a value for each requested column. It compares the values returned from the replicas and returns the value that has the latest timestamp. If Cassandra finds different values stored with the same timestamp, it will compare the values lexicographically and choose the one that has the greater value. This case should be exceedingly rare. The merged data is the value that is returned to the client.

Asynchronously, the coordinator identifies any replicas that return obsolete data and issues a read-repair request to each of these replicas to update their data based on the merged data.

The read repair may be performed either before or after the return to the client. If you are using one of the two stronger consistency levels (QUORUM or ALL), then the read repair happens *before* data is returned to the client. If the client specifies a weak consistency level (such as ONE), then the read repair is optionally performed in the background after returning to the client. The percentage of reads that result in background repairs for a given table is determined by the read_repair_chance and dc_local_read_repair_chance options for the table.

Transient Replication

Companies with large Cassandra deployments have developed a technique called *transient replication* (*https://oreil.ly/9r-61*) to help manage infrastructure costs for very large clusters. The feature works by adding a new type of replica known as a transient replica that only stores data when regular or *full replicas* are unavailable. When the full replicas are available, the data is moved to them through incremental repair, whereupon it can be deleted from transient replicas. This results in less disk storage to achieve the same availability and consistency and also reduces CPU and I/O load on nodes in the cluster. From a client perspective, the fact that you have enabled transient replication should be transparent.

Transient replication is an experimental feature in the 4.0 release and is disabled by default. You enable it by setting the `enable_transient_replication` property in the *cassandra.yaml* file. Doing this enables you to configure the replication strategy for each keyspace to specify how many of the total number of replicas will be designated as transient replicas; for example:

```
CREATE KEYSPACE reservation WITH REPLICATION =
    {'class': 'SimpleStrategy', 'replication_factor' : '5/2'};
```

The 5/2 denotes the request for five total replicas, with three full replicas and two transient replicas. This is a common usage for a single data center using RF=3; changing the strategy to 5/2, that is, three full and two transient replicas, results in the ability to have two additional replicas without increasing the number of nodes.

You can configure transient replicas on the `NetworkTopologyStrategy` as well:

```
CREATE KEYSPACE reservation WITH REPLICATION =
    {'class' : 'NetworkTopologyStrategy', 'DC1' : '3/1', 'DC2' : '3/1'};
```

For a two data center configuration with RF=3 per data center, changing the strategy to 3/1 per data center means there will be a total of four full replicas, which is sufficient to achieve QUORUM consistency.

Because transient replication is configured by keyspace, you can have keyspaces using transient replication and keyspaces that do not use it in the same cluster.

To understand how Cassandra designates which replicas are full versus transient, you'll need to recall what you learned about Cassandra's ring topology in Chapter 6. Each node in the cluster is assigned a token, which represents a range of hashed partition key values that designate what partitions will be stored on that replica. Remember that as you increase the replication factor, the nodes that have the next higher tokens (clockwise around the ring) will become replicas for a given partition as well. When you enable transient replication, the nodes with the tokens farthest from the original token will be the transient replica, as shown in Figure 9-5. In this way, each node will be a full replica for some tokens and a transient replica for others.

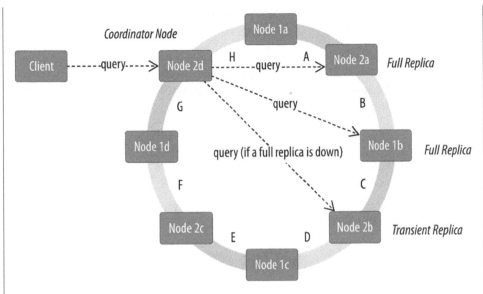

Figure 9-5. Transient replication and the ring

Let's see how this works on reads and writes. First, on a write, Cassandra attempts to write the data to each full replica. When full replicas are down, transient replicas will receive writes in order to achieve the requested consistency level. Transient replicas are just as eligible to count toward your desired consistency level as any other node; this is known as a *cheap quorum*. Later, when incremental repairs are run, full replicas that are back online will receive the data, and the transient replicas can discard their copies.

On reads, at least one full replica is required, but beyond that, any replicas, including full or transient, may be used to achieve the requested consistency level.

Because transient replication changes the nature of how Cassandra nodes interact, there are some challenges in reconciling its behavior with other features. For the 4.0 release, features including read repair, batches, lightweight transactions, and counters cannot be used within keyspaces that have transient replication set. Secondary indexes and materialized views are unlikely to ever be supported. Finally, remember that since transient replication is an experimental feature, it is not yet recommended for production use.

Range Queries, Ordering and Filtering

So far your read queries have been confined to very simple examples. Let's take a look at more of the options that Cassandra provides on the SELECT command, such as the WHERE and ORDER BY clauses.

First, let's examine how to use the WHERE clause that Cassandra provides for reading ranges of data within a partition, sometimes called *slices*.

In order to do a range query, however, it will help to have some data to work with. Although you don't have a lot of data yet, you can quickly get some by using cqlsh to load some sample reservation data into your cluster. We'll look at more advanced bulk loading options in Chapter 15.

You can access a simple *.csv* file in the GitHub repository for this book (*https:// github.com/jeffreyscarpenter/cassandra-guide*). The *reservations.csv* file contains a month's worth of inventory for two small hotels with five rooms each. Let's load the data into the cluster:

```
cqlsh:hotel> COPY available_rooms_by_hotel_date FROM
  'available_rooms.csv' WITH HEADER=true;

310 rows imported in 0.789 seconds.
```

If you do a quick query to read some of this data, you'll find that you have data for two hotels: "AZ123" and "NY229."

Now let's consider how to support the query labeled "Q4. Find an available room in a given date range" in Chapter 5. Remember that the available_rooms_by_hotel_date table was designed to support this query, with the primary key:

```
PRIMARY KEY (hotel_id, date, room_number)
```

This means that the hotel_id is the partition key, while date and room_number are clustering columns.

Here's a CQL statement that allows you to search for hotel rooms for a specific hotel and date range:

```
cqlsh:hotel> SELECT * FROM available_rooms_by_hotel_date
  WHERE hotel_id='AZ123' and date>'2016-01-05' and date<'2016-01-12';

 hotel_id | date       | room_number | is_available
----------+------------+-------------+--------------
    AZ123 | 2016-01-06 |         101 |         True
    AZ123 | 2016-01-06 |         102 |         True
    AZ123 | 2016-01-06 |         103 |         True
    AZ123 | 2016-01-06 |         104 |         True
    AZ123 | 2016-01-06 |         105 |         True
...
(30 rows)
```

Note that this query involves the partition key hotel_id and a range of values representing the start and end of your search over the clustering key date.

If you wanted to try to find the records for room number 101 at hotel AZ123, you might attempt a query like the following:

```
cqlsh:hotel> SELECT * FROM available_rooms_by_hotel_date
  WHERE hotel_id='AZ123' and room_number=101;
InvalidRequest: code=2200 [Invalid query] message="PRIMARY KEY column
  "room_number" cannot be restricted as preceding column "date" is not
  restricted"
```

As you can see, this query results in an error, because you have attempted to restrict the value of the second clustering key while not limiting the value of the first clustering key.

The syntax of the WHERE clause involves two rules. First, all elements of the partition key must be identified. Second, a given clustering key may only be restricted if all previous clustering keys are restricted by equality.

These restrictions are based on how Cassandra stores data on disk, which is based on the clustering columns and sort order specified on the CREATE TABLE command. The conditions on the clustering column are restricted to those that allow Cassandra to select a contiguous ordering of rows.

The exception to this rule is the ALLOW FILTERING keyword, which allows you to omit a partition key element. For example, you can search the room status across multiple hotels for rooms on a specific date with this query:

```
cqlsh:hotel> SELECT * FROM available_rooms_by_hotel_date
  WHERE date='2016-01-25' ALLOW FILTERING;

 hotel_id | date       | room_number | is_available
----------+------------+-------------+--------------
    AZ123 | 2016-01-25 |         101 |         True
    AZ123 | 2016-01-25 |         102 |         True
    AZ123 | 2016-01-25 |         103 |         True
    AZ123 | 2016-01-25 |         104 |         True
    AZ123 | 2016-01-25 |         105 |         True
    NY229 | 2016-01-25 |         101 |         True
    NY229 | 2016-01-25 |         102 |         True
    NY229 | 2016-01-25 |         103 |         True
    NY229 | 2016-01-25 |         104 |         True
    NY229 | 2016-01-25 |         105 |         True

(10 rows)
```

Usage of ALLOW FILTERING is not recommended, however, as it has the potential to result in very expensive queries. If you find yourself needing such a query, you will want to revisit your data model to make sure you have designed tables that support your queries.

The IN clause can be used to test equality with multiple possible values for a column. For example, you could use the following to find inventory on two dates a week apart with the command:

```
cqlsh:hotel> SELECT * FROM available_rooms_by_hotel_date
    WHERE hotel_id='AZ123' AND date IN ('2016-01-05', '2016-01-12');
```

Note that using the IN clause to specify multiple clustering column values can result in slower performance on queries, as the specified column values may correspond to noncontiguous areas within the row.

Similarly, if you use the IN clause to specify multiple partitions, that would cause the coordinator node to have to talk to a greater number of nodes to support your query. In such a case, you might consider kicking off separate requests for the different partitions in parallel threads in your application so that the driver can directly contact a replica as the coordinator for each query.

Finally, the SELECT command allows you to override the sort order that has been specified on the columns when you created the table. For example, you could obtain the rooms in descending order by date for any of your previous queries using the ORDER BY syntax:

```
cqlsh:hotel> SELECT * FROM available_rooms_by_hotel_date
    WHERE hotel_id='AZ123' and date>'2016-01-05' and date<'2016-01-12'
    ORDER BY date DESC;
```

More on the WHERE Clause

The DataStax blog post "A deep look at the CQL WHERE clause" (*https://oreil.ly/Y622e*) provides additional advice and examples on how to use the various options available on the WHERE clause.

Paging

In early releases of Cassandra, clients had to make sure to carefully limit the amount of data requested at a time. For a large result set, it is possible to overwhelm both nodes and clients even to the point of running out of memory.

Thankfully, Cassandra provides a paging mechanism that allows retrieval of result sets incrementally. A simple example of this is shown with the CQL keyword LIMIT. For example, the following command will return no more than 10 hotels:

```
cqlsh> SELECT * FROM reservation.reservations_by_hotel_date LIMIT 10;
```

Of course, the limitation of the LIMIT keyword (pun intended) is that there's no way to obtain additional pages containing the additional rows beyond the requested quantity.

The 2.0 release of Cassandra introduced a feature known as *automatic paging*. Automatic paging allows clients to request a subset of the data that would be returned by a query. The server breaks the result into pages that are returned as the client requests them.

You can view paging status in `cqlsh` via the `PAGING` command. The following output shows a sequence of checking paging status, changing the fetch size (page size), and disabling paging:

```
cqlsh> PAGING;
Query paging is currently enabled. Use PAGING OFF to disable
Page size: 100
cqlsh> PAGING 1000;
Page size: 1000
cqlsh> PAGING OFF;
Disabled Query paging.
cqlsh> PAGING ON;
Now Query paging is enabled
```

Now let's see how paging (*https://oreil.ly/zZ5NO*) works in the DataStax Java Driver. You can set a default fetch size globally for a `CqlSession` instance using the `basic.request.page-size` parameter, which defaults to 5000. The page size can also be set on an individual statement, overriding the default value:

```
Statement statement = SimpleStatement.builder("...").build();
statement.setPageSize(2000);
```

The page size is not necessarily exact; the driver might return slightly more or slightly fewer rows than requested. The driver handles automatic paging on your behalf, allowing you to iterate over a `ResultSet` without requiring knowledge of the paging mechanism. For example, consider the following code sample for iterating over a query for hotels:

```
SimpleStatement reservationsByHotelDateSelect = SimpleStatement.builder(
  "SELECT * FROM reservations_by_hotel_date").build();
ResultSet resultSet = cqlSession.execute(reservationsByHotelDateSelect);

for (Row row : resultSet) {
  // process the row
}
```

What happens behind the scenes is as follows: when your application invokes the `cqlSession.execute()` operation, the driver performs your query to Cassandra, requesting the first page of results. Your application iterates over the results, as shown in the `for` loop, and when the driver detects that there are no more items remaining on the current page, it requests the next page.

It is possible that the small pause of requesting the next page would affect the performance and user experience of your application, so the `ResultSet` provides additional operations that allow more fine-grained control over paging. Here's an example of how you could extend your application to do some pre-fetching of rows:

```
for (Row row : resultSet) {
  if (resultSet.getAvailableWithoutFetching() < 100 &&
      !resultSet.isFullyFetched())
```

```
        resultSet.fetchMoreResults();
    // process the row
    }
```

This additional statement checks to see if there are less than 100 rows remaining on the current page using `getAvailableWithoutFetching()`. If there is another page to be retrieved, which you determine by checking `isFullyFetched()`, you initiate an asynchronous call to obtain the extra rows via `fetchMoreResults()`.

The driver also exposes the ability to access the paging state more directly so it can be saved and reused later. This could be useful if your application is a stateless web service that doesn't sustain a session across multiple invocations.

You can access the paging state through the `ExecutionInfo` of the `ResultSet`, which provides the state as an opaque array of bytes contained in a `java.nio.ByteBuffer`:

```
    ByteBuffer nextPage = resultSet.getExecutionInfo().getPagingState();
```

You can then save this state within your application, or return it to clients. The paging state can be converted to a string using `toString()`, or a byte array using `array()`.

Note that in either string or byte array form, the state is not something you should try to manipulate or reuse with a different statement since it is not guaranteed to have the same format between different Cassandra versions. Doing so could result in an exception.

To resume a query from a given paging state, you set it on the `Statement`:

```
    SimpleStatement reservationsByHotelDateSelect = SimpleStatement.builder(
      "SELECT * FROM reservation.reservations_by_hotel_date").build();
    reservationsByHotelDateSelect.setPagingState(pagingState);
```

Deleting

Deleting data is not the same in Cassandra as it is in a relational database. In an RDBMS, you simply issue a delete statement that identifies the row or rows you want to delete. In Cassandra, a delete does not actually remove the data immediately. There's a simple reason for this: Cassandra's durable, eventually consistent, distributed design. If Cassandra had a traditional design for deletes, any nodes that were down at the time of a delete would not receive the delete. Once one of these nodes came back online, it would mistakenly think that all of the nodes that had received the delete had actually missed a write (the data that it still has because it missed the delete), and it would start repairing all of the other nodes. So Cassandra needs a more sophisticated mechanism to support deletes. That mechanism is called a *tombstone*.

A tombstone is a special marker issued in a delete, acting as a placeholder. If any replica did not receive the delete operation, the tombstone can later be propagated to those replicas when they are available again. The net effect of this design is that your data store will not immediately shrink in size following a delete. Each node keeps track of the age of all its tombstones. Once they reach the age configured in gc_grace_seconds (which is 10 days by default), then a compaction is run, the tombstones are garbage collected, and the corresponding disk space is recovered.

Because SSTables are immutable, the data is not deleted from the SSTable. On compaction, tombstones are accounted for, merged data is sorted, a new index is created over the sorted data, and the freshly merged, sorted, and indexed data is written to a single new file. The assumption is that 10 days is plenty of time for you to bring a failed node back online before compaction runs. If you feel comfortable doing so, you can reduce that grace period to reclaim disk space more quickly.

You've previously used the CQL DELETE command in Chapter 4. Here's what a simple delete of an entire row looks like using the DataStax Java Driver:

```
SimpleStatement reservationByConfirmationDelete = SimpleStatement.builder(
  "DELETE * FROM reservation.reservations_by_confirm
    WHERE confirm_number=?")
  .addPositionalValue("RS2G0Z")
  .build();

cqlSession.execute(reservationByConfirmationDelete);
```

You can also delete data using PreparedStatements, the QueryBuilder, and the Mapper. Here is an example of deleting an entire row using the QueryBuilder:

```
import static com.datastax.oss.driver.api.querybuilder.QueryBuilder.*;

SimpleStatement reservationByConfirmationDelete = deleteFrom("reservations",
    "reservations_by_confirmation")
  .whereColumn("confirm_number").isEqualTo("RS2G0Z")
  .build();

cqlSession.execute(reservationByConfirmationDelete);
```

Because a delete is a form of write, the consistency levels available for deletes are the same as those listed for writes.

Cassandra allows you to delete data at multiple levels of granularity. You can:

- Delete items from a collection (set, list, or map), as you learned in Chapter 4
- Delete nonprimary key columns by identifying them by name in your DELETE query
- Delete entire rows as shown earlier
- Delete ranges of rows using the same WHERE clauses as with the SELECT command
- Delete an entire partition

Because of how Cassandra tracks deletions, each of these operations will result in a single tombstone. The more data you are able to delete in a single command, the fewer tombstones you will have. If your application generates a large number of tombstones, Cassandra's read performance can begin to be impacted by having to traverse over these tombstones as it reads SSTable files. You'll learn in Chapter 11 how to detect this issue, but it's also wise to try to avoid it to begin with.

Here are a few techniques to help minimize the impact of tombstones on your cluster:

- Avoid writing NULL values into your tables, as these are interpreted as deletes. This can happen in cases where an unset attribute on a user interface or API is interpreted as a NULL value as it moves down through your application stack. While this is relatively simple to police in your own application code, mapping frameworks such as Spring Data Cassandra or the DataStax Java Driver's Mapper can tend to abstract this behavior, which can lead to the generation of many tombstones without your knowledge. Make sure you investigate and properly configure the null-handling behavior you expect when using frameworks that abstract CQL queries.

- Delete data at the largest granularity you can, ideally entire partitions at once. This will minimize the number of tombstones you create. Alain Rodriguez's blog post "About Tombstones and Deletes in Cassandra" (*https://oreil.ly/TCLFM*) explains this strategy in more depth.

- Exercise care when updating collections. If possible, avoid replacing the entire contents of a list, set, or map, as this will generate tombstones for all of the previous content. Instead, update only the elements you need to modify.

- Use Cassandra's time-to-live (TTL) feature when inserting data, which allows Cassandra to expire data automatically on your behalf.

- For tables that implement a time-series pattern, consider using the TimeWindow CompactionStrategy, which allows Cassandra to drop entire SSTable files at once. We'll discuss this strategy further in Chapter 13.

Summary

In this chapter, you saw how to read, write, and delete data using both cqlsh and client drivers. You also took a peek behind the scenes to learn how Cassandra implements these operations, which should help you to make more informed decisions as you design, implement, deploy, and maintain applications using Cassandra.

Configuring and Deploying Cassandra

In this chapter, you'll build your first cluster and look at the available options for configuring Cassandra nodes, including aspects of Cassandra that affect node behavior in a cluster, such as partitioning, snitches, and replication. We will also share a few pieces of advice as you work toward deploying Cassandra in production. We'll discuss options to consider in planning deployments and deploying Cassandra in various cloud environments.

Cassandra Cluster Manager

Out of the box, Cassandra works with no configuration at all; you can simply download, decompress, and execute the program to start the server with its default configuration. However, one of the things that makes Cassandra such a powerful technology is its emphasis on configurability and customization. At the same time, the number of options may seem confusing at first.

In order to get practice in building and configuring a cluster, let's take advantage of a tool called the Cassandra Cluster Manager or ccm. Built by Sylvain Lebresne and several other contributors, this tool is a set of Python scripts that allow you to run a multinode cluster on a single machine. This allows you to quickly configure a cluster without having to provision additional hardware. It's also a great way to introduce some of the most commonly configured options, as discussed in the Cassandra documentation (*https://oreil.ly/KOLvb*).

Creating Cassandra Clusters for Testing

It's often convenient when developing applications with Cassandra to use real clusters for unit and integration testing. Docker and ccm are both great options for creating small test clusters that you can quickly build and tear down for use in your tests.

A quick way to get started with ccm is to use the Python installer *pip* in a terminal window:

```
$ pip install ccm
```

Alternatively, a Homebrew package is available for macOS users: brew install ccm.

Once you've installed ccm, it should be on the system path. To get a list of supported commands, you can type ccm or ccm -help. If you need more information on the options for a specific cluster command, type ccm <command> -h. You'll use several of these commands in the following sections as you create and configure a cluster. You can also invoke the scripts directly from automated test suites.

The source is available in this GitHub repository (*https://github.com/riptano/ccm*). You can dig into the Python script files to learn more about what ccm is doing.

Creating a Cluster

The *cassandra.yaml* file is the primary configuration file for a Cassandra node, and where you specify the configuration values that define a cluster. You can find this file in the *conf* directory under your Cassandra installation.

The key values in configuring a cluster are the cluster name, the partitioner, the snitch, and the seed nodes. The cluster name, partitioner, and snitch must be the same in all of the nodes participating in the cluster. The seed nodes are not strictly required to be exactly the same for every node across the cluster, but it is a good idea to have a common set of seeds per data center; we'll discuss configuration best practices momentarily.

Cassandra clusters are given names to prevent machines in one cluster from joining another cluster that you don't want them to be a part of. The name of the default cluster in the *cassandra.yaml* file is Test Cluster. You can change the name of the cluster by updating the cluster_name property—just make sure that you have done this on all nodes that you want to participate in this cluster.

Changing the Cluster Name

If you have written data to an existing Cassandra cluster and then change the cluster name, Cassandra will warn you with a cluster name mismatch error as it tries to read the datafiles on startup, and then it will shut down.

Let's try creating a cluster using ccm for use with the Reservation Service we've discussed in previous chapters (some of the output has been reduced for brevity):

```
$ ccm create -v 4.0.0 -n 3 reservation_cluster --vnodes
  ...
Current cluster is now: reservation_cluster
```

This command creates a cluster based on the version of Cassandra you select—in this case, 4.0.0. The cluster is named my_cluster and has three nodes. You must specify explicitly when you want to use virtual nodes, because ccm defaults to creating single-token nodes. ccm designates your cluster as the current cluster that will be used for subsequent commands. You'll notice that it downloads the source for the version requested to run and compiles it. This is because it needs to make minor modifications to the Cassandra source in order to support running multiple nodes on a single machine. You could also have used the copy of the source downloaded in Chapter 3. If you'd like to investigate additional options for creating a cluster, run the command ccm create -h.

Running ccm on macOS

ccm uses loopback addresses for each node in a cluster according to the pattern 127.0.0.1, 127.0.0.2, and so on. If you're using ccm to create clusters on macOS, you'll need to manually create loopback addresses 127.0.0.2 and greater. See the ccm README (*https://github.com/riptano/ccm*) if you need instructions for creating these addresses.

Once you've created the cluster, you'll see it is the only cluster in your list of clusters (and marked as the currently selected cluster with an asterisk), and you can learn about its status:

```
$ ccm list
 *reservation_cluster

$ ccm status
Cluster: 'reservation_cluster'
--------------------
node1: DOWN (Not initialized)
node3: DOWN (Not initialized)
node2: DOWN (Not initialized)
```

At this point, none of the nodes have been initialized. Start your cluster and then check the status again:

```
$ ccm start

$ ccm status
Cluster: 'reservation_cluster'
--------------------
node1: UP
node3: UP
node2: UP
```

This is the equivalent of starting each individual node using the *bin/cassandra* script. To dig deeper on the status of an individual node, enter the following command:

```
$ ccm node1 status

Datacenter: datacenter1
========================
Status=Up/Down
|/ State=Normal/Leaving/Joining/Moving
--  Address    Load        Tokens  Owns (effective)  Host ID        Rack
UN  127.0.0.1  115.13 KiB  256     67.5%             9019859a-...   rack1
UN  127.0.0.2  115.14 KiB  256     63.3%             5650bfa0-...   rack1
UN  127.0.0.3  115.13 KiB  256     69.2%             158a78c2-...   rack1
```

This is equivalent to running the command `nodetool status` on the individual node. The output shows that all of the nodes are up and reporting normal status (UN means "up normal"). Each of the nodes has 256 tokens and a very small amount of metadata, since you haven't inserted any data yet. (We've shortened the `Host ID` somewhat for brevity.)

You run the `nodetool ring` command in order to get a list of the tokens owned by each node. To do this in ccm, enter the command:

```
$ ccm node1 ring

Datacenter: datacenter1
==========
Address     Rack     Status State    ...  Token
                                           9171899284504323785
127.0.0.1   rack1    Up     Normal   ...  -9181802192617819638
127.0.0.2   rack1    Up     Normal   ...  -9119747148344833344
127.0.0.2   rack1    Up     Normal   ...  -9114111430148268761
127.0.0.3   rack1    Up     Normal   ...  -9093245859094984745
127.0.0.2   rack1    Up     Normal   ...  -9093095684198819851
```

The command requires us to specify a node. This doesn't affect the output; it just indicates what node `nodetool` is connecting to in order to get the ring information. As you can see, the tokens are allocated randomly across the three nodes. (As before, we've abbreviated the output and omitted the `Owns` and `Load` columns for brevity.)

A Closer Look at Cluster Configuration

It's quite interesting to take a look under the hood to see what configuration changes ccm makes in order to get a cluster running on your local machine. By default, ccm stores metadata and configuration files for your clusters in a directory under your home directory called *.ccm*; it also uses this directory to store the source files for versions of Cassandra you have run. Take a look in this directory to see what you can find there:

```
$ cd ~/.ccm; ls
CURRENT            reservation_cluster repository
```

The *repository* directory contains the source that ccm downloaded. Diving deeper into the *my_cluster* directory, you'll see a directory for each node:

```
$ cd reservation_cluster; ls
cluster.conf      node1      node2      node3
```

The *cluster.conf* file contains a list of options selected when creating the cluster. To see the configuration options that are different between nodes, try using the diff command to compare the contents of the directories. For example:

```
$ diff node1/conf/ node2/conf/
```

The output highlights the differences in the configuration files, including the directories used for storage of data, commit logs, and output logs, the addresses used for network communications, and the JMX port exposed for remote management. We'll examine these settings in more detail throughout the rest of the chapter.

Adding Nodes to a Cluster

Now that you understand what goes into configuring each node of a Cassandra cluster, you're ready to learn how to add nodes. As we've already discussed, to add a new node manually, you need to configure the *cassandra.yaml* file for the new node to set the seed nodes, partitioner, snitch, and network ports. If you've elected to create single-token nodes, you'll also need to calculate the token range for the new node and make adjustments to the ranges of other nodes.

If you're using ccm, the process of adding a new node is quite simple. Run the following command:

```
$ ccm add node4 -i 127.0.0.4 -j 7400
```

This creates a new node, node4, with another loopback address and JMX port set to 7400. To see additional options for this command, you can type ccm add -h. Now that you've added a node, check the status of your cluster:

```
$ ccm status
Cluster: 'reservation_cluster'
--------------------
node1: UP
node3: UP
node2: UP
node4: DOWN (Not initialized)
```

The new node has been added but has not been started yet. If you run the nodetool ring command again, you'll see that no changes have been made to the tokens. Now you're ready to start the new node by typing ccm node4 start (after double-checking that the additional loopback address is enabled). If you run the `nodetool ring` command once more, you'll see output similar to the following:

```
Datacenter: datacenter1
==========
Address     Rack      Status  State   ...  Token
                                           9218701579919475223
127.0.0.1   rack1     Up      Normal  ...  -9211073930147845649
127.0.0.4   rack1     Up      Normal  ...  -9190530381068170163
...
```

If you compare this with the previous output, you'll notice a couple of things. First, the tokens have been reallocated across all of the nodes, including the new node. Second, the token values have changed, representing smaller ranges. In order to give your new node its 256 tokens (`num_tokens`), there are now 1,024 total tokens in the cluster.

You can observe what it looks like to other nodes when `node4` starts up by examining the log file. On a standalone node, you might look at the *system.log* file in */var/log/cassandra* (or *$CASSANDRA_HOME/logs*), depending on your configuration. `ccm` provides a handy command to examine the log files from any node. Look at the log for `node1` using the `ccm node1 showlog` command. This brings up a view similar to the standard Unix `more` command that allows you to page through or search the log file contents. Searching for gossip-related statements in the log file near the end (for example, by typing `/127.0.0.4`), you'll find something like this:

```
INFO  [GossipStage:1] 2019-11-27 15:40:51,176 Gossiper.java:1222 -
   Node 127.0.0.4:7000 is now part of the cluster
INFO  [GossipStage:1] 2019-11-27 15:40:51,203 TokenMetadata.java:490 -
   Updating topology for 127.0.0.4:7000
INFO  [GossipStage:1] 2019-11-27 15:40:51,206 StorageService.java:2524 -
   Node 127.0.0.4:7000 state jump to NORMAL
INFO  [GossipStage:1] 2019-11-27 15:40:51,213 Gossiper.java:1180 -
   InetAddress 127.0.0.4:7000 is now UP
```

These statements show `node1` successfully gossiping with `node4`, and that `node4` is considered up and part of the cluster. At this point, the bootstrapping process begins to allocate tokens to `node4` and stream any data associated with those tokens to `node4`.

Dynamic Ring Participation

Nodes in a Cassandra cluster can be brought down and back up without disrupting the rest of the cluster (assuming a reasonable replication factor and consistency level). Say that you've started a two-node cluster, as described in "Creating a Cluster" on page 214. You can cause an error to occur that will take down one of the nodes, and then make sure that the rest of the cluster is still OK.

You can simulate this situation by taking one of the nodes down using the `ccm stop` command. You can run the `ccm status` command to verify the node is down, and then check a log file as you did earlier via the `ccm showlog` command. If you stop node4 and examine the log file for another node, you'll see something like the following:

```
INFO  [GossipStage:1] 2019-11-27 15:44:09,564 Gossiper.java:1198 -
    InetAddress 127.0.0.4:7000 is now DOWN
```

Now bring node4 back up and recheck the logs at another node. Sure enough, Cassandra has automatically detected that the other participant has returned to the cluster and is again open for business:

```
INFO  [GossipStage:1] 2019-11-27 15:45:34,579 Gossiper.java:1220 -
    Node 127.0.0.4:7000 has restarted, now UP
```

The state jump to normal for node4 indicates that it's part of the cluster again. As a final check, run the `status` command again:

```
$ ccm status
Cluster: 'reservation_cluster'
--------------------
node1: UP
node2: UP
node3: UP
node4: UP
```

As you see, the node is back up.

Node Configuration

There are many other properties that can be set in the *cassandra.yaml* file. We'll look at a few highlights related to cluster formation, networking, and disk usage in this chapter, and save some of the others for treatment in Chapter 13 and Chapter 14.

A Guided Tour of the cassandra.yaml File

The Cassandra documentation provides a helpful guide (*https:// oreil.ly/t1y3Q*) to configuring the various settings in the *cassandra.yaml* file.

Seed Nodes

A new node in a cluster needs what's called a *seed node*. A seed node is used as a contact point for other nodes, so Cassandra can learn the topology of the cluster—that is, what hosts have what ranges. For example, if node A acts as a seed for node B, when node B comes online, it will use node A as a reference point from which to get data. This process is known as *bootstrapping*, or sometimes *auto-bootstrapping* because it is an operation that Cassandra performs automatically. Seed nodes do not auto-bootstrap because it is assumed that they will be the first nodes in the cluster.

By default, the *cassandra.yaml* file will have only a single `seed` entry set to the local host:

```
- seeds: "127.0.0.1"
```

To add more seed nodes to a cluster, just add another seed element. You can set multiple servers to be seeds just by indicating the IP address or hostname of the node. For an example, if you look in the *cassandra.yaml* file for node3, you'll find the following:

```
- seeds: 127.0.0.1, 127.0.0.2, 127.0.0.3
```

In a production cluster, these would be the IP addresses of other hosts rather than loopback addresses. To ensure high availability of Cassandra's bootstrapping process, it is considered a best practice to have at least two seed nodes in each data center. This increases the likelihood of having at least one seed node available should one of the local seed nodes go down during a network partition between data centers.

As you may have noticed if you looked in the *cassandra.yaml* file, the list of seeds is actually part of a larger definition of the seed provider. The `org.apache.cassandra.locator.SeedProvider` interface specifies the contract that must be implemented. Cassandra provides the `SimpleSeedProvider` as the default implementation, which loads the IP addresses of the seed nodes from the *cassandra.yaml* file. If you use a service registry as part of your infrastructure, you could register seed nodes in the registry and write a custom provider to consult that registry. This is an approach commonly used in Kubernetes operators, as we'll discuss in "Cassandra Kubernetes Operators" on page 299.

Snitches

Snitches gather some information about your network topology so that Cassandra can efficiently route requests. The snitch will figure out where nodes are in relation to other nodes. You configure the endpoint snitch implementation to use by updating the `endpoint_snitch` property in the *cassandra.yaml* file.

Changing the Snitch

You can configure any snitch you prefer on a new cluster, but once you've inserted data into a cluster, changing the snitch may involve some additional steps, as described in the DataStax documentation (*https://oreil.ly/0CGoC*).

SimpleSnitch

By default, Cassandra uses org.apache.cassandra.locator.SimpleSnitch. This snitch is not rack aware (a term we'll explain in just a minute), which makes it unsuitable for multiple data center deployments. If you choose to use this snitch, you should also use the SimpleStrategy replication strategy for your keyspaces.

PropertyFileSnitch

The org.apache.cassandra.locator.PropertyFileSnitch is a *rack-aware* snitch, meaning that it uses information that you provide about the topology of your cluster as key-value properties in the *cassandra-topology.properties* configuration file. Here's an example configuration:

```
# Cassandra Node IP=Data Center:Rack
175.56.12.105=DC1:RAC1
175.50.13.200=DC1:RAC1
175.54.35.197=DC1:RAC1

120.53.24.101=DC1:RAC2
120.55.16.200=DC1:RAC2
120.57.102.103=DC1:RAC2

# default for unknown nodes
default=DC1:RAC1
```

Notice that there there is a single data center (DC1) with two racks (RAC1 and RAC2). Any nodes that aren't identified here will be assumed to be in the default data center and rack (DC1, RAC1). These are the same rack and data center names that you will use in configuring the NetworkTopologyStrategy settings per data center for your keyspace replication strategies.

Update the values in this file to record each node in your cluster to specify the IP address of each node in your cluster and its location by data center and rack. The manual configuration required in using the PropertyFileSnitch trades away a little flexibility and ease of maintenance in order to give you more control and better runtime performance, as Cassandra doesn't have to figure out where nodes are. Instead, you just tell it where they are.

GossipingPropertyFileSnitch

The org.apache.cassandra.locator.GossipingPropertyFileSnitch is another rack-aware snitch. The data exchanges information about its own rack and data center location with other nodes via gossip. The rack and data center locations are defined in the *cassandra-rackdc.properties* file. The GossipingPropertyFileSnitch also uses the *cassandra-topology.properties* file, if present. This is simpler to configure since you only have to configure the data center and rack on each node; for example:

```
dc=DC1
rack=RAC1
```

The `GossipingPropertyFileSnitch` is the most commonly used snitch for multiple data center clusters in private clouds, as well as multicloud clusters.

RackInferringSnitch

The `org.apache.cassandra.locator.RackInferringSnitch` assumes that nodes in the cluster are laid out in a consistent network scheme. It operates by simply comparing different octets in the IP addresses of each node. If two hosts have the same value in the second octet of their IP addresses, then they are determined to be in the same data center. If two hosts have the same value in the third octet of their IP addresses, then they are determined to be in the same rack. This means that Cassandra has to guess based on an assumption of how your servers are located in different VLANs or subnets.

DynamicEndpointSnitch

As discussed in Chapter 6, Cassandra wraps your selected snitch with `org.apache.cassandra.locator.DynamicEndpointSnitch` to select the highest performing nodes for queries. The `dynamic_snitch_badness_threshold` property defines a threshold for changing the preferred node. The default value of 0.1 means that the preferred node must perform 10% worse than the fastest node in order to lose its status. The dynamic snitch updates this status according to the `dynamic_snitch_update_interval_in_ms` property, and resets its calculations at the duration specified by the `dynamic_snitch_reset_interval_in_ms` property. The reset interval should be a much longer interval than the update interval because it is a more expensive operation, but it does allow a node to regain its preferred status without having to demonstrate performance superior to the badness threshold.

Cassandra also comes with several snitches designed for use in cloud deployments, such as `Ec2Snitch`, `Ec2MultiRegionSnitch` for deployments in Amazon Web Services (AWS), `GoogleCloudSnitch` for Google Cloud Platform (GCP), and `AlibabaS nitch` for Alibaba Cloud. The `CloudstackSnitch` is designed for use in public or private cloud deployments based on the Apache Cloudstack project. We'll discuss several of these snitches in "Cloud Deployment" on page 236.

Partitioners

Now we'll get into some of the configuration options that are changed less frequently, starting with the partitioner. You can't change the partitioner once you've inserted data into a cluster, so take care before deviating from the default!

The purpose of the partitioner is to allow you to specify how partition keys are mapped to token values, which determines how data will be distributed across your nodes. You set the partitioner by updating the value of the partitioner property in the *cassandra.yaml* file.

Changing the Partitioner

While it is possible to change the partitioner on an existing cluster, it's a complex procedure, and the recommended approach is to migrate data to a new cluster with your preferred partitioner using techniques we discuss in Chapter 15.

Murmur3Partitioner

The default partitioner is org.apache.cassandra.dht.Murmur3Partitioner, which uses the murmur hash algorithm to generate tokens. This has the advantage of spreading partition keys evenly across your cluster, because the distribution is random. However, it does inefficient range queries, because keys within a specified range might be placed in a variety of disparate locations in the ring, and key range queries will return data in an essentially random order.

New clusters should always use the Murmur3Partitioner. However, Cassandra provides the additional partitioners listed below for backward compatibility.

RandomPartitioner

The org.apache.cassandra.dht.RandomPartitioner was Cassandra's default in Cassandra 1.1 and earlier. It uses a BigIntegerToken with an MD5 cryptographic hash applied to it to determine where to place the keys on the node ring. Although the RandomPartitioner and Murmur3Partitioner are both based on random hash functions, the cryptographic hash used by RandomPartitioner is considerably slower, which is why the Murmur3Partitioner replaced it as the default.

OrderPreservingPartitioner

The org.apache.cassandra.dht.OrderPreservingPartitioner represents tokens as UTF-8 strings calculated from the partition key. Rows are therefore stored by key order, aligning the physical structure of the data with your sort order. Configuring your column family to use order-preserving partitioning (OPP) allows you to perform range slices.

Because of the ordering aspect, users are sometimes attracted to the OrderPreservingPartitioner. However, it isn't actually more efficient for range queries than random partitioning. More importantly, it has the potential to create an unbalanced cluster with some nodes having more data. These *hotspots* create an additional operational burden—you'll need to manually rebalance nodes using the nodetool move operation.

`ByteOrderedPartitioner`

The `ByteOrderedPartitioner` is an additional order-preserving partitioner that treats the data as raw bytes, instead of converting them to strings the way the order-preserving partitioner and collating order-preserving partitioner do. The `ByteOrderedPartitioner` represents a performance improvement over the `OrderPreservingPartitioner`.

Avoiding Partition Hotspots

Although `Murmur3Partitioner` selects tokens randomly, it can still be susceptible to hotspots; however, the problem is significantly reduced compared to the order-preserving partitioners. In order to minimize hotspots, additional knowledge of the topology is required. An improvement to token selection was added in 3.0 to improve the allocation of vnodes. Configuring the `allo cate_tokens_for_local_replication_factor` property in *cassandra.yaml* with a replication factor for the local data center instructs the partitioner to optimize token selection based on the specified number of replicas. This value may vary according to the replication factor assigned to the data center for each keyspace, but is most often 3. This option is only available for the `Murmur3Parti tioner`.

Tokens and Virtual Nodes

By default, Cassandra is configured to use virtual nodes (vnodes). The number of tokens that a given node will service is set by the `num_tokens` property. Generally this should be left at the default value, but may be increased to allocate more tokens to more capable machines, or decreased to allocate fewer tokens to less capable machines.

How Many vnodes?

Many experienced Cassandra operators have recommended that the default `num_tokens` be changed from the historic default of 256 to a lower value such as 16 or even 8. They argue that having fewer tokens per node provides adequate balance between token ranges, while requiring significantly less bandwidth to coordinate changes. The Jira request CASSANDRA-13701 (*https://oreil.ly/-PPRi*) represents a potential change to this default in a future release.

To disable vnodes and configure the more traditional token ranges, you'll first need to set `num_tokens` to 1, or you may also comment out the property entirely. Then you'll need to calculate tokens for each node in the cluster and configure the `initial_token` property on each node to indicate the range of tokens that it will own. There is a handy calculator available at Geroba.com (*https://oreil.ly/qhNL4*) that you can use to calculate ranges based on the number of nodes in your cluster and the partitioner in use.

In general, we recommend using vnodes, due to the effort required to recalculate token assignments and manually reconfigure the tokens to rebalance the cluster when adding or deleting single-token nodes.

Network Interfaces

There are several properties in the *cassandra.yaml* file that relate to the networking of the node. Cassandra uses separate ports and protocols for internode and client-to-node communications. Let's look at the internode settings first:

`listen_address`

The `listen_address` controls which IP address Cassandra listens on for incoming connections from other nodes. You can see how this is configured in your ccm cluster, as follows:

```
$ cd ~/.ccm
$ find . -name cassandra.yaml -exec grep -H 'listen_address' {} \;
./node1/conf/cassandra.yaml:listen_address: 127.0.0.1
./node2/conf/cassandra.yaml:listen_address: 127.0.0.2
./node3/conf/cassandra.yaml:listen_address: 127.0.0.3
```

If you'd prefer to bind via an interface name, you can use the `listen_interface` property instead of `listen_address`. For example, `listen_interface=eth0`. You may not set both of these properties. If you leave this property undefined, Cassandra will assign an address based on the Java method `InetAddress.getLocal Host()`. See the instructions in the *cassandra.yaml* file for more details.

`broadcast_address`

The `broadcast_address` is the IP address advertised to other nodes. If not set, it defaults to the `listen_address`. This is typically overridden in multiple data center configurations where there is a need to communicate within a data center using private IP addresses, but across data centers using public IP addresses. Set the `listen_on_broadcast_address` property to `true` to enable the node to communicate on both interfaces.

`storage_port`

The `storage_port` property designates the port used for internode communications, typically 7000. If you will be using Cassandra in a network environment that traverses public networks, or multiple regions in a cloud deployment, you should configure the `ssl_storage_port` (typically 7001). Configuring the secure port also requires configuring internode encryption options, which we'll discuss in Chapter 14.

Now let's consider the client-to-node settings. The term *native transport* refers to the transport that clients use to communicate with Cassandra nodes via CQL:

rpc_address

> The rpc_address is the IP address to which the native transport is bound. If not set, Cassandra assigns a default using the same approach used for the default lis ten_address. Alternatively, you may set the rpc_interface property to bind to a named interface.

broadcast_rpc_address

> The broadcast_rpc_address is the IP address advertised to clients for the native transport. If not set, it defaults to the rpc_address.

native_transport_port

> The native transport defaults to port 9042, as specified by the native_trans port_port property.

> The rpc_keepalive property defaults to true, which means that Cassandra will allow clients to hold connections open across multiple requests. Other properties are available to limit the threads, connections, and frame size, which we'll examine in Chapter 13.

Deprecation of Thrift RPC Properties

Historically, Cassandra supported two different client interfaces: the original Thrift API, also known as the Remote Procedure Call (RPC) interface, and the CQL native transport first added in 0.8. For releases through 2.2, both interfaces were supported and enabled by default. Starting with the 3.0 release, Thrift was disabled by default and has been removed entirely as of the 4.0 release. If you're using an earlier version of Cassandra, know that properties prefixed with rpc generally refer to the Thrift interface, but to sim-plify upgrading from older versions, properties such as rpc_address, rpc_interface, and broadcast_rpc_address now apply to the native transport.

Data Storage

Cassandra allows you to configure how and where its various datafiles are stored on disk, including datafiles, commit logs, hints, and saved caches. The default is the *data* directory under your Cassandra installation (*$CASSANDRA_HOME/data* or *%CASSANDRA_HOME%/data*).

You'll remember from Chapter 6 that the *commit log* is used as short-term storage for incoming writes. As Cassandra receives updates, every write value is written immediately to the commit log in the form of raw sequential file appends. If you shut down the database or it crashes unexpectedly, the commit log can ensure that data is not lost. That's because the next time you start the node, the commit log gets replayed. In fact, that's the only time the commit log is read; clients never read from it. Commit logs are stored in the location specified by the `commitlog_directory` property.

The *datafile* represents the Sorted String Tables (SSTables). Unlike the commit log, data is written to this file asynchronously. The SSTables are periodically merged during major compactions to free up space. To do this, Cassandra will merge keys, combine columns, and delete expired tombstones.

Datafiles are stored in the location specified by the `data_file_directories` property. You can specify multiple values if you wish, and Cassandra will spread the datafiles evenly across them. This is how Cassandra supports a "just a bunch of disks" (JBOD) deployment, where each directory represents a different disk mount point. You can read about the pros and cons of JBOD configuration in Anthony Grasso's blog post (*https://oreil.ly/Z-xIE*).

Other configuration options are available to override the locations of saved key and row caches, and change data capture logs, which are discussed in Chapter 9 and Chapter 15, respectively.

Storage File Locations on Windows

You don't need to update the default storage file locations for Windows, because Windows will automatically adjust the path separator and place them under *C:*. Of course, in a real environment, it's a good idea to specify them separately, as indicated.

For testing, you might not see a need to change these locations. However, in production environments using spinning disks, it's recommended that you store the datafiles and the commit logs on separate disks for maximum performance and availability.

Cassandra is robust enough to handle loss of one or more disks without an entire node going down, but gives you several options to specify the desired behavior of nodes on disk failure. The behavior on disk failure impacting datafiles is specified by the `disk_failure_policy` property, while failure response for commit logs is specified by `commit_failure_policy`. The default behavior `stop` is to disable client interfaces while remaining alive for inspection via JMX. Other options include `die`, which stops the node entirely (JVM exit), and `ignore`, which means that filesystem errors are logged and ignored. Use of `ignore` is not recommended. The `best_effort` option is available for datafiles, allowing operations on SSTables stored on disks that are still available.

Startup and JVM Settings

So far, this chapter has focused on settings in the *cassandra.yaml* file, but there are other configuration files you should examine as well. Cassandra's startup scripts embody a lot of hard-won logic to optimize configuration of the various options for your chosen JVM (recall the note on "Required Java Version" from Chapter 3).

The key file to look at is *conf/jvm.options*. This file contains settings to configure the JVM version (if multiple versions are available on your system), heap size, and other JVM options. Most of these options you'll rarely need to change from their default settings, with the possible exception of the JMX settings. The environment script allows you to set the JMX port and configure security settings for remote JMX access. We'll examine these settings in more detail in Chapter 13.

Cassandra's logging configuration is found in the *conf/logback.xml* file. This file includes settings such as the log level, message formatting, and log file settings, including locations, maximum sizes, and rotation. Cassandra uses the Logback logging framework, which you can learn more about at *http://logback.qos.ch*. The logging implementation was changed from Log4j to Logback in the 2.1 release.

We'll examine logging and JMX configuration in more detail in Chapter 11, and JVM memory configuration in Chapter 13.

Creating a Cluster in Docker

We discussed how to create a single Cassandra node in a Docker container in Chapter 3. It's also simple to create a small cluster on your local machine from multiple Docker containers. Let's say you want to create a cluster that runs on its own network but exposes the standard CQL port for application access. First, you'll need to create a Docker network, which could be as simple as:

```
$ docker network create my-network
```

Then you can create Cassandra nodes attached to that network, using the CASSAN DRA_SEEDS environment variable to specify a seed node for nodes after the first:

```
$ docker run --name node1 --network my-network -p 9042:9042 -d cassandra
$ docker run --name node2 -d --network my-network -p 9042:9042 -d
    -e CASSANDRA_SEEDS=node1 cassandra
$ docker run --name node3 -d --network my-network -p 9042:9042 -d
    -e CASSANDRA_SEEDS=node1,node2 cassandra
...
```

There are additional environment variables you can use to override configuration settings, including the listen and broadcast addresses, the cluster name, the number of vnodes (num_tokens), and the snitch. If you set CASSANDRA_ENDPOINT_SNITCH=Gossi pingPropertyFileSnitch, you may also set the data center and rack via the environment variables CASSANDRA_DC and CASSANDRA_RACK, respectively.

Alternatively, you could override the entire *cassandra.yaml* file with a file on your host:

```
$ docker run <other options> cassandra
    -Dcassandra.config=/path/to/cassandra.yaml
```

When running Cassandra in Docker, you'll want to remember that storage for Docker containers is ephemeral by default. If you delete a container, its data will be lost as well. If you desire to maintain your data beyond the container life cycle, you can mount a directory on your host as the Cassandra data directory in the image:

```
$ docker run <other options> -v /path/to/datadir:/var/lib/cassandra cassandra
```

You can find additional options for running the Cassandra Docker image on Docker Hub (*https://oreil.ly/XCYfa*).

Planning a Cluster Deployment

Now that you've learned some of the basics of configuring nodes and forming a small cluster, let's move toward configuring more complex deployments.

A successful deployment of Cassandra starts with good planning. You'll want to consider the topology of the cluster in data centers and racks, the amount of data that the cluster will hold, the network environment in which the cluster will be deployed, and the computing resources (whether physical or virtual) on which the instances will run. This section will consider each of these factors in turn.

Cluster Topology and Replication Strategies

The first thing to consider is the topology of the cluster. This includes factors such as how many data centers the cluster will span, and the location and ownership of these clusters. Many Cassandra deployments span multiple data centers in order to maximize data locality, comply with data protection regulations such as the European Union's General Data Protection Regulation (GDPR), or isolate workloads. Some of the common variations include:

- Clusters that span one or more private data centers.
- Clusters that span one or more data centers in a public cloud provider, such as Amazon Web Services, Google Cloud Platform, Microsoft Azure, Alibaba Cloud, and others.
- *Hybrid cloud* clusters that span both public cloud and private data centers. These are commonly used for deployments that run core workloads on private infrastructure but use public clouds to add capacity during seasons of peak usage.
- *Multicloud* or *intercloud* clusters that span multiple public cloud providers. These deployments are frequently used to locate data close to customers in geographic

areas unique to a particular cloud provider region, or close to services that are provided by a specific public cloud.

In addition to these options, it's a common practice to use additional data centers in a Cassandra cluster that are separated logically (if not physically) in order to isolate particular workloads, such as analytic or search integrations. You'll see some of these configurations in Chapter 15.

The cluster topology dictates how you configure the replication strategy for the keyspaces the cluster will contain. The choice of replication strategy determines which nodes are responsible for which key ranges. The first replica will always be the node that claims the range in which the token falls, but the remainder of the replicas are placed according to your replication strategy and cluster topology. Let's examine the implication of the two commonly used replication strategies you learned in Chapter 6, the SimpleStrategy and NetworkTopologyStrategy.

First, the SimpleStrategy is designed to place replicas in a single data center, in a manner that is not aware of their placement on a data center rack. This is shown in Figure 10-1.

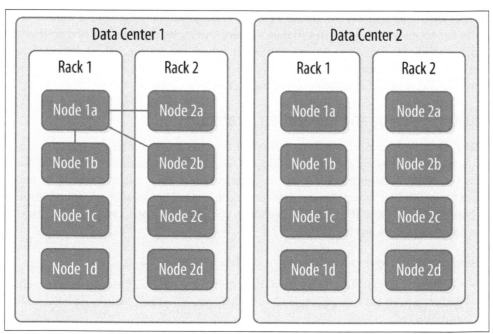

Figure 10-1. *The* SimpleStrategy *places replicas in a single data center, without respect to topology*

What's happening here is that the next N nodes on the ring are chosen to hold replicas, and the strategy has no notion of data centers. A second data center is shown in the diagram to highlight the fact that the strategy is unaware of it.

Now let's say you want to spread replicas across multiple data centers in case one of the centers suffers some kind of catastrophic failure or network outage. The Network TopologyStrategy allows you to request that some replicas be placed in DC1, and some in DC2. Within each data center, the NetworkTopologyStrategy distributes replicas on distinct racks, because nodes in the same rack (or similar physical grouping) often fail at the same time due to power, cooling, or network issues.

The NetworkTopologyStrategy distributes the replicas as follows: the first replica is placed according to the selected partitioner. Subsequent replicas are placed by traversing the nodes in the ring, skipping nodes in the same rack until a node in another rack is found. The process repeats for additional replicas, placing them on separate racks. Once a replica has been placed in each rack, the skipped nodes are used to place replicas until the replication factor has been met.

The NetworkTopologyStrategy allows you to specify a replication factor for each data center. Thus, the total number of replicas that will be stored is equal to the sum of the replication factors for each data center. The results of the NetworkTopology Strategy are depicted in Figure 10-2.

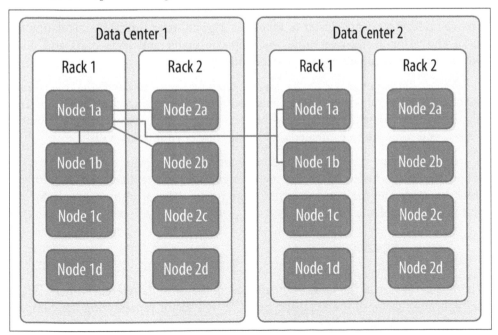

Figure 10-2. The NetworkTopologyStrategy places replicas in multiple data centers according to the specified replication factor per data center

To take advantage of additional data centers, you'll need to update the replication strategy for the keyspaces in your cluster accordingly. For example, you might issue an ALTER KEYSPACE command to change the replication strategy for the reservation keyspace used by the Reservation Service:

```
cqlsh> ALTER KEYSPACE reservation
  WITH REPLICATION = {'class' : 'NetworkTopologyStrategy',
    'DC1' : '3', 'DC2' : '3'};
```

Changing the Cluster Topology

While planning the cluster topology and replication strategy is an important design task, you're not locked into a specific topology forever. When you take actions to add or remove data centers or change replication factors within a data center, these are maintenance operations that will require tasks that include running repairs on affected nodes. You'll learn about nodetool commands that help perform tasks such as repair and cleanup in Chapter 12.

Sizing Your Cluster

To properly size your cluster, you'll want to consider the amount of data that your cluster will need to store, as well as the expected read and write load and latency goals, which we'll address in Chapter 13. You will, of course, be able to add and remove nodes from your cluster to adjust its capacity over time, but calculating the initial and planned size over time will help you better anticipate costs and make sound decisions as you plan your cluster configuration.

To calculate the required size of the cluster, you'll first need to determine the storage size of each of the supported tables using the formulas introduced in Chapter 5. This calculation is based on the columns within each table as well as the estimated number of rows, and results in an estimated size of one copy of your data on disk.

In order to estimate the actual physical amount of disk storage required for a given table across your cluster, you'll also need to consider the replication factor for the table's keyspace and the compaction strategy in use. The resulting formula for the total size T_t is as follows:

$$T_t = S_t \times RF_k \times CSF_t$$

Where S_t is the size of the table calculated using the formula referenced here, RF_k is the replication factor of the keyspace, and CSF_t is a factor representing the compaction strategy of the table, whose value is as follows:

- 2 for the `SizeTieredCompactionStrategy`. The worst-case scenario for this strategy is that there is a second copy of all the data required for a major compaction.

- 1.25 for other compaction strategies, which have been estimated to require 20% overhead during a major compaction. The actual overhead will vary based on your data, but this is a reasonable starting point.

Once you know the total physical disk size of the data for all tables, you can then sum those values across all keyspaces and tables to arrive at the total data size for the cluster.

You can then divide this total by the amount of usable storage space per disk to estimate a required number of disks. A reasonable estimate for the usable storage space of a disk is 90% of the disk size. Historically, Cassandra operators have recommended 1 TB as a maximum data size per node. This tends to provide a good balance between compute costs and time to complete operations such as compaction or streaming data to a new or replaced node. This may change in future releases.

Note that this calculation is based on the assumption of providing enough overhead on each disk to handle a major compaction of all keyspaces and tables. It's possible to reduce the required overhead if you can ensure such a major compaction will never be executed by an operations team, but this seems like a risky assumption. Another item to note is that this calculation does not take compression of SStables into account, which is an option we'll discuss in Chapter 14.

Sizing Cassandra's System Keyspaces

Alert readers may wonder about the disk space devoted to Cassandra's internal data storage in the various `system` keyspaces. This is typically insignificant when compared to the size of the disk. For example, you just created a three-node cluster and measured the size of each node's data storage at about 18 MB with no additional keyspaces.

Although this could certainly grow considerably if you are making frequent use of tracing, the `system_traces` tables do use TTL to allow trace data to expire, preventing these tables from overwhelming your data storage over time.

Once you've calculated the required size and number of nodes, you'll be in a better position to decide on an initial cluster size. The amount of capacity you build into your cluster is dependent on how quickly you anticipate growth, which must be balanced against cost of additional hardware, whether it be physical or virtual.

Selecting Instances

It is important to choose the right computing resources for your Cassandra nodes, whether you're running on physical hardware or in a virtualized cloud environment. The recommended computing resources for modern Cassandra releases (2.0 and later) tend to differ for development versus production environments:

Development environments
> Cassandra nodes in development environments should generally have CPUs with at least two cores and 8 GB of memory. Although Cassandra has been successfully run on smaller processors such as Raspberry Pi with 512 MB of memory, this does require a significant performance-tuning effort.

Production environments
> Cassandra nodes in production environments should have CPUs with at least eight cores and at least 32 GB of memory. Having additional cores and memory tends to increase the throughput of both reads and writes.

Storage

There are a few factors to consider when selecting and configuring storage, including the type and quantities of drives to use:

HDDs versus SSDs
> Cassandra supports both hard disk drives (HDDs, also called *spinning drives*) and *solid state drives* (SSDs) for storage. Although Cassandra's usage of append-based writes is conducive to sequential writes on spinning drives, SSDs provide higher performance overall because of their support for low-latency random reads.
>
> Historically, HDDs have been the more cost-effective storage option, but the cost of using SSDs has continued to come down, especially as more and more cloud platform providers support this as a storage option. As appropriate for your deployment, configure the `disk_optimization_strategy` in the *cassandra.yaml* file to either `ssd` (the default) or `spinning`.

Disk configuration
> If you're using spinning disks, it's best to use separate disks for data and commit log files. If you're using SSDs, the data and commit log files can be stored on the same disk.

JBOD versus RAID
> Using servers with multiple disks is a recommended deployment pattern, with Just a Bunch of Disks (JBOD) or Redundant Array of Independent Disks (RAID) configurations. Because Cassandra uses replication to achieve redundancy across multiple nodes, the RAID 0 (or *striped volume*) configuration is considered

sufficient. The JBOD approach provides the best overall performance and is a good choice if you have the ability to replace individual disks.

Use caution when considering shared storage

The standard recommendation for Cassandra deployments has been to avoid using storage area networks (SAN) and network-attached storage (NAS). These storage technologies don't scale as effectively as local storage—they consume additional network bandwidth in order to access the physical storage over the network, and they require additional I/O wait time on both reads and writes. However, we'll consider possible exceptions to this rule in "Cloud Deployment" on page 236.

Network

Because Cassandra relies on a distributed architecture involving multiple networked nodes, here are a few things you'll need to consider:

Throughput

First, make sure your network is sufficiently robust to handle the traffic associated with distributing data across multiple nodes. The recommended network bandwidth is 1 Gbps or higher.

Network configuration

Make sure that you've correctly configured firewall rules and IP addresses for your nodes and network appliances to allow traffic on the ports used for the CQL native transport, internode communication (the listen_address), JMX, and so on. This includes networking between data centers (we'll discuss cluster topology momentarily). It's recommended to run internode and client-to-node traffic on different interfaces.

The clocks on all nodes and clients should be synchronized using the Network Time Protocol (NTP) or other methods. Remember that Cassandra only overwrites columns if the timestamp for the new value is more recent than the timestamp of the existing value. Without synchronized clocks, writes from nodes or clients that lag behind can be lost.

Avoid load balancers

Load balancers are a feature of many computing environments. While these are frequently useful to spread incoming traffic across multiple service or application instances, it's not recommended to use load balancers with Cassandra. Cassandra already provides its own mechanisms to balance network traffic between nodes, and the DataStax drivers spread client queries across replicas, so strictly speaking a load balancer won't offer any additional help. Besides this, putting a load balancer in front of your Cassandra nodes potentially introduces a single point of failure, which could reduce the availability of your cluster.

Timeouts

> If you're building a cluster that spans multiple data centers, it's a good idea to measure the latency between data centers and tune timeout values in the *cassandra.yaml* file accordingly.

A proper network configuration is key to a successful Cassandra deployment, whether it is in a private data center, a public cloud spanning multiple data centers, or even a hybrid cloud environment.

Cloud Deployment

Now that you've learned the basics of planning a cluster deployment, let's examine options for deploying Cassandra in some of the most popular public cloud providers.

There are a couple of key advantages that you can realize by using commercial cloud computing providers. First, you can select from multiple data centers in order to maintain high availability. If you extend your cluster to multiple data centers in an active-active configuration and implement a sound backup strategy, you can avoid having to create a separate disaster recovery system.

Second, using commercial cloud providers allows you to situate your data in data centers that are closer to your customer base, thus improving application response time. If your application's usage profile is seasonal, you can expand and shrink your clusters in each data center according to the current demands.

You may want to save time by using a prebuilt image that already contains Cassandra. There are also companies that provide Cassandra as a managed service in a Software-as-a-Service (SaaS) offering, as discussed in Chapter 3.

Don't Forget Cloud Resource Costs

In planning a public cloud deployment, you'll want to make sure to estimate the cost to operate your cluster. Don't forget to account for resources, including compute services, node and backup storage, and networking.

Amazon Web Services

Amazon Web Services (AWS) has long been a popular deployment option for Cassandra, as evidenced by the presence of AWS-specific extensions in the Cassandra project, such as the `Ec2Snitch`, `Ec2MultiRegionSnitch`, and `EC2MultiRegionAddressTranslator` in the DataStax Java Driver:

Cluster layout

AWS is organized around the concepts of regions and availability zones, which are typically mapped to the Cassandra constructs of data centers and racks, respectively. A sample AWS cluster topology spanning the us-east-1 (Virginia) and eu-west-1 (Ireland) regions is shown in Figure 10-3. The node names are notional—this naming is not a required convention.

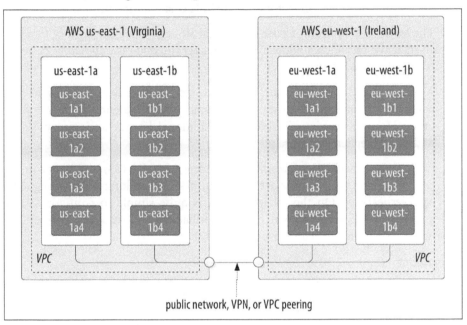

Figure 10-3. Topology of a cluster in two AWS regions

EC2 instances

The Amazon Elastic Compute Cloud (EC2) provides a variety of different virtual hardware instances grouped according to various classes. The two classes most frequently recommended for production Cassandra deployments are the C-class and the I-class, while the more general-purpose T-class and M-class instances are suitable for development and smaller production clusters.

The I-class instances are SSD-backed and designed for high I/O. These instances are ideal when using ephemeral storage, while the C-class instances are compute-optimized and suitable when using block storage. We'll discuss these storage options later in this section.

You can find more information about the various instance types available at *https://oreil.ly/yRTrq*.

Bitnami provides prebuilt Amazon Machine Images (AMIs) to simplify deployment, which you can find on its website (*https://oreil.ly/6TA5u*) or in the AWS Martketplace (*https://oreil.ly/_zUiB*).

Data storage

The two options for storage in AWS EC2 are ephemeral storage attached to virtual instances and Amazon Elastic Block Store (EBS). The right choice for your deployment depends on factors that include cost and operations.

The lower-cost option is to use ephemeral storage. The drawback of this is that if an instance on which a node is running is terminated (as happens occasionally in AWS), the data is lost.

Alternatively, EBS volumes are a reliable place to store data that doesn't go away when EC2 instances are dropped, and you can enable encryption on your volumes. However, reads will have some additional latency and your costs will be higher than ephemeral storage.

AWS services such as Amazon Simple Storage Service (S3) and Amazon S3 Glacier are a good option for short- to medium-term and long-term storage of backups, respectively. On the other hand, it is quite simple to configure automatic backups of EBS volumes, which simplifies backup and recovery. You can create a new EBS volume from an existing snapshot.

Networking

If you're running a multiregion configuration, you'll want to make sure you have adequate networking between the regions. Many have found that using elements of the Amazon Virtual Private Cloud (VPC) provides an effective way of achieving reliable, high-throughput connections between regions. AWS Direct Connect provides dedicated private networks, and there are virtual private network (VPN) options available as well. These services, of course, come at an additional cost.

If you have a single region deployment or a multiregion deployment using VPC peering, you can use the `Ec2Snitch`. If you have a multiregion deployment that uses public IP between regions, use the `Ec2MultiRegionSnitch`. Both EC2 snitches use the *cassandra-rackdc.properties* file, with data centers named after AWS regions (i.e., `us-east-1`) and racks named after availability zones (i.e., `us-east-1a`). Use the `GossipingPropertyFileSnitch` if you anticipate including data centers outside of AWS in your cluster.

Use Scripting to Automate Cassandra Deployments

If you find yourself operating a cluster with more than just a few nodes, you'll want to start thinking about automating deployment as well as other cluster maintenance tasks we'll consider in Chapter 12. A best practice is to use a scripting approach, sometimes known as "Infrastructure as Code." For example, if using AWS CloudFormation (*https://oreil.ly/1cwDq*), you might create a single CloudFormation template that describes the deployment of Cassandra nodes within a data center, and then reuse that in a CloudFormation StackSet to describe a cluster deployed in multiple AWS regions.

To get a head start on building scripts using tools like Puppet, Chef, Ansible, and Terraform, you can find plenty of open source examples on repositories such as GitHub (*https://github.com/*) and the DataStax Examples page (*https://oreil.ly/ZCigV*).

Additional guidance for deploying Cassandra on AWS can be found on the AWS website (*https://oreil.ly/9Cr3M*).

Google Cloud Platform

Google Cloud Platform (GCP) provides cloud computing, application hosting, networking, storage, and various Software-as-a-Service (SaaS) offerings. In particular, GCP is well known for its big data and Cloud Machine Learning services. You may wish to deploy (or extend) a Cassandra cluster into GCP to bring your data closer to these services:

Cluster layout
The Google Compute Engine (GCE) provides regions and zones, corresponding to Cassandra's data centers and racks, respectively. Similar conventions for cluster layout apply as in AWS. Google Cloud Stackdriver also provides a nice Cassandra integration for collecting and analyzing metrics.

Virtual machine instances
You can launch Cassandra quickly on the Google Cloud Platform using the Cloud Launcher. For example, if you search the launcher at the Google Cloud Platform site (*https://oreil.ly/sJsRk*), you'll find options for creating a cluster in just a few button clicks based on available VM images.

If you're going to build your own images, GCE's *n1-standard* and *n1-highmem* machine types are recommended for Cassandra deployments.

Data storage

GCE provides a variety of storage options (*https://oreil.ly/kZMmq*) for instances ranging from local spinning disk, and SSD options for both ephemeral drives and network-attached drives.

Networking

You can deploy your cluster in a single global VPC network that can span regions on Google's private network. You can also create connections between your own data centers and a Google VPC using Dedicated Interconnect or Partner Interconnect.

The `GoogleCloudSnitch` is a custom snitch designed just for the GCE, which also uses the *cassandra-rackdc.properties* file. The snitch may be used in a single region or across multiple regions. VPN networking is available between regions.

Microsoft Azure

Microsoft Azure is known as a cloud that is particularly well suited for enterprises, partly due to the large number of supported regions. Similar to GCP, there are a number of quick deployment options available in the Azure Marketplace (*https://oreil.ly/nGzDw*):

Cluster layout

Azure provides data centers in locations worldwide, using the same term *region* as AWS. The concept of *availability sets* is used to manage collections of VMs. Azure manages the assignment of the VMs in an availability set across *update domains*, which equate to Cassandra's racks.

Virtual machine instances

The Azure Resource Manager is recommended if you will be managing your own cluster deployments, since it enables specifying required resources declaratively.

Similar to AWS, Azure provides several classes of VMs. The D series VMs provide general-purpose, SSD-backed instances appropriate for most Cassandra deployments. The H series VMs provide additional memory as might be required for integrations such as the Apache Spark integration described in Chapter 15. You can find more information about Azure VM types on the Azure site (*https://oreil.ly/X_XG4*).

Data storage

Azure provides SSD, Premium SSD, and HDD options on the previously mentioned instances. Premium SSDs are recommended for Cassandra nodes.

Networking

There is not a dedicated snitch for Azure. Instead, use the `GossipingPropertyFi` `leSnitch` to allow your nodes to detect the cluster topology. For networking you may use public IPs, VPN gateways, or Azure Virtual Network (VNet) peering. VNet peering is recommended as the best option, with peering of VNets within a region or global peering across regions available.

Summary

In this chapter, you learned how to create Cassandra clusters and add additional nodes to a cluster. You learned how to configure Cassandra nodes via the *cassandra.yaml* file, including setting the seed nodes, the partitioner, the snitch, and other settings. You also learned how to configure replication for a keyspace and how to select an appropriate replication strategy. Finally, you learned how to plan a cluster and deploy in environments, including multiple public clouds. Now that you've deployed your first cluster, you're ready to learn how to monitor it.

Monitoring

The term *observability* is often used to describe a desirable attribute of distributed systems. Observability means having visibility into the various components of a system in order to detect, predict, and perhaps even prevent the complex failures that can occur in distributed systems. Failures in individual components can affect other components in turn, and multiple failures can interact in unforeseen ways, leading to system-wide outages. Common elements of an observability strategy for a system include metrics, logging, and tracing.

In this chapter, you'll learn how Cassandra supports these elements of observability and how to use available tools to monitor and understand important events in the life cycle of your Cassandra cluster. We'll look at some simple ways to see what's going on, such as changing the logging levels and understanding the output.

To begin, let's discuss how Cassandra uses the Java Management Extensions (JMX) to expose information about its internal operations and allow the dynamic configuration of some of its behavior. That will give you a basis to learn how to monitor Cassandra with various tools.

Monitoring Cassandra with JMX

Cassandra makes use of JMX to enable remote management of your nodes. JMX started as Java Specification Request (JSR) 160 and has been a core part of Java since version 5.0. You can read more about the JMX implementation in Java by examining the `java.lang.management` package.

JMX is a Java API that provides management of applications in two key ways. First, it allows you to understand your application's health and overall performance in terms of memory, threads, and CPU usage—things that apply to any Java application.

Second, it allows you to work with specific aspects of your application that you have instrumented.

Instrumentation refers to putting a wrapper around application code that provides hooks from the application to the JVM in order to allow the JVM to gather data that external tools can use. Such tools include monitoring agents, data analysis tools, profilers, and more. JMX allows you not only to view such data but also, if the application enables it, to manage your application at runtime by updating values.

Many popular Java applications are instrumented using JMX, including the JVM itself, the Tomcat application server, and Cassandra. Figure 11-1 shows the JMX architecture as used by Cassandra.

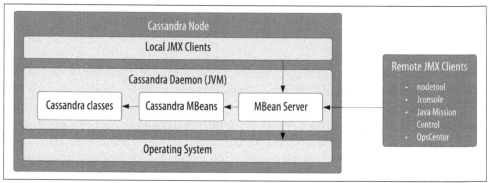

Figure 11-1. The JMX architecture

The JMX architecture is simple. The JVM collects information from the underlying operating system. The JVM itself is instrumented, so many of its features are exposed, including memory management and garbage collection, threading and deadlock detection, classloading, and logging.

An instrumented Java application (such as Cassandra) runs on top of this, also exposing some of its features as manageable objects. The Java Development Kit (JDK) includes an MBean server that makes the instrumented features available over a remote protocol to a JMX management application. The JVM also offers management capabilities via the Simple Network Monitoring Protocol (SNMP), which may be useful if you are using SMTP monitoring tools such as Nagios or Zenoss.

Connecting Remotely via JMX

By default, Cassandra runs with JMX enabled for local access only. To enable remote access, edit the file *<cassandra-home>/cassandra-env.sh* (or *cassandra-env.ps1* on Windows). Search for "JMX" to find the section of the file with options to control the JMX port and other local/remote connection settings. For example, in public cloud deployments it is often required to override the setting of the `java.rmi.server.hostname` command-line argument passed to the JVM to enable remote clients to access JMX.

Within a given application, you can manage only what the application developers have made available for you to manage. Luckily, the Cassandra developers have instrumented large parts of the database engine, making management via JMX fairly straightforward.

JMX Clients

In this chapter we'll focus on Nodetool, but there are plenty of other JMX clients available:

JConsole
> The JConsole tool ships with the standard Java Development Kit. It provides a graphical user interface client for working with MBeans and can be used for local or remote management. JConsole is an easy choice when you're looking for a JMX client, because it's easy to use and doesn't require a separate install.

Oracle Java Mission Control and Visual VM
> These tools also ship with the Oracle JDK and provide more robust metrics, diagnostics, and visualizations for memory usage, threads, garbage collection, and others. The main comparison between the two is that Visual VM is an open source project available under the GNU license, while Mission Control provides a deeper level of integration with the Oracle JVM via a framework called Flight Control.
>
> Java Mission Control can be run via the command `$JAVA_HOME/bin/jmc`, and Visual VM via the command `$JAVA_HOME/bin/jvisualvm`. Both are suitable for usage in development and production environments.

MX4J
> The Management Extensions for Java (MX4J) project provides an open source implementation of JMX, including tooling, such as an embedded web interface to JMX using HTTP/HTML. This allows interactions with JMX via a standard web browser.
>
> To integrate MX4J into a Cassandra installation, download the *mx4j_tools.jar* library (*http://mx4j.sourceforge.net/*), save the JAR file in the *lib* directory of your

---

Cassandra installation, and configure the `MX4J_ADDRESS` and `MX4J_PORT` options in *conf/cassandra-env.sh*.

Jmxterm
Jmxterm is a command-line JMX client that allows access to a JMX server without a graphical interface. This can be especially useful when working in cloud environments, as the graphical tools are typically more resource intensive.

Jmxterm is an open source Java project available from the CyclopsGroup (*https://oreil.ly/bqnE3*).

IDE Integrations
You can also find JMX clients that integrate with popular IDEs; for example, eclipse-jmx (*https://oreil.ly/N68Rl*).

Cassandra's MBeans

A *managed bean*, or MBean, is a special type of Java bean that represents a single manageable resource inside the JVM. MBeans interact with an MBean server to make their functions remotely available. Many classes in Cassandra are exposed as MBeans, which means in practical terms that they implement a custom interface that describes attributes they expose and operations that need to be implemented and for which the JMX agent will provide hooks.

```
public interface CompactionManagerMBean
{
    public List<Map<String, String>> getCompactions();
    public List<String> getCompactionSummary();
    public TabularData getCompactionHistory();

    public void forceUserDefinedCompaction(String dataFiles);
    public void stopCompaction(String type);
    public void stopCompactionById(String compactionId);

    public int getCoreCompactorThreads();
    public void setCoreCompactorThreads(int number);

    ...
}
```

Some simple values in the application are exposed as *attributes*. An example of this is the `coreCompactorThreads` attribute, for which getter and setter operations are provided. Other attributes that are read-only are the current `compactions` in progress, the `compactionSummary`, and the `compactionHistory`. You can refresh to see the most recent values, but that's pretty much all you can do with them. Because these values are maintained internally in the JVM, it doesn't make sense to set them externally (they're derived from actual events, and are not configurable).

MBeans can also make *operations* available to the JMX agent that let you execute some useful action. The `forceUserDefinedCompaction()` and `stopCompaction()` methods are operations that you can use to force a compaction to occur or stop a running compaction from a JMX client.

As you can see by this MBean interface definition, there's no magic going on. This is just a regular interface defining the set of operations. The `CompactionManager` class implements this interface and does the work of registering itself with the MBean server for the JMX attributes and operations that it maintains locally:

```
public static final String MBEAN_OBJECT_NAME =
    "org.apache.cassandra.db:type=CompactionManager";

static
{
    instance = new CompactionManager();
    MBeanWrapper.instance.registerMBean(instance, MBEAN_OBJECT_NAME);
}
```

Note that the MBean is registered in the domain `org.apache.cassandra.db` with a type of `CompactionManager`. The attributes and operations exposed by this MBean appear under `org.apache.cassandra.db` > `CompactionManager` in JMX clients.

In the following sections, you'll learn about some of the key MBeans that Cassandra exposes to allow monitoring and management via JMX. Many of these MBeans correspond to the services and managers introduced in Chapter 6. In most cases, the operations and attributes exposed by the MBeans are accessible via `nodetool` commands discussed throughout this book.

Database MBeans

These are the Cassandra classes related to the core database itself that are exposed to clients in the `org.apache.cassandra.db` domain. There are many MBeans in this domain, but we'll focus on a few key ones related to the data the node is responsible for storing, including caching, the commit log, and metadata about specific tables.

Storage Service MBean

Because Cassandra is a database, it's essentially a very sophisticated storage program; therefore, Cassandra's storage engine as implemented in the `org.apache.cassandra.service.StorageService` is an essential focus of monitoring and management. The corresponding MBean for this service is the `StorageServiceMBean`, which provides many useful attributes and operations.

The MBean exposes identifying information about the node, including its host ID, the cluster name, and partitioner in use. It also allows you to inspect the node's `OperationMode`, which reports `normal` if everything is going smoothly (other possible states are leaving, joining, decommissioned, and client). These attributes are used by nodetool commands such as describecluster and info.

You can also view the current set of live nodes, as well as the set of unreachable nodes in the cluster. If any nodes are unreachable, Cassandra will tell you their IP addresses in the UnreachableNodes attribute.

To get an understanding of how much data is stored on each node, you can use the getLoadMapWithPort() method, which will return a Java Map with keys of IP addresses with values of their corresponding storage loads. You can also use the effectiveOwnershipWithPort(String keyspace) operation to access the percentage of the data in a keyspace owned by each node. This information is used in the nodetool ring and status commands.

If you're looking for which nodes own a certain partition key, you can use the getNaturalEndpointsWithPort() operation. Pass it the keyspace name, table name, and the partition key for which you want to find the endpoint value, and it will return a list of IP addresses (with port number) that are responsible for storing this key.

You can also use the describeRingWithPortJMX() operation to get a list of token ranges in the cluster, including their ownership by nodes in the cluster. This is used by the nodetool describering operation.

There are many standard maintenance operations that the StorageServiceMBean affords you, including resumeBootstrap(), joinRing(), flush(), truncate(), repairAsync(), cleanup(), scrub(), drain(), removeNode(), decommission(), and operations to start and stop gossip, and the native transport. We'll dig into the nodetool commands that correspond to these operations in Chapter 12.

If you want to change Cassandra's logging configuration at runtime without interrupting service (as you'll see in "Logging" on page 266), you can invoke the getLoggingLevels() method to see the currently configured levels, and then use the setLoggingLevel(String classQualifier, String level) method to override the log level for classes matching the pattern you provide.

Storage Proxy MBean

As you learned in Chapter 6, the org.apache.cassandra.service.StorageProxy provides a layer on top of the StorageService to handle client requests and internode communications. The StorageProxyMBean provides the ability to check and set timeout values for various operations, including read and write. Along with many other attributes exposed by Cassandra's MBeans, these timeout values would originally be specified in the *cassandra.yaml* file. Setting these attributes takes effect only until the next time the node is restarted, whereupon they'll be initialized to the values in the configuration file.

This MBean also provides access to hinted handoff settings such as the maximum time window for storing hints. Hinted handoff statistics include `getTotalHints()` and `getHintsInProgress()`. You can disable hints for nodes in a particular data center with the `disableHintsForDC()` operation.

You can also turn this node's participation in hinted handoff on or off via `setHintedHandoffEnabled()`, or check the current status via `getHintedHandoffEnabled()`. These are used by nodetool's `enablehandoff`, `disablehandoff`, and `statushandoff` commands, respectively.

Hints Service MBean

In addition to the hinted handoff operations on the `StorageServiceMBean`, Cassandra provides more hinted handoff controls via the `org.apache.cassandra.hints.HintsServiceMBean`. The MBean exposes the ability to pause and resume hint delivery. You can delete hints that are stored up for a specific node with `deleteAllHintsForEndpoint()`.

Additionally, you can pause and resume hint delivery to all nodes with `pauseDispatch()` and `resumeDispatch()`. You can delete stored hints for all nodes with the `deleteAllHints()` operation, or for a specific node with `deleteAllHintsForEndpoint()`. These are used by nodetool's `pausehandoff`, `resumehandoff`, and `truncate hints` commands.

Column Family Store MBean

Cassandra registers an instance of the `org.apache.cassandra.db.ColumnFamilyStoreMBean` for each table stored in the node under `org.apache.cassandra.db > Tables` (this is a legacy name: tables were known as column families in early versions of Cassandra).

The `ColumnFamilyStoreMBean` provides access to the compaction and compression settings for each table. This allows you to temporarily override these settings on a specific node. The values will be reset to those configured on the table schema when the node is restarted.

The MBean also exposes a lot of information about the node's storage of data for this table on disk. The `getSSTableCountPerLevel()` operation provides a list of how many SStables are in each tier. The `estimateKeys()` operation provides an estimate of the number of partitions stored on this node. Taken together, this information can give you some insight as to whether invoking the `forceMajorCompaction()` operation for this table might help free space on this node and increase read performance.

There is also a `trueSnapshotsSize()` operation that allows you to determine the size of SSTable shapshots that are no longer active. A large value here indicates that you should consider deleting these snapshots, possibly after making an archive copy.

Because Cassandra stores indexes as tables, there is also a `ColumnFamilyStoreMBean` instance for each indexed column, available under `org.apache.cassandra.db > IndexTables` (previously `IndexColumnFamilies`), with the same attributes and operations.

Commit Log MBean

The `org.apache.cassandra.db.commitlog.CommitLogMBean` exposes attributes and operations that allow you to learn about the current state of commit logs. The `CommitLogMBean` also exposes the `recover()` operation, which can be used to restore database state from archived commit log files.

The default settings that control commit log recovery are specified in the *conf/commitlog_archiving.properties* file, but can be overridden via the MBean. You'll learn more about data recovery in Chapter 12.

Compaction Manager MBean

You've already taken a peek inside the source of the `org.apache.cassandra.db.compaction.CompactionManagerMBean` to see how it interacts with JMX, but we didn't really talk about its purpose. This MBean allows you to get statistics about compactions performed in the past, and the ability to force compaction of specific SSTable files we identify by calling the `forceUserDefinedCompaction` method of the `CompactionManager` class. This MBean is leveraged by `nodetool` commands, including `compact`, `compactionhistory`, and `compactionstats`.

Cache Service MBean

The `org.apache.cassandra.service.CacheServiceMBean` provides access to Cassandra's key, row, chunk, and counter caches under the domain `org.apache.cassandra.db > Caches`. The information available for each cache includes the maximum size and time duration to cache items, and the ability to invalidate each cache.

Cluster-Related MBeans

There are plenty of additional MBeans outside the core database engine that help manage how a Cassandra node relates to other nodes in its cluster, including snitching, gossip and failure detection, hinted handoff, messaging, and streaming.

Gossiper MBean

The `org.apache.cassandra.gms.GossiperMBean` provides access to the work of the Gossiper.

We've already discussed how the `StorageServiceMBean` reports which nodes are unreachable. Based on that list, you can call the `getEndpointDowntime()` operation on the `GossiperMBean` to determine how long a given node has been down. The downtime is measured from the perspective of the node whose MBean you're inspecting, and the value resets when the node comes back online. Cassandra uses this operation internally to know how long it can wait to discard hints.

The `getCurrentGenerationNumber()` operation returns the generation number associated with a specific node. The generation number is included in gossip messages exchanged between nodes and is used to distinguish the current state of a node from the state prior to a restart. The generation number remains the same while the node is alive and is incremented each time the node restarts. It's maintained by the `Gossiper` using a timestamp.

The `assassinateEndpoint()` operation attempts to remove a node from the ring by telling the other nodes that the node has been permanently removed, similar to the concept of "character assassination" in human gossip. Assassinating a node is a maintenance step of last resort when a node cannot be removed from the cluster normally. This operation is used by the `nodetool assassinate` command.

Failure Detector MBean

The `org.apache.cassandra.gms.FailureDetectorMBean` provides attributes describing the states and Phi scores of other nodes, as well as the Phi conviction threshold.

Snitch MBeans

Cassandra provides two MBeans to monitor and configure behavior of the snitch. The `org.apache.cassandra.locator.EndpointSnitchInfoMBean` provides the name of the rack and data center for a given host, as well as the name of the snitch in use.

If you're using the `DynamicEndpointSnitch`, the `org.apache.cassandra.locator.DynamicEndpointSnitchMBean` is registered. This MBean exposes the ability to reset the badness threshold used by the snitch to determine when to change its preferred replica for a token range, as well as allowing you to see the scores for various nodes.

Stream Manager MBean

The `org.apache.cassandra.streaming.StreamManagerMBean` allows us to see the SSTable streaming activities that occur between a node and its peers. There are two basic ideas here: a stream source and a stream destination. Each node can stream its data to another node in order to perform load balancing, and the `StreamManager` class supports these operations. The `StreamManagerMBean` gives a necessary view into the data that is moving between nodes in the cluster.

The `StreamManagerMBean` supports two modes of operation. The `getCurrentStreams()` operation provides a snapshot of the current incoming and outgoing streams, and the MBean also publishes notifications associated with stream state changes, such as initialization, completion, or failure. You can subscribe to these notifications in your JMX client in order to watch the streaming operations as they occur.

So in conjunction with the `StorageServiceMBean`, if you're concerned that a node is not receiving data as it should, or that a node is unbalanced or even down, these two MBeans working together can give you very rich insight into exactly what's happening in your cluster.

Messaging Service MBean

As you learned in Chapter 6, the `org.apache.cassandra.net.MessagingService` manages messages to and from other nodes other than streaming. The `MessagingServiceMBean` exposes attributes that include data about pending and dropped messages, as well as operations to manage backpressure.

Internal MBeans

The final MBeans we'll consider describe internal operations of the Cassandra node, including threading, garbage collection, security, and exposing metrics.

Thread Pool MBeans

Cassandra's thread pools are implemented via the `JMXEnabledThreadPoolExecutor` and `JMXConfigurableThreadPoolExecutor` classes in the `org.apache.cassandra.concurrent` package. The MBeans for each stage implement the `JMXEnabledThreadPoolExecutorMBean` and `JMXConfigurableThreadPoolExecutorMBean` interfaces, respectively, which allow you to view and configure the number of core threads in each thread pool as well as the maximum number of threads. The MBeans for each type of thread pool appear under the `org.apache.cassandra.internal` domain to JMX clients.

Garbage Collection MBeans

The JVM's garbage collection processing can impact tail latencies if not tuned properly, so it's important to monitor its performance, as you'll see in Chapter 13. The `GCInspectorMXBean` appears in the `org.apache.cassandra.service` domain. It exposes the operation `getAndResetStats()`, which retrieves and then resets garbage collection metrics that Cassandra collects on its JVM, which is used by the `nodetool` `gcstats` command. It also exposes attributes that control the thresholds at which `INFO` and `WARN` logging messages are generated for long garbage collection pauses.

Security MBeans

The `org.apache.cassandra.auth` domain defines the `AuthCacheMBean`, which exposes operations used to configure how Cassandra caches client authentication records. We'll discuss this MBean in Chapter 14.

Metrics MBeans

The ability to access metrics related to application performance, health, and key activities has become an essential tool for maintaining web-scale applications. Fortunately, Cassandra collects a wide range of metrics on its own activities to help you understand the behavior. JMX supports several different styles of metrics, including counters, gauges, meters, histograms, and timers.

To make its metrics accessible via JMX, Cassandra uses the Dropwizard Metrics open source Java library (*http://metrics.dropwizard.io*). Cassandra uses the `org.apache.cas` `sandra.metrics.CassandraMetricsRegistry` to register its metrics with the Dropwizard Metrics library, which in turn exposes them as MBeans in the `org.apache.cassandra.metrics` domain. You'll see in "Metrics" on page 263 a summary of the specific metrics that Cassandra reports and learn how these can be exposed to metrics aggregation frameworks.

Monitoring with nodetool

You've already explored a few of the commands offered by `nodetool` in previous chapters, but let's take this opportunity to get properly acquainted.

`nodetool` ships with Cassandra and can be found in *<cassandra-home>/bin*. This is a command-line program that offers a rich array of ways to look at your cluster, understand its activity, and modify it. `nodetool` lets you get statistics about the cluster, see the ranges each node maintains, move data from one node to another, decommission a node, and even repair a node that's having trouble.

Behind the scenes, `nodetool` uses JMX to access the MBeans described previously using a helper class called `org.apache.cassandra.tools.NodeProbe`. The `NodeProbe` class connects to the JMX agent at a specified node by its IP address and JMX port, locates MBeans, retrieves their data, and invokes their operations. The `NodeToolCmd` class in the same package is an abstract class that is extended by each `nodetool` command to provide access to administrative functionality in an interactive command-line interface.

`nodetool` uses the same environment settings as the Cassandra daemon: *bin/cassandra.in.sh* and *conf/cassandra-env.sh* on Unix (or *bin/cassandra.in.bat* and *conf/cassandra-env.ps1* on Windows). The logging settings are found in the *conf/logback-tools.xml* file; these work the same way as the Cassandra daemon logging settings found in *conf/logback.xml*.

Starting `nodetool` is a breeze. Just open a terminal, navigate to *<cassandra-home>*, and enter the following command:

```
$ bin/nodetool help
```

This causes the program to print a list of available commands, several of which we will cover momentarily. Running `nodetool` with no arguments is equivalent to the `help` command. You can also execute help with the name of a specific command to get additional details.

Connecting to a Specific Node

With the exception of the `help` command, `nodetool` must connect to a Cassandra node in order to access information about that node or the cluster as a whole.

You can use the `-h` option to identify the IP address of the node to connect to with `nodetool`. If no IP address is specified, the tool attempts to connect to the default port on the local machine.

If you have a `ccm` cluster available, as discussed in Chapter 10, you can run `nodetool` commands against specific nodes; for example:

```
ccm node1 nodetool help
```

To get more interesting statistics from a cluster as you try out the commands in this chapter yourself, you might want to run your own instance of the Reservation Service introduced in Chapter 7 and Chapter 8.

Getting Cluster Information

You can get a variety of information about the cluster and its nodes, which we look at in this section. You can get basic information on an individual node or on all the nodes participating in a ring.

describecluster

The `describecluster` command prints out basic information about the cluster, including the name, snitch, and partitioner. For example, here's a portion of the output when run against the cluster created for the Reservation Service using `ccm`:

```
$ ccm node1 nodetool describecluster

Cluster Information:
        Name: reservation_service
        Snitch: org.apache.cassandra.locator.SimpleSnitch
        DynamicEndPointSnitch: enabled
        Partitioner: org.apache.cassandra.dht.Murmur3Partitioner
        Schema versions:
                2b88dbfd-6e40-3ef1-af11-d88b6dff2c3b: [127.0.0.4, 127.0.0.3,
                127.0.0.2, 127.0.0.1]
    ...
```

We've shortened the output a bit for brevity. The `Schema versions` portion of the output is especially important for identifying any disagreements in table definitions, or schema, between nodes. While Cassandra propagates schema changes through a cluster, any differences are typically resolved quickly, so any lingering schema differences usually correspond to a node that is down or unreachable and needs to be restarted, which you should be able to confirm via the summary statistics on nodes that are also printed out.

status

A more direct way to identify the nodes in your cluster and what state they're in, is to use the `status` command:

```
$ ccm node1 nodetool status

Datacenter: datacenter1
========================
Status=Up/Down
|/ State=Normal/Leaving/Joining/Moving
--  Address    Load        Tokens  Owns (effective)  Host ID       Rack
UN  127.0.0.1  251.77 KiB  256     48.7%             d23716cb...   rack1
UN  127.0.0.2  250.28 KiB  256     50.0%             635f2ab7...   rack1
UN  127.0.0.3  250.47 KiB  256     53.6%             a1cd5663...   rack1
UN  127.0.0.4  403.46 KiB  256     47.7%             b493769e...   rack1
```

The status is organized by data center and rack. Each node's status is identified by a two-character code: the first character indicates whether the node is up (currently available and ready for queries) or down, and the second character indicates the state or operational mode of the node. The `load` column represents the byte count of the data each node is holding. The `owns` column indidates the effective percentage of the token range owned by the node, taking replication into account.

info

The `info` command tells `nodetool` to connect with a single node and get basic data about its current state. Just pass it the address of the node you want info for:

```
$ ccm node2 nodetool info

ID                       : 635f2ab7-e81a-423b-a566-674d8010c819
Gossip active            : true
Native Transport active: true
Load                     : 250.28 KiB
Generation No            : 1574894395
Uptime (seconds)         : 146423
Heap Memory (MB)         : 191.69 / 495.00
Off Heap Memory (MB)     : 0.00
Data Center              : datacenter1
Rack                     : rack1
Exceptions               : 0
Key Cache                : entries 10, size 896 bytes, capacity 24 MiB,
                           32 hits, 44 requests, 0.727 recent hit rate,
                           14400 save period in seconds
Row Cache                : entries 0, size 0 bytes, capacity 0 bytes,
                           0 hits, 0 requests, NaN recent hit rate,
                           0 save period in seconds
Counter Cache            : entries 0, size 0 bytes, capacity 12 MiB,
                           0 hits, 0 requests, NaN recent hit rate,
                           7200 save period in seconds
Chunk Cache              : entries 16, size 256 KiB, capacity 91 MiB,
                           772 misses, 841 requests, 0.082 recent hit rate,
                           NaN microseconds miss latency
Percent Repaired         : 100.0%
Token                    : (invoke with -T/--tokens to see all 256 tokens)
```

The information reported includes the memory and disk usage (Load) of the node and the status of various services offered by Cassandra. You can also check the status of individual services with the `nodetool` commands `statusgossip`, `statusbinary`, and `statushandoff` (note that handoff status is not part of `info`).

ring

To determine what nodes are in your ring and what state they're in, use the `ring` command on `nodetool`, like this:

```
$ Datacenter: datacenter1
==========
Address    Rack   Status  State   Load        Owns     Token
                                                        9218490134647118760
127.0.0.1  rack1  Up      Normal  251.77 KiB  48.73%   -9166983985142207552
127.0.0.4  rack1  Up      Normal  403.46 KiB  47.68%   -9159867377343852899
127.0.0.2  rack1  Up      Normal  250.28 KiB  49.99%   -9159653278489176223
127.0.0.1  rack1  Up      Normal  251.77 KiB  48.73%   -9159520114055706114
...
```

This output is organized in terms of virtual nodes (vnodes). Here you see the IP addresses of all the nodes in the ring. In this case, there are three nodes, all of which are up (currently available and ready for queries). The load column represents the byte count of the data each node is holding. The output of the describering command is similar but is organized around token ranges.

Other useful status commands provided by nodetool include:

- The getLoggingLevels and setLoggingLevels commands allow dynamic configuration of logging levels, using the Logback JMXConfiguratorMBean we discussed previously.

- The gossipinfo command prints the information this node disseminates about itself and has obtained from other nodes via gossip, while failuredetector provides the Phi failure detection value calculated for other nodes.

- The version command prints the version of Cassandra this node is running.

Getting Statistics

nodetool also lets you gather statistics about the state of your server in the aggregate level as well as down to the level of specific keyspaces and tables. Two of the most frequently used commands are tpstats and tablestats, both of which we examine now.

Using tpstats

The tpstats tool gives us information on the thread pools that Cassandra maintains. Cassandra is highly concurrent, and optimized for multiprocessor/multicore machines, so understanding the behavior and health of the thread pools is important to good Cassandra maintenance.

To find statistics on the thread pools, execute nodetool with the tpstats command:

```
$ bin/nodetool tpstats
ccm node1 nodetool tpstats

Pool Name           Active  Pending  Completed  Blocked  All time blocked
ReadStage                0        0        399        0                 0
MiscStage                0        0          0        0                 0
CompactionExecutor       0        0      95541        0                 0
MutationStage            0        0          0        0                 0
...

Message type    Dropped  Latency waiting in queue (micros)
                           50%      95%      99%      Max
READ_RSP              0   0.00     0.00     0.00     0.00
RANGE_REQ            0   0.00     0.00     0.00     0.00
```

```
PING_REQ              0     0.00    0.00    0.00    0.00
_SAMPLE               0     0.00    0.00    0.00    0.00
```

The top portion of the output presents data on tasks in each of Cassandra's thread pools. You can see directly how many operations are in what stage, and whether they are active, pending, or completed. For example, by reviewing the number of active tasks in the MutationStage, you can learn how many writes are in progress.

The bottom portion of the output indicates the number of dropped messages for the node. Dropped messages are an indicator of Cassandra's load shedding implementation, which each node uses to defend itself when it receives more requests than it can handle. For example, internode messages that are received by a node but not processed within the rpc_timeout are dropped, rather than processed, as the coordinator node will no longer be waiting for a response.

Seeing lots of zeros in the output for blocked tasks and dropped messages means that you either have very little activity on the server or that Cassandra is doing an exceptional job of keeping up with the load. Lots of nonzero values are indicative of situations where Cassandra is having a hard time keeping up, and may indicate a need for some of the techniques described in Chapter 13.

Using tablestats

To see overview statistics for keyspaces and tables, you can use the tablestats command. You may also recognize this command from its previous name, cfstats. Here is sample output on the reservations_by_confirmation table:

```
$ ccm node1 nodetool tablestats reservation.reservations_by_confirmation

Total number of tables: 43
----------------
Keyspace : reservation
        Read Count: 0
        Read Latency: NaN ms
        Write Count: 0
        Write Latency: NaN ms
        Pending Flushes: 0
                Table: reservations_by_confirmation
                SSTable count: 0
                Old SSTable count: 0
                Space used (live): 0
                Space used (total): 0
                Space used by snapshots (total): 0
                Off heap memory used (total): 0
                SSTable Compression Ratio: -1.0
                Number of partitions (estimate): 0
                Memtable cell count: 0
                Memtable data size: 0
                Memtable off heap memory used: 0
                Memtable switch count: 0
```

```
Local read count: 0
Local read latency: NaN ms
Local write count: 0
Local write latency: NaN ms
Pending flushes: 0
Percent repaired: 100.0
Bloom filter false positives: 0
Bloom filter false ratio: 0.00000
Bloom filter space used: 0
Bloom filter off heap memory used: 0
Index summary off heap memory used: 0
Compression metadata off heap memory used: 0
Compacted partition minimum bytes: 0
Compacted partition maximum bytes: 0
Compacted partition mean bytes: 0
Average live cells per slice (last five minutes): NaN
Maximum live cells per slice (last five minutes): 0
Average tombstones per slice (last five minutes): NaN
Maximum tombstones per slice (last five minutes): 0
Dropped Mutations: 0
```

You can see the read and write latency, and total number of reads and writes. You can also see detailed information about Cassandra's internal structures for the table, including memtables, Bloom filters, and SSTables. You can get statistics for all the tables in a keyspace by specifying just the keyspace name, or specify no arguments to get statistics for all tables in the cluster.

Virtual Tables

In the 4.0 release, Cassandra added a *virtual tables* feature. Virtual tables are so named because they are not actual tables that are stored using Cassandra's typical write path, with data written to memtables and SSTables. Instead, these virtual tables are views that provide metadata about nodes and tables via standard CQL.

This metadata is available via two keyspaces, which you may have noticed in earlier chapters when you used the DESCRIBE KEYSPACES command, called system_views and system_virtual_schema:

```
cqlsh> DESCRIBE KEYSPACES;

reservation    system_traces  system_auth  system_distributed    system_views
system_schema  system         system_virtual_schema
```

These two keyspaces contain virtual tables that provide different types of metadata. Before we look into them, here are a couple of important things you should know about virtual tables:

- You may not define your own virtual tables.
- The scope of virtual tables is the local node.

- When interacting with virtual tables through `cqlsh`, results will come from the node that `cqlsh` connected to, as you'll see next.

- Virtual tables are not persisted, so any statistics will be reset when the node restarts.

System Virtual Schema

Let's look first at the tables in the `system_virtual_schema`:

```
cqlsh:system> USE system_virtual_schema;
cqlsh:system_virtual_schema> DESCRIBE TABLES;

keyspaces  columns  tables
```

If you examine the schema and contents of the `keyspaces` table, you'll see that the schema of this table is extremely simple—it's just a list of keyspace names:

```
cqlsh:system_virtual_schema> SELECT * FROM KEYSPACES;

 keyspace_name
-----------------------
           reservation
          system_views
 system_virtual_schema

(3 rows)
```

The design of the `tables` table is quite similar, consisting of `keyspace_name`, `table_name`, and `comment` columns, in which the primary key is (`keyspace_name`, `table_name`).

The `columns` table is more interesting. We'll focus on a subset of the available columns:

```
cqlsh:system_virtual_schema> SELECT column_name, clustering_order, kind,
  position, type FROM columns WHERE keyspace_name = 'reservation' AND
  table_name = 'reservations_by_hotel_date';
```

column_name	clustering_order	kind	position	type
confirm_number	none	regular	-1	text
end_date	none	regular	-1	date
guest_id	none	regular	-1	uuid
hotel_id	none	partition_key	0	text
room_number	asc	clustering	0	smallint
start_date	none	partition_key	1	date

```
(6 rows)
```

As you can see, this query provides enough data to describe the schema of a table, including the columns and primary key definition. Although it does not include the table options, the response is otherwise quite similar in content to the output of the cqlsh DESCRIBE operations.

Interestingly, cqlsh traditionally scanned tables in the system keyspace to implement these operations, but is updated in the 4.0 release to use virtual tables.

System Views

The second keyspace containing virtual tables is the system_views keyspace. Let's get a list of the available views:

```
cqlsh:system_virtual_schema> SELECT * FROM tables WHERE
  keyspace_name = 'system_views';

 keyspace_name | table_name                | comment
---------------+---------------------------+----------------------------
 system_views  |                    caches |               system caches
 system_views  |                   clients | currently connected clients
 system_views  |   coordinator_read_latency |
 system_views  |   coordinator_scan_latency |
 system_views  |  coordinator_write_latency |
 system_views  |                disk_usage |
 system_views  |         internode_inbound |
 system_views  |        internode_outbound |
 system_views  |        local_read_latency |
 system_views  |        local_scan_latency |
 system_views  |       local_write_latency |
 system_views  |        max_partition_size |
 system_views  |             rows_per_read |
 system_views  |                  settings |            current settings
 system_views  |             sstable_tasks |        current sstable tasks
 system_views  |              thread_pools |
 system_views  |        tombstones_per_read |

(17 rows)
```

As you can see, there is a mix of tables that provide latency histograms for reads and writes to local storage, and for when this node is acting as a coordinator.

The max_partition_size and tombstones_per_read tables are particularly useful in helping to identify some of the situations that lead to poor performance in Cassandra clusters, which we'll address in Chapter 12.

The disk_usage view provides the storage expressed in mebibytes (1,048,576 bytes). Again, remember this is how much storage there is for each table on that individual node. Related to this is the max_partition_size, which can be useful in determining if a node is affected by a wide partition. You'll learn more about how to detect and address these in Chapter 13.

Let's look a bit more closely at a couple of these tables. First, let's have a look at a few of the columns in the `clients` table:

```
cqlsh:system_virtual_schema> USE system_views;
cqlsh:system_views> SELECT address, port, hostname, request_count
  FROM clients;

 address   | port  | hostname  | request_count
-----------+-------+-----------+---------------
 127.0.0.1 | 50631 | localhost |           261
 127.0.0.1 | 50632 | localhost |           281
```

As you can see, this table provides information about each client with an active connection to the node, including its location and number of requests. Other columns not shown here provide information about the client's identity and encryption settings, and the protocol version in use. This information is useful to make sure the list of clients and their level of usage is in line with what you expect for your application.

Another useful table is `settings`. This allows you to see the values of configurable parameters for the node set via the *cassandra.yaml* file or subsequently modified via JMX:

```
cqlsh:system_views> SELECT * FROM settings LIMIT 10;

 name                                         | value
----------------------------------------------+-----------------------
              allocate_tokens_for_keyspace |                  null
 allocate_tokens_for_local_replication_factor |                  null
         audit_logging_options_audit_logs_dir |        /var/logs/audit/
               audit_logging_options_enabled |                 false
    audit_logging_options_excluded_categories |
     audit_logging_options_excluded_keyspaces | system,system_schema,
                                              | system_virtual_schema
         audit_logging_options_excluded_users |
     audit_logging_options_included_categories |
      audit_logging_options_included_keyspaces |
         audit_logging_options_included_users |

(10 rows)
```

You'll notice that much of this same information could be accessed via various node tool commands. However, the value of virtual tables is that they may be accessed through any client using the CQL native protocol, including applications you write using the DataStax Java Drivers. Of course, some of these values you may not wish to allow your clients access to; we'll discuss how to secure access to keyspaces and tables in Chapter 14.

If you're interested in the implementation of virtual tables, you can find the code in the `org.apache.cassandra.db.virtual` package. For more detail on using virtual tables, see Alexander Dejanovski's blog post, "Virtual tables are coming in Cassandra 4.0" (*https://oreil.ly/HxxDr*).

 More Virtual Table Functionality

While the 4.0 release provides a very useful set of virtual tables, the Cassandra community has proposed several additional virtual tables that may be added in future releases, which you can find in the Cassandra Jira:

CASSANDRA-15254 (https://oreil.ly/B8jFo)
Set the configuration values on the `settings` table

CASSANDRA-14795 (https://oreil.ly/DP0jX)
Hints metadata

CASSANDRA-14572 (https://oreil.ly/dCIIg)
Additional table metrics

CASSANDRA-12367 (https://oreil.ly/PJdFD)
Access to individual partition sizes

CASSANDRA-15241 (https://oreil.ly/XRw22)
Get a listing of current running queries

CASSANDRA-15399 (https://oreil.ly/V9cFR)
Repair status

We expect that the data available via virtual tables will eventually catch up with JMX, and even surpass it in some areas.

Metrics

As we mentioned at the start of this chapter, metrics are a vital component of the observability of the system. It's important to have access to metrics at the OS, JVM, and application level. The metrics Cassandra reports at the application level include:

- *Buffer pool metrics* describing Cassandra's use of memory
- *CQL metrics*, including the number of prepared and regular statement executions
- *Cache metrics* for key, row, and counter caches, such as the number of entries versus capacity, as well as hit and miss rates
- *Client metrics*, including the number of connected clients, and information about client requests such as latency, failures, and timeouts
- *Commit log metrics*, including the commit log size and statistics on pending and completed tasks

- *Compaction metrics*, including the total bytes compacted and statistics on pending and completed compactions
- *Connection metrics* to each node in the cluster, including gossip
- *Dropped message metrics* that are used as part of `nodetool tpstats`
- *Read repair metrics* describing the number of background versus blocking read repairs performed over time
- *Storage metrics*, including counts of hints in progress and total hints
- *Streaming metrics*, including the total incoming and outgoing bytes of data streamed to other nodes in the cluster
- *Thread pool metrics*, including active, completed, and blocked tasks for each thread pool
- *Table metrics*, including caches, memtables, SSTables, and Bloom filter usage, and the latency of various read and write operations, reported at 1-, 5-, and 15-minute intervals
- *Keyspace metrics* that aggregate the metrics for the tables in each keyspace

Many of these metrics are used by `nodetool` commands such as `tpstats`, `tablehisto grams`, and `proxyhistograms`. For example, `tpstats` is simply a presentation of the thread pool and dropped message metrics.

Resetting Metrics

Note that in Cassandra releases through 4.0, the metrics reported are lifetime metrics since the node was started. To reset the metrics on a node, you have to restart it. The Jira issue CASSANDRA-8433 (*https://oreil.ly/p1quJ*) requests the ability to reset the metrics via JMX and `nodetool`.

Metrics Aggregation

You've read how Cassandra exposes metrics via JMX and Dropwizard, and how to view some of these metrics via tools, including `nodetool` and `cqlsh` (via virtual tables). These tools are a great help for looking at the state of one node at a time. Cassandra's metrics can also fit into a broader observability strategy for your applications.

If you've had experience building cloud applications, you may be familiar with metrics aggregation frameworks such as Prometheus and metrics visualization tools such as Grafana. There's a simple integration (*https://oreil.ly/ogqEi*) available on GitHub that you can use to aggregate Cassandra and operating system metrics from across your cluster. This repository provides configuration files for running Prometheus and Grafana in Docker, and instructions for how to install agents that will expose metrics from your nodes to Prometheus. There are four built-in Grafana dashboards that provide useful sets of metrics to observe:

C* Cluster Overview
> This dashboard provides a top-level summary of the health of your cluster, highlighting cluster size, total data stored, node compute data in terms of CPU, memory, disk, and network, and Cassandra statistics.

C* Cluster Metrics
> This dashboard provides a deeper look into Cassandra-specific metrics, including read and write load and latencies, and information about active, pending, and blocked tasks per node, as shown in Figure 11-2.

C* Table Metrics
> This dashboard allows you to slice read and write metrics by keyspace and table to get a more fine-grained view.

System Metrics
> This dashboard provides a deeper look into the compute metrics of nodes as collected from the host operating system.

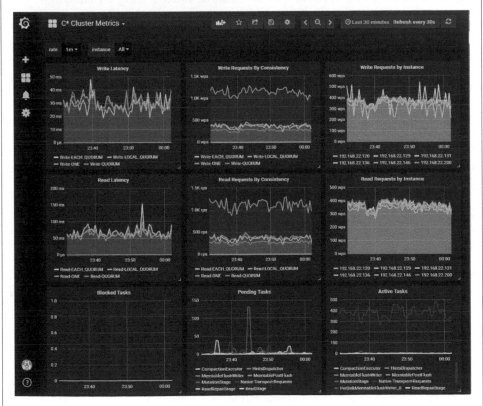

Figure 11-2. Cassandra metrics dashboard in Grafana

These dashboards enable you to assess the overall health of Cassandra clusters and get early indication of potential issues. Another powerful technique is to create dashboards that combine Cassandra cluster and application-level metrics such as those made available via the DataStax drivers, as you learned in Chapter 8. This will give you a deeper understanding of how Cassandra and your application code interact to affect the overall performance and health of your system.

Logging

While you can learn a lot about the overall health of your cluster from metrics, logging provides a way to get more specific detail about what's happening in your database so that you can investigate and troubleshoot specific issues. Cassandra uses the Simple Logging Facade for Java (SLF4J) API for logging, with Logback as the implementation. SLF4J provides a facade over various logging frameworks such as Logback, Log4j, and Java's built-in logger (`java.util.logging`).

You can learn more about Logback here (*http://logback.qos.ch/*). Cassandra's default logging configuration is found in the file *<cassandra-home>/conf/logback.xml*.

The SLF4J API is built around the concepts of *loggers* and *appenders*. Each class in a Java application has a dedicated logger, plus there are loggers for each level of the package hierarchy, as well as a root logger. This allows fine-grained control over logging; you can configure the log level for a particular class or any level in the package hierarchy, or even the root level.

The API uses a progression of log levels: `ALL < DEBUG < INFO < WARN < ERROR < FATAL < OFF`. When you configure a log level for a logger, messages at that log level and greater will be output via appenders (which we'll introduce later in this section). You can see how the logging level for Cassandra's classes is set in the *logback.xml* file:

```
<logger name="org.apache.cassandra" level="DEBUG"/>
```

Note that the root logger defaults to the `INFO` logging level, so that is the level at which all other classes will report.

An appender is responsible for taking generated log messages that match a provided filter and outputting them to some location. According to the default configuration found in *logback.xml*, Cassandra provides appenders for logging into three different files:

system.log

Contains logging messages at the INFO logging level and greater. You've already seen some of the contents of the *system.log* in Chapter 10 as you were starting and stopping a node, so you know that this log will contain information about nodes joining and leaving a cluster. It also contains information about schema changes.

debug.log

Contains more detailed messages useful for debugging, incorporating the DEBUG log level and above. This log can be pretty noisy but provides a lot of useful information about internal activity within a node, including memtable flushing and compaction.

gc.log

Contains messages related to the JVM's garbage collection. This is a standard Java garbage collection log file and is particularly useful for identifying long garbage collection pauses. We'll discuss garbage collection tuning in Chapter 13.

The default configuration also describes an appender for the console log, which you can access in the terminal window where you start Cassandra by setting the -f flag (to keep output visible in the foreground of the terminal window).

By default, Cassandra's log files are stored in the *logs* directory under the Cassandra installation directory. If you want to change the location of the *logs* directory, you can override this value using the CASSANDRA_LOG_DIR environment variable when starting Cassandra, or you can edit the *logback.xml* file directly.

The default configuration does not pick up changes to the logging settings on a live node. You can ask Logback to rescan the configuration file once a minute, by setting properties in the *logback.xml* file:

```
<configuration scan="true" scanPeriod="60 seconds">
```

You may also view the log levels on a running node through the nodetool getloggin glevels command, and override the log level for the logger at any level of the Java package and class hierarchy using nodetool setlogginglevel.

Other settings in the *logback.xml* file support rolling log files. By default, the logs are configured to use the SizeAndTimeBasedRollingPolicy. Each log file will be rolled to an archive once it reaches a size of 50 MB or at midnight, whichever comes first, with a maximum of 5 GB across all system logs. For example, look at the configuration of the rolling policy for the *system.log*:

```
<rollingPolicy class="ch.qos.logback.core.rolling.SizeAndTimeBasedRollingPolicy">
  <fileNamePattern>
    ${cassandra.logdir}/system.log.%d{yyyy-MM-dd}.%i.zip
  </fileNamePattern>
```

```
<maxFileSize>50MB</maxFileSize>
<maxHistory>7</maxHistory>
<totalSizeCap>5GB</totalSizeCap>
</rollingPolicy>
```

Each log file archive is compressed in zip format and named according to the pattern we've described, which will lead to files named *system.log.2020-05-30.0.zip, system.log. 2020-05-30.1.zip*, and so on. These archived log files are kept for seven days by default. The default settings may well be suitable for development and production environments; just make sure you account for the storage that will be required in your planning.

Examining Log Files

You can examine log files in order to determine things that are happening with your nodes. One of the most important tasks in monitoring Cassandra is to regularly check log files for statements at the WARN and ERROR log levels. Several of the conditions under which Cassandra generates WARN log messages are configurable via the *cassandra.yaml* file:

- The `tombstone_warn_threshold` property sets the maximum number of tombstones that Cassandra will encounter on a read before generating a warning. This value defaults to 1,000.

- The `batch_size_warn_threshold_in_kb` property sets the maximum size of the total data in a batch command, which is useful for detecting clients that might be trying to insert a quantity of data in a batch that will negatively impact the coordinator node performance. The default value is 5 kb.

- The `gc_warn_threshold_in_ms` property sets the maximum garbage collection pause that will cause a warning log. This defaults to 1,000 ms (1 second), and the corresponding setting for INFO log messages `gc_log_threshold_in_ms` is set at 200 ms.

Here's an example of a message you might find in the logs for a query that encounters a large number of tombstones:

```
WARN  [main] 2020-04-08 14:30:45,111 ReadCommand.java:598 -
   Read 0 live rows and 3291 tombstone cells for query
   SELECT * FROM reservation.reservations_by_hotel_date
   (see tombstone_warn_threshold)
```

Log Aggregation and Distributed Tracing

As with the use of metrics aggregation, it's also frequently helpful to aggregate logs across multiple microservices and infrastructure components in order to analyze threads of related activity correlated by time. There are many commercial log aggregation solutions available, and the ELK stack consisting of Elasticsearch, Logstash, and Kibana is a popular combination of open source projects used for log aggregation and analysis.

An additional step beyond basic aggregation is the ability to perform distributed traces of calls throughout a system. This involves incorporating a correlation ID into metadata passed on remote calls or messages between services. The correlation ID is a unique identifier, typically assigned by a service at the entry point into the system. The correlation ID can be used as a search criteria through aggregated logs to identify work performed across a system associated with a particular request. You'll learn more about tracing with Cassandra in Chapter 13.

You can also observe the regular operation of the cluster through the log files. For example, you could connect to a node in a cluster started using ccm, as described in Chapter 10, and write a simple value to the database using cqlsh:

```
$ ccm node2 cqlsh
cqlsh> INSERT INTO reservation.reservations_by_confirmation
  (confirm_number, hotel_id, start_date, end_date, room_number,
  guest_id) VALUES ('RS2G0Z', 'NY456', '2020-06-08', '2020-06-10',
  111, 1b4d86f4-ccff-4256-a63d-45c905df2677);
```

If you execute this command, cqlsh will use node2 as the coordinator, so you can check the logs for node2:

```
$ tail ~/.ccm/reservation_service/node2/logs/system.log
INFO  [Messaging-EventLoop-3-5] 2019-12-07 16:00:45,542
  OutboundConnection.java:1135 - 127.0.0.2:7000(127.0.0.3:7000)->
  127.0.0.3:7000(127.0.0.3:62706)-SMALL_MESSAGES-627a8d80 successfully
  connected, version = 12, framing = CRC, encryption = disabled
INFO  [Messaging-EventLoop-3-10] 2019-12-07 16:00:45,545
  OutboundConnection.java:1135 - 127.0.0.2:7000(127.0.0.4:7000)->
  127.0.0.4:7000(127.0.0.4:62707)-SMALL_MESSAGES-5bc34c55 successfully
  connected, version = 12, framing = CRC, encryption = disabled
INFO  [Messaging-EventLoop-3-8] 2019-12-07 16:00:45,593
  InboundConnectionInitiator.java:450 - 127.0.0.1:7000(127.0.0.2:62710)->
  127.0.0.2:7000-SMALL_MESSAGES-9e9a00e9 connection established,
  version = 12, framing = CRC, encryption = disabled
INFO  [Messaging-EventLoop-3-7] 2019-12-07 16:00:45,593
  InboundConnectionInitiator.java:450 - 127.0.0.3:7000(127.0.0.2:62709)->
  127.0.0.2:7000-SMALL_MESSAGES-e037c87e connection established,
  version = 12, framing = CRC, encryption = disabled
```

This output shows connections initiated from node2 to the other nodes in the cluster to write replicas, and the corresponding responses. If you examine the debug.log, you'll see similar information, but not the details of the specific query that was executed.

Full Query Logging

If you want more detail on exact CQL query strings that are used by client applications, use the full query logging feature introduced in Cassandra 4.0. The full query log is a binary log designed to be extremely fast and add the minimum possible overhead to your queries. Full query logging is also useful for live traffic capture and replay.

To enable full query logging on a node, create a directory to hold the logs and then set the full_query_logging_options in the *cassandra.yaml* file to point to the directory:

```
full_query_logging_options:
    log_dir: /var/tmp/fql_logs
```

Other configuration options allow you to control how often the log is rolled over to a new file (hourly by default), specify a command used to archive the log files, and set a limit for full query logs. The full query log will not be enabled until you run the node tool enablefullquerylog command.

Cassandra provides a tool to read the logs under the *tools/bin/fqltool* directory. Here's an example of what the output looks like after running some simple queries:

```
$ tools/bin/fqltool dump /var/tmp/fql_logs
Type: single-query
Query start time: 1575842591188
Protocol version: 4
Generated timestamp:-9223372036854775808
Generated nowInSeconds:1575842591
Query: INSERT INTO reservation.reservations_by_confirmation
  (confirm_number, hotel_id, start_date, end_date, room_number,
  guest_id) VALUES ('RS2G0Z', 'NY456', '2020-06-08', '2020-06-10', 111,
  1b4d86f4-ccff-4256-a63d-45c905df2677);
Values:

Type: single-query
Query start time: 1575842597849
Protocol version: 4
Generated timestamp:-9223372036854775808
Generated nowInSeconds:1575842597
Query: SELECT * FROM reservation.reservations_by_confirmation ;
Values:
```

Once you're done collecting full query logs, run the nodetool disablefullquerylog command.

Summary

In this chapter, you learned ways you can monitor and manage your Cassandra cluster. In particular, you learned the rich variety of operations Cassandra makes available via JMX to the MBean server. You also learned how to use `nodetool`, virtual tables, metrics, and logs to view what's happening in your Cassandra cluster. You are now ready to learn how to perform routine maintenance tasks to help keep your Cassandra cluster healthy.

Maintenance

In this chapter, we look at some things you can do to keep your Cassandra cluster healthy. Our goal here is to provide an overview of the various maintenance tasks available. Because the specific procedures for these tasks tend to change slightly from release to release, you'll want to make sure to consult the Cassandra documentation (*https://oreil.ly/EpZyq*) for the release you're using to make sure you're not missing any new steps.

Let's put our operations hats on and get started!

Health Check

There are some basic things that you'll want to look for to ensure that nodes in your cluster are healthy:

- Use `nodetool status` to make sure all of the nodes are up and reporting normal status. Check the `load` column for each node to make sure the cluster is well balanced. An uneven number of nodes per rack can lead to an imbalanced cluster.

- Check `nodetool tpstats` on your nodes for dropped messages, especially mutations, as this indicates that data writes may be lost. A growing number of blocked flush writers indicates the node is ingesting data into memory faster than it can be flushed to disk. Both of these conditions can indicate that Cassandra is having trouble keeping up with the load. As is usual with databases, once these problems begin, they tend to continue in a downward spiral. Three things that can improve the situation are a decreased load, scaling up (adding more hardware), or scaling out (adding another node and rebalancing).

If these checks indicate issues, you may need to dig deeper to get more information about what is going on:

- Check the logs to see that nothing is reporting at ERROR or WARN level (e.g., an OutOfMemoryError). Cassandra generates warning logs when it detects bad or obsolete configuration settings, operations that did not complete successfully, and memory or data storage issues.

- Review the configuration of the *cassandra.yaml* and *cassandra-env.sh* files for your Cassandra nodes to make sure that they match your intended settings, especially those for JVM and network configuration.

- Verify keyspace settings to make sure they match the topology of your cluster, and the table configuration to make sure each table reflects your intended compaction strategy and other settings. For example, a frequent configuration error is to forget to update keyspace replication strategies when adding a new data center.

- Beyond the health of your Cassandra nodes, it is always helpful to have a sense of the overall health and configuration of your system, including ensuring network connectivity and that Network Time Protocol (NTP) servers are functioning correctly.

These are a few of the most important things that experienced Cassandra operators have learned to look for, and the Cassandra documentation (*https://oreil.ly/roQi4*) on locating unhealthy nodes may also be helpful. As you gain experience with your own deployments, you can augment these with additional health checks that are appropriate for your own environment.

Common Maintenance Tasks

There are a few basic tasks that you'll need to perform as part of sequences involving other more impactful tasks. For example, it makes sense to take a snapshot only after you've performed a flush. We'll introduce a few such tasks in this section so we can reference them in the rest of the chapter.

Many of the tasks we look at in this chapter work somewhat differently depending on whether you're using virtual nodes (vnodes) or single-token nodes. Because vnodes are the default, we'll focus primarily on maintenance of those nodes, but provide pointers if you're using single-token nodes.

Flush

To force Cassandra to write data from its memtables to SSTables on the filesystem, you use the nodetool flush command:

```
$ nodetool flush
```

If you check the *debug.log* file, you'll see a series of output statements similar to this, one per table stored on the node:

```
DEBUG [RMI TCP Connection(2)-127.0.0.1] 2019-12-09 17:43:19,958
  StorageService.java:3751 - Forcing flush on keyspace reservation,
  CF reservations_by_confirmation
```

You can selectively flush specific keyspaces or even specific tables within a keyspace by naming them on the command line:

```
$ nodetool flush reservation
$ nodetool flush reservation reservations_by_hotel_date
```

Running flush also allows Cassandra to clear commitlog segments, as the data has been written to SSTables.

The nodetool drain command is similar to flush. This command actually performs a flush and then directs Cassandra to stop listening to commands from the client and other nodes. The drain command is typically used as part of an orderly shutdown of a Cassandra node and helps the node startup to run more quickly, as there is no commitlog to replay.

Cleanup

The nodetool cleanup command is a special case of compaction. It scans all of the data on a node and discards any data that is no longer owned by the node. You might ask why a node would have any data that it doesn't own.

Say that you've had a cluster running for some time, and you want to change the replication factor or the replication strategy. If you decrease the number of replicas for any data center, then there will be nodes in that data center that no longer serve as replicas for secondary ranges.

Or perhaps you've added a node to a cluster and reduced the size of the token range(s) owned by each node. Then each node may contain data from portions of token ranges it no longer owns.

In both of these cases, Cassandra does not immediately delete the excess data, in case a node goes down while you're in the middle of your maintenance. Instead, the normal compaction processes will eventually discard this data.

However, you may wish to reclaim the disk space used by this excess data more quickly to reduce the strain on your cluster. To do this, you can use the nodetool cleanup command. To complete as quickly as possible, you can allocate all compaction threads to the cleanup by adding the -j 0 option. As with the flush command, you can select to clean up specific keyspaces and tables.

Repair

As you learned in Chapter 6, Cassandra's tuneable consistency means that it is possible for nodes in a cluster to get out of sync over time. For example, writes at consistency levels less than ALL may succeed even if some of the nodes don't respond, especially when a cluster is under heavy load. It's also possible for a node to miss mutations if it is down or unreachable for longer than the time window for which hints are stored. The result is that different replicas for a different partition may have different versions of your data.

This is especially challenging when the missed mutations are deletions. A node that is down when the deletion occurs and remains offline for longer than the gc_grace_sec onds defined for the table in question can "resurrect" the data when it is brought back online.

Fortunately, Cassandra provides multiple anti-entropy mechanisms to help mitigate against inconsistency. You've already learned how read repair and higher consistency levels on reads can be used to increase consistency. The final key element of Cassandra's arsenal is the anti-entropy repair or manual repair, which you perform using the nodetool repair command.

You can execute a basic repair as follows:

```
$ nodetool repair
[2019-12-09 17:53:01,741] Starting repair command #1 (6aa75460-...
...
[2019-12-09 17:53:06,213] Repair completed successfully
[2019-12-09 17:53:06,219] Repair command #1 finished in 4 seconds
[2019-12-09 17:53:06,231] Replication factor is 1. No repair is needed...
[2019-12-09 17:53:06,240] Starting repair command #2 (6d56bcf0-...
...
```

You'll be able to see additional logging statements in the debug log referencing the same repair session identifiers. The output of these logs will vary, of course, based on the current state of your cluster. This particular command iterates over all of the keyspaces and tables in the cluster, repairing each one. You can also specify specific keyspaces and even one or more specific tables to repair via the syntax: nodetool repair <keyspace> {<table(s)>}; for example, nodetool repair reservation reservations_by_hotel_date.

Limiting Repair Scope

The repair command can be restricted to run in the local data center via the -local option (which you may also specify via the longer form --in-local-dc), or in a named data center via the -dc <name> option (or --in-dc <name>).

Let's look at what is happening behind the scenes when you run `nodetool repair` on a node. The node on which the command is run serves as the coordinator node for the request. The `org.apache.cassandra.service.ActiveRepairService` class is responsible for managing repairs on the coordinator node and processes the incoming request. The `ActiveRepairService` first executes a read-only version of a major compaction, also known as a *validation compaction*. During a validation compaction, the node examines its local data store and creates Merkle trees containing hash values representing the data in one of the tables under repair. This part of the process is generally expensive in terms of disk I/O and memory usage.

Next, the node initiates a TreeRequest/TreeResponse conversation to exchange Merkle trees with neighboring nodes. If the trees from the different nodes don't match, they have to be reconciled in order to determine the latest data values they should all be set to. If any differences are found, the nodes stream data to each other for the ranges that don't agree. When a node receives data for repair, it stores it in new SSTables.

Note that if you have a lot of data in a table, the resolution of Merkle trees (see "What's a Merkle Tree?" on page 120) will not go down to the individual partition. For example, in a node with a million partitions, each leaf node of the Merkle tree will represent about 30 partitions. Each of these partitions will have to be streamed together even if only a single partition requires repair. This behavior is known as *overstreaming*. For this reason, the streaming part of the process is generally expensive in terms of network I/O, and can result in duplicate storage of data that did not actually need repair.

This process is repeated on each node, for each included keyspace and table, until all of the token ranges in the cluster have been repaired.

Although repair can be an expensive operation, Cassandra provides several options to give you flexibility in how the work is spread out.

Full repair, incremental repair, and anti-compaction

In Cassandra releases prior to 2.1, performing a repair meant that all SSTables in a node were examined; this is now referred to as a *full repair*. The 2.1 release introduced *incremental repair*. With incremental repairs, data that has been repaired is separated from data that has not been repaired, a process known as *anti-compaction*.

This incremental approach improves the performance of the repair process, since there are fewer SSTables to search on each repair. Also, the reduced search means that fewer partitions are in scope, leading to smaller Merkle trees and less overstreaming.

Incremental Repair Improvements

Alex Dejanovski's excellent blog post, "Incremental Repair Improvements in Cassandra 4" (*https://oreil.ly/4JxtR*), explains the causes of overstreaming in some detail, including why the process of anti-compaction was not enough by itself to handle these issues in earlier releases, and how incremental repairs have been improved in the 4.0 release to be more reliable and efficient.

Cassandra adds a bit of metadata to each SSTable file in order to keep track of its repair status. You can view the repair time by using the `sstablemetadata` tool. For example, examining an SSTable for your reservation data indicates the data it contains has not been repaired:

```
$ tools/bin/sstablemetadata data/data/reservation/reservations_by_confirmation-
  ae8e00601a0211ea82980de3aa109b1d/na-1-big-Data.db
SSTable: data/data/reservation/reservations_by_confirmation-
  ae8e00601a0211ea82980de3aa109b1d/na-1-big
Partitioner: org.apache.cassandra.dht.Murmur3Partitioner
Bloom Filter FP chance: 0.01
...
SSTable Level: 0
Repaired at: 1575939181899 (12/09/2019 17:53:01)
Pending repair: --
...
```

Transitioning to Incremental Repair

Incremental repair became the default in the 2.2 release, and you must use the `-full` option to request a full repair. If you are using a version of Cassandra prior to 2.2, make sure to consult the release documentation for any additional steps to prepare your cluster for incremental repair.

Sequential and parallel repair

A sequential repair works on repairing one node at a time, while parallel repair works on repairing multiple nodes with the same data simultaneously. Sequential repair was the default for releases through 2.1, and parallel repair became the default in the 2.2 release.

When a sequential repair is initiated using the `-seq` option, a snapshot of data is taken on the coordinator node and each replica node, and the snapshots are used to construct Merkle trees. The repairs are performed between the coordinator node and each replica in sequence. During sequential repairs, Cassandra's dynamic snitch helps maintain performance. Because replicas that aren't actively involved in the current repair are able to respond more quickly to requests, the dynamic snitch will tend to route requests to these nodes.

A parallel repair is initiated using the `-par` option. In a parallel repair, all replicas are involved in repair simultaneously, and no snapshots are needed. Parallel repair places a more intensive load on the cluster than sequential repair, but also allows the repair to complete more quickly.

Partitioner range repair

When you run repair on a node, by default Cassandra repairs all of the token ranges for which the node is a replica. This is appropriate for the situation where you have a single node that is in need of repair—for example, a node that has been down and is being prepared to bring back online.

However, if you are doing regular repairs for preventative maintenance, as recommended, repairing all of the token ranges for each node means that you will be doing multiple repairs over each range. For this reason, the `nodetool repair` command provides the `-pr` option, which allows you to repair only the primary token range or *partitioner range*. If you repair each node's primary range, the whole ring will be repaired.

Subrange repair

Even with the `-pr` option, a repair can still be an expensive operation, as the primary range of a node can represent a large amount of data. For this reason, Cassandra supports the ability to repair by breaking the token range of a node into smaller chunks, a process known as *subrange repair*.

Subrange repair also addresses the issue of overstreaming. Because the full resolution of a Merkle tree is applied to a smaller range, Cassandra can precisely identify individual rows that need repair.

To initiate a subrange repair operation, you will need the start token (`-st`) and end token (`-et`) of the range to be repaired:

```
$ nodetool repair -st <start token> -et <end token>
```

You can obtain the assigned token ranges for your cluster using the `nodetool ring` command. You can also obtain your cluster's token ranges programmatically via the DataStax Cassandra drivers. For example, the Java driver provides operations to get the token ranges for a given host and keyspace, and to split a token range into subranges. You could use these operations to automate a repair request for each subrange, or just print out the ranges, as shown in this example:

```
for (TokenRange tokenRange :
    cqlSession.getMetadata().getTokenRanges())
{
```

```
    for (TokenRange splitRange : tokenRange.splitEvenly(SPLIT_SIZE))
    {
      System.out.println("Start: " + splitRange.getStart().toString() +
                          ", End: " + splitRange.getEnd().toString());
    }
  }
}
```

However, it's much more common to use one of the available tools, such as Reaper or the OpsCenter Repair Service, rather than attempting to implement your own subrange repair scheme.

Reaper: A Tool for Repairs

Cassandra Reaper (*http://cassandra-reaper.io*), an automated repair tool created by Spotify, has a web-based user interface added by The Last Pickle. Reaper orchestrates repairs across one or more clusters, and lets you pause, resume, or cancel repairs and track repair status. It uses a subrange repair approach as well as a backpressure mechanism to optimize repair performance. It uses a pluggable storage approach for its own record keeping, allowing you to store state in memory, the Java-based H2 database, Postgres, or Cassandra.

Best practices for repair

In practice, selecting and executing the proper repair strategy is one of the more difficult tasks in maintaining a Cassandra cluster. Here's a checklist to help guide your decision making:

Repair frequency
> Remember that the data consistency your applications will observe depends on the read and write consistency levels you use, the gc_grace_seconds defined for each table, and the repair strategy you put in place. If you're willing to use read/ write consistency levels that don't guarantee immediate consistency, you'll want to do more frequent repairs.

Repair scheduling
> Minimize the impact of repairs on your application by scheduling them at off-peak times for your application. Alternatively, spread the process out by using subrange repairs, or stagger repairs for various keyspaces and tables at different start times. Even better, use one of the tools mentioned previously to schedule your repairs.

Operations requiring repair
> Don't forget that some operations will require a full repair, such as changing the snitch on a cluster, changing the replication factor on a keyspace, or recovering a node that has been down.

Avoiding conflicting repairs

Cassandra does not allow multiple simultaneous repairs over a given token range, as repair by definition involves interactions between nodes. For this reason, it's best to manage repairs from a single location external to the cluster, rather than trying to implement automated processes on each node to repair their locally owned ranges.

Tracking Repair Status

Until a more robust repair status mechanism is put in place (for example, see the JIRA issue CASSANDRA-10302 (*https://oreil.ly/ xIodR*)), you can monitor repairs in progress using `nodetool net stats`.

Rebuilding Indexes

If you're using secondary indexes, they can get out of sync just like any other data. While it is true that Cassandra stores secondary indexes as tables behind the scenes, the index tables only reference values stored on the local node. For this reason, Cassandra's repair mechanisms aren't helpful for keeping indexes up to date.

Because secondary indexes can't be repaired and there is no simple way to check their validity, Cassandra provides the ability to rebuild them from scratch using `nodetool`'s `rebuild_index` command. It is a good idea to rebuild an index after repairing the table on which it is based, as the columns on which the index is based could have been represented among the values repaired. As with repair, remember that rebuilding indexes is a CPU- and I/O-intensive procedure.

Moving Tokens

If you have configured your cluster to use vnodes (which has been the default configuration since the 2.0. release), Cassandra handles the assignment of token ranges to each of the nodes in your cluster. This includes changing these assignments when nodes are added or removed from the cluster. However, if you're using single-token nodes, you'll need to reconfigure the tokens manually.

To do this, you first need to recalculate the token ranges for each node using the technique described in Chapter 10. Then you use the `nodetool move` command to assign the ranges. The `move` command takes a single argument, which is the new start token for the node:

```
$ nodetool move 3074457345618258600
```

After adjusting the token of each node, complete the process by running `nodetool cleanup` on each node.

Adding Nodes

You learned in Chapter 10 how to add a node using the Cassandra Cluster Manager (ccm), which was a great way for you to get started quickly. Now let's dig a little deeper to discuss some of the motivations and procedures for adding new nodes and data centers.

Adding Nodes to an Existing Data Center

If your application is successful, sooner or later you'll need to add nodes to your cluster. This might be as part of a planned increase in capacity. Alternatively, it might be in reaction to something you've observed in a health check, such as running low on storage space, nodes that are experiencing high memory and CPU utilization, or increasing read and write latencies.

Whatever the motivation for your expansion, you'll start by installing and configuring Cassandra on the machines that will host the new nodes. The process is similar to what we outlined in Chapter 10, but keep the following in mind:

- The Cassandra version must be the same as the existing nodes in the cluster. If you want to do a version upgrade, upgrade the existing nodes to the new version first and then add new nodes.

- You'll want to use the same configuration values as you did for other nodes in files such as *cassandra.yaml* and *cassandra-env.sh*, including the cluster_name, dynamic_snitch, and partitioner.

- Use the same seed nodes as in the other nodes. Typically, the new nodes you add won't be seed nodes, so there is no need to add the new nodes to the seeds list in your previously existing nodes.

- If you have multiple racks in your configuration, it's a good idea to add nodes to each rack at the same time to keep the number of nodes in each rack balanced. For some reason, this always reminds us of the rule in the classic board game Monopoly that requires houses to be spread evenly across properties.

- If you're using single-token nodes, you'll have to manually calculate the token range that will be assigned to each node, as you learned in "Moving Tokens" on page 281. A simple and effective way to keep the cluster balanced is to divide each token range in half, doubling the number of nodes in the cluster.

- In most cases, you'll want to configure your new nodes to begin bootstrapping immediately—that is, claiming token ranges and streaming the data for those ranges from other nodes. This is controlled by the autobootstrap property, which defaults to true. You can add this to your *cassandra.yaml* file to explicitly enable or disable auto bootstrapping.

Once the nodes are configured, you can start them, and use `nodetool status` to determine when they are fully initialized.

You can also watch the progress of a bootstrap operation on a node by running the `nodetool bootstrap` command. If you've started a node with auto bootstrapping disabled, you can also kick off bootstrapping remotely at the time of your choosing with the command `nodetool bootstrap resume`.

After all new nodes are running, make sure to run a `nodetool cleanup` on each of the previously existing nodes to clear out data that is no longer managed by those nodes.

Adding a Data Center to a Cluster

There are several reasons you might want to add an entirely new data center to your cluster. For example, let's say that you are deploying your application to a new data center in order to reduce network latency for clients in a new market. Or perhaps you need an active-active configuration to support disaster recovery requirements for your application. A third popular use case is to create a separate data center that can be used for analytics without impacting online customer transactions.

Let's explore how you can extend your cluster to a new data center. The same basic steps for adding a node in an existing data center apply to adding nodes in a new data center. Here are a few additional things you'll want to consider as you configure the *cassandra.yaml* file for each node:

- Make sure to configure an appropriate snitch for your deployment environment using the `endpoint_snitch` property and any configuration files associated with the snitch, for example, the *cassandra-rackdc.properties* file for the `GossipingPro pertyFileSnitch`. Hopefully you planned for this when first setting up your cluster, but if not, you will need to change the snitch in the initial data center. If you do need to change the snitch, you'll first want to change it on nodes in the existing data center and perform a repair before adding the new data center.

- Select a couple of the nodes in the new data center to be seeds, and configure the `seeds` property in the other nodes accordingly. Each data center should have its own seeds independent of the other data centers.

- The new data center is not required to have the same token range configuration as any existing data centers within the cluster. You can select a different number of vnodes or use single-token nodes if so desired.

After all of the nodes in the new data center have been brought online, you then configure replication options for the `NetworkTopologyStrategy` for all keyspaces that you wish to replicate to the new data center.

For example, to extend the `reservation` keyspace into an additional data center, you might execute the command:

```
cqlsh> ALTER KEYSPACE reservation WITH REPLICATION =
    {'class' : 'NetworkTopologyStrategy', 'DC1' : 3, 'DC2' : 3};
```

Note that the `NetworkTopologyStrategy` allows you to specify a different number of replicas for each data center.

Next, run the `nodetool rebuild` command on each node in the new data center. For example, the following command causes a node to rebuild its data by streaming from data center DC1:

```
$ nodetool rebuild -- DC1
```

You can rebuild multiple nodes in parallel if desired; just remember to consider the impact on your cluster before doing this. The `nodetool abortrebuild` command can be used to stop a rebuild that is in progress.

Once the rebuilding is complete, your new data center is ready to use.

Don't Forget Your Clients

You'll also want to consider how adding another data center affects your existing clients and their usage of LOCAL_* and EACH_* consistency levels. For example, if you have clients using the QUORUM consistency level for reads or writes, queries that used to be confined to a single data center will now involve multiple data centers. You may wish to switch to LOCAL_QUORUM to limit latency, or to EACH_QUORUM to ensure strong consistency in each data center. To maintain high availability from your clients, make sure they have designated the existing data center as the local data center, before changing the keyspace replication factor to extend to the new data center.

Handling Node Failure

From time to time, a Cassandra node may fail. Failure can occur for a variety of reasons, including hardware failure, a crashed Cassandra process, or a virtual machine that has been stopped or destroyed. A node that is experiencing network connectivity issues may be marked as failed in gossip and reported as down in `nodetool status`, although it may come back online if connectivity improves.

Taking Nodes Offline

If you wish to investigate issues with a node that is still running but not behaving normally, use the nodetool disablegossip and disablebinary commands to disable gossip and the CQL protocol, respectively. This will make the node appear down without actually killing it. Note that the node will still be accessible via JMX, so you can use other nodetool commands to diagnose and fix issues, before re-enabling via nodetool enablegossip and enablebinary. Similarly, the nodetool commands enablehandoff, disablehandoff, enablehintsfordc, and disablehintsfordc give you the ability to control a node's participation in hinted handoff.

In this section, we'll examine how to repair or replace failed nodes, as well as how to remove nodes from a cluster gracefully.

Repairing Failed Nodes

The first thing to do when you observe there is a failed node is to try to determine how long the node has been down. Here are some quick rules of thumb to know if repair or replacement may be required:

- If the node has been down for less than the hints delivery window specified by the max_hint_window_in_ms property, the hinted handoff mechanism should be able to recover the node. Restart the node and see whether it is able to recover. You can watch the node's logs or track its progress using nodetool status.

- If the node has been down for more than the hints window and less than the repair window defined lowest value of gc_grace_seconds for any of its contained tables, then restart the node. If it comes up successfully, run a nodetool repair.

- If the node has been down for longer than the repair window, it should be rebuilt or replaced to avoid tombstone resurrection.

Recovering from disk failure

A disk failure is one form of hardware failure from which a node may be able to recover. If your node is configured to use Cassandra with multiple disks (JBOD), the disk_failure_policy setting determines what action is taken when a disk failure occurs, and how you may be able to detect the failure:

- If the policy is set to the default (stop), the node will stop gossiping and accepting queries, which will cause it to appear as a downed node in nodetool status. You can still connect to the node via JMX.

- The policy setting `stop_paranoid` is similar to `stop`, with the addition that if any failures are detected on startup, the node will shut down the JVM.

- If the policy is set to `die`, the JVM exits and the node will appear as a downed node in `nodetool status`.

- If the policy is set to `ignore`, there's no immediate way to detect the failure.

- If the policy is set to `best_effort`, Cassandra continues to operate using the other disks, but a WARN log entry is written, which can be detected if you are using a log aggregation tool. Alternatively, you can use a JMX monitoring tool to monitor the state of the `org.apache.cassandra.db.BlacklistedDirectoriesM Bean`, which lists the directories for which the node has recorded failures.

Once you've detected a disk failure, you may want to try restarting the Cassandra process or rebooting the server. But if the failure persists, you'll have to replace the disk and delete the contents of the *data/system* directory in the remaining disks so that when you restart the node, it comes up in a consistent state. See the DataStax documentation (*https://oreil.ly/2DQKS*) for full instructions on recovering the node.

Replacing Nodes

If you've determined that a node can't be repaired or recovered after hardware failure, you will most likely want to replace it to keep your cluster balanced and maintain the same capacity.

While you could replace a node by removing the old node (as in the next section) and adding a new node, this is not a very efficient approach. Removing and then adding nodes results in excess streaming of data.

The more efficient approach is to add a node that takes over the token ranges of an existing node. To do this, you follow the previously outlined procedure for adding a node, with one addition. Edit the *jvm.options* file for the new node to add the following JVM option (where `<address>` is the IP address or hostname of the node that is being replaced):

```
JVM_OPTS="$JVM_OPTS -Dcassandra.replace_address_first_boot=<address>"
```

You can monitor the progress of bootstrapping by running `nodetool netstats` on the replacement node. After the replacement node finishes bootstrapping, you can remove this option, as it is not required for any subsequent restarts of the node.

If you're using the `PropertyFileSnitch`, you'll need to add the address of your new node to the properties file on each node and do a rolling restart of the nodes in your cluster. It is recommended that you wait 72 hours before removing the address of the old node to avoid confusing the gossiper.

Replacing a Seed Node

If the node you're replacing is a seed node, select an existing non-seed node to promote to a seed node. You'll need to add the promoted seed node to the `seeds` property in the *cassandra.yaml* file of existing nodes.

Typically, these will be nodes in the same data center, assuming you follow the recommendation of using a different seed list per data center. In this way, the new node you create will be a nonseed node and can bootstrap normally.

There are some additional details if you are using a package installation of Cassandra; consult the documentation for your specific release for additional details.

Removing Nodes

If you decide not to replace a downed node right away, or just want to shrink the size of your cluster, you'll need to remove or decommission the node. The proper technique for removal depends on whether the node being removed is online or can be brought online. We'll look at three techniques, in order of preference: decommission, remove, and assassinate.

Decommissioning a node

If the node is reporting as up, you *decommission* the node. Decommissioning a node means pulling it out of service. When you execute the `nodetool decommission` command, you're calling the `decommission()` operation on Cassandra's `StorageService` class. This operation assigns the token ranges that the node was responsible for to other nodes and then streams the data to those nodes. This is effectively the opposite of the bootstrapping operation.

If you still have access to the cluster created using `ccm` in Chapter 10, you can perform this operation with the command `ccm node4 nodetool decommission`. For other commands in this section we'll omit the `ccm <node>` part of the command for simplicity.

While the decommission is running, the node will report that it is in a leaving state in `nodetool status` via the code `UL` (up, leaving). You can check this in another terminal window:

```
$ nodetool status

Datacenter: datacenter1
=======================
Status=Up/Down
|/ State=Normal/Leaving/Joining/Moving
--  Address     Load        Tokens  Owns (effective)  Host ID       Rack
```

```
UN  127.0.0.1  712 KiB      256     76.3%         9019859a-...  rack1
UN  127.0.0.2  773.07 KiB   256     74.0%         5650bfa0-...  rack1
UN  127.0.0.3  770.18 KiB   256     72.3%         158a78c2-...  rack1
UL  127.0.0.4  140.69 KiB   256     77.4%         073da652-...  rack1
```

You can examine the server log of the decommissioned node to see the progress. For example, you'll see log statements indicating the node is leaving and streaming data to other nodes, followed by a series of statements summarizing the nodes to which data is being streamed:

```
INFO  [RMI TCP Connection(7)-127.0.0.4] 2019-12-11 22:02:20,815
    StorageService.java:1523 - LEAVING: sleeping 30000 ms for batch
    processing and pending range setup
INFO  [RMI TCP Connection(7)-127.0.0.4] 2019-12-11 22:02:50,975
    StorageService.java:1523 - LEAVING: replaying batch log and streaming
    data to other nodes
INFO  [RMI TCP Connection(7)-127.0.0.4] 2019-12-11 22:02:51,110
    StreamResultFuture.java:90 - [Stream #a5c6b340-1c9c-11ea-9fc3-c5e7d446c8a2]
    Executing streaming plan for Unbootstrap
INFO  [RMI TCP Connection(7)-127.0.0.4] 2019-12-11 22:02:51,110
    StreamSession.java:277 - [Stream #a5c6b340-1c9c-11ea-9fc3-c5e7d446c8a2]
    Starting streaming to 127.0.0.1:7000
...
```

After this, you'll see another log statement indicating the streaming of hints:

```
INFO  [RMI TCP Connection(7)-127.0.0.4] 2019-12-11 22:02:51,137
    StorageService.java:1523 - LEAVING: streaming hints to other nodes
```

You can also use `nodetool netstats` to monitor the progress of data streaming to the new replicas.

When the streaming is complete, the node announces its departure to the rest of the cluster for a period of 30 seconds, and then stops:

```
INFO  [RMI TCP Connection(7)-127.0.0.4] 2019-12-11 22:02:53,623
    StorageService.java:4231 - Announcing that I have left the ring for 30000ms
INFO  [RMI TCP Connection(7)-127.0.0.4] 2019-12-11 22:03:23,629
    Server.java:213 - Stop listening for CQL clients
WARN  [RMI TCP Connection(7)-127.0.0.4] 2019-12-11 22:03:23,630
    Gossiper.java:1822 - No local state, state is in silent shutdown, or node
    hasn't joined, not announcing shutdown
INFO  [RMI TCP Connection(7)-127.0.0.4] 2019-12-11 22:03:23,630
    MessagingService.java:500 - Waiting for messaging service to quiesce
```

Finally, the decommission is complete:

```
INFO  [RMI TCP Connection(7)-127.0.0.4] 2019-12-11 22:03:25,806
    StorageService.java:1523 - DECOMMISSIONED
```

If you call `decommission` on a node that can't be decommissioned (such as one that isn't part of the ring yet, or on the only node available), you'll see an error message to that effect.

Decommissioning Does Not Remove Datafiles

Be warned that data is not automatically removed from a decommissioned node. If you decide that you want to reintroduce a previously decommissioned node into the ring with a different range, you'll need to manually delete its data first.

Removing a node

If the node is down, you'll have to use the `nodetool removenode` command instead of `decommission`. If your cluster uses vnodes, the `removenode` command causes Cassandra to recalculate new token ranges for the remaining nodes and stream data from current replicas to the new owner of each token range.

If your cluster does not use vnodes, you'll need to manually adjust the token ranges assigned to each remaining node (as discussed in "Moving Tokens" on page 281) prior to running `removenode` to perform the streaming. The `removenode` command also provides a `--status` option to allow you to monitor the progress of streaming.

Most `nodetool` commands operate directly on the node identified via the `-h` flag. The syntax of the `removenode` command is a bit different, because it has to run on a node that is not the one being removed.

If you're following along, you can simulate a node being down by stopping it using the `nodetool stop` command on the actual node, for example, `ccm node3 nodetool stop`.

Rather than the IP address, the target node is identified via its host ID, which you can obtain via the `nodetool status` command:

```
$ nodetool status
Datacenter: datacenter1
=======================
Status=Up/Down
|/ State=Normal/Leaving/Joining/Moving
--  Address    Load        Tokens  Owns (effective)  Host ID       Rack
UN  127.0.0.1  712 KiB     256     100.0%            9019859a-...  rack1
UN  127.0.0.2  773.07 KiB  256     100.0%            5650bfa0-...  rack1
DN  127.0.0.3  770.18 KiB  256     100.0%            158a78c2-...  rack1

$ nodetool removenode  158a78c2-4a41-4eaa-b5ea-fb9747c29cc3
```

Assassinating a node

If the `nodetool removenode` operation fails, you can also attempt a `removenode -force`, and if that fails then run `nodetool assassinate` as a last resort. The `assassinate` command is similar to `removenode`, except that it does not re-replicate the removed node's data. This leaves your cluster in a state where repair is needed.

Another key difference from removenode is that the assassinate command takes the IP address of the node to assassinate, rather than the host ID:

```
$ nodetool assassinate 127.0.0.3
```

Don't Forget to Clean Up Seed Node Configuration

Whenever you remove a seed node, make sure you update the *cassandra.yaml* files on remaining nodes to remove the IP address of the node that was removed. You'll also want to make sure you still have an adequate number of seed nodes (at least two per data center).

Removing a data center

Should you wish to reduce the capacity of your cluster by eliminating an entire data center, the procedure uses commands you've already learned. Before starting, you'll want to make sure that no clients are connecting to nodes in the cluster. One way to check this would be to query the system_views.clients virtual table on each node, as you learned in Chapter 11. You'll want to run a full repair to make sure that all data from the data center being decommissioned is preserved.

To begin decommissioning the data center, alter all of the keyspaces that reference the data center to change the replication factor for the data center to zero. Then stop each of the nodes. You can check your work when complete using nodetool status.

Upgrading Cassandra

Because Cassandra continues to thrive and grow, new releases are made available on a regular basis, offering new features, improved performance, and bug fixes. You'll want to plan your adoption of these releases to take advantage of these improvements. As with any software upgrade, it's highly recommended to put the new version through its paces on your workload on development and test clusters before you move to deployment on production systems.

When you determine it is time for an upgrade, be careful to consult the *NEWS.txt* file found in the base directory of the new release and follow the upgrade instructions for releases between your current and new releases. An upgrade can be a complex process, and it's easy to cause a lot of damage to your cluster if you don't follow the instructions carefully.

A Cassandra cluster is upgraded via a process known as a *rolling upgrade*, as each node is upgraded one at a time. To perform a rolling upgrade:

1. First, run a nodetool drain on the node to clear out any writes that still need to be flushed to disk and stop receiving new writes.

2. Stop the node.

3. Make a backup copy of configuration files, such as *cassandra.yaml*, *jvm.options*, and *cassandra-env.sh*, so they don't get overwritten.

4. Install the new version.

5. Update the configuration files to match your specific deployment.

Best Practices for Updating Configuration Files

If you're upgrading your version of Cassandra, you may be tempted to try to reuse the *cassandra.yaml* and other configuration files from your previous deployment. The problem with this approach is that new releases frequently include additional configuration options. In addition, default values of configuration parameters occasionally change. In both of these cases, you won't be able to take advantage of the changes. If you are making a significant jump, there's even a chance that Cassandra won't function correctly with your old configuration file.

The best practice for an upgrade is to start with the *cassandra.yaml* file that comes with the new release and merge custom changes you've made for your environment from your old configuration file, such as the cluster name, seeds list, and the partitioner. Remember that the partitioner cannot be changed on a cluster that has data in it.

If you are on a Unix-based system, the merge can typically be done fairly simply by hand by using the `diff` command to identify the changes. Alternatively, you can use merge tools provided by your source code configuration tool or integrated development environment (IDE).

Upgrading a major version number (and some minor version upgrades) requires you to run the `nodetool upgradesstables` command to convert your stored datafiles to the latest format. It's also a good idea to use this command to ensure your SSTables are on the current version before beginning an upgrade. As with other `nodetool` commands you've examined, you can specify a keyspace or even tables within a keyspace to be upgraded, but in general you'll need to upgrade all of the node's tables. You can also update a node's tables when it is offline via the *bin/sstableupgrade* script.

These steps are repeated for each node in the cluster. Although the cluster remains operational while the rolling upgrade is in process, you should carefully plan your upgrade schedule, taking into account the size of the cluster. While there are still active nodes running the old version, you should avoid making schema changes or running any repairs. To minimize the upgrade window, you can defer running `upgradesstables` until after all the nodes are running the new version.

Backup and Recovery

Cassandra is built to be highly resilient to failure, with its support for configurable replication and multiple data centers. However, there are still a number of good reasons for backing up data:

- Human error or defects in application logic could cause good data to be overwritten and replicated to all nodes before the situation becomes known.
- SSTables can become corrupted.
- A multiple data center failure could wipe out your disaster recovery plan.

Cassandra provides two mechanisms for backing up data: *snapshots* and *incremental backups*. Snapshots provide a full backup, while incremental backups provide a way to back up changes a little at a time.

Full, Incremental, and Differential Backups

Database backup approaches typically take one of three forms:

- A *full backup* includes the entire state of a database (or specific tables within a database) and is the most expensive to create.
- An *incremental backup* includes the changes made over a period of time, typically the period of time since the last incremental backup. Taken together, a series of incremental backups provides a differential backup.
- A *differential backup* includes all of the changes made since the previous full backup.

Note that Cassandra does not provide a built-in differential backup mechanism, focusing instead on full and incremental backups.

Cassandra's snapshots and backups are complementary techniques that are used together to support a robust backup and recovery approach.

Both the snapshot and backup mechanisms create hard links to SSTable files, which avoids creating extra files in the short term. However, these files can accumulate over time as compaction occurs and files that are deleted from the data directory are still preserved via the hard links.

The tasks of copying these files to another location and deleting them so they do not fill up disk space are left to the user. However, these tasks are easy to automate and there are various tools that support this, such as Medusa or Jeremy Grosser's Tablesnap (*https://oreil.ly/RTSfx*).

Taking a Snapshot

The purpose of a snapshot is to make a copy of some or all of the keyspaces and tables in a node and save it to what is essentially a separate database file. This means that you can back up the keyspaces elsewhere or leave them where they are in case you need to restore them later. When you take a snapshot, Cassandra first performs a flush, and then makes a hard link for each SSTable file.

Taking a snapshot is straightforward:

```
$ nodetool snapshot
Requested creating snapshot(s) for [all keyspaces] with snapshot name
  [1576202815095] and options {skipFlush=false}
Snapshot directory: 1576202815095
```

Here, a snapshot has been taken for all of the keyspaces on the server, including Cassandra's internal `system` keyspaces. If you want to specify only a single keyspace to take a snapshot of, you can pass it as an additional argument: `nodetool snapshot reservation`. Alternatively, you can use the `-cf` option to list the name of a specific table.

You can list the snapshots that have been taken with the `nodetool listsnapshots` command:

```
$ nodetool listsnapshots
Snapshot Details:
Snapshot name Keyspace name   Column family name    True size  Size on disk
1576202815095 system_schema   columns               12.66 KiB  12.69 KiB
...

    Total TrueDiskSpaceUsed: 160.66 MiB
```

To find these snapshots on the filesystem, remember that the contents of the data directory are organized in subdirectories for keyspaces and tables. There is a snapshots directory under each table's directory, and each snapshot is stored in a directory named for the timestamp at which it was taken. For example, you can find the `reser vations_by_confirmation` table snapshots at:

CASSANDRA_HOME/data/data/reservation/
reservations_by_confirmationreservations_by_confirmation-
ae8e00601a0211ea82980de3aa109b1d/snapshots/

Each snapshot also contains a *manifest.json* file that lists the SSTable files included in the snapshot. This is used to make sure that the entire contents of a snapshot are present.

Point-in-Time Snapshots Across Multiple Nodes

The `nodetool snapshot` command only operates on a single server. You will need to run this command at the same time on multiple servers if you want a point-in-time snapshot, using a parallel *ssh* tool such as *pssh* or one of the utilities listed.

Cassandra also provides an *auto snapshot* capability that takes a snapshot on every `DROP KEYSPACE`, `DROP TABLE`, or `TRUNCATE` operation. This capability is enabled by default via the `auto_snapshot` property in the *cassandra.yaml* file to prevent against accidental data loss. There is an additional property, `snapshot_before_compaction`, which defaults to false.

Clearing a Snapshot

You can also delete any snapshots you've made, say, after you've backed them up to permanent storage elsewhere. It is a good idea to delete old snapshots before creating a new one.

To clear your snapshots, you can manually delete the files or use the `nodetool clear snapshot` command, which takes an optional keyspace option.

Enabling Incremental Backup

After you perform a snapshot, you can enable Cassandra's incremental backup using the `nodetool enablebackup` command. This command applies to all keyspaces and tables in the node.

You can also check whether incremental backups are enabled with `nodetool status backup`, and disable incremental backups with `nodetool disablebackup`.

When incremental backups are enabled, Cassandra creates backups as part of the process of flushing SSTables to disk. The backup consists of a hard link to each data-file Cassandra writes under a *backups* directory; for example:

CASSANDRA_HOME/data/data/reservation/
reservations_by_confirmationreservations_by_confirmation-
ae8e00601a0211ea82980de3aa109b1d/backups/

To enable backups across a restart of the node, set the `incremental_backups` property to `true` in the *cassandra.yaml* file.

You can safely clear incremental backups after you perform a snapshot and save the snapshot to permanent storage.

Restoring from Snapshot

The process of restoring a node from backups begins with collecting the most recent snapshot plus any incremental backups since the snapshot. There is no difference in how datafiles from snapshots and backups are treated.

Before starting a restore operation on a node, you will most likely want to truncate the tables to clear any data changes made since the snapshot.

Don't Forget to Restore the Schema!

Be aware that Cassandra does not include the database schema as part of snapshots and backups. You will need to make sure that the schema is in place before doing any restore operations. Fortunately, this is easy to do using the `cqlsh`'s DESCRIBE TABLES operation, which can easily be scripted.

If your cluster topology is the same as when the snapshots were taken, there have been no changes to the token ranges for each node, and there are no changes to the replication factor for the tables in question, you can copy the SSTable datafiles into the data directory for each node. If the nodes are already running, running the `node tool import` command will cause Cassandra to load the data. In releases prior to Cassandra 4.0, you'll use `nodetool refresh` instead.

If there has been a change to the topology, token ranges, or replication, you'll need to use a tool called `sstableloader` to load the data. In some ways, the `sstableloader` behaves like a Cassandra node: it uses the gossip protocol to learn about the nodes in a cluster, but it does not register itself as a node. It uses Cassandra's streaming libraries to push SSTables to nodes. The `sstableloader` does not copy SSTable files directly to every node, but inserts the data in each SSTable into the cluster, allowing the partitioner and replication strategy of the cluster to do their work.

The `sstableloader` is also useful for moving data between clusters.

SSTable Utilities

There are several utilities found in the *bin* and *tools/bin* directories that operate directly on SSTable datafiles on the filesystem of a Cassandra node. These files have a *.db* extension. For example:

CASSANDRA_HOME/data/hotels-b9282710a78a11e5a0a5fb1a2fbefd47/ma-1-big-Data.db/

In addition to the `sstablemetadata`, `sstableloader`, and `sstableupgrade` tools you've seen already, here are a few other SSTable utilities:

sstableutil
> This utility lists the SSTable files for a provided table name.

sstabledump
> This utility outputs a given SSTable file in JSON format.

sstableverify
> This utility verifies the SSTable files for a provided keyspace and table name, identifying any files that exhibit errors or data corruption. This is an offline version of the `nodetool verify` command.

sstablescrub
> This utility is an offline version of the `nodetool scrub` command. Because it runs offline, it can be more effective at removing corrupted data from SSTable files. If the tool removes any corrupt rows, you will need to run a repair.

sstablerepairedset
> This marks specific SSTables as repaired or unrepaired to enable transitioning a node to incremental repair. Because incremental repair is the default as of the 2.2 release, clusters created on 2.2 or later will not need to use this tool.

Several of the utilities help assist in managing compaction, which we'll examine further in Chapter 13:

sstableexpiredblockers
> This utility reveals blocking SSTables that prevent an SSTable from being deleted. This class outputs all SSTables that are blocking other SSTables from getting dropped so you can determine why a given SSTable is still on disk.

sstablelevelreset
> This utility resets the level to 0 on a given set of SSTables, which will force the SSTable to be compacted as part of the next compaction operation.

`sstableofflinerelevel`
> This utility reassigns SSTable levels for tables using the `LeveledCompactionStrat egy`. This is useful when a large amount of data is ingested quickly, such as with a bulk import.

`sstablesplit`
> This utility splits SSTables files into multiple SSTables of a maximum designated size. This is useful if a major compaction has generated large tables that otherwise would not be compacted for a long time.

Under normal circumstances, you probably won't need to use these tools very often, but they can be quite useful in debugging and gaining a greater understanding of how Cassandra's data storage works. Utilities that modify SSTables, such as `sstablelevel reset`, `sstablerepairedset`, `sstablesplit`, and `sstableofflinerelevel`, must be run when Cassandra is not running on the local host.

Maintenance Tools

While it is certainly possible to maintain a Cassandra cluster entirely via `nodetool`, many organizations, especially those with larger installations, have found it helpful to make use of advanced tools that provide automated maintenance features and improved visualizations. There are other community tools available, in addition to "Medusa: A Backup and Restore Tool" on page 293 and "Reaper: A Tool for Repairs" on page 280.

Netflix Priam

Priam (*https://oreil.ly/xswy1*) is a tool built by Netflix to help manage its Cassandra clusters. Priam was the King of Troy in Greek mythology, and the father of Cassandra. Priam automates the deployment, starting, and stopping of nodes, as well as backup and restore operations.

Priam is also well integrated with the Amazon Web Services (AWS) cloud environment, although AWS deployment is not required. For example, Priam supports deployment of Cassandra in Auto Scaling groups (ASGs), automated backup of snapshots to the Simple Storage Service (S3), and configuration of networking and security groups for Cassandra clusters that span multiple regions.

While Priam does not include a user interface, it does provide a RESTful API that you can use to build your own frontend or access directly via `curl`. The API provides the ability to start and stop nodes, access `nodetool` commands (with JSON-formatted output), and perform backup and restore operations.

DataStax OpsCenter

DataStax OpsCenter is a web-based management and monitoring solution for clusters using the DataStax Enterprise distribution of Cassandra. OpsCenter provides metrics dashboards for tracking cluster health, and repair and backup services to automate maintenance tasks discussed in this chapter.

Cassandra Sidecars

Cassandra has traditionally been known as extremely powerful, but difficult to operate. One difficulty is the number of different tools, interfaces (JMX, CQL), and configuration files (XML, YAML, properties files) that an operator must learn. In addition to the configuration, monitoring, and management of each individual node, there are activities that involve interactions between multiple nodes in a cluster. For example, deploying a cluster involves planning which nodes will be seeds, token assignments (for single-token clusters), and setting topology properties. Upgrading the Cassandra version across a cluster involves rolling restarts as individual nodes are updated, and so on.

Many Cassandra operators have built tools that automate specific cluster maintenance activities, and we've cited several of them in this chapter. Many of these tools require a *co-process* or *sidecar* that is resident on the same host as the Cassandra daemon.

In 2018, community members articulated multiple competing proposals for an official Cassandra sidecar. Several of these began collaborating toward a unified approach that became the first Cassandra Enhancement Proposal, also known as CEP-1 (*https://oreil.ly/w2Ros*). The goals of this enhancement proposal are to produce a minimum viable product (MVP) implementation, with other CEPs likely to extend the performance of the sidecar. This initial implementation will be an experimental feature and is expected to automate:

- Health checks for determining if a node can serve as a coordinator or receive writes, or if a cluster can achieve required consistency for a given keyspace

- Bulk commands to be executed on some or all nodes, such as getting and retrieving settings

- Life cycle commands to start and stop nodes according to best practices, for example, executing a drain during stop

- Desire-based orchestration, such as rolling restarts, or in the future, a rolling version upgrade

- Automating scheduled maintenance, such as cleanup in the initial implementation, and compaction and backups in future releases

- Exposing a standard metrics agent, such as Prometheus

Design constraints for sidecars include:

- Sidecar processes should be separately installable or deployable from the Cassandra daemon and run in their own JVM.
- Changes to the Cassandra daemon should be minimized.
- Sidecars should expose HTTP-based RESTful APIs for maximum accessibility by other tools and avoid usage of SSH and JMX due to the security vulnerabilities of these interfaces.

The Cassandra sidecar(s) will provide a much-needed building block for improving the management of Cassandra, including integrability with other management tools and frameworks.

Cassandra Kubernetes Operators

We've previously discussed the deployment of Cassandra nodes in Docker containers in Chapter 3 and creating clusters of these nodes in Chapter 10. Now it's time to learn about managing containerized Cassandra clusters in Kubernetes.

Kubernetes (*https://kubernetes.io*) (or K8s for short) is a system for automating the deployment and management of containerized applications. It is an open source system based on Borg, Google's system built up over many years to run and manage billions of containers within its internal infrastructure. Kubernetes has become the leading platform, surging in popularity ahead of similar platforms, such as Docker Swarm or Apache Mesos.

Kubernetes provides the building blocks for describing distributed systems that are portable across cloud providers and supports hybrid cloud and multicloud deployments. These building blocks include automated deployment and scaling, self healing, service discovery, load balancing, secret management, and others.

Figure 12-1 shows a few key K8s concepts and how they apply to managing a Cassandra cluster. This is not intended as prescriptive but only to illustrate K8s features and concepts that are useful for managing Cassandra.

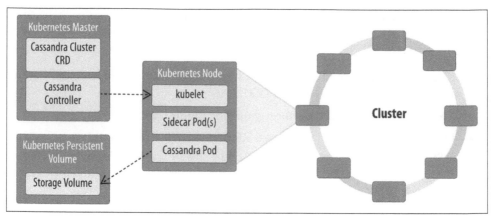

Figure 12-1. Running Cassandra in Kubernetes

A Kubernetes cluster is composed of *master* and *worker* nodes. A worker node is a physical or virtual machine that can host *pods*, the basic execution unit of a K8s application. A pod can run a single container or multiple related containers; for example, Cassandra and sidecars could run in a single pod.

Kubernetes does not provision nodes; they must be created externally and registered with the Kubernetes master. Each node has an agent known as a *kubelet* that is responsible for running pods that are allocated to it on an underlying container runtime, such as Docker, as well as agents that support cross-cutting concerns, such as logging.

A Kubernetes application consists of a collection of pods that together provide some logical capability. Applications can expose *services*, and you can define *namespaces* to help define application boundaries.

The Kubernetes control plane consists of the *Kubernetes Master* and the kubelet running on each node. The master is typically run on dedicated hardware (although it is not required to do so), and you can run multiple masters for high availability. The K8s Master contains an *API server* for the K8s API, a data store (typically *etcd*) used to track cluster status, a scheduler, and controllers. You use the *kubectl* client to communicate with the master.

Kubernetes is a declarative system—you specify the desired state of your cluster rather than providing the detailed instructions for how to get there. A *controller* is a loop that observes the K8s cluster to detect differences between the current and desired state and executes actions that move toward the desired state. There are controllers that manage the deployment of pods to nodes, tracking node health, the configuration of networking and load balancers, exposing pod interfaces as services, interfacing with cloud infrastructure, and more.

While Kubernetes can be used to deploy infrastructure such as messaging frameworks or databases, it does not know how to operate this infrastructure. A Kubernetes *operator* represents an implementation of the knowledge human operators typically have about deploying applications, their expected behavior, and how to detect and correct issues.

An operator consists of a controller and a *custom resource definition* (CRD). Thus, a Cassandra operator would consist of a Cassandra controller and a CRD that defines the contents of a Cassandra cluster, consisting of multiple pods, network infrastructure, and storage. A CRD allows the definition of a cluster as a single resource based on a provided cluster name, Kubernetes namespace, node count, persistent volumes to use, and custom Cassandra configuration settings for the *cassandra.yaml* file. These parameters are used to configure each pod via the kubelet. Cassandra CRDs typically use a feature called *anti-affinity* to ensure that nodes in a Cassandra cluster are started on separate worker nodes to ensure high availability.

A Kubernetes *deployment* describes how to deploy pods based on a provided container image, where each pod is essentially the same and could be deployed to any worker node or even replaced by a pod running the same container image on another node at the direction of the scheduler. A *stateful set* is similar to a deployment but includes the ability to have a fixed identity for each pod, with stable network endpoints and persistent storage.

Cassandra and the Origin of Stateful Sets

The concept of stateful sets was added to facilitate the deployment of Cassandra and other databases. In fact, Cassandra is now the featured database in the Kubernetes tutorial on stateful sets (*https://oreil.ly/2QjHR*).

For storage, Kubernetes provides *volumes* that have the same life cycle as the pod, but for Cassandra nodes you'll need storage that is more long-lasting. Thankfully, Kubernetes also allows you to configure *persistent volumes* representing external storage provided as a resource to the Kubernetes cluster. A Cassandra CRD can define a *persistent volume claim* for each Cassandra pod that Kubernetes will use to allocate storage on a persistent volume.

A *service* is an abstraction of an application interface, where the implementation might consist of multiple pods behind a load balancer. A Cassandra CRD can describe a service that represents exposed endpoints of one or more Cassandra nodes for your client applications to use as contact points.

The *operator* is a common pattern in Kubernetes for providing automated management of complex applications such as databases. Operators typically consist of one or more custom resources that extend the Kubernetes API and a controller to manage the state of each type of resource. Operators are often packaged with a script known as a *Helm chart* to describe a typical deployment using a Cassandra operator.

Several organizations have written Cassandra operators to automate the maintenance operations discussed in this chapter, such as scaling clusters up and down, performing automated repair and backup, restarting or replacing downed nodes, and rolling restarts and upgrades:

- Orange has released an operator called CassKop (*https://oreil.ly/3tavg*). This is arguably the most mature of the operators, with an extension for managing multiregion clusters (*https://oreil.ly/lfkdy*) in progress. You can read more about this operator on the blog.

- The Instaclustr Cassandra operator (*https://oreil.ly/VAl_v*) leverages experience from providing Cassandra-as-a-Service on multiple clouds. You can read more about this operator and its design on *DZone* (*https://oreil.ly/UmQnM*).

- DataStax has an open source operator called cass-operator (*https://github.com/k8ssandra/cass-operator*), which is based on the code it uses to manage its Astra service. cass-operator supports deployment of both Cassandra and DataStax Enterprise clusters.

After initially working independently, these organizations and other community members began collaborating through the Cassandra Enhancement Proposal (CEP) process under CEP-2 (*https://oreil.ly/LDk6D*). As a result of this process, cass-operator was selected as the operator that the community would rally behind, and the operator has been incorporated as part of the K8ssandra project.

K8ssandra, A Data Platform for Kubernetes

The open-source K8ssandra project was created by John Sanda and other engineers at DataStax in late 2020 as a complete data platform for running Cassandra on Kubernetes, bringing cass-operator together with other tools typically needed for production deployments. These tools include Cassandra sidecars for management and metrics (see "Cassandra Sidecars" on page 298), Prometheus and Grafana for metrics collection and aggregation, Medusa for backup and restore (see "Medusa: A Backup and Restore Tool" on page 293), and Reaper for performing regular repair operations (see "Reaper: A Tool for Repairs" on page 280). K8ssandra also deploys the Stargate data gateway (see "Stargate, An Open Source Data Gateway" on page 184) to provide developer-friendly APIs on top of Cassandra.

While the K8ssandra 1.x release series relies on the Helm package manager for deploying resources on Kubernetes clusters, performing more complex management tasks and extending Cassandra clusters across multiple Kubernetes clusters has proven more difficult (*https://oreil.ly/PJFKR*), so the team began implementing a K8ssan-

---

dra operator (*https://github.com/k8ssandra/k8ssandra-operator*) in mid-2021, working toward a 2.0 release.

Summary

In this chapter, you learned some of the ways you can interact with Cassandra to perform routine maintenance tasks; add, remove, and replace nodes; back up and recover data with snapshots, and more. You also looked at some tools that help automate these tasks to speed up maintenance and reduce errors. Now you're ready to apply the knowledge you've obtained about configuring, monitoring, and maintaining Cassandra clusters to tune your clusters for optimal performance.

Performance Tuning

In this chapter, you'll learn how and why to tune Cassandra to improve performance, and a methodology for setting performance goals, monitoring your cluster's performance, simulating stress loads, and troubleshooting performance goals. You'll also learn about specific settings in Cassandra's configuration files, and options on individual tables, and how they affect the performance and resource utilization of your cluster.

Managing Performance

To be effective at achieving and maintaining a high level of performance in your cluster, it's helpful to think of managing performance as a process that begins with the architecture of your application and continues through development and operations.

Setting Performance Goals

Before beginning any performance tuning effort, it is important to have clear goals in mind, whether you are just getting started on deploying an application, or maintaining an existing one.

When planning a cluster, it's important to understand how the cluster will be used: the number of clients, intended usage patterns, expected peak periods, and so on. This is useful in planning the initial cluster capacity and for planning cluster growth, as discussed in Chapter 10.

An important part of this planning effort is to identify clear performance goals in terms of both throughput (the number of queries serviced per unit time) and latency (the time to complete a given query). Usually, you will be trying to increase throughput while reducing latency. A good place to start is with the use cases that you anticipate will put the greatest load on your cluster.

For example, let's say that you're building an ecommerce website for hotel reservations that uses the data model designed in Chapter 5. If you're following a process of setting performance goals for various operations on the website, you might anticipate that most of the traffic will come from customers browsing the site, shopping for available hotel rooms. As a result, you set a goal for the site to respond to each search for available rooms in under a second. Through the process of allocating that performance budget to various services and layers, you might then arrive at the following goal for shopping queries on your Cassandra cluster:

> The cluster must support 30,000 read operations per second from the `avail able_rooms_by_hotel_date` table with a 99th percentile read latency of 5 ms.

This is a statement that includes both throughput and latency goals. Throughput goals are typically expressed in terms of number of operations per second that can be supported by the cluster as a whole. Latency goals are expressed in terms of percentile distribution: for example, the goal that 99% of all queries complete in under 5 milliseconds.

In this chapter, you'll learn how to measure performance goals similar to the one here using `nodetool tablestats`. It's useful to have similar goals for each of the access patterns and resulting Cassandra queries that your application must support. You can use the techniques identified in Chapter 11 to track performance against these goals and identify when performance is trending in the wrong direction.

The USE Method

Brendan Gregg has created a methodology known for analyzing system performance based on the utilization, saturation, and errors (USE) of each system resource, including CPU, memory, and disk and network I/O. By tracking performance metrics and thresholds across multiple resources, you can have a better awareness of the state of your system holistically, identifying and addressing root causes instead of making naive attempts to optimize individual resources in isolation.

For example, tracking CPU and disk I/O in parallel, you might identify a period of increased CPU activity corresponding to saturation of disk I/O corresponding to increased query latency. Further investigation of this might point to a high compaction workload, especially if you can correlate the high-activity period with warning messages in Cassandra's logs. This might lead you to identifying issues with your data model or application, such as usage that results in a very wide partition or a large number of tombstones. You can read more about the USE method at Brendan Gregg's website (*https://oreil.ly/T2Ld2*).

Regardless of your specific performance goals, it's important to remember that performance tuning is all about trade-offs. Having well-defined performance goals will help you articulate what trade-offs are acceptable for your application. For example:

- Enabling SSTable compression in order to conserve disk space, at the cost of reading more data than necessary and additional CPU processing
- Throttling network usage and threads, which can be used to keep network and CPU utilization under control, at the cost of reduced throughput and increased latency
- Increasing or decreasing the number of threads allocated to specific tasks such as reads, writes, or compaction in order to affect the priority relative to other tasks or to support additional clients
- Increasing heap size in order to decrease query times
- Reducing the read or write consistency level required by your application in order to increase throughput

These are just a few of the trade-offs that you will find yourself considering in performance tuning. We'll highlight others throughout the rest of this chapter.

Benchmarking and Stress Testing

Once you have set performance targets, it's helpful to create some load on your cluster to get an idea of the performance you can expect in your production deployment. There are two main approaches to consider: benchmarking and stress testing.

Benchmarking
This is the process of measuring the performance of software under a defined load. The purpose of this might be to compare one database against another, or to compare different configurations of the same system. There are standard database benchmarks available, such as the Yahoo Cloud Serving Benchmark (YCSB), which has proven popular for benchmarking distributed NoSQL databases. However, it can be difficult to get an apples-to-apples comparison between different databases without a significant amount of tuning.

Stress testing
This is similar to benchmarking in that you are generating a load on the system. However, in this case the goal is slightly different. Instead of measuring performance for comparison against a baseline, in a stress test you increase the load on the system in order to discover errors and performance degradations, such as bottlenecks.

Our recommendation is to focus on creating benchmarks and stress tests that exercise your Cassandra data models on test clusters resembling your desired production topology and configuration options, with loads resembling your expected nominal and peak operating conditions. It's especially important to have tests available that can verify there is no performance degradation when you make significant changes to your data models, cluster configuration and topology, or application.

Using cassandra-stress

The first tool to examine is one that ships with Cassandra. You can use `cassandra-stress` to run a stress test on your Cassandra cluster. To run `cassandra-stress`, navigate to the *<cassandra-home>/tools/bin* directory and run the command:

```
$ cassandra-stress write n=1000000
```

First, the stress tool will print out a detailed description of your chosen configuration, including how the tool will connect to the cluster, the mix of CQL commands that will be run, and the schema to be used for testing, including how random values will be generated. Then you'll see a few lines indicating the test is starting:

```
Connected to cluster: reservation_cluster, max pending requests per connection
    128, max connections per host 8
Datacenter: datacenter1; Host: localhost/127.0.0.1:9042; Rack: rack1
Datacenter: datacenter1; Host: /127.0.0.2:9042; Rack: rack1
Datacenter: datacenter1; Host: /127.0.0.3:9042; Rack: rack1
Created keyspaces. Sleeping 1s for propagation.
Sleeping 2s...
Warming up WRITE with 50000 iterations...
Running WRITE with 200 threads for 1000000 iteration
...
```

If you're using the `ccm` tool introduced in Chapter 10 to run a local cluster, you could run `ccm node1 stress write n=1000000`.

The output lists the nodes to which the tool is connected (in this case, a cluster created using ccm) and creates a sample keyspace and table to which it can write data. The test warms up by doing 50,000 writes, and then the tool begins to output metrics as it continues to write, which we've omitted for brevity. The tool creates a pool of threads (defaulting to 200) that perform one write after another, until it inserts one million rows. Finally, it prints a summary of results:

```
Results:
Op rate                    :    22,187 op/s  [WRITE: 22,187 op/s]
Partition rate             :    22,187 pk/s   [WRITE: 22,187 pk/s]
Row rate                   :    22,187 row/s [WRITE: 22,187 row/s]
Latency mean               :     9.0 ms [WRITE: 9.0 ms]
Latency median             :     1.0 ms [WRITE: 1.0 ms]
Latency 95th percentile    :    50.9 ms [WRITE: 50.9 ms]
Latency 99th percentile    :   131.9 ms [WRITE: 131.9 ms]
Latency 99.9th percentile  :   267.9 ms [WRITE: 267.9 ms]
Latency max                :   628.6 ms [WRITE: 628.6 ms]
Total partitions           :   1,000,000 [WRITE: 1,000,000]
```

```
Total errors             :             0 [WRITE: 0]
Total GC count           : 0
Total GC memory          : 0.000 KiB
Total GC time            :     0.0 seconds
Avg GC time              :     NaN ms
StdDev GC time           :     0.0 ms
Total operation time     : 00:00:45
```

Let's unpack these results. They summarize the insertion of one million values into a completely untuned three-node cluster running on a single machine using ccm. The insertions completed in about 45 seconds, which represents a rate over 20,000 writes per second. The median latency per write operation was 1 millisecond, although a small number of writes took longer. Your results will, of course, vary depending on the configuration of your cluster, including topology and choice of hardware.

Now that you have all of this data in the database, use the test to read some values, too:

```
$ cassandra-stress read n=200000
...
Warming up READ with 50000 iterations...
Thread count was not specified

Running with 4 threadCount
Running READ with 4 threads for 200000 iteration
...
```

If you examine the output, you will see that it first performs a run using a small number of threads (4) and ramps up the number of threads used on each subsequent run, printing the results of each run and comparing the results with the previous run. Here's an example of a run that used 121 client threads:

```
Running with 121 threadCount
Running READ with 121 threads for 200000 iteration
...

Results:
Op rate                   :      23,493 op/s  [READ: 23,493 op/s]
Partition rate            :      23,493 pk/s  [READ: 23,493 pk/s]
Row rate                  :      23,493 row/s [READ: 23,493 row/s]
Latency mean              :       5.1 ms [READ: 5.1 ms]
Latency median            :       0.9 ms [READ: 0.9 ms]
Latency 95th percentile   :      22.0 ms [READ: 22.0 ms]
Latency 99th percentile   :      88.8 ms [READ: 88.8 ms]
Latency 99.9th percentile :     146.3 ms [READ: 146.3 ms]
Latency max               :     305.1 ms [READ: 305.1 ms]
Total partitions          :     200,000 [READ: 200,000]
Total errors              :           0 [READ: 0]
Total GC count            : 0
Total GC memory           : 0.000 KiB
Total GC time             :     0.0 seconds
Avg GC time               :     NaN ms
```

```
StdDev GC time            :    0.0 ms
Total operation time      : 00:00:08
```

```
Improvement over 81 threadCount: 6%
```

The tool periodically prints out statistics about the last several writes. As you can see, Cassandra doesn't read quite as fast as it writes; the mean read latency was around 5 ms. Remember, though, that these results were generated with default configuration options on a regular workstation running other programs. Regardless, this is a great tool to help you do performance tuning for your environment and to get a set of numbers that indicates what to expect in your cluster.

You can also run `cassandra-stress` on your own tables by creating a specification in a *yaml* file. For example, you could create a *cqlstress-hotel.yaml* file to describe read and write queries on tables in the `hotel` keyspace. This file defines queries that you could use to stress the `available_rooms_by_hotel_date` table:

```
keyspace: hotel
table: available_rooms_by_hotel_date

columnspec:
  - name: date
    cluster: uniform(20..40)

insert:
  partitions: uniform(1..50)
  batchtype: LOGGED
  select: uniform(1..10)/10

queries:
    simple1:
      cql: select * from available_rooms_by_hotel_date
        where hotel_id = ? and date = ?
      fields: samerow
    range1:
      cql: select * from available_rooms_by_hotel_date
        where hotel_id = ? and date >= ? and date <= ?
      fields: multirow
```

You can then execute these queries in a run of `cassandra-stress`. For example, you might run a mixed load of writes, single item queries, and range queries, as follows:

```
$ cassandra-stress user profile=~/cqlstress-hotel.yaml
  ops\(simple1=2,range1=1,insert=1\) no-warmup
```

The numbers associated with each query indicate the desired ratio of usage. This command performs three reads for every write.

Additional Help on cassandra-stress

You can execute `cassandra-stress help` to get the list of supported commands and options, and `cassandra-stress help <command>` to get more information on a specific command.

Additional load testing tools

There are a few additional tools for load and stress testing that you may find useful:

`tlp-stress`
> The Last Pickle have released `tlp-stress` (*https://oreil.ly/YCEas*), which is available on GitHub (*https://oreil.ly/JXfdw*). First created by Jon Haddad, `tlp-stress` is a command-line tool similar to `cassandra-stress`, but with simpler syntax. It comes with built-in workloads for common data model patterns such as time-series and key-value data models. These workloads offer parameters that allow you to tailor behavior such as the number of requests and the read/write mix. It also includes workloads that demonstrate the performance impact of features that can make Cassandra work harder, such as materialized views, lightweight transactions, and queries using `ALLOW FILTERING`. Planned improvements include the ability to add your own custom workloads.

NoSQLBench
> NoSQLBench (previously known as DSBench), is a performance and load testing platform provided by DataStax for Cassandra and DataStax Enterprise. The goal of the project is to provide an extensible framework for running tests ranging from a simple set of preconfigured tests, to tests based on your application schema that emulate your anticipated access patterns. NoSQLBench is built on the extensible concept of workloads that allow you to compose more complex test scenarios. You can read more about this tool on the DataStax blog (*https://oreil.ly/YDCgk*) and find usage instructions on the project's GitHub page (*https://oreil.ly/6sNnQ*).

Apache JMeter
> JMeter is an open source Java framework designed for functional and load testing. Originally designed for testing web applications, it has been extended to allow testing of applications via a variety of applications and protocols, and works with many continuous integration frameworks. You can see an example of stress testing a Cassandra cluster using Groovy scripts and the DataStax Java Driver in Alain Rastoul's blog post (*https://oreil.ly/BeoQB*).

Monitoring Performance

As the size of your cluster grows, the number of clients increases, and more keyspaces and tables are added, the demands on your cluster will begin to pull in different directions. Taking frequent baselines to measure the performance of your cluster against its goals will become increasingly important.

You learned in Chapter 11 about the various metrics that are exposed via JMX, including performance-related metrics for Cassandra's `StorageProxy` and individual tables. In that chapter, you also examined `nodetool` commands that publish performance-related statistics such as `nodetool tpstats` and `nodetool tablestats`, and saw how these can help identify loading and latency issues.

Now let's look at two additional `nodetool` commands that present performance statistics formatted as histograms: `proxyhistograms` and `tablehistograms`. First, examine the output of the `nodetool proxyhistograms` command:

```
$ nodetool proxyhistograms

proxy histograms
Percentile      Read Latency    Write Latency    Range Latency  ...
                (micros)        (micros)         (micros)       ...
50%                654.95          450.12           1629.72     ...
75%                943.13          504.35           5839.59     ...
95%               4055.27          608.40          62479.63     ...
98%              62479.63          692.77         107964.79     ...
99%             107964.79          888.01         129557.75     ...
Min                263.21          229.89            545.79     ...
Max             107964.79        66871.26         155469.30     ...
```

The output shows the latency of reads, writes, and range requests for which the requested node has served as the coordinator. We've shortened the output to omit the additional columns *CAS Read Latency*, *CAS Write Latency*, and *View Write Latency*. These columns track read and write latency associated with Cassandra's lightweight transactions (*CAS* is an abbreviation of *Check and Set*), and latency for writing to materialized view tables. These columns are only applicable if you are using these features.

The output is expressed in terms of percentile rank as well as minimum and maximum values, in microseconds. Running this command on multiple nodes can help identify the presence of slow nodes in the cluster. A large range latency (in the hundreds of milliseconds or more) can be an indicator of clients using inefficient range queries, such as those requiring the ALLOW FILTERING clause or index lookups.

While the view provided by `proxyhistograms` is useful for identifying general performance issues, you'll frequently need to focus on performance of specific tables. This is what `nodetool tablehistograms` allows you to do. Let's look at the output of this command against the `available_rooms_by_hotel_date` table:

```
nodetool tablehistograms hotel available_rooms_by_hotel_date

hotel/available_rooms_by_hotel_date histograms
Percentile  SSTables  Write Latency  Read Latency  Partition Size  Cell Count
                         (micros)       (micros)       (bytes)
50%          1.00         146.83         654.95          2759          179
75%          1.00         157.77        1358.10          6742          179
95%          1.00         801.59        5839.59         19034          179
98%          1.00        1684.31       12719.37         31559          179
99%          1.00        2841.44       12719.37         40520          179
Min          1.00          72.93         219.34          2300          179
Max          1.00        2841.44       12719.37        223548          179
```

The output of this command is similar. It omits the range latency statistics and instead provides counts of SSTables read per query. The partition size and cell count are provided, where cells are values stored in a partition. These metrics provide another way of identifying large partitions.

Once you've gained familiarity with these metrics and what they tell you about your cluster, you should identify key metrics to monitor and even implement automated alerts that indicate your performance goals are not being met. You can accomplish this via frameworks, discussed in Chapter 11.

Analyzing Performance Issues

It's not unusual for the performance of a cluster that has been working well to begin to degrade over time. When you detect a performance issue, you'll want to begin analyzing it quickly to ensure the performance doesn't continue to deteriorate. Your goal in these circumstances should be to determine the root cause and address it.

In this chapter, you'll learn many configuration settings that you can use to tune the performance of each node in a cluster as a whole, across all keyspaces and tables. It's also important to narrow performance issues down to specific tables and even queries.

In fact, the quality of the data model is usually the most influential factor in the performance of a Cassandra cluster. For example, a table design that results in partitions with a growing number of rows can begin to degrade the performance of the cluster and manifest in failed repairs, or streaming failures on addition of new nodes. Conversely, partitions with partition keys that are too restrictive can result in rows that are too narrow, requiring many partitions to be read to satisfy a simple query.

Beware the Large Partition

In addition to the `nodetool tablehistograms` discussed earlier, you can detect large partitions by searching logs for WARN messages that reference "Writing large partition" or "Compacting large partition." The threshold for warning on compaction of large partitions is set by the `compaction_large_partition_warning_thres hold_mb` property in the *cassandra.yaml* file.

You'll also want to learn to recognize instances of the anti-patterns discussed in Chapter 5, such as queues, or other design approaches that generate a large amount of tombstones.

Tracing

In Chapter 11, we described tracing as one of the key elements of an overall observability strategy for your applications. Now you're ready to explore how tracing fits into the strategy. The idea is to use metrics and logging to narrow your search down to a specific table and query of concern, and then to use tracing to gain detailed insight. Tracing is an invaluable tool for understanding the communications between clients and nodes involved in each query and the time spent in each step. This helps you see the performance implications of design decisions you make in your data models and choice of replication factors and consistency levels.

There are several ways to access trace data. Let's start by looking at how tracing works in `cqlsh`. First, enable tracing, and then execute a simple command:

```
cqlsh:hotel> TRACING ON
Now Tracing is enabled
cqlsh:hotel> SELECT * from hotels where id='AZ123';

 id    | address | name                          | phone           | pois
-------+---------+-------------------------------+-----------------+------
 AZ123 |    null | Super Hotel Suites at WestWorld | 1-888-999-9999 | null

(1 rows)

Tracing session: 6669f210-de99-11e5-bdb9-59bbf54c4f73

 activity            | timestamp                  | source    | source_elapsed
---------------------+----------------------------+-----------+----------------
 Execute CQL3 query  | 2019-12-23 21:03:33.503000 | 127.0.0.1 |              0
 Parsing SELECT *... | 2019-12-23 21:03:33.505000 | 127.0.0.1 |          16996
 ...
```

We've truncated the output quite a bit for brevity, but if you run a command like this, you'll see activities such as preparing statements, read repair, key cache searches, data lookups in memtables and SSTables, interactions between nodes, and the time associated with each step, in microseconds.

You'll want to be on the lookout for queries that require a lot of internode interaction, as these may indicate a problem with your schema design. For example, a query based on a secondary index will likely involve interactions with most or all of the nodes in the cluster.

Once you are done using tracing in cqlsh, you can turn it off using the TRACING OFF command. Tracing visualization is also supported in tools including DataStax DevCenter and DataStax Studio, as well as your application code using DataStax drivers. Taking the DataStax Java Driver as an example, tracing is individually enabled or disabled on a Statement using the setTracing() operation.

To obtain the trace of a query, take a look at the ResultSet object. You may have noticed in previous examples that the CqlSession.execute() operation always returns a ResultSet, even for queries other than SELECT queries. This enables you to obtain metadata about the request via the getExecutionInfo() operation, even when there are no results to be returned. The resulting ExecutionInfo includes the consistency level that was achieved, the coordinator node and other nodes involved in the query, and information about tracing via the getQueryTrace() operation.

The available query trace information includes the trace ID, coordinator node, and a list of events representing the same information available in cqlsh. Because this operation triggers a read from the tables in the system_traces keyspace, there is also an asynchronous variant: getQueryTraceAsync(). Additional configuration options are available under the datastax-java-driver.advanced.request.trace namespace.

Traces Aren't Forever

Cassandra stores query trace results in the system_traces keyspace. Since the 2.2 release, Cassandra also uses tracing to store the results of repair operations. Cassandra limits the TTL on these tables to prevent them from filling up your disk over time. You can configure these TTL values by editing the tracetype_query_ttl and tracetype_repair_ttl properties in the *cassandra.yaml* file.

On the server side, you can configure individual nodes to trace some or all of their queries via the nodetool settraceprobability command. This command takes a number between 0.0 (the default) and 1.0, where 0.0 disables tracing and 1.0 traces every query. This does not affect tracing of individual queries as requested by clients. Exercise care in changing the trace probability, as a typical trace session involves 10 or more writes. Setting a trace level of 1.0 could easily overload a busy cluster, so a value such as 0.01 or 0.001 is typically appropriate.

Distributed Tracing Frameworks

As microservice architectures have gained in popularity, developers have recognized the challenge of analyzing and debugging the interactions across multiple services and infrastructure components that are typically required to satisfy a client request. Google's Dapper paper (*https://oreil.ly/JumKC*) from 2010 introduced the concept of *distributed tracing* as an approach for tracking these interactions in order to identify sources of error and poor performance. Distributed tracing solutions use a correlation identifier generated at the entry point to the system that is passed as metadata between the various networked components. The correlation identifier is included in log entries at each component. Log aggregation tools can then pull the logging statements with the same correlation ID to assemble a distributed trace of what happened. This can be useful to dig into the overall context of your application to identify any cases where Cassandra may be impacting performance.

The Cassandra 3.4 release introduced the improvement documented in CASSANDRA-10392 (*https://oreil.ly/bqkmV*) for pluggable query trace logging. You can override the default tracing implementation found in the `org.apache.cassan dra.tracing` package by setting the system property `cassandra.custom_trac ing_class` with the name of a class that extends the abstract `Tracing` class and adding the implementation to Cassandra's classpath.

You can read about an implementation Mick Semb Wever created using Zipkin query tracing on The Last Pickle blog (*https://oreil.ly/dnz4O*). The implementation is available on GitHub (*https://oreil.ly/EQCdl*). The Zipkin tracing implementation leverages the ability provided by client drivers to add custom metadata to CQL queries, including a client-provided correlation identifier, and sends tracing data to a Zipkin service instead of writing it to Cassandra, reducing the impact of write amplification.

Infracloud has provided an alternate implementation using Jaeger (*https://oreil.ly/_SFiS*), and more options are likely to become available as the OpenTracing project (*https://opentracing.io/*) has emerged to provide standard APIs for distributed tracing frameworks.

Tuning Methodology

Once you've identified the root cause of performance issues related to one of your established goals, it's time to begin tuning performance. The suggested methodology for tuning Cassandra performance is to change one configuration parameter at a time and test the results.

It is important to limit the amount of configuration changes you make when tuning so that you can clearly identify the impact of each change. You may need to repeat the change process multiple times until you've reached the desired performance goal.

In some cases, it may be that you can get the performance back in line simply by adding more resources such as memory or extra nodes, but make sure that you aren't simply masking underlying design or configuration issues. In other cases, you may find that you can't reach your desired goals through tuning alone, and that design changes are needed.

With this methodology in mind, let's look at some of the various options that you can configure to tune your Cassandra clusters, including node configuration properties in the *cassandra.yaml* and *jvm.options* files, as well as options that are configured on individual tables using CQL.

Caching

Caches are used to improve responsiveness to read operations. Additional memory is used to hold data, to minimize the number of disk reads that must be performed. As the cache size increases, so does the number of "hits" that can be served from memory.

The caches built into Cassandra include the key cache, row cache, chunk cache, and counter cache. The row cache caches a configurable number of rows per partition. If you are using a row cache for a given table, you will not need to use a key cache on it as well.

Your caching strategy should therefore be tuned in accordance with a few factors:

- Consider your queries, and use the cache type that best fits your queries. Row caching is only recommended for read-heavy workloads, say 95% reads.
- Consider the ratio of your heap size to your cache size, and do not allow the cache to overwhelm your heap.
- Consider the size of your rows against the size of your keys. Typically keys will be much smaller than entire rows.

Let's consider some specific tuning and configuration options for each cache.

Key Cache

Cassandra's key cache stores a map of partition keys to row index entries, facilitating faster read access into SSTables stored on disk. You configure usage of the key cache on a per-table basis. For example, use `cqlsh` to examine the caching settings on the hotels table:

```
cqlsh:hotel> DESCRIBE TABLE hotels;

CREATE TABLE hotel.hotels (
    id text PRIMARY KEY,
```

```
        address frozen<address>,
        name text,
        phone text,
        pois set<text>
) WITH bloom_filter_fp_chance = 0.01
    AND caching = {'keys': 'ALL', 'rows_per_partition': 'NONE'}
    ...
```

Because the key cache greatly increases read performance without consuming a lot of additional memory, it is enabled by default; that is, key caching is enabled if you don't specify a value when creating the table. You can disable key caching for this table with the ALTER TABLE command:

```
cqlsh:hotel> ALTER TABLE hotels
    WITH caching = { 'keys' : 'NONE', 'rows_per_partition' : 'NONE' };
```

The legal options for the keys attribute are ALL or NONE.

Some key cache behaviors can be configured via settings in the *cassandra.yaml* file. The key_cache_size_in_mb setting indicates the maximum amount of heap memory that will be devoted to the key cache, which is shared across all tables. The default value is either 5% of the total JVM heap, or 100 MB, whichever is less.

Row Cache

With the row cache, you can cache entire rows and speed up read access for frequently accessed rows, at the cost of more memory usage.

You'll want to configure the row cache size setting carefully, as the wrong setting can easily lead to more performance issues than it solves. In many cases, a row cache can yield impressive performance results for small data sets when all the rows are in memory, only to degrade on larger data sets when the data must be read from disk.

If your table gets far more reads than writes, then configuring an overly large row cache will needlessly consume considerable server resources. If your table has a lower ratio of reads to writes, but has rows with lots of data in them (hundreds of columns), then you'll need to do some math before setting the row cache size. And unless you have certain rows that get hit a lot and others that get hit very little, you're not going to see much of a boost here.

For these reasons, row caching tends to yield fewer benefits than key caching. You may want to explore file caching features supported by your operating system as an alternative to row caching.

As with key caching, you can configure usage of the row cache on a per-table basis. The rows_per_partition setting specifies the number of rows that will be cached per partition. By default, this value is set to NONE, meaning that no rows will be cached.

Other available options are positive integers or ALL. The following CQL statement sets the row cache to 200 rows:

```
cqlsh:hotel> ALTER TABLE hotels
    WITH caching = { 'keys' : 'NONE', 'rows_per_partition' : '200' };
```

The implementation of the row cache is pluggable via the `row_cache_class_name` property. This defaults to the off-heap cache provider implemented by the `org.apache.cassandra.OHCProvider` class. The previous implementation was the `SerializingCacheProvider`. Third-party solutions are available, such as the CAPI-RowCache (*https://oreil.ly/tDZ57*) (CAPI stands for Coherent Accelerator Processor Interface, a Linux extension for Flash memory access).

Chunk Cache

The chunk cache, also known as the in-process uncompressed page cache, stores chunks of data that have been read from SSTable files and decompressed. To understand why this cache exists, let's revisit what happens on the read path. In processing reads, Cassandra uses its in-memory indexes in order to identify offsets into SSTable files at which to read. It then reads chunks of data and decompresses them. The size of each chunk is set in the compression options for each table by the `chunk_length_in_kb` property, as you'll see. Since an entire chunk is read at a time, reading a single row from a large chunk that is accessed frequently could be quite wasteful in terms of I/O (for file access) and CPU (for decompression). The chunk cache stores arrays of uncompressed bytes to make reads more efficient.

The chunk cache is considered to be more helpful than the the row cache in most cases since it is more granular; the contents of the row cache are invalidated for an entire partition each time there is a write to the partition. The chunk cache is enabled by default and you can configure its size using the `file_cache_size_in_mb` property.

The chunk cache was added to Cassandra in the 3.6 release. The implementation is based on the Caffeine (*https://oreil.ly/a6fnI*) Java cache created by Ben Manes. You can find more details in the Jira issue CASSANDRA-5863 (*https://oreil.ly/0efCO*).

Counter Cache

The counter cache improves counter performance by reducing lock contention for the most frequently accessed counters. There is no per-table option for configuration of the counter cache.

The `counter_cache_size_in_mb` setting determines the maximum amount of memory that will be devoted to the counter cache, which is shared across all tables. The default value is either 2.5% of the total JVM heap, or 50 MB, whichever is less.

Saved Cache Settings

Cassandra provides the ability to periodically save caches to disk, so that they can be read on startup as a way to quickly warm the cache. The saved cache settings are similar across all three cache types:

- Cache files are saved under the directory specified by the saved_caches property. The files are written at the interval in seconds specified by the key_cache_ save_period, row_cache_save_period, and counter_cache_save_period properties, which default to 14,000 (4 hours), 0 (disabled), and 7,200 (2 hours), respectively.

- Caches are indexed by key values. The number of keys to save in the file are indicated by the key_cache_keys_to_save, row_cache_keys_to_save, and counter_cache_keys_to_save properties.

Managing Caches via nodetool

You'll want to monitor your caches to make sure they are providing the value you expect. The output of the nodetool info command includes information about each of Cassandra's caches, including the recent hit rate metrics. These metrics are also available via JMX. If you've enabled tracing, you'll be able to see caches in use, for example, when a row is loaded from cache instead of disk.

Cassandra also provides capabilities for managing caches via node tool:

- You can clear caches using the invalidatekeycache, invalida terowcache, and invalidatecountercache commands.

- Use the setcachecapacity command to override the configured settings for key, row, and counter cache capacity.

- Use the setcachekeystosave command to override the configured settings for how many key, row, and counter cache elements to save to a file.

Remember that these settings will revert to the values set in the *cassandra.yaml* file on a node restart.

Memtables

Cassandra uses memtables to speed up writes, holding a memtable corresponding to each table it stores. Cassandra flushes memtables to disk as SSTables when either the commit log threshold or memtable threshold has been reached.

Cassandra stores memtables either on the Java heap, off-heap (native) memory, or both. The limits on heap and off-heap memory can be set via the properties `mem table_heap_space_in_mb` and `memtable_offheap_space_in_mb`, respectively. By default, Cassandra sets each of these values to one-quarter of the total heap size set in the *cassandra-env.sh* file. Changing the ratio of memory used for memtables reduces the memory available for caching and other internal Cassandra structures, so tune carefully and in small increments. We'll discuss the overall heap size settings in "Memory" on page 332.

You can influence how Cassandra allocates and manages memory via the `mem table_allocation_type` property. This property configures another of Cassandra's pluggable interfaces, selecting which implementation of the abstract class `org.apache.cassandra.utils.memory.MemtablePool` is used to control the memory used by each memtable. The default value `heap_buffers` causes Cassandra to allocate memtables on the heap using the Java New I/O (NIO) API, while `offheap_buffers` uses Java NIO to allocate a portion of each memtable both on and off the heap. The `offheap_objects` directs Cassandra to use native memory directly.

Another element related to tuning the memtables is `memtable_flush_writers`. This setting, which is 2 by default, indicates the number of threads used to write out the memtables when it becomes necessary. If your data directories are backed by SSD, you should increase this to the number of cores, without exceeding the maximum value of 8. If you have a very large heap, it can improve performance to set this count higher, as these threads are blocked during disk I/O.

You can also enable metered flushing on each table via the CQL `CREATE TABLE` or `ALTER TABLE` command. The `memtable_flush_period_in_ms` option sets the interval at which the memtable will be flushed to disk.

Setting this property results in more predictable write I/O, but will also result in more SSTables and more frequent compactions, possibly impacting read performance. The default value of 0 means that periodic flushing is disabled, and flushes will only occur based on the commit log threshold or memtable threshold being reached.

Commit Logs

There are two sets of files that Cassandra writes to as part of handling update operations: the commit log and the SSTable files. Their different purposes need to be considered in order to understand how to treat them during configuration. You would typically look at tuning commit log settings for write-heavy workloads.

Remember that the *commit log* can be thought of as short-term storage that helps ensure that data is not lost if a node crashes or is shut down before memtables can be flushed to disk. That's because when a node is restarted, the commit log gets replayed. In fact, that's the only time the commit log is read; clients never read from it.

You can set the value for how large the commit log is allowed to grow before it stops appending new writes to a file and creates a new one. This value is set with the `commi tlog_segment_size_in_mb` property. By default, the value is 32 MB. Note that if you change this property, you will also want to make sure it is set to at least twice the size of the `max_mutation_size_in_kb`, which controls the largest size value Cassandra will accept on a write.

The total space allocated to the commit log is specified by the `commi tlog_total_space_in_mb` property. Setting this to a larger value means that Cassandra will need to flush tables to disk less frequently.

The commit logs are periodically removed, following a successful flush of all their appended data to the dedicated SSTable files. For this reason, the commit logs will not grow to anywhere near the size of the SSTable files, so the disks don't need to be as large; this is something to consider during hardware selection.

To increase the amount of writes that the commit log can hold, you'll want to enable log compression via the `commitlog_compression` property. The supported compression algorithms are LZ4, Snappy, Deflate, and Zstd (added in Cassandra 4.0). Using compression comes at the cost of additional CPU time to perform the compression.

Additional settings relate to the commit log sync operation, represented by the `commi tlog_sync` element. There are two possible settings for this: `periodic` and `batch`. The default is `periodic`, meaning that the server will make writes durable only at specified intervals. The interval is specified by the `commitlog_sync_period_in_ms` property, which defaults to 10,000 (10 seconds).

In order to guarantee durability for your Cassandra cluster, you may want to examine this setting. When the server is set to make writes durable periodically, you can potentially lose the data that has not yet been synced to disk from the write-behind cache.

If your commit log is set to `batch`, it will block until the write is synced to disk (Cassandra will not acknowledge write operations until the commit log has been completely synced to disk). Changing this value will require taking some performance metrics, as there is a necessary trade-off here: forcing Cassandra to write more immediately constrains its freedom to manage its own resources. If you do set `commitlog_sync` to `batch`, you need to provide a suitable value for `com mit_log_sync_batch_window_in_ms`, where `ms` is the number of milliseconds between each sync effort.

SSTables

Unlike the commit log, Cassandra writes SSTable files to disk asynchronously. If you're using hard disk drives, it's recommended that you store the datafiles and the commit logs on separate disks for maximum performance. If you're deploying on solid state drives (SSDs), it is fine to use the same disk.

Cassandra, like many databases, is particularly dependent on the speed of the disk and CPUs. It's more important to have several processing cores than one or two very fast ones, to take advantage of Cassandra's highly concurrent construction. So make sure for QA and production environments to get the fastest disks you can—preferably SSDs. If you're using hard disks, make sure there are at least two so that you can store commit log files and the datafiles on separate disks, and avoid competition for I/O time.

When reading SSTable files from disk, Cassandra sets aside a portion of 32 MB of off-heap memory known a *buffer cache* (also known as a *buffer pool*), to help reduce database file I/O. This buffer cache is part of a larger file cache that is also used for caching uncompressed chunks of SSTables, which you'll see momentarily. The file cache size can be set by the file_cache_size_in_mb property in *cassandra.yaml*, but defaults to either 512 MB, or one-quarter of the Java heap, whichever is smaller. You can also allow Cassandra to use the Java heap for file buffers once the off-heap cache is full by setting buffer_pool_use_heap_if_exhausted to true.

By default, Cassandra compresses data contained in SSTables using the LZ4 compression algorithm. The data is compressed in chunks according to the value of the chunk_length_in_kb property set on each table as part of the compression options:

```
CREATE TABLE reservation.reservations_by_confirmation (...)
  WITH ... compression = {'chunk_length_in_kb': '16',
  'class': 'org.apache.cassandra.io.compress.LZ4Compressor'}
  ...
```

The remaining portion of the file cache not used for the buffer cache is used for caching uncompressed chunks to speed up reads. The default chunk length is 16 kb in Cassandra 4.0, which provides a good trade-off between the lesser amount of disk I/O required to read and write compressed data versus the CPU time expended to encrypt and decrypt each chunk. You can alter the compression options on a table, but they will only take effect on SSTables written after the options are set. To update existing SSTable files to use the new compression options, you'll need to use the node tool scrub command.

As discussed in Chapter 9, Cassandra uses SSTable index summaries and Bloom filters to improve performance of the read path. Cassandra maintains a copy of the Bloom filters in memory, although you may recall that the Bloom filters are stored in files alongside the SSTable datafiles so that they don't have to be recalculated if the node is restarted.

The Bloom filter does not guarantee that the SSTable contains the partition, only that it might contain it. You can set the `bloom_filter_fp_chance` property on each table to control the percentage of false positives that the Bloom filter reports. This increased accuracy comes at the cost of additional memory use as the number of unique partition keys grows.

Index summaries are kept in memory in order to speed access into SSTable files. By default, Cassandra allocates 5% of the Java heap to these indexes, but you can override this via the `index_summary_capacity_in_mb` property in *cassandra.yaml*. In order to stay within the allocated limit, Cassandra will shrink indexes associated with tables that are read less frequently. Because read rates may change over time, Cassandra also resamples indexes from files stored on disk at the frequency specified by the `index_summary_resize_interval_in_minutes` property, which defaults to 60.

Cassandra also provides a mechanism to influence the relative amount of space allocated to indexes for different tables. This is accomplished via the `min_index_inter val` and `max_index_interval` properties, which can be set per table via the CQL `CREATE TABLE` or `ALTER TABLE` commands. These values specify the minimum and maximum number of index entries to store per SSTable.

Hinted Handoff

Hinted handoff is one of several mechanisms that Cassandra provides to keep data in sync across the cluster. As you learned in Chapter 6, a coordinator node can keep a copy of data on behalf of a node that is down for some amount of time. You can tune hinted handoff in terms of the amount of disk space you're willing to use to store hints, and how quickly hints will be delivered when a node comes back online.

You can control the bandwidth utilization of hint delivery using the property `hin ted_handoff_throttle_in_kb`, or at runtime via `nodetool sethintedhandoff throttlekb`.

This throttling limit has a default value of 1,024, or 1 MB per second, and is used to set an upper threshold on the bandwidth that would be required of a node receiving hints. For example, in a cluster of three nodes, each of the two nodes delivering hints to a third node would throttle its hint delivery to half of this value, or 512 KB per second.

Note that configuring this throttle is a bit different than configuring other Cassandra features, as the behavior that will be observed by a node receiving hints is entirely based on property settings on other nodes. You'll definitely want to use the same values for these settings in sync across the cluster to avoid confusion.

In releases prior to 3.0, Cassandra stores hints in a table that is not replicated to other nodes, but starting with the 3.0 release, Cassandra stores hints in a directory specified by the hints_directory property, which defaults to the *data/hints* directory under the Cassandra installation. You can set a cap on the amount of disk space devoted to hints via the max_hints_file_size_in_mb property.

You can clear out any hints awaiting delivery to one or more nodes using the node tool truncatehints command with a list of IP addresses or hostnames. Hints eventually expire after the value expressed by the max_hint_window_in_ms property.

It's also possible to enable or disable hinted handoff between specific data centers, or entirely, as you learned in Chapter 11. While some would use this as a way to conserve disk and bandwidth, in general the hinted handoff mechanism does not consume a lot of resources in comparison to the extra layer of consistency it helps to provide, especially compared to the cost of repairing a node.

Compaction

Cassandra provides configuration options for compaction, including the resources used by compaction on a node, and the compaction strategy to be used for each table.

Choosing the right compaction strategy for a table can certainly be a factor in improving performance. Let's review the available strategies and discuss when they should be used:

SizeTieredCompactionStrategy

> The SizeTieredCompactionStrategy (STCS) is the default compaction strategy, and it should be used in most cases. This strategy groups SSTables into tiers organized by size. When there is a sufficient number of SSTables in a tier (4 or more by default), a compaction is run to combine them into a larger SSTable. As the amount of data grows, more and more tiers are created. STCS performs especially well for write-intensive tables, but less so for read-intensive tables, as the data for a particular row may be spread across an average of 10 or so SSTables.

LeveledCompactionStrategy

> The LeveledCompactionStrategy (LCS) creates SSTables of a fixed size (160 MB by default) and groups them into levels, with each level holding 10 times as many SSTables as the previous level. LCS guarantees that a given row appears in at most one SSTable per level. LCS spends additional effort on I/O to minimize the number of SSTables a row appears in; the average number of SSTables for a given row is 1.11. This strategy should be used if there is a high ratio of reads to writes (more than 90% reads), or predictable latency is required. LCS will tend to not perform as well if a cluster is already I/O bound. If writes dominate reads, Cassandra may struggle to keep up.

TimeWindowCompactionStrategy

The TimeWindowCompactionStrategy (TWCS) introduced in the 3.8 release is designed to improve read performance for time-series data. It works by grouping SSTables in windows organized by the write time of the data. Compaction is performed within the most recent window using STCS, and TWCS inherits most of its configuration parameters from STCS. Although processes such as hints and repair could cause the generation of multiple SSTables within a time bucket, this causes no issues because SSTables from one time bucket are never compacted with an SSTable from another bucket. Because this compaction strategy is specifically designed for time-series data, you are strongly recommended to set time to live (TTL) on all inserted rows, avoid updating existing rows, and to prefer allowing Cassandra to age data out via TTL rather than deleting it explicitly. You should also tune the compaction_window_unit and compaction_window_size options so that you have a target of 20–30 windows at once.

DateTieredCompactionStrategy Deprecated

TWCS replaces the DateTieredCompactionStrategy (DTCS) introduced in the 2.0.11 and 2.1.1 releases, which had similar goals but also some rough edges that made it difficult to use and maintain. DTCS is now considered deprecated as of the 3.8 release. New tables should use TWCS.

Each strategy has its own specific parameters that can be tuned. Check the documentation for your release for further details.

Testing Compaction Strategies with Write Survey Mode

If you'd like to test out using a different compaction strategy for a table, you don't have to change it on the whole cluster in order to see how it works. Instead, you can create a test node running in *write survey mode* to see how the new compaction strategy will work.

To do this, add the following options to the *jvm.options* file for the test node:

```
JVM_OPTS="$JVM_OPTS -Dcassandra.write_survey=true"
JVM_OPTS="$JVM_OPTS -Djoin_ring=false"
```

Once the node is up, you can then access the org.apache.cassandra.db.ColumnFami lyStoreMBean for the table under org.apache.cassandra.db > Tables in order to configure the compaction strategy. Set the CompactionParameters attribute, which is a map of parameter names and values similar to what you might see in a CREATE or ALTER TABLE command:

```
CREATE TABLE reservation.reservations_by_confirmation (...)
  WITH ...
```

```
        AND compaction = {'class': 'org.apache.cassandra.db.compaction
          .SizeTieredCompactionStrategy', 'max_threshold': '32',
          'min_threshold': '4'}
...
```

After this configuration change, add the node to the ring via nodetool join so that it can start receiving writes. Writes to the test node place a minimal additional load on the cluster and do not count toward consistency levels. You can now monitor the performance of writes to the node using nodetool tablestats and tablehistograms.

You can test the impact of new compaction strategy on reads by stopping the node, bringing it up as a standalone machine, and then testing read performance on the node.

Write survey mode is also useful for testing out other configuration changes or even a new version of Cassandra.

Another per-table setting is the *compaction threshold*. The compaction threshold refers to the number of SSTables that are in the queue to be compacted before a minor compaction is actually kicked off. By default, the minimum number is 4 and the maximum is 32. You don't want this number to be too small, or Cassandra will spend time fighting with clients for resources to perform many frequent, unnecessary compactions. You also don't want this number to be too large, or Cassandra could spend a lot of resources performing many compactions at once, and therefore will have fewer resources available for clients.

The compaction threshold is set per table using the CQL CREATE TABLE or ALTER TABLE commands. However, you can inspect or override this setting for a particular node using the nodetool getcompactionthreshold or setcompactionthreshold commands:

```
$ nodetool getcompactionthreshold reservation reservations_by_confirmation
Current compaction thresholds for reservation/reservations_by_confirmation:
 min = 4,  max = 32
$ nodetool setcompactionthreshold reservation reservations_by_confirmation 8 32
```

Compaction can be intensive in terms of I/O and CPU, so Cassandra provides the ability to monitor the compaction process and influence when compaction occurs.

You can monitor the status of compaction on a node using the nodetool compaction stats command, which lists the completed and total bytes for each active compaction (we've omitted the ID column for brevity):

```
$ nodetool compactionstats

pending tasks: 1
   id  compaction type  keyspace  table   completed  total      unit   progress
   ... Compaction                 hotel    hotels  57957241   127536780  bytes  45.44%
Active compaction remaining time :    0h00m12s
```

If you see that the pending compactions are starting to stack up, you can use the node tool commands getcompactionthroughput and setcompactionthroughput to check and set the throttle that Cassandra applies to compactions across the cluster. This corresponds to the property compaction_throughput_mb_per_sec in the *cassandra.yaml* file. Setting this value to 0 disables throttling entirely, but the default value of 16 MBps is sufficient for most cases that are not write-intensive.

If this does not fix the issue, you can increase the number of threads dedicated to compaction by setting the concurrent_compactors property in the *cassandra.yaml* file, or at runtime via the CompactionManagerMBean. This property defaults to the minimum of the number of disks and number of cores, with a minimum of 2 and a maximum of 8.

Although it is not very common, a large compaction could negatively impact the performance of the cluster. You can use the nodetool stop command to stop all active compactions on a node. You can also identify a specific compaction to stop by ID, where the ID is obtained from the compactionstats output. Cassandra will reschedule any stopped compactions to run later. By default, compaction is run on all keyspaces and tables, but you can use the nodetool disableautocompaction and enableautocompaction commands for more selective control.

You can force a major compaction via the nodetool compact command. Before kicking off a major compaction manually, remember that this is an expensive operation. The behavior of nodetool compact during compaction varies depending on the compaction strategy in use. If using the SizeTieredCompactionStrategy, it's recommended to use the -s option to request that Cassandra create multiple, smaller SSTable files rather than a single, large SSTable file. If your concern is specifically related to cleanup of deleted data, you may use nodetool garbagecollect as an alternative to a major compaction.

The nodetool compactionhistory command prints statistics about completed compactions, including the size of data before and after compaction, and details for each partition about the merging of rows from existing SSTables. The output is pretty verbose, so we've omitted it here.

Concurrency and Threading

Cassandra differs from many data stores in that it offers much faster write performance than read performance. There are two settings related to how many threads can perform read and write operations: concurrent_reads and concurrent_writes. In general, the defaults provided by Cassandra out of the box are very good.

The concurrent_reads setting determines how many simultaneous read requests the node can service. This defaults to 32, but should be set to the number of drives used for data storage times 16. This is because when your data sets are larger than available memory, the read operation is I/O bound.

The `concurrent_writes` setting behaves somewhat differently. This should correlate to the number of clients that will write concurrently to the server. If Cassandra is backing a web application server, you can tune this setting from its default of 32 to match the number of threads the application server has available to connect to Cassandra. It is common in Java application servers to prefer database connection pools no larger than 20 or 30, but if you're using several application servers in a cluster, you'll need to factor that in as well.

Two additional settings—`concurrent_counter_writes` and `concurrent_material ized_view_writes`—are available for tuning special forms of writes. Because counter and materialized view writes both involve a read before write, it is best to set this to the lower of `concurrent_reads` and `concurrent_writes`.

There are several other properties in the *cassandra.yaml* file that control the number of threads allocated to the thread pools Cassandra allocates for performing various tasks. You've seen some of these already, but here is a summary:

`max_hints_delivery_threads`
Maximum number of threads devoted to hint delivery

`memtable_flush_writers`
Number of threads devoted to flushing memtables to disk

`concurrent_compactors`
Number of threads devoted to running compaction

`native_transport_max_threads`
Maximum number of threads devoted to processing incoming CQL requests

Note that some of these properties allow Cassandra to dynamically allocate and deallocate threads up to a maximum value, while others specify a static number of threads. Tuning these properties up or down affects how Cassandra uses its CPU time and how much I/O capacity it can devote to various activities.

Networking and Timeouts

As Cassandra is a distributed system, it provides mechanisms for dealing with network and node issues including retries, timeouts, throttling, and message coalescing. We've already discussed a couple of the ways Cassandra implements retry logic, such as the `RetryPolicy` in the DataStax client drivers, and speculative read execution in drivers and nodes.

Now let's take a look at the timeout mechanisms that Cassandra provides to help it avoid hanging indefinitely waiting for other nodes to respond. The timeout properties listed in Table 13-1 are set in the *cassandra.yaml* file.

Table 13-1. Cassandra node timeouts

Property name	Default value	Description
read_request_timeout_in_ms	5000 (5 seconds)	How long the coordinator waits for read operations to complete
range_request_timeout_in_ms	10000 (10 seconds)	How long the coordinator should wait for range reads to complete
write_request_timeout_in_ms	2000 (2 seconds)	How long the coordinator should wait for writes to complete
counter_write_request_time out_in_ms	5000 (5 seconds)	How long the coordinator should wait for counter writes to complete
cas_contention_timeout_in_ms	1000 (1 second)	How long a coordinator should continue to retry a lightweight transaction
truncate_request_timeout_in_ms	60000 (1 minute)	How long the coordinator should wait for truncates to complete (including snapshot)
streaming_socket_timeout_in_ms	3600000 (1 hour)	How long a node waits for streaming to complete
request_timeout_in_ms	10000 (10 seconds)	The default timeout for other, miscellaneous operations

The values for these timeouts are generally acceptable, but you may need to adjust them slightly for your network environment.

Another property related to timeouts is cross_node_timeout, which defaults to false. If you have NTP configured in your environment, consider enabling this so that nodes can more accurately estimate when the coordinator has timed out on long-running requests, and release resources more quickly.

Cassandra also provides several properties that allow you to throttle the amount of network bandwidth it will use for various operations. Tuning these allows you to prevent Cassandra from swamping your network, at the cost of longer time to complete these tasks. For example, the stream_throughput_outbound_megabits_per_sec and inter_dc_stream_throughput_outbound_megabits_per_sec properties specify a per-thread throttle on streaming file transfers to other nodes in the local and remote data centers, respectively.

The throttles for hinted handoff and batchlog replay work slightly differently. The values specified by hinted_handoff_throttle_in_kb and batchlog_replay_throt tle_in_kb are considered maximum throughput values for the cluster and are therefore spread proportionally across nodes according to the formula:

$$T_x = \frac{T_t}{N_n - 1}$$

That is, the throughput of a node x (T_x) is equal to the total throughput (T_t) divided by one less than the number of nodes in the cluster (N_n).

There are several properties that you can use to limit traffic to the native CQL port on each node. These may be useful in situations where you don't have direct control over the client applications of your cluster. The default maximum frame size specified by the `native_transport_max_frame_size_in_mb` property is 256. Frame requests larger than this will be rejected by the node.

The node can also limit the maximum number of simultaneous client connections, via the `native_transport_max_concurrent_connections` property, but the default is −1 (unlimited). If you configure this value, you'll want to make sure it makes sense in light of the `concurrent_readers` and `concurrent_writers` properties.

To limit the number of simultaneous connections from a single source IP address, configure the `native_transport_max_concurrent_connections_per_ip` property, which defaults to −1 (unlimited).

JVM Settings

Cassandra allows you to configure a variety of options for how the server JVM should start up, how much Java memory should be allocated, and so forth. In this section, you'll learn how to tune the startup.

If you're using Windows, the startup script is called *cassandra.bat*, and on Unix systems it's *cassandra.sh*. You can start the server by simply executing this file, which detects the selected JVM and configures the Java classpath and paths for loading native libraries. The startup script sources (includes) additional files in the *conf* directory that allow you to configure a variety of JVM settings.

The *cassandra-env.sh* (*cassandra-env.ps1* on Windows) is primarily concerned with configuring JMX and Java heap options.

The Cassandra 3.0 release began a practice of moving JVM settings related to heap size and garbage collection to a dedicated settings file in the *conf* directory called *jvm.options*, as these are the settings that are tuned most frequently. In the 3.0 release, the *jvm.options* file is included (sourced) by the *cassandra-env.sh* file.

Since the Cassandra 4.0 release is intended to run against either JDK 8 or JDK 11, multiple options files are provided:

- The *conf/jvm-server.options* file contains settings that apply to running Cassandra regardless of your selected JVM.

- The *conf/jvm8-server.options* and *conf/jvm11-server.options* files contain settings that apply to running Cassandra using JDK 8 or JDK 11, respectively.

- The *conf/jvm-client.options*, *conf/jvm8-client.options*, and *conf/jvm11-client.options* files contain JVM settings for running clients such as nodetool and cqlsh, following the same conventions as the server options.

Memory

By default, Cassandra uses the following algorithm to set the JVM heap size: if the machine has less than 1 GB of RAM, the heap is set to 50% of RAM. If the machine has more than 4 GB of RAM, the heap is set to 25% of RAM, with a cap of 8 GB. To tune the minimum and maximum heap size yourself, use the -Xms and -Xmx flags. These should be set to the same value to allow the entire heap to be locked in memory and not swapped out by the OS. It is not recommended to set the heap larger than 12 GB if you are using the Concurrent Mark Sweep (CMS) garbage collector, as heap sizes larger than this value tend to lead to longer garbage collection pauses.

When performance tuning, it's a good idea to set only the heap min and max options, and nothing else at first. Only after real-world usage in your environment and some performance benchmarking with the aid of heap analysis tools and observation of your specific application's behavior should you dive into tuning the more advanced JVM settings. If you tune your JVM options and see some success, don't get too excited. You need to test under real-world conditions.

In general, you'll probably want to make sure that you've instructed the heap to dump its state if it hits an out-of-memory error, which is the default in *cassandra-env.sh*, set by the -XX:+HeapDumpOnOutOfMemory option. This is just good practice if you start experiencing out-of-memory errors.

Garbage Collection

Garbage collection (GC) is the process of reclaiming heap memory in the JVM that has been allocated for but is no longer used. Garbage collection has traditionally been a focus of performance tuning efforts for Java applications since it is an administrative process that consumes processing resources, and GC pauses can negatively affect latencies of remote calls in networked applications like Cassandra. The good news is that there is a lot of innovation in the area of Java garbage collection. Let's look at the available options based on the JVM you're using.

Default configuration (JDK 8 or JDK 11)

The default configuration for the 3.x and 4.0 releases uses two different garbage collection algorithms that work on different parts of the heap. In this approach, the Java heap is broadly divided into two object spaces: young and old. The young space is subdivided into one for new object allocation (called "eden space") and another for new objects that are still in use (the "survivor space").

Cassandra uses the parallel copying collector in the young generation; this is set via the -XX:+UseParNewGC option. Older objects still have some reference, and have therefore survived a few garbage collections, so the survivor ratio is the ratio of eden space to survivor space in the young object part of the heap. Increasing the ratio makes sense for applications with lots of new object creation and low object preservation; decreasing it makes sense for applications with longer-living objects. Cassandra sets this value to 8 via the -XX:SurvivorRatio option, meaning that the ratio of eden to survivor space is 1:8 (each survivor space will be 1/8 the size of eden). This is fairly low, because the objects are living longer in the memtables.

Every Java object has an age field in its header, indicating how many times it has been copied within the young generation space. Objects are copied into a new space when they survive a young generation garbage collection, and this copying has a cost. Because long-living objects may be copied many times, tuning this value can improve performance. By default, Cassandra has this value set at 1 via the -XX:MaxTenuringThreshold option. Set it to 0 to immediately move an object that survives a young generation collection to the old generation. Tune the survivor ratio together along with the tenuring threshold.

Modern Cassandra releases use the Concurrent Mark Sweep (CMS) garbage collector for the old generation; this is set via the -XX:+UseConcMarkSweepGC option. This setting uses more RAM and CPU power to do frequent garbage collections while the application is running, in order to keep the GC pause time to a minimum. When using this strategy, it's recommended to set the heap min and max values to the same value, in order to prevent the JVM from having to spend a lot of time growing the heap initially.

Garbage-First garbage collector (JDK 8 or JDK 11)

The Garbage-First garbage collector (also known as G1GC) was introduced in Java 7. It was intended to become the long-term replacement for the CMS garbage collection, especially on multiprocessor machines with more memory.

G1GC divides the heap into multiple, equal-size regions and allocates these to eden, survivor, and old generations dynamically, so that each generation is a logical collection of regions that need not be consecutive regions in memory. This approach enables garbage collection to run continually and require fewer of the "stop the world" pauses that characterize traditional garbage collectors.

G1GC generally requires fewer tuning decisions; the intended usage is that you need only define the min and max heap size and a pause time goal. A lower pause time will cause GC to occur more frequently.

There has been considerable discussion in the Cassandra community about switching to G1GC as the default. For example, G1GC was originally the default for the

Cassandra 3.0 release, but was backed out because it did not perform as well as the CMS for heap sizes smaller than 8 GB. The emerging consensus is that the G1GC performs well without tuning, but the default configuration of ParNew/CMS can result in shorter pauses when properly tuned.

If you'd like to experiment with using G1GC and a larger heap size on a Cassandra 2.2 or later release, the settings are readily available in the *jvm.options* file (or the *cassandra-env.sh* file for releases prior to 3.0).

Z Garbage Collector (JDK 11 and later)

The Z Garbage Collector (ZGC) was developed at Oracle and introduced in JDK 11. Its primary goals are to limit pause times to 10 ms or less, and to scale even to heaps in the multiple terabyte range. ZGC represents a new approach that does not rely on young and old generations. Instead, it divides the heap into regions and copies data into spare regions in order to perform collections in parallel while your application continues to execute. For this reason, ZGC is referred to as a concurrent compactor. ZGC does require that you maintain some headroom in your Java heap in order to support the copied data.

ZGC was originally only supported on Linux platforms, but Windows and macOS support is coming in JDK 14. To give ZGC a try on Cassandra 3 or 4, we recommend using the settings on the ZGC wiki page (*https://oreil.ly/KqSTi*).

Shenandoah Garbage Collector (JDK12)

Shenandoah Garbage Collector (SGC) is a new garbage collector developed by Red-Hat and included for the first time in JDK 12 (although backported versions are available for JDK 8 and JDK 11). SGC also uses a region-based approach similar to ZGC, but works better than ZGC on smaller heap sizes, especially when there is less headroom on the heap. While it has similar overall latency to ZGC, with most pauses under 10 ms, SGC can have worse tail latencies.

SGC is still considered experimental, but if you'd like to experiment, you can read more about how to configure it on the Shenandoah wiki (*https://oreil.ly/S5zp0*).

To get more insight on garbage collection activity in your Cassandra nodes, there are a couple of options. The `gc_warn_threshold_in_ms` setting in the *cassandra.yaml* file determines the pause length that will cause Cassandra to generate log messages at the WARN logging level. This value defaults to 1,000 ms (1 second). You can also instruct the JVM to print garbage collection details by setting options in the *cassandra-env.sh* or *jvm.options* files.

Operating System Tuning

If you're somewhat new to Linux systems and you want to run Cassandra on Linux (which is recommended), you may want to check out Amy Tobey's blog post on tuning Cassandra (*https://oreil.ly/ hvENt*). This walks through several Linux performance monitoring tools to help you understand the performance of your underlying platform so that you can troubleshoot in the right place. Although the post references Cassandra 2.1, the advice it contains is broadly applicable. The DataStax documentation (*https://oreil.ly/cl33M*) contains recommended Linux OS settings, and the Cassandra documentation (*https://oreil.ly/-XkFd*) also contain advice on using lower-level JVM and OS tools to tune performance.

Tuning Cassandra Clients

While the majority of this chapter has focused on tuning performance from the server side, there are options available to you on the client side as well. Let's consider performance-related features of the DataStax Java Driver that you should be aware of:

Prepared statements
> Make sure that you're using `PreparedStatements` for queries that are repeated multiple times in order to take advantage of the bandwidth savings and security benefits of only transmitting parameter values rather than full CQL statements.

Compression
> Another way to speed communications is to compress messages. By default, the Java driver does not use compression for communications with Cassandra nodes, but you can select to use either the LZ4 or Snappy algorithms by setting configuration options in the `advanced.protocol.compression` namespace. The trade-off you are making by transmitting fewer bytes over the network is the additional CPU effort for compression and decompression on each end. You might consider enabling compression if your queries involve a nontrivial amount of data.

Request tracking
> The Java driver provides a `RequestTracker` (*https://oreil.ly/znS_i*) interface. You can specify an implementation of your own or use the provided `RequestLogger` implementation by configuring the properties in the `datastax-java-driver.advanced.request-tracker` namespace. The `RequestLogger` tracks every query your application executes and has options to enable logging for successful, failed, and slow queries. Use the slow query logger to identify queries that are not within your defined performance SLAs.

Request tracing

As we discussed in "Tracing" on page 314, you can enable tracing on individual queries in order to obtain detailed information on the interactions between nodes. This is useful for debugging your slow queries to see what is happening.

Request throttling

If you're concerned about a client flooding the cluster with a large number of requests, you can use the Java driver's request throttling (*https://oreil.ly/KTTXz*) feature to limit the rate of queries to a value you define using configuration options in the `advanced.throttler` namespace. Queries in excess of the rate are queued until the utilization is back within range. This behavior is mostly transparent from the client perspective, but it is possible to receive a `RequestThrot tlingException` on executing a statement; this indicates that the `CqlSession` is overloaded and unable to queue the request.

For more details on these and other performance-related tips, check out the DataStax Java Driver Performance page (*https://oreil.ly/OCeuz*). Many of these features are available from other drivers as well; check the documentation of the driver you're using for more information.

Summary

In this chapter, you learned how to manage Cassandra performance and about the settings available in Cassandra to aid in performance tuning, including caching settings, memory settings, and hardware concerns. You also learned a methodology for planning, monitoring, and debugging performance and how to use stress tools to effectively simulate operational conditions on your clusters. Next, let's have a look at how to secure your Cassandra clusters.

Security

Making data accessible has been one of the key tenets of the Big Data movement, enabling huge strides in data analytics and bringing tangible benefits to business, academia, and the general public. At the same time, this data accessibility is held in tension with growing security and privacy demands. Internet-scale systems are exposed to an ever-changing collection of attacks, most of which target the data they hold. We're all aware of high-profile breaches resulting in significant losses of data, including personal data, payment information, military intelligence, and corporate trade secrets. And these are just the breaches that have made the news.

One result of this heightened threat environment has been increased regulatory and compliance regimens in many regions and industries:

- The European Union's General Data Protection Regulation (GDPR), which took effect in 2018, specifies data protections and privacy for all EU citizens, including limitations on transfer of personal data outside the EU. The California Consumer Privacy Act (CCPA), effective January 2020, is a similar provision reflecting trends toward data privacy in the United States.

- The US Health Insurance Portability and Accountability Act (HIPAA) of 1996 prescribes controls for the protection and handling of individual health information.

- The Payment Card Industry Data Security Standard (PCI DSS), first released in 2006, is an industry-defined set of standards for the secure handling of payment card data.

- The US Sarbanes-Oxley Act of 2002 regulates corporate auditing and reporting, including data retention, protection, and auditing.

These are just a few examples of regulatory and compliance standards. Even if none of these examples apply directly to your application, chances are there are regulatory guidelines of some kind that impact your system.

All of this publicity and regulatory rigor has resulted in a much increased level of visibility on enterprise application security in general, and more pertinently for our discussions, on NoSQL database security. Although a database is by definition only a part of an application, it certainly forms a vital part of the attack surface of the application, because it serves as the repository of the application's data.

Is Security a Weakness of NoSQL?

A 2012 Information Week report (*https://oreil.ly/Oks4d*) took the NoSQL community to task for what the authors argue is a sense of complacency, arguing that NoSQL databases fail to prioritize security. While the security of many NoSQL technologies, including Cassandra, has improved significantly since then, the paper serves as a healthy reminder of our responsibilities and the need for continued vigilance.

Fortunately, the Cassandra community has demonstrated a commitment to continuous improvement in security. Cassandra's security features include authentication, role-based authorization, encryption, and audit logging, as shown in Figure 14-1.

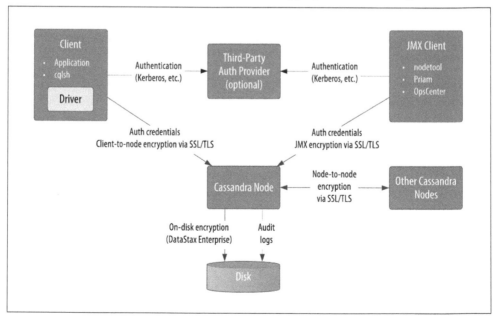

Figure 14-1. Cassandra's security features

In this chapter, we'll explore these security features and how to access them via `cqlsh` and other clients, with some thoughts along the way for how Cassandra fits into a broader application security strategy that protects against attack vectors such as unauthorized access and eavesdropping.

Authentication and Authorization

Let's take a look at Cassandra's authentication and authorization features.

Password Authenticator

By default, Cassandra allows any client on your network to connect to your cluster. This does not mean that no security is set up out of the box, but rather that Cassandra is configured to use an authentication mechanism that allows all clients, without requiring that they provide credentials. The security mechanism is pluggable, which means that you can easily swap out one authentication method for another, or write your own.

The authenticator that's plugged in by default is the `org.apache.cassandra.auth.AllowAllAuthenticator`. If you want to force clients to provide credentials, another alternative ships with Cassandra, the `org.apache.cassandra.auth.PasswordAuthenticator`. In this section, you'll learn how to use this second authenticator.

Configuring the authenticator

First, shut down your cluster so that you can change the security configuration. Open the *cassandra.yaml* file and search for "authenticator." You'll find the following line:

```
authenticator: AllowAllAuthenticator
```

Change this line to use the `PasswordAuthenticator`:

```
authenticator: PasswordAuthenticator
```

You'll want to repeat this action on each node in the cluster. If you're using Cassandra 2.2 or later, you'll see a note in the *cassandra.yaml* file indicating that the `CassandraRoleManager` must be used if the `PasswordAuthenticator` is used. The `CassandraRole Manager` is part of Cassandra's authorization capability, which we'll discuss in more depth momentarily.

Additional authentication providers

You can provide your own method of authenticating to Cassandra, such as a Kerberos ticket, or store passwords in a different location, such as an LDAP directory. In order to create your own authentication scheme, simply implement the `IAuthenticator` interface. DataStax Enterprise Edition provides additional authentication integrations, and Instaclustr has made its LDAP and Kerberos authenticators open source.

Cassandra also supports pluggable authentication between nodes via the `IInterno deAuthenticator` interface. The default implementation `AllowAllInternodeAuthen ticator` performs no authentication, but you are free to implement your own authenticator as a way to protect a node from making connections to untrusted nodes.

Adding users

Now, save the *cassandra.yaml* file, restart your node or cluster, and try logging in with `cqlsh`. Immediately you run into a problem:

```
$ bin/cqlsh
Connection error: ('Unable to connect to any servers',
  {'127.0.0.1': AuthenticationFailed('Remote end requires
  authentication.',)})
```

Prior versions of Cassandra might allow login, but would not allow any access. Versions of Cassandra 2.2 and later require a password even to log in. Cassandra comes with a default user known as *cassandra*, with "cassandra" as the password. Let's try logging in again with these credentials:

```
$ bin/cqlsh -u cassandra -p cassandra
Connected to reservation_cluster at 127.0.0.1:9042.
[cqlsh 6.0.0 | Cassandra 4.0.0 | CQL spec 3.4.5 | Native protocol v5]
Use HELP for help.
cassandra@cqlsh>
```

Once you've logged in successfully, you'll see that the prompt indicates that you are logged in as the user *cassandra*. One of the first things you'll want to do to begin securing your installation is to change the password for this very important user. We've used a random password generator here as an example:

```
cassandra@cqlsh> ALTER USER cassandra WITH PASSWORD 'Kxl0*nGpB6';
```

Make sure to store the *cassandra* user's password in a secure location.

 Don't Forget to Clear cqlsh History

Remember that `cqlsh` stores a history of your commands under your home directory at *.cassandra/cqlsh_history*, so the full clear-text password you provide is preserved there. You'll want to remove the command from the history after setting a password.

For a microservice-style application, as we've used for the examples in this book, you might want to create a user account specifically to give the service access to a single keyspace. To create this new user, you'll start by specifying a username and password. The password is optional, but of course recommended:

```
cassandra@cqlsh> CREATE USER reservation_service WITH PASSWORD 'i6XJsj!k#9';
```

The CREATE USER command also supports the IF NOT EXISTS syntax to avoid errors on multiple attempts to create a user. Now, check to see that you've created the user successfully by using the LIST USERS command:

```
cassandra@cqlsh> LIST USERS ;

 name                 | super | datacenters
----------------------+-------+-------------
           cassandra  | True  |         ALL
 reservation_service  | False |         ALL
(2 rows)
```

You'll note that the user *cassandra* is listed as being a superuser. The superuser designates the ability to perform all supported actions. Only a superuser can create other users. You've already changed the password for the built-in user *cassandra*. You may also want to create another superuser and remove the *cassandra* account's superuser status for additional security. This is considered a best practice for securing Cassandra.

 Configuring Automatic Login

To avoid having to enter a username and password on every login to cqlsh, create a file in your home directory called *.cqlshrc*. You can enter login credentials with lines like this:

```
; Sample ~/.cqlshrc file.
[authentication] username = reservation_service
    password = i6XJsj!k#9
```

Obviously, you'll want to make sure this file is secure so that only authorized users (such as your account) have access to the password.

Other operations on users include the ALTER USER command, which allows you to change a user's password or superuser status, as well as the DROP USER command, which you use to delete a user. A nonsuperuser can alter their own password using the ALTER USER command, but all other operations require superuser status.

You can use the LOGIN command to switch users within cqlsh without restart:

```
cassandra@cqlsh> login reservation_service 'i6XJsj!k#9'
reservation_service@cqlsh>
```

You may choose to omit the password from the command, in which case cqlsh will prompt you to enter the password. It's preferable to enter passwords at the shell prompt, rather than the command line, as `cqlsh` saves all of your commands to a file called *.cassandra/cqlsh_history* under your home directory, including any passwords you include on the command line when using the `LOGIN` command.

Authenticating via the DataStax Java Driver

Of course, your applications don't use `cqlsh` to access Cassandra, so it will be helpful to learn how to authenticate to the client using the DataStax client drivers. Building on the Reservation Service from Chapter 8, use the `CqlSessionBuilder.withCreden tials()` operation to provide the username and password when you construct your `Cluster` instance:

```
CqlSession = CqlSession.builder().addContactPoint("127.0.0.1").
  withAuthCredentials("reservation_service", "i6XJsj!k#9").
  build();
```

The login syntax is quite similar for other DataStax drivers. This is a simple example that hardcodes the login credentials, but you could just as easily use values provided by an application user or stored in a secure configuration file:

```
datastax-java-driver {
  advanced.auth-provider {
    username = reservation_service
    password = i6XJsj!k#9
}
```

If you've configured an authenticator on your nodes other than the default, you'll also need to configure a compatible authenticator in your clients. Client authentication providers implement the `com.datastax.oss.driver.api.core.auth.AuthProvider` interface. The default implementation is the `PlainTextAuthProvider` class, an instance of which is registered when you call the `CqlSessionBuilder.withCreden tials()` operation. You can override the provider when constructing your `Cluster` object by calling the `CqlSessionBuilder.withAuthProvider()` operation.

Using CassandraAuthorizer

It is certainly possible to only use authentication, although in most cases you'll want to make use of Cassandra's authorization capabilities as well. Cassandra's out-of-the-box configuration authorizes all clients to access all keyspaces and tables in your cluster. As with authentication, the authorization mechanism is pluggable.

The authorizer that's plugged in by default is the `org.apache.cassandra.auth.Allow AllAuthorizer`. To enable Cassandra's role-based access control, you'll need to configure the `org.apache.cassandra.auth.CassandraAuthorizer`.

Again, you'll shut down the cluster to change the authorizer. In the *cassandra.yaml* file, search for "authorizer." You'll find the line:

```
authorizer: AllowAllAuthorizer
```

and change it to:

```
authorizer: CassandraAuthorizer
```

Once you restart the cluster, you can log in to `cqlsh` again as your regular user to see what you can access, making use of the reservation data stored in your cluster in previous chapters:

```
$ cqlsh -u reservation_service -p 'i6XJsj!k#9'
...
reservation_service@cqlsh> DESCRIBE KEYSPACES;
system_schema    system              system_traces    system_virtual_schema
system_auth      system_distributed  reservation      system_views

reservation_service@cqlsh> USE reservation;
reservation_service@cqlsh:reservation> DESCRIBE TABLES;

reservations_by_confirmation   reservations_by_hotel_date
reservations_by_guest

reservation_service@cqlsh:reservation> SELECT * FROM
  reservations_by_confirmation;
Unauthorized: Error from server: code=2100 [Unauthorized]
  message="User reservation_service has no SELECT permission on <table
  reservation.reservations_by_confirmation> or any of its parents"
```

As you can see, you are able to navigate through `cqlsh` to view the names of the various keyspaces and tables, but once you attempt to access data, you are denied access.

To fix this, you'll need to switch back into a superuser role and grant your user some permissions. For example, let's allow the user to access tables in the reservations keyspace:

```
cassandra@cqlsh> GRANT SELECT ON KEYSPACE reservation TO reservation_service;
cassandra@cqlsh> GRANT MODIFY ON KEYSPACE reservation TO reservation_service;
```

This allows your Reservation Service account to read and write data, but no other operations. You could also have granted `SELECT ON TABLE` or `MODIFY ON TABLE` permissions to allow access to a specific table. Now, if you log back in as your regular user and run the `SELECT` command again, you'll see the data you stored previously.

Getting Help with Permissions

The `cqlsh` commands HELP GRANT and HELP PERMISSIONS provide additional information on configuring permissions such as:

CREATE, ALTER, DROP
> These permissions allow users to CREATE, ALTER, and DROP keyspaces, tables, functions and roles.

SELECT
> These permissions allow the ability to SELECT data from tables and keyspaces, as well as the ability to call get() operations on MBeans.

MODIFY
> These permissions group the INSERT, UPDATE, DELETE and TRUNCATE commands for modifying tables, as well as the ability to call set() operations on MBeans.

AUTHORIZE
> These permissions deal with the ability to GRANT and REVOKE other permissions. These are commonly used to create users and roles that have administrative privileges over some or all keyspaces, but not the ability to manage access of other accounts.

DESCRIBE
> Since it is possible for the database schema itself to contain sensitive information, these permissions restrict access to the various CQL DESCRIBE operations.

EXECUTE
> These permissions control the ability to execute functions and MBean actions.

The Cassandra Query Language specification (*https://oreil.ly/lEmK6*) contains a detailed listing of grantable permissions by CQL command and the resources to which they apply, which include keyspaces, tables, MBeans, functions (introduced in Chapter 15), and roles (which we discuss next).

Role-Based Access Control

In a large Cassandra cluster, there might be a lot of different keyspaces and tables, with many different potential users. It would be difficult to keep track of the permissions assigned to them all. While it's tempting to share login information with multiple support staff, there is a better way.

Starting with the 2.2 release, Cassandra provides role-based access control (RBAC). This allows you to create roles and assign permissions to these roles. Roles can be granted to individual users in any combination. Roles can themselves contain other roles.

It's a good practice to create separate roles in order to keep permissions to the minimum required for each user. For example, you might also wish to create a `reservation_maintenance` role that has permissions to modify the `reservation` keyspace and its tables, but not all of the power of the `cassandra` administrator role:

```
cassandra@cqlsh> CREATE ROLE reservation_maintenance;
cassandra@cqlsh> GRANT ALL ON KEYSPACE reservation TO reservation_maintenance;
```

You've created a simple role here to which you can't log in to directly. You can also create roles that have superuser privileges, and roles that support login and take a password. Now you could apply this role to some user account `jeff`:

```
cassandra@cqlsh> GRANT reservation_maintenance TO jeff;
```

Roles are additive in Cassandra, meaning that if any of the roles granted to a user have a specific permission granted, then that permission is granted to the user.

4.0 Feature: Network Authorization

Beginning with the 4.0 release, you can restrict roles to only have access to named data centers. Cassandra provides the `INetworkAuthorizer` interface to allow pluggable implementations, and two implementations, the `AllowAllNetworkAuthorizer` (which does not restrict role access), and the `CassandraNetworkAuthorizer`.

To enable network authorization, you'll want to edit the *cassandra.yaml* file to set the `network_authorizer` option:

```
network_authorizer: CassandraNetworkAuthorizer
```

Then, you can use the `ACCESS TO DATACENTERS` syntax when creating or altering users or roles to specify data centers they may access:

```
CREATE ROLE reservation_maintenance WITH ACCESS
   TO DATACENTERS {'DC1', 'DC2'};
```

The `CassandraNetworkAuthorizer` stores permissions in the `system_auth.network_permissions` table, which underlines the importance of setting the replication strategy appropriately on the `system_auth` keyspace, so that all nodes in the cluster will be aware of the network authorization configuration.

Behind the scenes, Cassandra stores users and roles in the `system_auth` keyspace. If you've configured authorization for your cluster, only administrative users can access this keyspace, so let's examine its contents in `cqlsh` using the administrator login:

```
cassandra@cqlsh> DESCRIBE KEYSPACE system_auth

CREATE KEYSPACE system_auth WITH replication = {'class': 'SimpleStrategy',
  'replication_factor': '1'} AND durable_writes = true;

...
```

We've truncated the output, but if you run this command, you'll see the tables that store the roles, their permissions, and role assignments. There is actually no separate concept of a user at the database level—Cassandra uses the role concept to track both users and roles.

Changing the system_auth Replication Factor

The system_auth keyspace is configured out of the box to use the SimpleStrategy with a replication factor of one.

This means that by default, any users, roles, and permissions you configure will not be distributed across the cluster until you reconfigure the replication strategy of the system_auth keyspace to match your cluster topology and run repair on the system_auth keyspace.

Encryption

Protecting user privacy is an important aspect of many systems, especially those that handle health, financial, and other personal data. Typically you protect privacy by encrypting data, so that if the data is intercepted, it is unusable to an attacker who does not have the encryption key. Data can be encrypted as it moves around the public internet and within internal systems, also known as *data in motion,* or it can be encrypted on systems where it is persisted (known as *data at rest*).

Starting with the 2.2.4 release, Cassandra provides the option to secure data in motion via encryption between clients and servers (nodes), and encryption between nodes using Secure Sockets Layer (SSL). As of Cassandra 4.0, encryption of datafiles (data at rest) is not supported; however, it is offered by DataStax Enterprise releases of Cassandra and can also be achieved by using storage options that support full-disk encryption, such as encrypted EBS volumes on AWS.

Datafile Encryption Roadmap

There are several Cassandra Jira requests targeted for the 3.X release series that provide encryption features. For example, the following were added in the 3.4 release:

CASSANDRA-11040 (https://oreil.ly/4FNeI)
  Encryption of hints

CASSANDRA-6018 (https://oreil.ly/Z3xs5)
  Encryption of commit logs

See also CASSANDRA-9633 (*https://oreil.ly/w20Al3*) on encryption of SSTables, and CASSANDRA-7922 (*https://oreil.ly/BqaVX*), which serves as an umbrella ticket for file-level encryption requests.

Before you start configuring nodes to enable encryption, there is some preparation work to do to create security certificates that are a key part of the machinery.

SSL, TLS, and Certificates

Cassandra uses Transport Layer Security (TLS) for encrypting data in motion. TLS is often referenced by the name of its predecessor, Secure Sockets Layer (SSL). TLS is a cryptographic protocol for securing communications between computers to prevent eavesdropping and tampering. More specifically, TLS makes use of public key cryptography (also known as asymmetric cryptography), in which a pair of keys is used to encrypt and decrypt messages between two endpoints: a client and a server.

Prior to establishing a connection, each endpoint must possess a certificate containing a public and private key pair. Public keys are exchanged with communication partners, while private keys are not shared with anyone.

To establish a connection, the client sends a request to the server indicating the cipher suites it supports. The server selects a cipher suite from the list that it also supports and replies with a certificate that contains its public key. The client validates the server's public key. The server may also require that the client provide its public key in order to perform two-way validation. The client uses the server's public key to encrypt a message to the server in order to negotiate a session key. The session key is a symmetric key generated by the selected cipher suite that is used for subsequent communications.

For most applications of public key cryptography, the certificates are obtained from a certificate authority, and this is the recommended practice for production Cassandra deployments as well. However, for small development clusters, you may find it useful to create your own certificates.

Generating Certificates for Development Clusters

Let's examine how to create your own certificates for development clusters. The following command gives an example of how you can use the -genkey switch on the JDK's keytool to generate a public/private key pair (substituting different keystore and key passwords and distinguished name when you run this yourself):

```
$ keytool -genkey -keyalg RSA -alias node1 -keystore node1.keystore
  -storepass cassandra -keypass cassandra
  -dname "CN=192.168.86.29, OU=None, O=None, L=Scottsdale, C=USA"

Warning:
The JKS keystore uses a proprietary format. It is recommended to migrate
  to PKCS12 which is an industry standard format using "keytool
  -importkeystore -srckeystore node1.keystore -destkeystore node1.keystore
  -deststoretype pkcs12".
```

This command generates the key pair for one of your Cassandra nodes, node1, and places the key pair in a *keystore* file called *node1.keystore*. You provide passwords for the keystore and for the key pair, and a distinguished name specified according to the Lightweight Directory Access Prototol (LDAP) format. It's recommended to use the IP address of the host for the common name (CN).

The example command shown here provides the bare minimum set of attributes for generating a key. You could also provide fewer attributes on the command line and allow keytool to prompt you for the remaining ones, which is more secure for entering passwords.

PKCS12 and the Java Cryptography Extension

You probably noticed the warning message in this output, which indicates a preference for using the the industry standard PKCS12 (*.pfx*) format over the Java keystore (JKS) format. When creating certificates for development clusters, the Java keystore (JKS) format is typically sufficient. However, if you're planning to use cqlsh with the development cluster or are developing clients in languages that don't support the JKS format, you'll want to import your server public keys into a PKCS12-compatible truststore for client use.

Once you have a certificate for each node, export the public key of each certificate to a separate file:

```
$ keytool -export -alias node1 -file node1.cer -keystore node1.keystore
Enter keystore password:
Certificate stored in file <node1.cer>
```

You identify the key you want to export from the keystore via the same alias as before, and provide the name of the output file. keytool prompts you for the keystore password and generates the certificate file. Repeat this procedure to generate keys for each node and client.

Then, configure options for a file similar to the keystore called the *truststore*. You'll generate a truststore for each node containing the public keys of all the other nodes in the cluster. For example, to add the certificate for node1 to the keystore for node2, you would use the command:

```
$ keytool -import -v -trustcacerts -alias node1 -file node1.cer
  -keystore node2.truststore
Enter keystore password:
Re-enter new password:
Owner: CN=192.168.86.29, OU=None, O=None, L=Scottsdale, C=USA
Issuer: CN=192.168.86.29, OU=None, O=None, L=Scottsdale, C=USA
Serial number: 3cc50090
Valid from: Mon Dec 16 18:08:57 MST 2019 until: Sun Mar 15 18:08:57 MST 2020
Certificate fingerprints:
        MD5:   3E:1A:1B:43:50:D9:E5:5C:7A:DA:AA:4E:9D:B9:9E:2A
        SHA1:  B4:58:21:73:43:8F:08:3C:D5:D6:D7:22:D9:32:04:7C:8F:E2:A6:C9
        SHA256: 00:A4:64:E9:C9:CA:1E:69:18:08:38:6D:8B:5B:48:6F:4C:9D:DB:62:17:
          8C:79:CC:ED:24:23:B8:81:04:41:59
Signature algorithm name: SHA256withRSA
Subject Public Key Algorithm: 2048-bit RSA key
Version: 3

Extensions:

#1: ObjectId: 2.5.29.14 Criticality=false
SubjectKeyIdentifier [
KeyIdentifier [
0000: 0E 95 97 B1 69 CF 57 50   C1 98 87 F4 06 28 A7 C1  ....i.WP.....(..
0010: 51 AC 35 18                                        Q.5.
]
]

Trust this certificate? [no]:  y
Certificate was added to keystore
[Storing truststore.node1]
```

keytool prompts you to enter a password for the new truststore and then prints out summary information about the key you're importing.

Once you have the keystore and truststore files for each node, deploy them to the nodes using remote copy or secure copy protocol (SCP) tools as per your environment. If you also intend to require certificates for your clients, the process of generating keystores and truststores is quite similar, and of course you'll want to add the client public certificates to your server truststores as well.

For more detailed instructions on generating your own certificates using keytool, see the DataStax documentation (*https://oreil.ly/cB9r-*).

Generating Certificates for Production Clusters

For managing production clusters (or even larger development clusters), it's recommended to use a certificate authority (CA) to generate your certificates. The DataStax documentation (*https://oreil.ly/kVb2u*) provides detailed instructions for creating a self-signed root CA using `openssl` and using that to sign the certificates for your nodes (and clients, if desired).

The procedure for creating distinguished names is similar to that described earlier, although you may wish to use the fully qualified domain name (FQDN) of the node or client as the CN, and the IP address as a subject alternative name (SAN), so that the certificate protects the IP address in addition to the domain name.

Whether you are using a self-signed root CA or a publicly trusted CA, you'll need to ensure there is a truststore for each node that provides the chain of trust for the CA. If you're using a public CA, it's likely that the CA's root certificate will be present in your JDK's default truststore. If you're using a self-signed CA, a common practice is to use the package manager for your operating system to install the CA on your nodes as part of your infrastructure deployment.

As with development clusters, you'll want to ensure you use a secure method to install certificates on your nodes and clients. Whatever scheme you choose to manage your certificates, the overall security of your Cassandra cluster depends on limiting access to the computers on which your nodes are running so that the configuration can't be tampered with.

4.0 Feature: Hot Certificate Reloading

In 2018 the software industry adopted a recommended maximum validity of two years for SSL certificates, and many environments enforce even shorter validity periods. One ramification of this is that in a long-running production cluster you might have nodes that will be around long enough to need new certificates. As of the 4.0 release, Cassandra supports hot reloading of certificates, which enables certificate rotation without downtime. The `keystore` and `truststore` settings are reloaded every 10 minutes, or you can force a refresh with the `nodetool reloadssl` command.

Node-to-Node Encryption

Once you have keys for each of your Cassandra nodes, you are ready to enable node-to-node configuration by setting the `server_encryption_options` in the *cassandra.yaml* file:

```
server_encryption_options:
    enabled: false
    optional: false
```

```
enable_legacy_ssl_storage_port: false
internode_encryption: none
keystore: conf/.keystore
keystore_password: cassandra
truststore: conf/.truststore
truststore_password: cassandra
# protocol: TLS
# store_type: JKS
# cipher_suites: [TLS_RSA_WITH_AES_128_CBC_SHA,...]
# require_client_auth: false
# require_endpoint_verification: false
```

First, set the `enabled` option to `true`. You can also set the `optional` option to `true` to indicate that both encrypted and unencrypted connections should be allowed on the storage port; otherwise only encrypted connections will be allowed.

Deprecated SSL Storage Port

Versions of Cassandra prior to 4.0 used a separate `ssl_storage_port` for encrypted communications between nodes. Since Cassandra 4.0 and later may be configured to allow both encrypted and unencrypted connections on the storage port, the secure port is only needed in the context of upgrading a 3.x cluster to 4.0. In this case, the `ssl_storage_port` should be configured and `enable_legacy_ssl_storage_port` set to true.

Next, set the `internode_encryption` option. You can select `all` to encrypt all inter-node communications, `dc` to encrypt between data centers, and `rack` to encrypt between racks. Provide the password for the keystore and set its path, or place the keystore file you created earlier at the default location in the *conf* directory.

The *cassandra.yaml* file also presents you with a series of "advanced" options to configure the cryptography. These options provide you with the ability to select from Java's menu of supported cryptographic algorithms and libraries. For example, for Java 8, you can find the descriptions of these items in this Oracle documentation (*https://oreil.ly/Qt5Nd*).

The defaults will be sufficient in most cases, but it's helpful to understand what options are available. You can see how these options are used in Cassandra by examining the class `org.apache.cassandra.security.SSLFactory`, which Cassandra uses to generate secure sockets.

The `protocol` option specifies the protocol suite that will be used to instantiate a `javax.net.ssl.SSLContext`. As of Java 8, the supported values include SSLv2, SSLv3, TLSv1, TLSv1.1, or TLSv1.2. You can also use the shortcuts SSL or TLS to get the latest supported version of either suite.

The `store_type` option specifies the setting provided to obtain an instance of `java.security.KeyStore`. The default value JKS indicates a keystore built by key tool, but you can also use PKCS12 keystores as discussed previously.

The `cipher_suites` option is a list of encryption algorithms in order of preference. The cipher suite to use is determined by the client and server in negotiating their connection, based on the priority specified in this list. The same technique is used by your browser in negotiating with web servers when you visit websites using *https:* URLs. As demonstrated by the defaults, you'll typically want to prefer stronger cipher suites by placing them at the front of the list.

You can also enable two-way certificate authentication between nodes, in which the server node authenticates the client node, by setting `require_client_auth` to `true`. If `require_endpoint_verification` is set to `true`, Cassandra will verify whether the client node that is connecting matches the name in its certificate.

Client-to-Node Encryption

Client-to-node encryption protects data as it moves from client machines to nodes in the cluster. The `client_encryption_options` in the *cassandra.yaml* file are quite similar to the node-to-node options:

```
client_encryption_options:
    enabled: false
    optional: false
    keystore: conf/.keystore
    keystore_password: cassandra
    # require_client_auth: false
    # truststore: conf/.truststore
    # truststore_password: cassandra
    # More advanced defaults below:
    # protocol: TLS
    # store_type: JKS
    # cipher_suites: [TLS_RSA_WITH_AES_128_CBC_SHA,...]
```

The `enabled` option serves as the on/off switch for client-to-node encryption, while `optional` indicates whether clients may choose either encrypted or unencrypted connections.

The `keystore` and `truststore` settings will typically be the same as those in the `server_encryption_options`, although it is possible to have separate files for the client options.

Note that setting `require_client_auth` for clients means that the `truststore` for each node will need to have a public key for each client that will be using an encrypted connection.

The `cipher_suites` option works the same as for the server options. If you don't have total control over your clients, you may wish to remove weaker suites entirely to eliminate the threat of a downgrade attack.

Simplified Certificate Management

Configuring truststores for Cassandra nodes can become something of a logistical problem if you're adding nodes to your cluster or additional clients on a regular basis, or want to periodically rotate certificates.

One approach is to reuse the same certificate for all of the nodes in a cluster, and a second certificate for all of the clients. This approach greatly simplifies the process of managing your cluster as you won't have to update `truststores` with new certificates. This comes at the cost of fine-grained control over the trust you assign to individual nodes and clients.

As of the 4.0 release, Cassandra supports hot reloading of certificates, which enables certificate rotation without downtime. The `keystore` and `truststore` settings are reloaded every 10 minutes, or you can force a refresh with the `nodetool reloadssl` command.

Whatever scheme you choose to manage your certificates, the overall security of your Cassandra cluster depends on limiting access to the computers on which your nodes are running so that the configuration can't be tampered with.

JMX Security

You learned how Cassandra exposes a monitoring and management capability via Java Management Extensions (JMX) in Chapter 11. In this section, you'll learn how to make that management interface secure, and what security-related options you can configure using JMX.

Securing JMX Access

By default, Cassandra only makes JMX accessible from the local host. This is fine for situations where you have direct machine access, but if you're running a large cluster, it may not be practical to log in to the machine hosting each node in order to access them using tools such as `nodetool`.

For this reason, Cassandra provides the ability to expose its JMX interface for remote access. Of course, it would be a waste to invest your efforts in securing access to Cassandra via the native transport, but leave a major attack surface like JMX vulnerable. So let's see how to enable remote JMX access in a way that is secure.

First, stop your node or cluster and edit the *conf/cassandra-env.sh* file (or *cassandra-env.ps1* on Windows). Look for the setting LOCAL_JMX, and change it as follows:

```
LOCAL_JMX=no
```

Setting this value to anything other than "yes" causes several additional properties to be set, including properties that enable the JMX port to be accessed remotely:

```
JVM_OPTS="$JVM_OPTS -Dcom.sun.management.jmxremote.port=$JMX_PORT"
JVM_OPTS="$JVM_OPTS -Dcom.sun.management.jmxremote.rmi.port=$JMX_PORT"
```

There are also properties that configure remote authentication for JMX:

```
JVM_OPTS="$JVM_OPTS -Dcom.sun.management.jmxremote.authenticate=true"
JVM_OPTS="$JVM_OPTS -Dcom.sun.management.jmxremote.password.file=
    /etc/cassandra/jmxremote.password"
```

The location of the *jmxremote.password* file is entirely up to you. You'll configure the *jmxremote.password* file in just a minute, but first finish up your configuration edits by saving the *cassandra-env.sh* file.

Your JRE installation comes with a template *jmxremote.password* file under the *jre/lib/management* directory. Typically you will find installed JREs under *C:\Program Files\Java* on Windows, */Library/Java/JavaVirtualMachines* on macOS, and */usr/lib/java* on Linux. Copy the *jmxremote.password* file to the location you set previously in *cassandra-env.sh* and edit the file, adding a line with your administrator username and password, as shown in bold here:

```
...
# monitorRole   QED
# controlRole   R&D
cassandra cassandra
```

You'll also edit the *jmxremote.access* file under the *jre/lib/management* directory to add read and write MBean access for the administrative user:

```
monitorRole readonly
controlRole readwrite \
            create javax.management.monitor.*,javax.management.timer.* \
            unregister
cassandra readwrite
```

Configure the permissions on the *jmxremote.password* and *jmxremote.access*. Ideally, the account under which you run Cassandra should have read-only access to this file, and other nonadministrative users should have no access.

Finally, restart Cassandra and test that secure access is configured correctly by calling nodetool:

```
$ nodetool status -u cassandra -pw cassandra
```

You can also configure SSL for your JMX connection. To do this, you'll need to add a few more JVM options in the *cassandra-env* file:

```
JVM_OPTS="${JVM_OPTS} -Dcom.sun.management.jmxremote.ssl=true"
JVM_OPTS="${JVM_OPTS} -Djavax.net.ssl.keyStore=conf/node1.keystore"
JVM_OPTS="${JVM_OPTS} -Djavax.net.ssl.keyStorePassword=cassandra"
JVM_OPTS="${JVM_OPTS} -Djavax.net.ssl.trustStore=conf/node1.truststore"
JVM_OPTS="${JVM_OPTS} -Djavax.net.ssl.trustStorePassword=cassandra"
JVM_OPTS="${JVM_OPTS} -Dcom.sun.management.jmxremote.ssl.need.client.auth=true"
```

Accessing JMX via Cassandra Integrated Authentication and Authorization

As an alternative to the preceding JMX authentication configuration, releases 3.6 and later allow you to use Cassandra's authentication and authorization for the JMX interface.

You'll need to uncomment the following lines in the *cassandra-env.sh* file:

```
#JVM_OPTS="$JVM_OPTS -Dcassandra.jmx.remote.login.config=CassandraLogin"
#JVM_OPTS="$JVM_OPTS -Djava.security.auth.login.config=$CASSANDRA_HOME/conf/
   cassandra-jaas.config"
...
#JVM_OPTS="$JVM_OPTS -Dcassandra.jmx.authorizer=org.apache.cassandra.auth.
   jmx.AuthorizationProxy"
```

Disable the standard authentication and authorization by commenting out the lines:

```
JVM_OPTS="$JVM_OPTS -Dcom.sun.management.jmxremote.password.file=
   /etc/cassandra/jmxremote.password"
JVM_OPTS="$JVM_OPTS -Dcom.sun.management.jmxremote.access.file=
   /etc/cassandra/jmxremote.access"
```

Note that if you choose integrated auth for JMX, you won't be able to access JMX to monitor a node until it joins the ring and finishes initializing the authentication system.

Use the CQL GRANT operation to add permissions to users and roles, including:

- DESCRIBE ON MBEANS to allow listing of MBeans and operations

- SELECT ON MBEAN to allow usage of MBean set() operations

- MODIFY ON MBEAN to allow usage of MBean get() operations

- EXECUTE ON MBEAN to allow invocation of MBean actions

Security MBeans

You learned about the various MBeans exposed by Cassandra in Chapter 11. For understandable reasons, not many security-related configuration parameters are accessible remotely via JMX, but there are some capabilities exposed via the `org.apache.cassandra.auth` domain.

Authentication cache MBean

By default, Cassandra caches information about permissions, roles, and login credentials as a performance optimization, since it could be quite expensive to retrieve these values from internal tables or external sources on each call.

For example, the `org.apache.auth.PermissionsCache` caches permissions for the duration set in the *cassandra.yaml* file by the `permissions_validity_in_ms` property. This value defaults to 2,000 (2 seconds), and you can disable the cache entirely by setting the value to 0. There is also a `permissions_update_interval_in_ms`, which defaults to the same value as `permissions_validity_in_ms`. Setting a lower value configures an interval after which accessing a permission will trigger an asynchronous reload of the latest value.

Similarly, the `RolesCache` manages a cache of roles assigned to each user. It is configured by the `roles_validity_in_ms` and `roles_update_interval_in_ms` properties.

The `CredentialsCache` caches the password for each user or role so that they don't have to be reread from the `PasswordAuthenticator`. Since the `CredentialsCache` is tied to Cassandra's internal `PasswordAuthenticator`, it will not function if another implementation is used. It is configured by the `credentials_validity_in_ms` and `credentials_update_interval_in_ms` properties.

The `AuthCacheMBean` allows you to override the configured cache validity and refresh values, and also provides a command to invalidate all of the permissions in the cache. This could be a useful operation if you need to change permissions in your cluster and need them to take effect immediately.

Unified Authentication Caching

In releases prior to Cassandra 3.4, the permissions cache and roles cache were separate concepts with separate MBeans. In the Cassandra 3.4 release, the class `AuthCache` was introduced as a base class for all authentication-related classes, and the `PermissionsCacheM Bean` and `RolesCacheMBean` were deprecated and replaced by the `AuthCacheMBean`.

Audit Logging

Once you've configured security settings such as access control, you may need to verify that they've been implemented correctly, perhaps as part of a compliance regime. Fortunately, Cassandra 4.0 added an audit logging feature that you can use to satisfy these requirements. This logging capability is to be as lightweight as possible in order to minimize the impact on read and write latency without compromising the strict accuracy requirements of compliance laws.

Audit logging shares some of its implementation with full query logging (see "Full Query Logging" on page 270), also included in the 4.0 release. The code for both features is found in the `org.apache.cassandra.audit` package. The `IAuditLogger` interface describes a pluggable interface for audit loggers. Available implementations include the `FileAuditLogger`, which generates human-readable messages, and the `BinAuditLogger`, which writes in a compact binary format that can be read using the `fqltool` introduced in Chapter 11. The `AuditLogManager` provides a central location for managing registered implementations of the `IAuditLogger` interface. The `AuditLogManager.log()` operation exposes a single API for logging used by various portions of the Cassandra codebase that perform writes, reads, schema management, and other operations.

While full query logging and audit logging share some implementation, the concerns they address are distinct. While the full query logger focuses on the syntax of `SELECT`, `INSERT`, `UPDATE`, and `DELETE` queries, it ignores other CQL queries and does not include success or failure indications, or information about the source of queries.

Audit logging settings are found in the *cassandra.yaml* file:

```
audit_logging_options:
    enabled: false
    logger: BinAuditLogger
    # audit_logs_dir:
    # included_keyspaces:
    # excluded_keyspaces: system, system_schema, system_virtual_schema
    # included_categories:
    # excluded_categories:
    # included_users:
    # excluded_users:
    # roll_cycle: HOURLY
    # block: true
    # max_queue_weight: 268435456 # 256 MiB
    # max_log_size: 17179869184 # 16 GiB
    ## archive command is "/path/to/script.sh %path" where %path is replaced
      with the file being rolled:
    # archive_command:
    # max_archive_retries: 10
```

To enable audit logging, set the `enabled` option to `true` and select the desired logger. You can include (*whitelist*) or exclude (*blacklist*) specific keyspaces or users in order to narrow the focus of audit logging.

Audit log messages are grouped into categories that can also be included or excluded:

QUERY
Messages generated for CQL `SELECT` operations

DML *(or data manipulation language)*
Messages for CQL `UPDATE`, `DELETE`, and `BATCH` operations

DDL *(or data definition language)*

Messages for operations on keyspaces, tables, user-defined types, triggers, user-defined functions, and aggregates. These latter items will be discussed in Chapter 15

PREPARE

Messages concerning prepared statements (as you learned in Chapter 8)

DCL *(or data control language)*

Messages generated for operations related to users, roles, and permissions

AUTH

Messages tracking login success, failure, and unauthorized access attempts

ERROR

Messages for logging CQL request failure

OTHER

The final category, currently used only to track the CQL USE command

In addition to the configuration in *cassandra.yaml*, you can also enable and disable audit logging through nodetool using the enableauditlog and disableauditlog operations. The enableauditlog also allows you to update options on specific audit loggers such as the included or excluded categories, keyspaces, and users.

If you're using the BinAuditLogger, binary audit logs will be written to files in the specified directory, which defaults to the *logs* directory under the Cassandra installation. The options for audit file rolling and archiving are similar to those described for full query logging in Chapter 11.

As an example, you could configure the use of the FileQueryLogger to log operations on a node related to the reservation keyspace:

```
audit_logging_options:
    enabled: true
    logger: FileAuditLogger
    included_keyspaces: reservation
    included_categories: QUERY,DML
```

Then restart the node. After inserting some data, you will see entries in the *logs/ system.log* file, like this:

```
INFO  [Native-Transport-Requests-1] 2019-12-17 19:57:33,649
    FileAuditLogger.java:49 - user:reservation_service|
    host:127.0.0.2:7000|source:/127.0.0.2|port:52614|
    timestamp:1576637853616|type:SELECT|category:QUERY|
    ks:reservation|scope:reservations_by_hotel_date|
    operation:SELECT * FROM reservations_by_hotel_date
```

As you can see, audit logging statements include not only the actual text of the CQL statement but also the timestamp, identity of the user, and IP address of the source that made the query. You can direct audit logging statements to their own dedicated file by configuring the Log4j settings according to instructions provided in the Cassandra documentation (*https://oreil.ly/GMqW3*).

Summary

Cassandra is just one part of an enterprise application, but it performs an important role. In this chapter, you learned how to configure Cassandra's pluggable authentication and authorization capabilities, and how to manage and grant permissions to users and roles. You enabled encryption between clients and nodes, and learned how to secure the JMX interface for remote access. Finally, you learned how to use Cassandra's audit log feature to help ensure compliance. This should put you in a great position for our next topic: integrating Cassandra with other technologies.

Migrating and Integrating

Throughout this book we've looked at many aspects of Cassandra, including its origins (Chapter 2), query language (Chapter 4), and architecture (Chapter 6); how to create Cassandra data models (Chapter 5) and design (Chapter 7) and implement applications using Cassandra (Chapter 8); and how to effectively configure (Chapter 10), monitor (Chapter 11), maintain (Chapter 12), tune (Chapter 13), and secure (Chapter 14) Cassandra clusters.

Now it's time to recap what you've learned from a different angle: bringing Cassandra into your existing enterprise architecture. First, you'll apply your knowledge to the task of migrating a relational application to Cassandra, including adapting data models and application code. While the focus is migration from relational databases to Cassandra, the principles apply to migration from other database types as well. We'll finish up by taking a look at tools and integrations for getting data into and out of Cassandra, and searching and analyzing data stored in Cassandra clusters.

Knowing When to Migrate

The first consideration is how to know when you need to migrate an application or use case to Cassandra. A clear indication is when you encounter one or more of the challenges of relational databases highlighted in Chapter 1:

- Poor performance due to volume and complexity of queries
- Challenges scaling beyond a single database node
- Availability risk due to single-node or single-region deployments
- High licensing costs associated with sophisticated multinode solutions
- High software maintenance cost due to complex queries and stored procedures

- Limited ability to deploy in hybrid cloud or multicloud architectures

You don't have to have all of these challenges in order to start looking at Cassandra, but they certainly indicate where Cassandra's decentralized design, elastic scalability, flexible deployment, high availability, tuneable consistency, and high performance could be a great fit for your application, as you learned in Chapter 2.

So, how will you approach a migration project from a legacy database such as an RDBMS to Cassandra? The history of IT is littered with overly ambitious projects that failed by attempting to deliver too much functionality at once. To mitigate this risk, we recommend making your transition incrementally, perhaps one or two use cases at a time.

Adapting the Data Model

Suppose your task is to migrate a hotel reservation system to a new cloud-based system. You'll want to start by adapting your data model. Building on the relational data model for the hotel domain introduced in Chapter 5, Figure 15-1 designates primary keys (PK) and foreign keys (FK) as well as the multiplicity of each relationship.

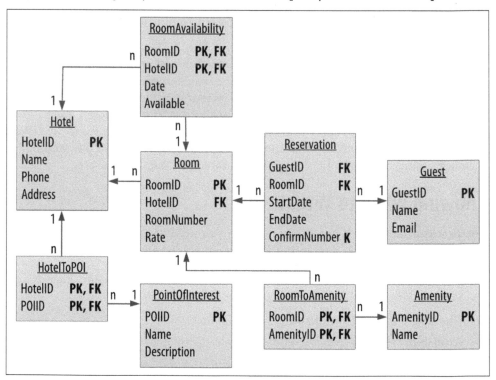

Figure 15-1. Reservation relational model

Considering how you might translate this relational model to Cassandra, there are two main approaches: *indirect translation* and *direct translation*. In indirect translation, you reverse engineer existing relational data models to produce a conceptual model, and analyze the workflows of the applications that exercise those data models to identify access patterns. As shown in Figure 15-2, the reverse engineered conceptual data model and access patterns become inputs to the familiar Cassandra data modeling process introduced in Chapter 5. That process begins with creating a conceptual data model and identifying access patterns, and proceeds to creating logical data models and physical data models, and eventually schema described in CQL.

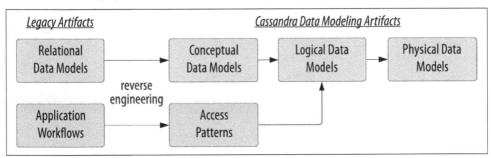

Figure 15-2. Indirect translation process

Since you've already learned this Cassandra data modeling process in Chapter 5, let's focus on direct translation, in which you translate directly from relational data models to Cassandra. In this method, the focus is on translating the entities and relationships from the source data models into Cassandra tables using patterns that we'll introduce in the following sections. As in the Cassandra data modeling approach, you will still want to review your table designs against access patterns to make sure you're identifying all the required queries.

Translating Entities

First, let's consider patterns for mapping entities to Cassandra tables. The relational `Hotel` table shown at the top of Figure 15-3 is an example entity table. Entities in this table might be accessed by an existing application by the relational key `HotelID`, so the first pattern is to create a `hotels` table in your Cassandra data model using a similar key design.

Over time, the legacy application likely identified the need to locate hotels by name, phone number, or other attributes, and may have created one or more indexes on relational tables to support these queries:

```
/* SQL */
CREATE INDEX idx_name ON Hotels (Name);
SELECT * FROM Hotels WHERE Name='My Hotel' ;
```

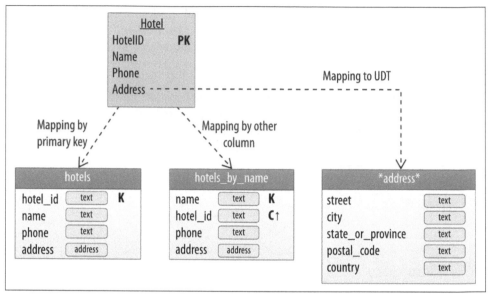

Figure 15-3. Entity translation

This leads to the second pattern, which is to create denormalized Cassandra tables representing the different search combinations. For example, the `hotels_by_name` table uses the `name` column as the partition key, and the `hotel_id` as a clustering column as a safeguard to ensure a unique row should another hotel have the same name. As you first learned in Chapter 4, the partition key and clustering column together make up a Cassandra primary key.

Use Secondary Indexes and Materialized Views Carefully

As you learned in Chapter 7, Cassandra does provide capabilities as an alternative to denormalization that those with a relational background will find familiar: secondary indexes and materialized views. Cassandra's pluggable secondary index capability allows you to create indexes on columns not included in a table's primary key, with multiple index implementations available. Remember that queries based on indexes involve a larger number of nodes and therefore do not scale as well as other queries. You'll want to stress test any intended usage using the techniques identified in Chapter 13.

Materialized views allow you to offload the work of maintaining multiple denormalized tables to Cassandra. There are some restrictions on views you can create, and this is still considered an experimental feature as of the 4.0 release.

The third pattern shown in Figure 15-3 involves the representation of complex types in Cassandra tables. While the type of the Address column in the SQL Hotels table has been left unspecified, it could be represented as a string (varchar) or user-defined type, depending on the SQL variant in use. In Cassandra it would be natural to use UDTs to describe a structure such as the Address type that can be referenced by multiple tables within a keyspace.

Translating Relationships

Next, consider that relationships between entities are frequently modeled as tables in relational models; these are also known as *join tables*. The RoomToAmenity table shown in Figure 15-4 is one such join table that describes the relationship between a hotel room in the Room table and an amenity that room offers to its guests in the Amenity table. This design provides a common definition of an amenity that could apply to rooms across many different hotels.

Note that while the RoomToAmenity table has no additional attributes beyond the RoomID and AmenityID that serve as foreign keys into the Room and Amenity tables, respectively, join tables may contain additional columns. For example, the Reservation table represents a more complex relationship between a hotel room and a guest who is reserving the room.

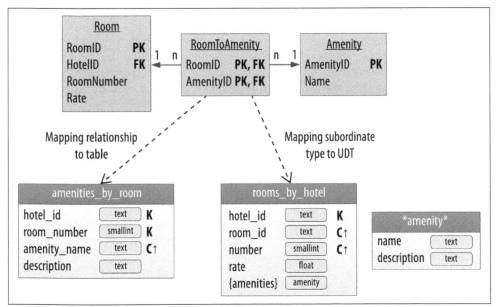

Figure 15-4. Relationship translation

The first pattern for translating relationships between entities is to map the relationship to a table. The `amenities_by_room` table is an example of this approach. Such a table could be used alongside entity tables for `amenities` and `rooms`.

The second pattern is to collapse one of the entity types as a user-defined type (UDT) within a containing entity table. For example, consider the design shown to the lower right of Figure 15-4. In this design, the `rooms_by_hotel` table contains a `set` of the `amenity` UDT.

Note that nothing prevents you from using both of these approaches in the same data model. You can use the intended access patterns of your application to determine if either or both would be appropriate. For example, the second design pattern would be appropriate if your application needs to retrieve information about hotel rooms and their amenities—this design allows that information to be retrieved in a single query. You'll want to balance this against the effort required to update amenities for each room when they change.

Additional Translation Patterns

In their paper, "A Big Data Modeling Methodology for Apache Cassandra," Artem Chebotko and Andrey Kashlev investigate additional translation patterns in their research and propose an approach for using these patterns to automate translation of relational models to Cassandra.

For example, your system might have hierarchical data models in which a base type is extended by multiple subtypes. Imagine a reservation application that could be used for both hotels and vacation rentals. The data model for a more generalized domain might include base type for a facility that could be extended with domain-specific attributes for hotels and vacation rentals.

One pattern for representing this in Cassandra would be to use a base table with columns for all possible subtypes, to take advantage of Cassandra's sparse storage model. Alternatively, a `string` column could be used to store a JSON blob containing subtype attributes, delegating the work of interpreting the blob to the application.

Whether you choose a direct or indirect translation approach, the resulting models should be largely the same, especially if you are evaluating your proposed designs against the queries needed by your application.

Adapting the Application

After updating your data model, the next step is to adapt (or create) the application code. You might identify inventory and reservation processing as the use cases to begin with, due to their impact on scalability.

You might then choose to use the microservice architecture style for the new implementation. You could identify and design a Reservation Service using the techniques discussed in Chapter 7, and assign responsibility for reservation data and associated Cassandra tables to it. One approach to migration toward a microservice architecture is to use a technique known as the *strangler pattern*, in which capabilities of the legacy system are gradually replaced one at a time by microservice implementations. The legacy system remains operational until all of its capabilities have been replaced, whereupon it can be decommissioned.

Figure 15-5 shows an early stage in this process, in which clients are first modified to talk to an API layer that abstracts access to the legacy application, either by emulating its API or by providing a modern API such as a REST or GraphQL. The API layer can delegate reservation-related requests to the Reservation Service while continuing to direct other requests to the legacy application.

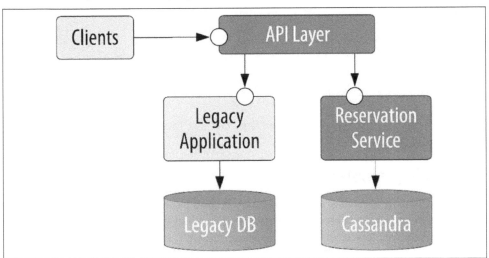

Figure 15-5. Application migration

The Reservation Service maintains its own data store based on Cassandra. Depending on the complexity of the design, the Reservation Service may require some coordination with the legacy application, but your goal should be to isolate the database level as much as possible. We'll discuss some approaches for message-based interaction in "Managing Data Flow with Apache Kafka" on page 379.

Refactoring Data Access

You'll recall we presented a design for the Reservation Service in Chapter 7 for a Java-based implementation. The view in Figure 15-6 is a more abstract view that highlights our recommendation to separate out layers within each microservice implementation. Provide one or more API endpoints using REST or GraphQL, centralize business logic such as validation and business processes, and use the Data Access Object (DAO) pattern to abstract the details of interactions with a specific database.

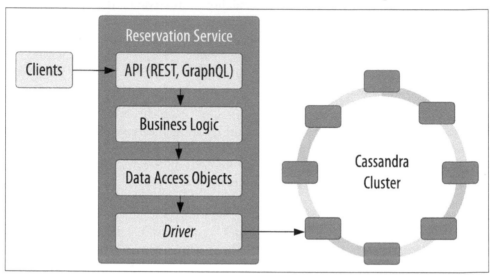

Figure 15-6. Data Access Object pattern

Using an object mapper as provided by the DataStax Java Driver is one way to implement a DAO layer.

Maintaining Consistency

As you write or update data access code, you'll need to consider the consistency needs of your application. Developers familiar with relational technology are accustomed to using transactions to accomplish writes to multiple related tables and often have concerns related to consistency in writing and reading data, including:

- "I've heard Cassandra is 'eventually consistent.' How can I make sure that I can read data immediately after it is written?"

- "How can I avoid race conditions when inserting or updating a row, or maintain consistency across writes to multiple tables without ACID transactions?"

- "How can I efficiently read data from multiple tables without joins?"

As you've learned in this book, Cassandra provides several mechanisms that allow you to gain a bit more control over the consistency of your reads and writes. Let's quickly review them here:

Configuring consistency levels to achieve strong consistency

Let's recap how you can use Cassandra's tuneable consistency to achieve the level of consistency you need. Cassandra allows you to specify a replication strategy at the keyspace level which includes the number of replicas of your data that will be stored per data center. You specify a consistency level on each CQL statement that describes how many of those nodes must respond; typically this includes setting a default consistency level in the driver you're using, and overriding on individual statements as needed.

We introduced the available consistency levels in Chapter 9 and discussed how you can achieve strong consistency (that is, the ability to guarantee that a read gets the most recently written data) using the QUORUM or LOCAL_QUORUM consistency level for both reads and writes. If your use case doesn't require this level of consistency, you can use lower consistency levels such as ONE or LOCAL_ONE to increase write throughput.

Using batches to coordinate writes to multiple tables

New Cassandra users accustomed to relational databases are often uncomfortable with the idea of storing multiple copies of data in denormalized tables. Typically users become comfortable with the idea that storage is relatively cheap in modern cloud architectures and are less concerned with these additional copies than with how to ensure data is written consistently across these different tables.

Cassandra provides a BATCH query that allows you to group mutations to multiple tables in a single query. You can include CQL INSERT, UPDATE, and even DELETE statements in a batch. The guarantee of a batch is that if all the statements are valid CQL, once any of the statements complete successfully, the coordinator will continue to work in the background to make sure that all the statements are executed successfully, using mechanisms such as hinted handoff (see "Hinted Handoff" on page 118) where needed.

Keep in mind the amount of data that is in a batch. Thankfully, Cassandra provides a configurable threshold batch_size_warn_threshold_in_kb property that you can use to detect when clients are submitting large batches, as discussed in Chapter 9 and Chapter 11.

Using lightweight transactions for exclusivity and uniqueness

One of the first things relational users learn about Cassandra is that it does not support transactions with ACID semantics due to the challenges of implementing the required locking in a distributed system. However, Cassandra provides a more limited capability called a *lightweight transaction* that is scoped to a single partition; a small number of nodes are involved in the lightweight transaction.

As you learned in Chapter 9, Cassandra provides two forms of lightweight transactions: one for guaranteeing unique rows, and one for implementing check-and-set style operations. You can use the IF NOT EXISTS syntax on an INSERT statement to make sure a row with the same primary key does not already exist. For example, when inserting into the reservations_by_confirmation table, you can use this syntax to ensure the confirmation number is unique. You use the IF <conditions> syntax to ensure that one or more values satisfy the conditions you supply before performing an UPDATE, for example, making sure that an available inventory count matches your expected value before decrementing it.

Using denormalization to avoid joins

Working around Cassandra's lack of joins actually begins back in data modeling, prior to application development. You saw an example of this in the design of the amenities_by_room table, which is intended to allow the retrieval of information about a hotel room and its amenities in a single query. This avoids the need for a join on rooms and amenities tables.

There may be cases where you can't anticipate the joins that will be needed in the future. In microservice architectures, separate data types may be owned by different services with their own data stores, meaning that you wouldn't have been able to join the data in any case. In both of these situations you'll most likely end up implementing application-level joins. The emergence of GraphQL as a standard for interfaces has helped application-level joins feel less threatening. We'll address more complex analytics queries in "Analyzing Data with Apache Spark" on page 382.

Migrating Stored Procedures

A final aspect you'll want to consider in migrating an application from a relational database is whether some of the business logic might actually be implemented within the database as stored procedures. Many legacy applications make use of stored procedures for reasons including: the desire to promote reuse of common queries, an attempt to achieve some performance benefit, or even because a DBA tasked with helping application developers write queries wanted to abstract some complexity away. The benefits of stored procedures are often traded against reduced application portability and maintainability, as there may be different tools and processes required to deploy, monitor, and debug the stored procedure.

Cassandra 2.2 introduced two features that will look familiar to those looking for stored procedures: user-defined functions (UDFs) and user-defined aggregates (UDAs) allow clients to shift some processing to the coordinator node. Using these features can improve performance in some situations by reducing the amount of data that has to be returned to the client and reducing processing load on the client, at the cost of additional processing on the server.

User-defined functions

UDFs are functions that are applied on Cassandra nodes to stored data as part of query processing. Before using UDFs in your cluster, enable them in the *cassandra.yaml* file on each node:

```
enable_user_defined_functions: true
```

Here's a quick summary of how this works: create a UDF using the CQL CREATE FUNC TION command, which causes the function to be propagated to every node in the cluster. When you execute a query that references the UDF, it is applied to each row of the query result.

Let's create an example UDF to count the number of available rooms in the avail able_rooms_by_hotel_date table:

```
cqlsh:hotel> CREATE FUNCTION count_if_true(input boolean)
    RETURNS NULL ON NULL INPUT
    RETURNS int
    LANGUAGE java AS 'if (input) return 1; else return 0;';
```

Let's dissect this command a bit at a time. You've created a UDF named count_if_true, which operates on a boolean parameter and returns an integer. You've also included a null check to make sure the function works effectively just in case the value is not defined. Note that if a UDF fails, execution of the query is aborted, so this can be an important check.

 UDF Security

The 3.0 release added a security feature to run UDF code in a separate sandbox so that malicious functions can't gain unauthorized access to a node's Java runtime.

Next, note that you've declared this to be a Java implementation with the LANGUAGE clause. Cassandra natively supports functions and aggregates defined in Java and JavaScript. They can also be implemented using any language supported by the Java Scripting API specified in JSR 223, including Python, Ruby, and Scala. Functions defined in these languages require adding additional scripting engine JAR files to Cassandra's Java CLASSPATH.

Finally, you include the actual Java syntax of the function with the AS clause. Now this function is somewhat trivial by itself, because all you're doing is counting true values as 1. You'll do something more powerful with this UDF in a bit.

First, however, try your UDF out on the available_rooms_by_hotel_date table to
see how it works:

```
cqlsh:hotel> SELECT room_number, count_if_true(is_available)
  FROM available_rooms_by_hotel_date
  WHERE hotel_id='AZ123' and date='2016-01-05';

 room_number | hotel.count_if_true(is_available)
-------------+-----------------------------------
         101 |                                 1
         102 |                                 1
         103 |                                 1
         104 |                                 1
         105 |                                 1

(5 rows)
```

As you can see, the column with the function result is qualified with the hotel key‐
space name. This is because each UDF is associated with a specific keyspace. If you
were to execute a similar query in the DataStax Java Driver, you would find a Column
in each Row with the name hotel_count_if_true_is_available.

User-defined aggregates

As you've just learned, user-defined functions operate on a single row. In order to
perform operations across multiple rows, you create a user-defined aggregate. The
UDA leverages two UDFs: a state function and an optional final function. A state
function is executed against every row, while the final function, if present, operates
on the results of the state function.

Let's look at a simple example to help investigate how this works. First, you'll need a
state function. The count_if_true function is close, but you need to make a small
change to allow the available count to be summed across multiple rows. Let's create a
new function that allows a running total to be passed in, incremented, and returned:

```
cqlsh:hotel> CREATE FUNCTION state_count_if_true(total int, input boolean)
   RETURNS NULL ON NULL INPUT
   RETURNS int
   LANGUAGE java AS 'if (input) return total+1; else return total;';
```

Note that the total parameter is passed as the first parameter, with its type matching
the return type of the function (int). For a UDF to be used as a state function, the
first parameter type and return types must match. The second parameter is the
boolean returned by the count_if_true UDF.

Now you can create an aggregate that uses this state function:

```
cqlsh:hotel> CREATE AGGREGATE total_available (boolean)
   SFUNC state_count_if_true
   STYPE int
   INITCOND 0;
```

Let's break down this statement piece by piece: first, you've declared a UDA called total_available, which operates on columns of type boolean.

The SFUNC clause identifies the state function used by this query—in this case, state_count_if_true.

Next, you identify the type that is used to accumulate results from the state function by the STYPE clause. Cassandra maintains a value of this type, which it passes to the state function as it is called on each successive row. The STYPE must be the same as the first parameter and return type of the state function. The INITCOND clause allows you to set the initial value of the result; here, you set the initial count to zero.

In this case, you've omitted the final function, but you could have included a function that took an argument of the STYPE and returned any other type, such as a function that accepts an integer argument and returns a boolean indicating if the inventory is at a low level that should generate an alert.

Now use your aggregate to get a count of available rooms returned by one of your previous queries. Note that your query must only include the UDA, with no other columns or functions:

```
cqlsh:hotel> SELECT total_available(is_available)
  FROM available_rooms_by_hotel_date
  WHERE hotel_id='AZ123' and date='2016-01-05';

 hotel.total_available(is_available)
-------------------------------------
                                   5

(1 rows)
```

As you can see, this query yields a result of five available rooms for the specified hotel and date.

Additional UDF/UDA Command Options

You can use the familiar IF NOT EXISTS syntax when creating UDFs and UDAs to avoid error messages for attempts to create functions and aggregates with duplicate signatures. Alternatively, you can use the CREATE OR REPLACE syntax when you actually intend to override the current function or aggregate.

Use the DESCRIBE FUNCTIONS command or the DESCRIBE AGGRE GATES command to learn which UDFs and UDAs have been defined already. This can be especially useful when there are functions with the same name but different signatures.

Finally, you can delete UDFs and UDAs using the DROP FUNCTION and DROP AGGREGATE commands.

Built-in functions and aggregates

In addition to user-defined functions and aggregates, Cassandra also provides some built-in, or *native*, functions and aggregates:

COUNT

> The COUNT function counts the number of rows returned by a query. For example, to count the number of hotels in the database:
>
> ```
> SELECT COUNT(*) FROM hotel.hotels;
> ```
>
> This command can also count the number of nonnull values of a specified column. For example, the following could be used to count how many guests provided an email address:
>
> ```
> SELECT COUNT(emails) FROM reservation.guests;
> ```

MIN *and* MAX

> The MIN and MAX functions compute the minimum and maximum value returned by a query for a given column. For example, this query could be used to determine the minimum and maximum stay lengths (in nights) for reservations at a given hotel and arrival date:
>
> ```
> SELECT MIN(nights), MAX(nights) FROM reservations_by_hotel_date
>     WHERE hotel_id='AZ123' AND start_date='2016-09-09';
> ```

sum

> The sum function calculates the sum of the values returned by a query for a given column. You could sum the number of nights to be stayed across multiple reservations as follows:
>
> ```
> SELECT SUM(nights) FROM reservations_by_hotel_date
>     WHERE hotel_id='AZ123' AND start_date='2016-09-09';
> ```

avg

> The avg function computes the average of all the values returned by a query for a given column. To get the average stay length in nights, you might execute:
>
> ```
> SELECT AVG(nights) FROM reservations_by_hotel_date
>     WHERE hotel_id='AZ123' AND start_date='2016-09-09';
> ```

These built-in aggregates are technically part of the system keyspace. Therefore, the column name containing results of your last query would be system_avg_nights.

Managing UDF/UDA Scope

When migrating an application to Cassandra, it might seem a natural fit to convert each stored procedure into a Cassandra equivalent. That might or might not be a good case. A good rule of thumb is to avoid using stored procedures to implement business processes, data transformation, or validation. It's best to confine their usage to very basic analytical and statistical tasks like counting numbers of records meeting particular criteria, or calculating sums, averages, or other mathematical operators across multiple records.

Planning the Deployment

Along with adapting your data model and application code, planning your deployment is an important step in migrating from your existing database to Cassandra. You've learned many things throughout the course of this book that will help you in these steps:

Planning your cluster topology

As you learned in Chapter 10, your cluster topology will be primarily driven by the data centers in which you need to deploy your application. In addition to physical data centers, you'll read later in this chapter about some cases in which you may want to create additional logical Cassandra data centers within the same physical data centers.

Make sure to configure an appropriate replication strategy for each keyspace that includes the number of replicas you want per data center. The `NetworkTopology Strategy` is almost always the right choice unless you are sure your cluster will never extend beyond a single data center. Remember to adjust replication strategies for Cassandra's `system` keyspaces to reflect that as well.

Sizing your cluster

You'll want to size your cluster appropriately so that you have some headroom for growth without over-provisioning. To get an estimate of the data size you can expect for your various denormalized table designs, use the formulas described in Chapter 5.

You should also identify performance goals for your key queries, including desired read and write throughput and maximum latencies. Your data size and performance requirements will help you identify the number of nodes you'll need in each data center to store all your data and ensure response times are within your requirements. Use the stress testing tools and techniques described in Chapter 13 to gain confidence in your estimates.

Integration with your operational environment

Since Cassandra is just one part of your deployed system, you'll likely have infrastructure in place for collecting metrics and aggregating log files. You can use what you learned in Chapter 11 to incorporate Cassandra's metrics and logs into your overall monitoring platform.

You may also use scripts or an orchestration framework like Kubernetes in place for automated deployment and management of cloud applications and infrastructure. You can use what you learned in Chapter 12 to help manage your Cassandra clusters in keeping with your DevOps practices.

Setting your security posture

Your Cassandra clusters will become a key part of your overall enterprise security program, since they will be storing data that is likely of strategic business value and may have regulatory implications. You'll want to take advantage of features you learned about in Chapter 14, including encryption of data in motion and at rest. Make sure your use of Cassandra's authentication and authorization is integrated with any enterprise identity management capability you may have in place. Strive to create Cassandra users or roles for specific administrators, microservices, or applications that map to the fewest privileges required to do their work.

Migrating Data

Once you've planned and deployed a cluster, you're ready to begin moving your application and its data. There are multiple techniques you can use for data migration. These techniques are useful not only when you are migrating applications in production, but in other cases such as loading test data into a cluster, or when you need to add or modify tables (a process often known as *schema migration*).

Zero-Downtime Migration

Depending on your business requirements, you may need to transition from your current database to Cassandra without taking your systems offline. A common integration design pattern used to perform zero-downtime migrations is to deploy a special version of an application that performs writes to both the old database and the new database. This *dual write* technique, shown in Figure 15-7, is usually leveraged in combination with an initial data load using a bulk loading tool.

To execute the data migration, you first deploy the application version performing dual writes in order to capture new data, then migrate existing data using one of the bulk loading approaches discussed next. If there is a failure during the migration and you need to roll it back, the legacy database will still have all the data. Once the data migration is complete, you disable writes to the legacy database and perhaps decommission the legacy application.

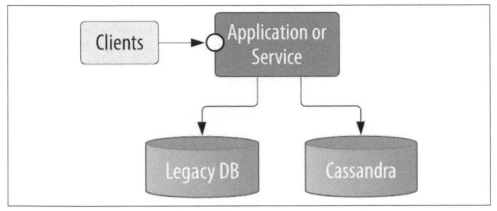

Figure 15-7. Dual write example

This approach could be combined with this application migration example, in which the API layer or another intermediate service performs the dual writes.

As an alternate approach to dual writes, you could enable the change data capture (CDC) capabilities of your legacy database and configure or write a component to consume the CDC events and push them into Cassandra. You'll see one example of how to do this in "Managing Data Flow with Apache Kafka" on page 379.

Bulk Loading

In using Cassandra, you'll often find it useful to be able to load data into a cluster, whether test data or data used by your application. Fortunately, there are a couple of easy ways to bulk-load formatted data to and from Cassandra:

The cqlsh COPY *command*

As you learned in Chapter 9, cqlsh supports loading and unloading of comma-separated value (CSV) files via the COPY command. For example, you could use the following command to save the contents of the reservations_by_confirma tion table to a file:

```
cqlsh:hotel> COPY reservations_by_confirmation TO 'reservations.csv'
    WITH HEADER=TRUE;
```

The TO value specifies the file to write to, and the HEADER option set to TRUE causes the column names to be printed in the output file. You could edit this file and read the contents back in with this command:

```
cqlsh:hotel> COPY reseravtions_by_confirmation FROM 'reservations.csv'
    WITH HEADER=true;
```

The COPY command supports other options to configure how quotes, escapes, and times are represented.

DataStax Bulk Loader (DSBulk)

The DataStax Bulk Loader (*https://oreil.ly/3w-7_*) is similar to `cqlsh COPY` in that it provides a command-line interface and inputs and outputs files, but with faster performance. DSBulk is available as a free download from the DataStax Downloads (*https://oreil.ly/zTP_d*) site. While the tool originally only supported unloading from open source Cassandra clusters, in December 2019 DataStax updated the tool to support loading into open source Cassandra clusters. DSBulk supports both JSON and CSV formats, and can read input from a web URL or `stdin`, and output to `stdout`. It provides flexible formats for dates and times, and handles user-defined types as well.

Other useful features of DSBulk include its status logging and error handling. Instead of failing immediately on a bad input line (or worse, failing silently and continuing), the bad lines are output to a log file so you can examine them, fix them, and try loading again. You can also configure a threshold for the maximum number of failures encountered before the import aborts. The tool also calculates summary statistics on every run.

The design of DSBulk was inspired by the work of Brian Hess on Cassandra Loader (*https://oreil.ly/ZGQVc*). Brian has produced a series of blog posts (*https://oreil.ly/KA-Nk*) with over 40 examples of how to use DSBulk for various use cases.

Apache Spark

While we'll cover the integration in more detail in "Analyzing Data with Apache Spark" on page 382, it's worth noting here that you can use Apache Spark to run distributed jobs that spread the work of reading from a source database and writing into Cassandra across multiple machines. Note that the source database could be another Cassandra cluster or even another table in the same cluster, which makes this is a popular approach for schema migration.

Validating Data Migration

No matter what tool you use to migrate data, you may want to have some checks in place to make sure all of your data has been moved correctly. The DSBulk error logging features are useful here, but you could also write Spark jobs to manually compare data between source and target databases a row at a time. If both your source and target systems are Cassandra-based, the Cassandra diff (*https://oreil.ly/31HRd*) project provides a useful starting point.

Common Integrations

Whether you're migrating an existing application to Cassandra or creating something entirely new, you'll likely have other infrastructure that you need Cassandra to work alongside in order to get the most out of your data. This might already be in place, or you might be adding it for a new application. In this final section we'll examine a few of the most popular integrations, many of which happen to be with other Apache Software Foundation projects with distributed architectures.

Managing Data Flow with Apache Kafka

Apache Kafka is a distributed streaming platform that is used to build real-time data pipelines and streaming applications. It supports a publish and subscribe style of messaging, in which messages are published to topics in a key-value format. Similar to Cassandra, Kafka partitions data using the key and replicates data across multiple nodes, known as *brokers* in Kafka.

Cassandra and Kafka are used together frequently in microservice architectures as shown in Figure 15-8. Revisiting the Reservation Service design from Chapter 7, you can see one common interaction pattern. In this design, the Reservation Service receives an API request to perform some action, such as creating, updating, or deleting a reservation. After persisting the change to Cassandra, the Reservation Service produces a message to a `reservations` topic in a Kafka cluster.

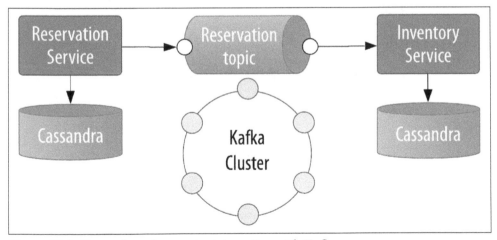

Figure 15-8. Cassandra microservice integration with Kafka

Other services consume the `reservations` topic and perform various actions in response to each message: for example, the Inventory Service updating inventory tables to mark the dates as reserved, or perhaps an Email Service sending an email thanking the guest for making a reservation. In this style of interaction, Cassandra and Kafka are not connected directly, but are used in a complementary fashion.

Kafka provides some storage capability for its topics and the ability to perform queries and joins via the KSQL query language. However, it does not provide all of the features of a database and is primarily suitable for short-term storage. In many cases involving larger data sets, it will be appropriate to replicate data to a database for longer-term storage and more flexible querying. Kafka Connect is a pluggable framework for building reusable producers or consumers that connect Kafka topics to existing databases or applications. You can find a wide variety of connectors for both open source Kafka and the enterprise Confluent Platform at the Confluent Hub (*https://www.confluent.io/hub*).

For our discussion here, we'll focus on connectors provided by DataStax that work with both Apache Kafka and Confluent Platform. The DataStax Apache Kafka Connector is a sink connector that you deploy in Kafka Connect that will automatically take messages from Kafka topics and write them to Cassandra or DataStax Enterprise. You could use the sink connector in a live migration of reservation data from another system, as shown in Figure 15-9. Configure a source connector for the legacy system database, which will write data into Kafka topics, and the DataStax Apache Kafka Connector as a sink to write data to Cassandra.

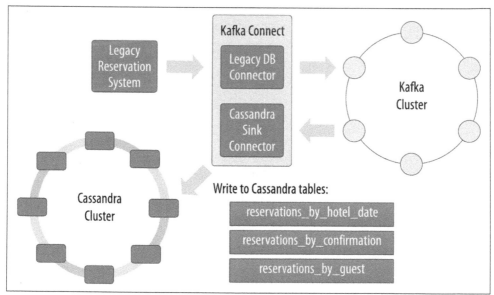

Figure 15-9. Streaming data into Cassandra with Kafka Connect

The connector uses a configuration file to map messages from Kafka topics to one or more Cassandra tables. This is useful for performing writes into multiple denormalized tables such as the various tables in the reservation keyspace. The connector supports multiple serialization formats for the source message, including Avro and JSON, and the ability to set the CQL `writetime` and `TTL` attributes on writes to Cassandra. Because the DataStax Kafka Connector is built on the DataStax Java Driver, all the configuration options provided by the driver are available as well.

Change Data Capture

As you read about streaming data into Cassandra, you may be wondering if the reverse is possible—streaming data out of Cassandra. You can do this using Cassandra's change data capture (CDC) feature, but there is an interesting challenge given Cassandra's distributed architecture, which we'll explain shortly.

Cassandra introduced the CDC feature in the 3.8 release that tracks all mutations, including CQL `INSERT`, `UPDATE`, and `DELETE` queries, by capturing portions of the commit log for selected tables. The original design was based on archiving segments of the commit log after the data was flushed to disk. The 4.0 release improved this behavior to store an index of locations into commit log files as the commit logs are written, increasing speed and reliability.

You enable CDC on a cluster by setting `cdc_enabled: true`, and your desired location for archived commit log segments via the `cdc_raw_directory` option in the *cassandra.yaml* file. You then specify the individual tables to capture via the `ALTER TABLE` command; for example:

```
cqlsh> ALTER TABLE reservation.reservations_by_confirmation WITH cdc=true;
```

If you enable CDC, you'll want to make sure there is a consumer that is processing and then deleting the commit logs. The `cdc_total_space_in_mb` option specifies the maximum size of the CDC logs, and if the value exceeds this then CDC will stop. You can write your own consumer using the `org.apache.cassandra.db.commitlog.CommitLogReader` class.

CDC provides a good starting point for streaming data from Cassandra into other locations such as Kafka, but the key challenge of doing this is ordering and deduplicating the CDC logs from the various nodes in the cluster, since each write should appear in as many nodes as your replication factor specifies.

DataStax has provided an early access version of a Kafka source connector known as DataStax CDC for Apache Kafka (*https://oreil.ly/TEKoi*). This CDC connector does not yet work with open source Cassandra clusters at the time of writing, as it depends on the Advanced Replication feature of DataStax Enterprise for deduplication.

Searching with Apache Lucene, SOLR, and Elasticsearch

Even if you follow the best practices for Cassandra data modeling and design multiple denormalized tables to support different queries, you may encounter cases where you need more advanced search semantics than just querying data by a primary key. For example, you may require full text search features such as case insensitivity, substring search, or fuzzy mapping. Or you might have location data and need to perform geospatial queries such as finding all the hotels within a certain radius from a specific latitude/longitude.

Distributed search capability can be added to Cassandra via Apache Lucene (*https://oreil.ly/J6jg9*), which provides an engine for distributed indexing and searching, and its subproject, Apache Solr (*https://oreil.ly/Kt5VT*), which adds REST and JSON APIs to the Lucene search engine. DataStax Enterprise Search provides an implementation of Cassandra's pluggable secondary index interface. It maintains Lucene indexes on each node in the cluster and uses Solr's APIs to implement searching. This integrated approach is more efficient than running a separate search cluster. Stratio has provided a plug-in (*https://oreil.ly/WObzc*) that uses a similar approach.

Elasticsearch (*https://oreil.ly/334x1*) is another popular open source search framework built on top of Apache Lucene. It supports multitenancy and provides Java and JSON over HTTP APIs. The Elassandra (*https://www.elassandra.io/*) project provides a forked version of Elasticsearch that works as a secondary index implementation for Cassandra.

Analyzing Data with Apache Spark

with Patrick McFadin

In a successful deployment of any application, you can expect your business partners to approach you with questions that require in-depth analysis of your data. There are many commercial analytics and business intelligence products that can ingest data from Cassandra, including Stream Analytix, Tableau, and Teradata. You can also use ETL tools such as Informatica or Talend to extract data from your Cassandra clusters into a data lake or data warehouse for future analysis.

In this section, we'll focus on the most popular open source analytics integration, Apache Spark (*http://spark.apache.org/*). Spark is a data analytics framework that provides a massively parallel processing framework to enable simple API calls across large volumes of data. Originally developed in 2009 at UC Berkeley as an improvement to MapReduce, Spark was open sourced in 2010, and became an Apache project in 2014.

Unlike Apache Hadoop, which writes intermediate results to disk, the Spark core processing engine is designed to maximize memory usage while minimizing disk and network access. Spark uses streaming instead of batch-oriented processing to achieve processing speeds up to 100 times faster than Hadoop. In addition, Spark's API is much simpler to use than Hadoop.

Spark provides multiple APIs for working with data at different levels of abstraction. The base level of data representation in Spark is the *Resilient Distributed Dataset* (RDD). The RDD is a description of the data to be processed, such as a file or data collection. Once an RDD is created, the data contained can be transformed with API calls as if all of the data were contained in a single machine. However, in reality, the RDD can span many nodes in the network by partitioning. Each partition can be operated on in parallel to produce a final result. The RDD supports the familiar map and reduce operations plus additional operations such as count, filter, union, and distinct. For a full list of transformations, see the Spark documentation (*https:// oreil.ly/mYU69*).

Spark provides two additional APIs on top of RDDs: Datasets and DataFrames. A *Dataset* provides the functionality of an RDD and adds the ability to query data using Spark SQL. A *DataFrame* is a Dataset that is organized into named columns, similar to a table in relational databases or Cassandra. DataFrames can be constructed from structured datafiles, existing RDDs, tables in Hive, or external databases.

Spark provides API support in Java, Scala, Python, and the R statistics language. In addition to the core engine, Spark includes further libraries for different types of processing requirements, including Spark SQL for SQL and structured data processing, MLlib for machine learning, GraphX for graph processing, and Spark Streaming. For a more fulsome introduction, we suggest the O'Reilly book *Spark: The Definitive Guide*, by Matei Zaharia and Bill Chambers.

Use cases for Spark with Cassandra

Apache Cassandra is a great choice for transactional workloads that require high scale and maximum availability. Apache Spark is a great choice for analyzing large volumes of data at scale. Combining the two enables many interesting use cases that exploit the power of both technologies.

An example use case is high-volume time-series data. A system for ingesting weather data from thousands of sensors with variable volume is a perfect fit for Cassandra. Once the data is collected, further analysis on data stored in Cassandra may be difficult given that the analytics capabilities available using CQL are limited. At this point, adding Spark to the solution will open many new uses for the collected data. For example, you can pre-build aggregations from the raw sensor data and store those results in Cassandra tables for use in frontend applications. This brings analytics closer to users without the need to run complex data warehouse queries at runtime.

Or consider the hotel application discussed throughout this book. You can use Spark to implement various analytic tasks on reservation and guest data, such as generating reports on revenue trends, or demographic analysis of anonymized guest records to determine where your company should build a new hotel.

One use case to avoid is using Spark-Cassandra integration as an alternative to a Hadoop workload. Cassandra is suited for transactional workloads at high volume and shouldn't be considered as a data warehouse. When approaching a use case where both technologies might be needed, first apply Cassandra to solving a problem suited for Cassandra, such as those discussed in Chapter 2. Then consider incorporating Spark as a way to analyze and enrich the data stored in Cassandra without the cost and complexity of extract, transform, and load (ETL) processing.

Deploying Spark with Cassandra

A Spark cluster consists of a Spark Cluster Manager and Spark Workers. Clients create `SparkContext` objects used to submit jobs to the Spark Cluster Manager, which distributes the work to the Spark Executors on each node. Several Cluster Managers are available, including implementations for Apache Mesos, Hadoop YARN, and Kubernetes. There is also a standalone Cluster Manager useful for test and development work on a single-node cluster.

Now let's look at deploying Spark and Cassandra together. While it is possible to deploy Spark and Cassandra clusters independently, you can gain performance and efficiency by co-locating a Spark Worker on each Cassandra node in a data center, as shown in Figure 15-10. Because Cassandra places data per node based on token assignment, this existing data distribution can be used as an advantage to parallelize Spark jobs. This is the architecture used by DataStax Enterprise Analytics, which you can also emulate in your own deployments of Cassandra and Spark.

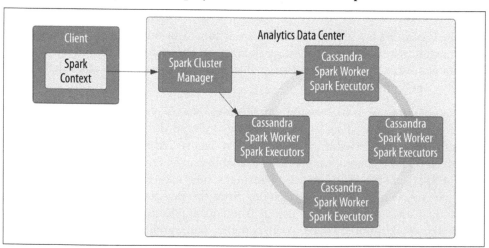

Figure 15-10. Topology of a Spark-Cassandra cluster

Here's how this works: when a job is submitted to the Spark Cluster Manager, the Spark Workers on each node spawn Spark Executors to complete the work. Using the `spark-cassandra-connector` as a conduit, the data required for each job is sourced from the local node as much as possible. You'll learn more about the connector momentarily.

Because each node contains a portion of the entire data in the cluster, each Spark Worker will only need to process that local subset of data: for example, a count action on a table. Each node will have a range of the table's data. The count is calculated locally and then merged from every node to produce the total count.

This design maximizes data locality, resulting in improved throughput and lower resource utilization for analytic jobs. The Spark Executors only communicate over the network when data needs to be merged from other nodes. As cluster sizes get larger, the efficiency gains of this design are much more pronounced.

> ## Using a Separate Data Center for Analytics
>
> A common deployment model for Cassandra and analytics toolsets such as Spark is to create a separate data center for analytic processing. This has the advantage of isolating the performance impact of analytics workloads from the rest of the cluster. The analytics data center can be constructed as a "virtual" data center where the actual hardware exists in the same physical location as another data center within the cluster. Using the `NetworkTopologyStrategy`, you can specify a lower replication factor for the analytics data center, since your required availability in this data center will typically be lower.

The spark-cassandra-connector

The `spark-cassandra-connector` (*https://oreil.ly/nIRpn*) is an open source project sponsored by DataStax on GitHub. The connector can be used by clients as a conduit to read and write data from Cassandra tables via Spark. The connector provides features including SQL queries and server-side filtering. The connector is implemented in Scala, but a Java API is available as well. API calls from the `spark-cassandra-connector` provide direct access to data in Cassandra in a context related to the underlying data. As Spark accesses data, the connector translates to and from Cassandra as the data source.

To start using the `spark-cassandra-connector`, you'll need to download both the connector and Spark. The connector documentation provides a useful quick start guide (*https://oreil.ly/fUNvk*). You can either download a pre-built version of Spark, or build Spark yourself from the source, from the Apache Spark website (*https://spark.apache.org*). If you'd just like to experiment, you can also download a copy of

DataStax Enterprise from the DataStax downloads page (*https://oreil.ly/2xHXX*) and enable analytics mode, as it is free for nonproduction use.

Let's review the common API elements used for most Spark jobs accessing data in Cassandra. The `spark-shell` is a great way to get started, which is available in the *bin* directory of your Spark installation. (The `pyspark` shell is another option if you're more comfortable with Python.) You'll need to provide the location of the connector jar files on the classpath and the location of at least one node in the Cassandra cluster using the `spark.cassandra.connection.host` property. If you have authorization enabled on your Cassandra cluster, as you learned about in Chapter 14, you'll need to include your login credentials via the properties `spark.cassandra.auth.username` and `spark.cassandra.auth.password`, respectively.

For example, you might point to the Cassandra node on local host like this (some output lines omitted for clarity):

```
$ spark-shell --conf spark.cassandra.connection.host=127.0.0.1
  --packages com.datastax.spark:spark-cassandra-connector_2.11:2.4.3
...
Spark context available as 'sc' (master = local[*], app id = local-1584302262471).
Spark session available as 'spark'.
Welcome to
      ____              __
     / __/__  ___ _____/ /__
    _\ \/ _ \/ _ `/ __/  '_/
   /___/ .__/\_,_/_/ /_/\_\   version 2.4.5
      /_/

Using Scala version 2.11.12 (OpenJDK 64-Bit Server VM, Java 1.8.0_232)
Type in expressions to have them evaluated.
Type :help for more information.

scala>
```

You'll note from the info messages that the `SparkContext` is available. Before you do anything else, you'll want to import libraries to enable the `SparkContext` to talk to your Cassandra cluster (from this point forward we'll omit the `scala>` prompt, except when we need to distinguish input from output):

```
import com.datastax.spark.connector._
import org.apache.spark.sql.cassandra._
```

Running Examples Using DataStax Enterprise Analytics

If you want to run these examples using DataStax Enterprise, you'll start the nodes in your cluster in analytics mode using the syntax `dse cassandra -k`, which automatically starts a Spark Worker on each node and designates one node as the Spark Cluster Manager. To run the Spark Shell, use the command `dse spark` on one of the nodes. The spark-cassandra-connector is already integrated, so you don't need to specify its location on the classpath when starting `spark-shell`, or import libraries at the Scala prompt, as in the commands above.

Once the `SparkContext` is created, you can then operate on Cassandra data using the Spark RDDs and DataFrames. For example, here's how you create a DataFrame representing the `reservations_by_hotel_date` table from the `reservation` keyspace introduced in Chapter 5 (note you should enter this on a single line):

```
val reservationDf = spark.read.format("org.apache.spark.sql.cassandra")
  .options(Map("keyspace" -> "reservation",
    "table" -> "reservations_by_hotel_date"))
  .load()
```

You can also use the `cassandraFormat()` method, which is simpler (note the table name comes first, followed by the keyspace name):

```
val reservationDf = spark.read.cassandraFormat("reservations_by_hotel_date",
  "reservation")
  .load()
```

To see the schema that Spark infers for your DataFrame, use the `printSchema()` operation (output included):

```
scala> reservationDf.printSchema()
root
 |-- hotel_id: string (nullable = true)
 |-- start_date: date (nullable = true)
 |-- room_number: short (nullable = true)
 |-- confirm_number: string (nullable = true)
 |-- end_date: date (nullable = true)
 |-- guest_id: string (nullable = true)
```

Now that you've created a DataFrame, you can perform transformations and actions on it. For example, to get the total number of reservations, create the following action to count every record in the table:

```
println("Number of reservations: " + reservationDf.count)
```

Because this is running as an analytics job in parallel with Cassandra, it is much more efficient than running a `SELECT count(*) FROM reservations` from `cqlsh`, especially as the size of your cluster grows.

As the underlying structure of the DataFrame is a Cassandra table, you can use CQL to filter the data and select rows. In Cassandra, filter queries using native CQL require a partition key to be efficient, but that restriction is removed when running queries as Spark jobs.

For example, you might derive a use case to produce a report listing reservations by end date, so that each hotel can know who is checking out on a given day. In this example, end_date is not a partition key or clustering column, but you can scan the entire cluster's data looking for reservations with a checkout date of September 8, 2020:

```
val reservationsByEndDate = reservationDf.filter($"end_date" === "2020-09-08")

// Invoke the action to run the Spark job
reservationsByEndDate.collect.foreach(println)
```

Finding and retrieving data is only half of the functionality available—you can also save data back to Cassandra. Traditionally, data in a transactional database would require extraction to a separate location in order to perform analytics. With the spark-cassandra-connector, you can extract data, transform in place, and save it directly back to a Cassandra table, eliminating the costly and error-prone ETL process.

For example, we might use the following code to create a report on the number of guests departing on each date and save the results to a Cassandra table:

```
val departureReport = reservationDf.groupBy("end_date")
  .agg(Map("*" -> "count"))
  .withColumnRenamed("COUNT(1)", "total_departures")

departureReport.createCassandraTable(
  "reservation",
  "departures_by_date",
  partitionKeyColumns = Some(Seq("end_date")))

departureReport.write.cassandraFormat("departures_by_date", "reservation")
  .save()
```

This is a simple example, but the basic syntax applies to any data. A more advanced example would be to calculate the average daily revenue for a hotel and write the results to a new Cassandra table. In a sensor application, you might calculate high and low temperatures for a given day and write those results back out to Cassandra.

Querying data is not just limited to Spark APIs. With SparkSQL, you can use familiar SQL syntax to perform complex queries on data in Cassandra, including query options not available in CQL. It's easy to create enhanced queries such as aggregations, ordering, and joins using the spark object, which is automatically available to you in the spark-shell. For example, if you wanted to create a report for guests arriving on a certain date, you could perform this query using a join, after first creating temporary views to represent the Cassandra tables being joined:

```
spark.sql("""CREATE TEMPORARY VIEW reservations_by_confirmation
    USING org.apache.spark.sql.cassandra
    OPTIONS (
    table "reservations_by_confirmation",
    keyspace "reservation",
    pushdown "true")""")

spark.sql("""CREATE TEMPORARY VIEW reservations_by_confirmation
    USING org.apache.spark.sql.cassandra
    OPTIONS (
    table "guests",
    keyspace "reservation",
    pushdown "true")""")

val arrivalList = spark.sql("""
  SELECT * from reservations_by_confirmation
  JOIN guests
  ON reservations_by_confirmation.guest_id = guests.guest_id
  WHERE end_date = '2020-09-08'""")

arrivalList.show()
```

The `arrivalList` returned from the `spark.sql()` operation is a `DataFrame` that you can manipulate using `DataFrame` APIs, for example to `show()` the results as was done here.

Once you've developed queries using `spark-shell`, you're ready to implement them in application code. If you're building an application in Java or Scala and using Maven, you'll want to add dependencies such as the following to your project's *pom.xml* file to access the Spark core and connector:

```
<dependency>
    <groupId>org.apache.spark</groupId>
    <artifactId>spark-sql_2.11</artifactId>
    <version>2.4.5</version>
    <scope>provided</scope>
</dependency>
<dependency>
    <groupId>com.datastax.spark</groupId>
    <artifactId>spark-cassandra-connector_2.11</artifactId>
    <version>2.4.3</version>
</dependency>
```

You've just scratched the surface of what you can accomplish with Cassandra and Spark. For example, you can use Cassandra as input to machine learning using Spark ML in order to gain additional insights from your data.

Summary

In this chapter, we've provided a roadmap for migrating applications to Cassandra and just scratched the surface of the many integration options available for Cassandra. Hopefully we've piqued your interest in the wide range of directions you can take your applications using Cassandra and related technologies.

And now we've come to the end of our journey together. If we've achieved our goal, you now have an in-depth understanding of the right problems to solve using Cassandra, and how to design, implement, deploy, and maintain successful applications.

Index

Cassandra's data model, 57-59, 63-66
creating a table, 50
partition size calculation, 97
secondary index pitfalls, 147
static, 97
commit logs
in Cassandra architecture, 122
data storage, 226
performance tuning, 321
writing data, 187, 190, 191
CommitLogMBean, 250
commitlog_compression property, 322
commitlog_directory property, 227
commitlog_sync element, 322
commitlog_sync_period_in_ms property, 322
commit_failure_policy property, 227
commit_log_sync_batch_window_in_ms, 322
compaction
in Cassandra architecture, 125
large partition warning, 314
nodetool cleanup command, 275
performance tuning, 325-328
tombstones and, 211
validation, 120, 277
compaction strategies, 126, 232, 325
compaction threshold, 327
CompactionManager class, 126, 247
CompactionManagerMBean class, 250, 328
CompactionParameters attribute, 326
compaction_throughput_mb_per_sec property,
    328
compensation for two-phase commit, defined,
    8
complex event processing system, 9
composite key, 57
compression
client–node messages, 177
commit log, 322
performance tuning, 335
SSTables, 124, 323
CompressionInfo.db, SSTable component, 192
conceptual data modeling, 81
concurrency, performance tuning, 328
Concurrent Mark Sweep garbage collector (see
    CMS)
concurrent_compactors property, 328
conditional write statements, 195
conf directory, 36
conferences, Cassandra community, 33

configuration files, 228, 291
    (see also cassandra.yaml file)
configuring Cassandra, 213-228
connection errors, installing Cassandra, 46
connection heartbeat, DataStax Java Driver, 177
connection pooling, 176
consensus algorithms, 121
consistency
Cassandra's tuneable, 20-23
defined, 6
LWT and Paxos, 120
maintaining among microservices, 154
relationship to availability and partition tol-
    erance, 23-27
scalability challenge and, 3
SERIAL and LOCAL_SERIAL, 196
types of, 21-23
CONSISTENCY command, 188
consistency levels
in Cassandra architecture, 115
deletes, 211
maintaining during migration, 368
performance tuning, 369
reading data, 200, 203
repairs, 276, 280
replication factors and, 116, 314, 346
writing data, 187-188, 195
ConstantReconnectionPolicy, 175
ConstantSpeculativeExecutionPolicy, 176
container deployments, 44
coordinator nodes, 117, 121, 189-191, 201
COUNT function, 374
counter batches, 196
counter cache, 125, 319
counter data type, 71
counters, 196
counter_cache_size_in_mb, 319
CP, primarily supporting consistency and parti-
    tion tolerance, 26
CQL (Cassandra Query Language), 55-79
Cassandra's data model, 56-66
client drivers and, 158
CQL data types, 66-79
defining database schema, 101-105
introduction of, 28
relational data model, 55
representing other database models in, 141
tools to manage, 103-105
CQL data types, 66-79

num_tokens property, 113, 228

O

object databases, 14
object mappers, 167-171
object-relational mapping (ORM) frameworks
 (see ORM)
objects, 9, 10, 332
ODBC (Open Database Connectivity), 184
OHCProvider class, 319
OldNetworkTopologyStrategy class, 115
ONE consistency level, 116, 188, 200
Open Database Connectivity (see ODBC)
OpenJDK, 40
operating systems, 35
 (see also Windows systems)
 extraction utilities, 36
 JVM settings, 331
 running ccm, 215
 setting the environment, 41
 storage file locations, 227
 updating configuration files, 291
 ZGC, 334
OPP (order-preserving partitioning), 223
OpsCenter, 298
Oracle Java Mission Control and Visual VM,
 245
Oracle JDK, 40
orchestration, 155
ORDER BY clause, 86, 208
ordering data, 208
OrderPreservingPartitioner, 223
org.apache.cassandra.concurrent package, 252
org.apache.cassandra.db package, 129
org.apache.cassandra.dht package, 114
org.apache.cassandra.internal domain, 252
org.apache.cassandra.locator package, 111
org.apache.cassandra.service.paxos package,
 121
org.apache.cassandra.transport package, 131
ORM (object-relational mapping) frameworks,
 10
overstreaming, 279

P

PaaS (Platform-as-a-Service), 5
PAGING command, 209
paging, reading data, 208-210
parallel repair, 278

parallel ssh tool, 294
partition index, 203
partition keys, 57, 100, 102, 202, 206, 317
partition recovery, 26
partition summary, 203
partition tolerance, 23-27, 108
partitioner range repair, 279
partitioners, 113, 222-224
partitions
 Cassandra's data model, 27, 57
 optimal storage design, 85
 Paxos state, 121
 performance tuning, 313
 size calculation, 97-98
 splitting, 100
 system keyspaces, 133
Partner Interconnect, 240
PasswordAuthenticator, 339-342
passwords, 341
patterns and anti-patterns, data modeling, 91,
 92
Paxos consensus algorithm, 121, 133
"Paxos Made Simple" (Lamport), 121
performance tuning, 305-336
 caching, 317-320
 commit logs, 321
 compaction, 325-328
 concurrency, 328
 hinted handoff, 324
 JVM settings, 331-336
 managing performance, 305-317
 memtables, 320
 networking, 329
 SSTables, 323
 threading, 328
 timeouts, 329
permissions, 343
persistence, designing with microservice architecture, 140
Pfeil, Matt, 29
pgrep tool, 43
Phi Accrual Failure Detection, 110, 111
PHP, DataStax Ruby and, 184
physical data modeling, 93-96
pip (Python installer), 214
PKCS12, 348
PlainTextAuthProvider, 177
Platform-as-a-Service (see PaaS)
polyglot persistence, 15, 140

services
    ActiveRepairService, 277
    AWS, 14, 236-239
    CRUD services, 155
    EmbeddedCassandraService, 129
    keyspaces and, 153
    messaging, 130, 252
    microservice architecture, 135-156
    S3, 14
    storage, 121, 129, 287
session key, 347
sessions, 160-162
set data type, 72
SGC (Shenandoah Garbage Collector), 334
sharding, 10-12
shared storage, 153, 235
shared-nothing architecture, 10-12
Shenandoah Garbage Collector (see SGC)
SHOW VERSION command, 47
Simple Logging Facade for Java (see SLF4J)
Simple Network Monitoring Protocol (see
    SNMP)
Simple Storage Service (see S3)
SimpleSeedProvider class, 220
SimpleSnitch class, 111, 221
SimpleStatement, DataStax Java Driver, 163,
    164
SimpleStatement.newInstance() method, 162
SimpleStrategy class, 115, 230
single point of failure, avoiding, 18
sizeOf() function, 99
SizeTieredCompactionStrategy (see STCS)
Slack chat, Cassandra community, 32
SLF4J (Simple Logging Facade for Java), 180,
    266
slices, 206
smallint data type, 67
snake case, 49
SNAPPY compression, 177
snapshots, 250, 293-295
snapshot_before_compaction property, 294
snitches
    adding a data center, 283
    in Cassandra architecture, 110
    configuring, 220-222
    creating a cluster, 214
    MBean, 251
    networking, 238, 240
    repair role of, 278

SNMP (Simple Network Monitoring Protocol),
    244
soft deletes, 128
Sorted String Table (see SSTables)
sorting data, 207
    designing ahead, 88
    in RDBMS vs. Cassandra, 85
Spark, 378, 382-389
Spark DataFrame, 389
Spark RDD (Resilient Distributed Dataset), 383
SpeculativeExecutionPolicy, 176
SQL (Structured Query Language)
    compared to CQL, 28, 55
    meta-database maintenance, 131
    support for and adoption of, 5
SSL (Secure Sockets Layer), 347
SSL certificates, 350
SSLContext object, 351
SSLFactory class, 351
SSTable Attached Secondary Index (see SASI)
sstableloader, 295
sstablemetadata tool, 278
SSTables
    in Cassandra architecture, 123
    compaction of, 125
    datafile and, 227
    deleting data, 211
    flush and restore for backup, 295
    MBean information, 249
    partition size and, 99
    performance tuning, 323
    reading data, 202
    repairs, 278
    streaming, 130
    upgrading, 291
    utilities, 296
    writing files to disk, 191-193
sstableupgrade script, 291
SSTableWriter interface, 192
"Starbucks Does Not Use Two-Phase Commit"
    (Hohpe), 9
starting the server, 41-43
startup scripts, 228
state function, 372
stateful sets, 301
statements, DataStax Java Driver, 161-165
static columns, 58, 97
statistics, nodetool monitoring, 257
Statistics.db, SSTable component, 193

STCS (SizeTieredCompactionStrategy), 126,
233, 325, 328
Stonebreaker, Michael
  "The Case for Shared Nothing", 12
stop-server command, 43
stopping Cassandra, 43
storage
  Amazon EC2, 238
  append-only storage model, 127
  cluster deployment, 235
  commit log as, 321
  data directory, 40
  designing for optimal, 85
  Kafka, 380
  Kubernetes, 301
  node configuration, 226
  shared vs. dedicated, 153, 235
storage engine, 129
StorageProxy class, 130, 131
StorageProxyMBean, 248
StorageService class, 121, 129, 287
StorageServiceMBean, 248, 252
stored procedures, migrating, 370-375
stream processing system, 9
streaming, 130, 279
StreamManager class, 130
StreamManagerMBean, 252
stress testing, performance tuning, 308-311
stress-build target, 39
strict consistency, 21
strings
  creating a table, 50
  enumerated types and, 67
strong consistency, 116, 156, 200
subrange repair, 279
sum function, 374
Summary.db, SSTable component, 193
superuser, 343
survivor space, 332
suspicion level, 109, 110
system keyspaces, 47, 131-134, 233, 313
system.log file, 218, 267

T

tables, 57
  (see also SSTables)
  Bigtable, 17, 26
  Cassandra's data model, 57-63
  creating in keyspace, 49

defined, 57, 59
freezing, 77
lookup tables, use in sharding, 11
memtables, 122-124, 127, 202, 274, 320
nesting, 77
system.hints table removal, 134
virtual tables for monitoring, 259-263
Tablesnap, 292
tempdb (SQL Server), 131
test (build target), 39
text data type, 68, 94
textAsBlob() function, 70
textual data types, 67
thread pools, 252, 257, 329
threading
  MBeans, 252
  performance tuning, 328
THREE consistency level, 116, 188, 200
throttling, 324, 330, 336
time data type, 68
time series pattern, data modeling, 92
time to live (see TTL)
timeouts, performance tuning, 329
timestamp data type, 68
timestamps, 63, 99
timeuuid data type, 69, 75
TimeWindowCompactionStrategy (see TWCS)
tinyint data type, 67
TLS (Transport Layer Security), 347
TOC.txt, SSTable component, 193
token ranges, 111, 133, 224, 279
token() function, 112
token-generator tool, 223
TokenAwarePolicy, 174
tokens, 111-113
  adding nodes, 282
  moving, 281
  node configuration, 224
  transient replication and, 204
tombstones, 128, 210
tools directory, 37
tracing, 314, 336
training and conferences, 33
"The Transaction Concept: Virtues and Limitations" (Gray), 6
transactions
  lightweight, 120, 193-196
  RDBMS and SQL support for, 6-9
  system keyspaces, 133

About the Authors

Eben Hewitt is chief technology officer for Choice Hotels International, one of the largest hotel companies in the world. He is the author of several books on architecture, distributed systems, and programming. He has consulted for venture capital firms, and is a frequently invited speaker on technology and strategy.

Jeff Carpenter works in developer relations at DataStax. He was previously a systems architect for Choice Hotels International, and has 20 years of experience in the hospitality and defense industries. Jeff's interests include SOA/microservices, architecting large-scale systems, and data architecture. He has worked on projects ranging from complex battle planning systems to a cloud-based hotel reservation system. Jeff is passionate about disruptive projects that change industries, mentoring architects and developers, and the next challenge.

Colophon

The bird on the cover of *Cassandra: The Definitive Guide* is an Indian paradise flycatcher (*Terpsiphone paradisi*). One of three species of the family of paradise flycatchers, the Indian paradise flycatcher is found in India, central Asia, and Myanmar. paradise flycatchers are passerine (perching) insectivores.

Paradise flycatchers are sexually dimorphic, meaning that males and females look different. Females tend to be less brilliantly colored than their male counterparts, which have long tail feathers. For example, the male Indian paradise flycatcher's tail streamers can be approximately 15 inches long. Female flycatchers are believed to select their mate based on tail length. Paradise flycatchers are monogamous, which makes their distinctive coloring and plumage unusual, as this form of sexual display is usually reserved for nonmonogamous species.

Because they're so widely distributed, paradise flycatchers can be found in a variety of habitats, including savannas, forests, and even cultivated gardens. They are insectivores and catch their food on the wing, thanks in part to their quick reflexes and sharp eyesight.

The color illustration on the cover is by Karen Montgomery, based on a black and white engraving from *Cassell's Natural History, Vol. IV*. The cover fonts are Gilroy Semibold and Guardian Sans. The text font is Adobe Minion Pro; the heading font is Adobe Myriad Condensed; and the code font is Dalton Maag's Ubuntu Mono.

O'REILLY®

Learn from experts.
Become one yourself.

Books | Live online courses
Instant Answers | Virtual events
Videos | Interactive learning

Get started at oreilly.com.

Milton Keynes UK
Ingram Content Group UK Ltd.
UKHW050743070924
447943UK00003B/6

9 781492 097143